国际财经中心
International Economics and Finance Institute

U0960807

CHINA FINANCE 2019

中国财政2019

Budget Taxation Treasury

主编 叶建第

EDITOR-IN-CHIEF JIANDI YE

中国财经出版传媒集团

中国财政经济出版社

图书在版编目（CIP）数据

中国财政. 2019 = China Finance 2019：英文 / 叶建第主编. -- 北京：中国财政经济出版社，2020.10

ISBN 978-7-5223-0090-0

Ⅰ. ①中… Ⅱ. ①叶… Ⅲ. ①财政 - 概况 - 中国 - 2019 - 英文 Ⅳ. ①F812

中国版本图书馆 CIP 数据核字（2020）第 184796 号

责任编辑：罗亚洪　　责任校对：赵婵婷

封面设计：孔德惠　　版式设计：孔德惠

中国财政经济出版社 出版

URL：http：//www.cfeph.cn

E - mail：cfeph @ cfeph.cn

社址：北京市海淀区阜成路甲 28 号　邮政编码：100142

营销中心电话：010 - 88191537

北京鑫海金澳胶印有限公司印刷　各地新华书店经销

889×1194 毫米　16开　19.25印张　365 000字

2020 年 10 月第 1 版　2020 年 10 月北京第 1 次印刷

定价：150.00 元

ISBN 978-7-5223-0090-0

（图书出现印装问题，本社负责调换）

本社质量投诉电话：010 - 88190744

打击盗版举报热线：010-88191661、QQ：2242791300

Preface

2019 is the 70th anniversary of the founding of the People's Republic of China. The past 70 years have witnessed not only the continuous improvement of China's comprehensive national strength, economic prowess and people's living standards, but also profound changes in public finance as evidenced by the increasingly stronger fiscal capacity, more robust fiscal system, greater effects of fiscal policies and further deepened fiscal and tax reform. The finance authorities in China have continued to follow the general principle of pursuing progress while ensuring stability, applied the new development philosophy, pursued supply-side structural reform as the main task. Coordinated efforts were made to maintain stable growth, advance reform, make structural adjustments, improve living standards, guard against risks and preserve stability. The finance authorities have stepped up countercyclical adjustments of macroeconomic policies, took further steps to ensure stable employment, stable financial sector, stable foreign trade, stable foreign investment, stable domestic investment and stable expectations. Effective measures were adopted to keep economic performance generally stable, advance structural adjustments, and contribute to the significant progress in building a moderately prosperous society in all respects.

In 2019, the finance authorities in China continued to pursue a proactive fiscal policy with greater intensity and enhanced effects, creating conditions for the stable fiscal and economic operation. The finance authorities have maintained a relatively large scale of spending, increased transfer payments, revitalized the stock of funds and assets, vigorously cut general expenditures, and ensured the expenditures on the "three protections". The measures of tax and fee cut of an unprecedented scale were launched, saving a total of 2.36 trillion RMB of taxes and fees throughout the year. The finance authorities have also vigorously supported poverty alleviation, prevention and resolution of fiscal and financial risks, and prevention and control of pollution to secure notable outcomes in the three critical battles. The finance authorities have insisted on deepening the supply-side structural reform, supported the high-quality development of manufacturing industry, promoted the implementation of innovation-driven development strategy, further alleviated the difficulties of micro and small-sized enterprises in accessing affordable financing, and helped improve the quality of economic development steadily. The finance authorities have supported the implementation of major regional strategies, promoted the development of high-quality agriculture, helped deepen the rural reform and development, promoted coordinated regional development, and advanced the implementation of rural revitalization strategy. The finance authorities have endeavored to steadily improve people's livelihood, promoted stability and expanded employment, continued to increase financial investment in education, increased basic housing security, and promoted the development of cultural and sports undertakings, thus delivering greater benefits, happiness and security to the people. In addition, the finance authorities have accelerated the reform of the fiscal and tax system, steadily advanced the fiscal and tax legislation, and strengthened basic fiscal management, resulting in more law-based and science-based fiscal management. With the concerted efforts of finance authorities at all levels, we have successfully completed all the tasks for the year.

Over the past year, China has pursued higher-level opening up and further deepened international economic and financial cooperation and exchanges. Thanks to the continuous efforts in improving the business environment, China's position in the Doing Business ranking has risen to the 31st place in the world, and China has become one of the top 10 economies with the largest improvement for two consecutive years. The finance authorities in China have provided funding for the Second Belt and Road Forum for International Cooperation, successfully held a thematic session on financial connectivity, and established the Multilateral Cooperation Center for Development Finance; have successfully held the Fourth "1+6" Roundtable Dialogue; have participated in the Regional Comprehensive Economic Partnership (RCEP), China, Japan and South Korea FTA and other multilateral and bilateral free trade negotiations; have actively involved in global tax governance and the development of international accounting standards, and accelerated the process of joining the WTO's Government Procurement Agreement (GPA); have actively promoted the conclusion of the Phase One China-US Economic and Trade Agreement, successfully held the 10th China-UK Economic and Financial Dialogue, the 2nd China-Germany High-level Financial Dialogue, and the 1st China-Italy Finance Dialogue, so that macroeconomic policy coordination and bilateral financial cooperation with major economies and emerging economies was further strengthened.

2020 is a year of milestones. China will complete the task of poverty eradication and build a moderately prosperous society in all respects. At the same time, given the global spread of COVID-19 and the increasing risks of global economic recession, China's economic development is faced with unprecedented risks and challenges. In this year, the proactive fiscal policy will be more proactive and impactful. By raising the deficit ratio, issuing special treasury bonds for combating COVID-19, increasing the issuance of local government special bonds, consolidating and expanding the effects of tax and fee cut, we seek to further advance the supply-side structural reform, expand domestic demand, effectively respond to the shocks and challenges arising from economic operation, and achieve sustained and healthy economic and social development. The key tasks of this year include: supporting the fight against the three critical battles, promoting innovation-driven development and industrial upgrading, implementing the rural revitalization strategy, increasing the level of financial equalization among regions, protecting and improving people's livelihood, advancing the reform of the fiscal and tax system, strengthening fiscal management and supervision, and further deepening international economic and financial cooperation.

China Finance 2019 covers important fiscal and tax reform policies introduced by MOF and other authorities of China, activities related to international economic and financial cooperation, macroeconomic data, local practices in fiscal and tax reform, and the theoretical discussions among economic and financial officials at all levels and domestic financial and economic academics on issues related to fiscal and tax reform. This book is instrumental for the international community to better understand China's macroeconomic policy trends, fiscal and tax reform processes, international economic and financial cooperation, and the latest measures for reform and opening up.

Acronyms

ADB	Asian Development Bank
AIIB	Asian Infrastructure Investment Bank
AMRO	ASEAN+3 Macroeconomic Research Office
APEC	Asia-Pacific Economic Cooperation
ASEAN+3	Association of Southeast Asian Nations, China, Korea and Japan
BEPS	Base Erosion and Profit Shifting
BRI	Belt and Road Initiative
BRICS	Brazil, Russia, India, China and South Africa
CAC	Cyberspace Administration of China
CBIRC	China Banking and Insurance Regulatory Commission
CEPA	Closer Economic Partnership Arrangement
CMIM	Chiang Mai Initiative Multilateralization
CPA	Certified Public Accountant
CPC	Communist Party of China
CPI	Consumer Price Index
CPPCC	Chinese People's Political Consultative Conference
CSRC	China Securities Regulatory Commission
FDA	U.S. Food and Drug Administration
GAS	General Administration of Sports
GDP	Gross Domestic Product
IEFI	International Economics and Finance Institute, Ministry of Finance, China
IMF	International Monetary Fund
IPI	Industrial Production Index
IPR	Intellectual Property Rights
LICs	Low-Income Countries
MCA	Ministry of Civil Affairs, China
MCT	Ministry of Culture and Tourism, China
MEE	Ministry of Ecology and Environment, China
MIIT	Ministry of Industry and Information Technology, China
MNR	Ministry of Natural Resources, China
MOA	Ministry of Agriculture and Rural Affair, China
MOE	Ministry of Education, China
MOF	Ministry of Finance, China

MOFCOM	Ministry of Commerce, China
MOHRSS	Ministry of Human Resources and Social Security, China
MOHURD	Ministry of Housing and Urban-Rural Development, China
MOST	Ministry of Science and Technology, China
MVA	Ministry of Veteran Affairs, China
MWR	Ministry of Water Resource, China
NBS	National Bureau of Statistics, China
NDB	New Development Bank
NDRC	National Development and Reform Commission, China
NEA	National Energy Administration, China
NFSRA	National Food and Strategic Reserves Administration, China
NHSA	National Healthcare Security Administration, China
NMPA	National Medical Products Administration, China
NPC	National People's Congress, China
OECD	Organization for Economic Co-operation and Development
PBoC	People's Bank of China
PMI	Purchasing Managers' Index
PPI	Producer Price Index
PPP	Public-Private Partnership
QE	Quantitative Easing
QQE	Qualitative and Quantitative Ease
R&D	Research and Development
RCEP	Regional Comprehensive Economic Partnership
SAFE	State Administration of Foreign Exchange, China
SAMR	State Administration of Market Regulation, China
SASAC	State-owned Assets Supervision and Administration Commission of the State Council, China
SAR	Special Administrative Region
SAT	State Administration of Taxation, China
SMEs	Small and Medium Enterprises
SOEs	State-Owned Enterprises
VAT	Value-Added Tax
WTO	World Trade Organization

Contents

Policy Update 1

Facts & Figures 107

MOF Events 147

Local Finance 169

Remarks & Opinions 227

POLICY UPDATE

01 MOF published a circular on the *Measures for the Disclosure of Local Government Debt Information (Trial)*

On December 29, MOF published a circular on the *Measures for the Disclosure of Local Government Debt Information (Trial)*, which provided the following. First, it is applicable to the disclosure of local government debt information by finance departments at or above the county level. Second, the disclosure of local government debt information should follow the principle of openness. Third, regarding the disclosure channels, the information of local government debt limit, balance, usage arrangement and debt service within the scope of budget and final accounts disclosure shall be made public on the portal website of local government and finance department. If the finance department does not have a portal website, it shall make public the relevant information in a dedicated section of the local government's portal website. Local government bond information outside the scope of budget and final accounts disclosure shall be made public on the portal website of provincial finance departments and the issuing institution. MOF has set up a local government debt information disclosure platform or section to support local finance departments to disclose local government debt (bond) information. Fourth, local finance departments at or above the county level should disclose information of local government debt limit, balance, usage arrangement and debt service payment along with budget and final accounts. Fifth, the provincial finance department should disclose the new government bond issuance and refinancing arrangement for the next month before the 20th of each month, and encourage qualified regions to simultaneously disclose local government bond issuance arrangement for multiple months. Sixth, the provincial finance department should disclose relevant information more than five working days before the issuance of new general bonds, special bonds or refinancing bonds. Seventh, when it comes to the disclosure of the duration of general bonds and special bonds, local finance departments at all levels shall organize the work of information disclosure on the duration of general bonds and special bonds in their local region and at their own administrative level, and supervise and guide the departments that use general bonds or special bond funds to disclose relevant information no later than the end of June in each year. Eighth, any violation of laws and regulations should be disclosed, and if illegal debt guarantees are held accountable, the finance departments at all levels shall disclose the results of accountability review within 20 working days after receiving the accountability review decision. Ninth, other matters also include information disclosure on general bond, special bond and the use of bond funds, the financial and economic information, and the government debt management system.

In terms of division of responsibilities, MOF is responsible for guiding and supervising the disclosure of debt information of local governments. The local finance departments at all levels are responsible for organizing the disclosure of government debt information at the local level as well as guiding, supervising and coordinating the use of bond funds by departments at the same level and the disclosure of government debt information at lower levels. In addition, the circular also set out relevant requirements on performance evaluation, daily supervision, legal responsibility and social supervision, and required the

Source: MOF

finance departments of provinces, autonomous regions, municipalities and cities with independent planning status to formulate local implementation rules in accordance with the provisions of this circular. The circular comes into force starting from January 1, 2019. ■

POLICY 02

MOF published a circular on unifying the formats of national fiscal electronic notes and machine billing

On January 2, MOF published a circular on unifying the formats of national fiscal electronic notes and machine billing, which provided the following. First, starting from January 1, 2019, the nationally unified formats for fiscal electronic notes and machine billing will be launched. Second, the formats of nationally unified fiscal electronic notes and machine billing are applicable to all types of fiscal notes. The scope of application and other management requirements are not changed by the format of notes. The general payment letter of non-tax income is governed by the relevant regulations of MOF. Third, in order to ensure the uniqueness of the fiscal note code in the country, the fiscal electronic note code and the fiscal machine bill code should be compiled according to the nationally uniform coding rules. Fourth, the finance authorities at all levels should attach great importance to the launch of the nationally unified fiscal electronic note and machine billing, formulate practical and feasible implementation plans according to local conditions, make preparatory work for the launch of the new format and the write off of the old notes, so as to ensure the transitional is carried out in a smooth and orderly way. Fifth, the finance authorities at all levels should actively organize the account-keeping of fiscal electronic notes in their jurisdiction to promote the receipt and filing of fiscal electronic notes. ■

POLICY 03

MOF published a circular on matters related to the management of the tax authorities' penalty and confiscatory income and other governmental non-tax revenue

On January 2, MOF published a circular on matters related to the management of tax authorities' penalty and confiscatory income and other governmental non-tax revenue, which provided the following. First, the relevant penalty and confiscatory income, interest income and damages received or generated by the tax authorities during the tax collection process shall all be turned over in full to the central treasury. Second, the relevant penalty and confiscatory income refers to the various penalties and confiscatory incomes collected by the tax authorities and do not include the late payment fees and fines imposed alongside taxes; the interest income refers to the interest income generated by the fiduciary account of tax authorities; damage revenue refers to the damages paid to tax authorities by the defaulting parties entrusted with tax collection in accordance with the *Entrusted Collection Agreement.* Third, when the above-mentioned penalties and confiscatory incomes collected by the tax authorities are turned over to the central treasury, they shall fall under the "tax authorities' penalty and confiscatory income" (103050107) of the general public budget revenue; the interest income shall fall under the "other interest income" (103070599) of the general public budget revenue; and the damages shall fall under the "other income" (1039999) of the general public budget revenue. Fourth, all departments should strictly implement the above provisions to ensure that the relevant governmental non-tax revenues are turned over to the central treasury in a timely manner and in full amount. The circular shall come into force on January 1, 2019. ■

POLICY 04

MOF published the *Measures for the Accounting of the Fiscal Special Account of Social Security Fund*

On January 3, MOF published the *Measures for the Accounting of the Fiscal Special Account of Social Security Fund*, which provided the following. First, the finance department should keep separate account for the social security fund by the types of insurance and the different systems. Second, the accounting of fiscal special account is generally done on a cash basis, and the accounting of entrusted investment of basic old-age insurance fund should be done on an accrual basis. Third, the accounting elements of the fiscal special account include assets, liabilities, net assets, incomes and expenses. Fourth, the accounting of fiscal special account uses the debit and credit bookkeeping method. Fifth, the accounting of fiscal special account should keep accounts and prepare financial statements by different accounting periods, and the starting and ending date of the accounting period should be based on the Gregorian calendar. Sixth, the accounting of fiscal special account should be measured in RMB. ■

POLICY 05

MOF published a circular on further improving the implementation and management of the central government's budgetary funds for science and technology and education

On January 9, MOF published a circular on further improving the implementation and management of the central government's budgetary funds for science and technology and education, which provided the following. First, optimize the management of fund payment and increase the autonomy of budget units. Improve the efficiency of budget implementation and allow some scientific research programs and education funds to be transferred from the zero-balance account of the unit to the actual fund account of the unit or other budget units. Second, improve the management of official credit cards and relax the settlement requirements for official credit cards in scientific research programs. Personnel who participate for more than one year in the research programs funded by the central government and oversee the reimbursement of research expenditures may apply for and use official credit cards subject to the approval of the project management department and the finance department. Third, simplify the procurement management of scientific research instruments and equipment and improve the efficiency of government procurement. Simplify the record-filing of the import of scientific research instruments and equipment. Starting from January 1, 2019, for the import of scientific research instruments and equipment by the central universities and research institutes, the procurers may file records through the Government Procurement Planning and Management System and are no longer required to report content such as the main performance indicators and performance. ■

POLICY 06

MOF published a circular on the budgetary implementation and management of the central budget units in 2019

On January 9, MOF published a circular on the budgetary implementation and management of the central budget units in 2019, which provided the following. First, consolidate the foundational work for centralized treasury payment. The budget units should strengthen the pre-planning of budgetary implementation, prepare the fund-use plan in strict accordance with the budget of the unit and the actual need for funds, and improve the accuracy of the fund-use plan. When the budget units actually use the funds, they should choose the corresponding method of payment according to the standard payment method stipulated by MOF. Second, strictly control the transfer of funds to the actual financial account. All departments must strictly control the transfer of funds from the zero-balance account of the higher-level budget unit to the actual financial account of the grass-root budget unit. In principle, all budgets should be broken down to the grass-roots units at the beginning of the year. If it is indeed impossible to break down to the grass-root units, the budget shall be broken down in accordance with the budget adjustment procedures during implementation and the funds shall be disbursed according to the adjusted budget. Third, regulate the deposit and management of funds in the budget unit. Establish and improve scientific, standardized, fair and transparent fund deposit and management mechanism, carry out fund deposit in accordance with the principles of compliance, fairness, transparency, safety, scientific assessment, and match between rights and responsibilities, and prevent the security risks and corruption risks of fund deposit. Fourth, implement the reform of the economic classification of expenditures. All departments must continue to accurately fill out the economic classification of government budget in the payment instruction in accordance with the relevant requirements of MOF on the reform of the economic classification of expenditures. ■

POLICY 07

The State Council decided to introduce more measures to cut taxes for small and micro-sized enterprises

Source: MOF

On January 9, Premier Li Keqiang presided over an executive meeting of the State Council, which provided the following. First, expand the scope of small-scale and low-profit enterprises that can enjoy preferential corporate income tax, and further strengthen the income tax breaks. The portion of the annual taxable income of small-scale and low-profit enterprises that does not exceed 1 million RMB and the portion between 1 million RMB and 3 million RMB will be deducted by 25% and 50% respectively when included in the taxable income, so that the tax burden will be reduced to 5% and 10%. The adjusted preferential policy will cover more than 95% of tax-paying enterprises, 98% of which are private enterprises. Second, the VAT threshold will be raised from monthly sales of 30,000 RMB to 100,000 RMB for small-scale taxpayers, which mainly include small and micro enterprises, sole proprietors and other individuals. Third, allow provinces (autonomous regions and municipalities) to reduce the resource taxes, urban maintenance and construction taxes, stamp duties, urban land use taxes, cultivated land occupation taxes, education surcharges and local education surcharges by no more than 50% for small-scale VAT payers. Fourth, expand the scope of entities that enjoy preferential policies for investing in tech start-ups so that venture capital and angel investors who invest in such firms will enjoy more tax incentives. Fifth, in order to make up for the loss of local financial resources caused by large-scale reduction of taxes and fees, the central government will increase general transfer payments to local governments. ■

POLICY 08 MOF published the *Measures for the Administration of the Allocation of State-owned Assets of Central Administrative Institutions*

On January 10, MOF published the *Measures for the Administration of the Allocation of State-owned Assets of Central Administrative Institutions*, which provided the following. First, the allocation of the assets of central administrative institutions should be primarily done by means of transfer. If it is indeed impossible to carry out transfer, comprehensive analysis and feasibility study on the methods of renting, purchase and construction should be conducted on the principle of controlling cost, saving money and facilitating convenient use, in order to choose the most optimal way of allocation. Second, the new assets generated by the capital construction programs of central administrative institutions should apply for the relevant budget for new asset allocation. Third, once the budget for new asset allocation has been approved, it cannot be adjusted in principle. In the implementation of the budget, if it is necessary to adjust for special reasons, the central department shall propose to MOF for adjusting the budget for new asset allocation and shall only carry out the adjustment with the consent of MOF. ■

POLICY 09 MOF published a circular on further strengthening and improving the management of state-owned assets of administrative institutions

On January 10, MOF published a circular on further strengthening and improving the management of state-owned assets of administrative institutions, which provided the following. First, relevant departments and units must earnestly assume the main responsibility of asset management. All departments must earnestly perform their management responsibilities over their state-owned assets and rectify problems, place asset management at the equally important position as fund management, establish and improve the internal control mechanism for asset management, strengthen the division of responsibilities, and engage in close coordination and cooperation to build up the synergy for management. Second, step up the registration and management of assets such as public infrastructure. All units should classify and register assets such as public infrastructure, affordable housing, government reserved supplies and cultural relics, further standardize and strengthen the accounting of various assets, so that the accounts are consistent and the asset information is comprehensive, accurate and complete. Third, explore the establishment of asset sharing and transfer mechanism. It is necessary to strengthen the overall management of asset allocation and use, and explore the establishment of a mechanism for sharing and transferring long-standing inefficient and idle assets. ■

10 MOF published the *Measures for the Administration of Air Pollution Prevention and Control Funds*

Source: MOF

On January 11, MOF published the *Measures for the Administration of Air Pollution Prevention and Control Funds*, which provided the following. First, the areas supported by the special funds include Beijing-Tianjin-Hebei and surrounding areas, the Fen-Wei Plain and the Yangtze River Delta. Second, MEE and the relevant authorities are responsible for proposing annual arrangements for special funds. Based on the annual budget size and annual arrangement proposals, MOF will decide on the allcation of the funds. Third, MOF should allocate special funds to the provincial finance department within 90 days after the approval of the central budget by NPC, and copy to MEE and the local inspector's offices of MOF. Fourth, MOF will disclose the results of fund allocation to the public within 20 days after the special funds are disbursed. ■

11 MOF published the *Trial Measures for the Management of Subsidy Funds for Universal Telecommunication Services*

On January 14, MOF published the *Trial Measures for the Management of Subsidy Funds for Universal Telecommunication Services*, which provided the following. First, the special funds will focus on supporting the construction of broadband networks such as optical fiber or 4G in administrative villages, border areas and islands (reefs). Second, the special funds shall be included in the central government's special transfer payments by MOF, and be governed by the relevant regulations on the management of local special transfer payments. Third, the local finance authorities should coordinate with the communication management, industry and information technology authorities to ensure that the special funds are effectively allotted to the pilot programs and the special funds are used to support the pilot work in the region. Fourth, the implementing enterprises should use the special funds they received for the intended purpose and conduct accounting according to the relevant national regulations on financial management and accounting. ■

12 MOF published the *Interim Measures for the Performance Management of the Central Reservoir Resettlement Support Fund*

On January 15, MOF published the *Interim Measures for the Performance Management of the Central Reservoir Resettlement Support Fund*, which provided the following. First, MOF is responsible for the overall organization and guidance of performance management, such as reviewing performance targets; guiding and facilitating the supervision work on the implementation of performance targets; determines the central government's priorities and approaches in conducting a performance evaluation of provincial governments; determines the use of the results of performance evaluation; and guidance on performance management of local finance authorities. Second, local finance authorities are responsible for the overall work of performance management in their jurisdiction. They should review the setting of local performance targets; organize and monitor the performance evaluation; review the results of self-assessment and performance evaluation; and determine the application of performance evaluation results and supervise the timely rectification of the problems found in performance evaluation. Third, in budget implementation, the local finance authorities and the resettlement management agencies shall monitor the fulfillment of performance targets and the operation of funds, timely detect and correct the existing problems, and promote the fulfillment of performance targets as scheduled. ■

POLICY 13 MOF published the Interim *Measures for the Administration of Public Rental Housing Assets*

On January 15, MOF published the *Interim Measures for the Administration of Public Rental Housing Assets*, which provided the following. First, the allocation of public rental housing assets includes construction (including renovation and expansion), purchase, transfer and donation. Second, the local housing authorities shall organize the preparation of the public rental housing asset allocation plan at their level. The public rental housing asset allocation plan includes the increase and decrease of the units of public rental housing, the unitesize, the capital demand and source, the stock of the previous year's assets, the allocation, the operation and maintenance. The public rental housing asset allocation plan is reported to the finance authorities along with the departmental budget, and the applied funds are included in the departmental budget. Third, the local housing authorities may organize the establishment of a transfer and use mechanism for the public rental housing assets of different administrative districts in the same city, and enhance the efficiency of the use of public rental housing assets. Fourth, the non-residential assets of public rental housing projects should be rented out in an open manner. ■

POLICY 14 MOF published a circular on strengthening the management of high-frequency and fast-opening lottery game awards

On January 16, MOF published a circular on strengthening the management of high-frequency and fast-opening lottery game awards, which provided the following. First, starting from January 16, 2019, any form of awarding will be suspended. For the ongoing awarding activities, the announcement on suspension shall be issued in a timely manner. The award period shall not exceed 5 days, and shall be halted immediately after expiration. If the prize money of the last award is still in surplus, the award will be discontinued. For the award that has been announced but not yet enforced, a cancellation notice shall be issued in a timely manner. Second, starting from January 16, 2019, any form of promotion will be suspended. ■

POLICY 15

MOF published a circular on improving the management of the bookkeeping agency industry in 2019

On January 16, MOF published a circular on improving the management of the bookkeeping agency industry in 2019, which provided the following. First, organize the annual records-filing of the bookkeeping agencies in 2019. The bookkeeping agencies that have obtained the qualification before December 31, 2018 shall file records with the approval authority through the National Bookkeeping Agency Management System before April 30, 2019. If a bookkeeping agency has established a branch, the branch shall file records with the local approval authority. If a bookkeeping agency moves its office to another place before December 31, 2018, it shall file records with the approval authority of the place where it is moved. Second, strengthen the supervision of the bookkeeping agency industry association. The bookkeeping agency industry association established according to laws before December 31, 2018 should file records with the supervisory authorities through the National Bookkeeping Agency Management System before April 30, 2019. ■

POLICY 16

MOF revised and published the *Format for Consolidated Financial Statements 2018*

Source: MOF

On January 22, MOF revised and published the *Format for Consolidated Financial Statements 2018*, which provided the following. First, the revised *Format for Consolidated Financial Statements 2018* is applicable to enterprise groups that have implemented the new financial instrument standards and new income standards. Second, only the consolidated financial statement format has been revised. The format and its various items cover not only the parent company but the subsidiaries engaged in various economic businesses. Third, for the content that needs to be separately presented, an enterprise may add to the consolidated financial statement items; for the consolidated financial statement items that do not have the corresponding business, necessary deletion can be made. Fourth, the enterprise group comprised mainly of financial enterprises shall prepare consolidated financial statements on the basis of the financial statement format of financial enterprise taking into account the requirements of the financial statement format of general enterprise and the requirements of this circular, and after adjusting for the consolidated financial statement items. ■

17 MOF published the *Administrative Measures for the Examination and Review of Large-scale Scientific Research Instruments and Equipment at the Central Level*

On January 22, MOF published the *Administrative Measures for the Examination and Review of Large-scale Scientific Research Instruments and Equipment at the Central Level*, which provided the following. First, the units that apply for the budget for purchasing large-scale scientific instruments and equipment shall ask the competent authorities to examine and review the relevance, necessity and rationality of the purchase of large-scale scientific research equipment in accordance with the provisions of the Measures. Second, when the relevant units apply for the budget for purchasing large-scale scientific instruments, they must ask the examination and review authorities to conduct a review and submit the application for purchase. Third, the examination and review authorities are mainly responsible for the examination and review work. Fourth, the main contents and principles of examination and review work are publicized. Fifth, MOF and other ministries would punish the relevant units for submitting false materials for purchasing instruments and equipment, the examination and review authorities for failing to conduct examination and review in accordance with regulations, and third-party examination and review agencies for carrying out fraudulent practices. ■

18 MOF and MOFCOM jointly published the *Circular on Supporting the Service Trade Innovation and Development Guiding Fund to Improve the Project Pipeline*

On January 23, MOF and MOFCOM jointly published the *Circular on Supporting the Service Trade Innovation and Development Guiding Fund to Improve the Project Pipeline*, which provided the following. First, make a briefing on the state of the service trade fund, including the amount, operating model, investment field, investment decision and management. Second, use multiple channels such as annual work conference, training, research and symposium to promote the service trade fund to service trade enterprises; members of the inter-ministerial meeting of service trade development, provincial-level commerce and finance departments and relevant national-level industry associations may recommend to the competent authorities of the service trade fund the list of leading enterprises with great service export potential and related projects to be included in the project pipeline; establish a liaison mechanism and invite all units to strengthen contact with the competent authorities of the service trade fund. Third, improve the management of project pipeline. The competent authorities of the service trade fund are responsible for project pipeline construction, operation and maintenance, and should use the project pipeline to strengthen the classified management of projects. Fourth, strengthen policy coordination and form synergy for development. ■

19 MOF published the *Circular on Implementing the Relevant Documents on Giving Greater Autonomy to Scientific Research Institutions and Personnel*

On January 23, MOF published the *Circular on Implementing the Relevant Documents on Giving*

Greater Autonomy to Scientific Research Institutions and Personnel, which provided the following. First, attach great importance to and enhance the awareness of the importance of implementing the relevant documents on giving greater autonomy to scientific research institutions and personnel. Second, strictly implement the policy measures identified in the relevant documents. Comprehensively carry out self-examination; promptly revise and improve relevant policy measures; and strengthen policy linkages. Third, promote the optimization and improvement of relevant management measures in the spirit of reform. Fourth, effectively strengthen publicity, training and supervision, and pay close attention to policy implementation. ■

POLICY 20

MOF and SAT jointly published the *Circular on the Issues Concerning the Income Tax Policy of Individual Partners in Venture Capital Enterprises*

On January 23, MOF and SAT jointly published the *Circular on the Issues Concerning the Income Tax Policy of Individual Partners in Venture Capital Enterprises*, which provided the following. First, venture capital enterprises may use either the single investment fund or annual income of venture capital enterprise as the basis for calculating the personal income tax of individual partner's income from venture capital enterprise. Second, if a venture capital enterprise chooses the single investment fund method, individual partner's share of the equity transfer income and dividend income distributed from the fund shall be subject to the personal income tax at the rate of 20%. Third, the single investment fund method refers to the separate calculation and taxation of the single investment fund's (including the venture capital enterprise established not in the name of the fund) equity transfer income and dividend income from different venture capital projects within a tax year. Fourth, the overall calculation of the annual income of venture capital enterprise refers to the calculation of the income that should be allocated to individual partners after the venture capital enterprise deducts the costs, expenses and losses from the total income of each tax year. Fifth, once the venture capital enterprise chooses the single investment fund method or the method of the overall calculation of the annual income of venture capital enterprise, the method cannot be changed within 3 years. Sixth, if a venture capital enterprise chooses the single investment fund method, it shall file records with the competent tax authorities regarding its calculation method, within 30 days after completing the filing requirements in accordance with the provisions of Article 1 of this Circular; otherwise, it shall be deemed to have chosen the method of the overall calculation of the annual income of venture capital enterprise. ■

POLICY 21

MOF and SAT jointly published the *Circular on the Continued Implementation of the Preferential Policies for Real Estate Tax and Urban Land Use Tax of Agricultural Products Wholesale and Retail Markets*

On January 24, MOF and SAT jointly published the *Circular on the Continued Implementation of the Preferential Policies for Real Estate Tax and Urban Land Use Tax of Agricultural Products Wholesale and Retail Markets*, which provided the following. First, from January 1, 2019 to December 31, 2021, the real estate and land used by agricultural products wholesale *and retail*

Source: MOF

markets (including proprietary and leased ones) for trading agricultural products will be temporarily exempted from real estate tax and urban land use tax. Second, the real estate and land that enjoy the above-mentioned tax incentives refer to the real estate and land that directly provide services for agricultural products trading in the agricultural product wholesale *and retail markets*. Third, the enterprises that enjoy the tax exemption policy stipulated in this *Circular* shall apply for tax exemption according to the regulations, and keep the property ownership certificate, the relevant materials showing the original value of the real estate, the lease agreement, and the certificate showing the intended purpose of the use of the land or real estate for future reference. ■

POLICY 22

MOF, MCA the GAS jointly published the *Circular on Adjusting the Rules for the High-frequency and Fast-opening Lottery Games and the Quiz Lottery Games to Strengthen the Supervision of the Lottery Market*

On January 28, MOF, MCA and GAS jointly published the *Circular on Adjusting the Rules for the High-frequency and Fast-opening Lottery Games and the Quiz Lottery Games to Strengthen the Supervision of the Lottery Market*, which provided the following. First, starting from February 11, 2019, those with a sales period of less than 20 minutes will be adjusted to 20 minutes; the adjustment fund that withholds 1% will be canceled, and the withdrawing proportion for the lottery public welfare fund will be increased by 1 percentage point; any form of promotion for high-frequency and fast-opening games outside the physical stores will be banned. Second, the prize proportion for a single quiz game will be reduced from 73% to 71%, and the number of quiz games will be strictly controlled. Third, the betting multiple for a single lottery ticket of a high-frequency and fast-opening game is adjusted from 2-99 times to 2-20 times; the betting multiple for a single lottery ticket of a single quiz game is adjusted from 2-99 times to 2-50 times. Fourth, strengthen the management of sales terminals and strengthen the management over the number of sales terminals in physical stores. Strengthen the supervision over the quota of a single sales terminal. Fifth, stop the prize awards and promotions. ■

POLICY 23

MOF published the *Circular on Issuing the Measures for the Administration of Island and Sea Area Protection Funds*

On January 29, MOF published the *Circular on Issuing the Measures for the Administration of Island and Sea Area Protection Funds*, which provided the following. First, the island and sea area protection funds mentioned in the Measures refer to the funds arranged by the central government. Second, the protection funds will be implemented by MOF in conjunction with MNR and MEE. Third, the protection funds will support marine environment protection, ocean pollutant treatment and damage remediation. Fourth, MOF is responsible for reviewing the proposal for the allocation of protection funds, preparing and issuing the budget for protection funds, organizing the budget performance management, and guiding local efforts to strengthen fund management. Fifth, the allocation of protection funds may adopt the factor method and the project-based method. Sixth, MOF, MNR and MEE are responsible for organizing budget performance management of protection funds, and conducting performance self-assessment and key performance evaluation. Seventh, the protection funds shall be earmarked for intended purposes, and no unit or individual may intercept, occupy or misappropriate the funds. Eighth, the provincial finance authorities in the coastal areas, in conjunction with the marine administrative authorities, shall, in light of the actual local conditions, formulate detailed implementation rules for the management and use of protection funds in accordance with the Measures, and submit them to MOF and the Ministry of Natural Resources for record-keeping. ■

POLICY 24 MOF and SAT jointly published the *Circular on the VAT Policy for Enterprises Sponsoring the Winter Olympic and Paralympic Games*

Source: MOF

On January 29, MOF and SAT jointly published the *Circular on the VAT Policy for Enterprises Sponsoring the Winter Olympic and Paralympic Games*, which provided the following. First, the sponsoring enterprises and their affiliates participating in the sponsorship will be exempted from VAT when they provide free services related to the 2022 Beijing Winter Olympic, Paralympic and Test Games for the Beijing Winter Olympics Organizing Committee in accordance with the sponsorship agreement and supplementary sponsorship agreement. Second, the services applicable to the VAT exemption policy are limited to the services listed in the sponsorship agreement and the supplementary sponsorship agreement signed by the sponsoring enterprises and their affiliates with the Beijing Winter Olympics Organizing Committee. Third, the sponsoring enterprises and their affiliates shall keep separate accounting for the above services; otherwise, the tax exemption policy shall not be applied. ■

POLICY 25 MOF published the *Circular on Issuing the Regulations on the Accounting Treatment of Perpetual Bonds*

On January 30, MOF published the *Circular on Issuing the Regulations on the Accounting Treatment of Perpetual Bonds*, which provided the following. First, the accounting classification of perpetual bond issuers should consider the due date, the settlement order, the interest rate increase and the indirect obligations. Second, the holder of perpetual bonds should distinguish between the following situations for the accounting of perpetual bonds: the holder that has implemented the new financial instrument guidelines and the holder that has not implemented the new financial instrument guidelines. ■

26 MOF and MOST jointly published the *Circular on Further Optimizing the National Key R&D Programs and Fund Management*

On January 30, MOF and MOST jointly published the *Circular on Further Optimizing the National Key R&D Programs and Fund Management*, which provided the following. First, systematically sort through various links, optimize management processes and integrate various financial reports. Second, fully apply information technology and submit materials through the Information System for National Science and Technology Management. Third, the projects with an implementation cycle of fewer than three years are generally not subject to procedural inspection. The annual inspection plan is formulated in advance, and the inspection is carried out in a relatively concentrated time period. Fourth, give researchers greater power to make decisions on technical direction. Fifth, simplify budgeting requirements. Sixth, expand the authority of implementing agencies in adjusting the budget. Seventh, regulate financial audit. Eighth, implement the one-time comprehensive project performance evaluation. Ninth,focus on the evaluation of the representative results and project implementation effectiveness. Tenth, strengthen scientific ethics review and supervision. Eleventh, strengthen the responsibility of the implementing agencies and project management institutions. Twelfth, improve project policy coordination. ■

27 MOF and the other nine ministries jointly published the *Implementation Plan for Further Improving Supply to Promote Steady Growth of Consumption and Promote the Formation of a Strong Domestic Market (2019)*

On January 31, MOF and the other nine ministries jointly published the *Implementation Plan for Further Improving Supply to Promote Steady Growth of Consumption and Promote the Formation of a Strong Domestic Market (2019)*, which provided the following. First, take multi-pronged measures to promote automobile consumption and better meet the needs of residents. Second, shore up the weak links in urban consumption supply and better meet the needs of urbanization and aging. Third, promote the upgrading of rural consumption and promote the connected development of urban and rural consumption. Fourth, provide more guidance support to drive new consumption. Fifth, expand the supply of quality products and services to better meet consumer demand for high-quality. Sixth, improve the policy system and further optimize the consumer market environment. ■

POLICY 28

Three departments jointly published the *Circular on the Relevant Tax Policies for Further Supporting the Business Startup and Employment of Retired Soldiers*

On February 2, MOF.SAT and MVA jointly published the *Circular on the Relevant Tax Policies for Further Supporting the Business Startup and Employment of Retired Soldiers*, which provided the following. First, the retired soldiers who engage in self-employment, starting from the month of the registration of an individual industrial and commercial business, may deduct payable VAT, urban maintenance and construction tax, education surcharge, local education surcharge and personal income tax in the current year by up to 12,000 RMB per year in three years. Second, the enterprises that recruit, sign plus one-year labor contract with, and pay social insurance premiums for the retired soldiers, starting from the month of signing the labor contract and paying social insurance premiums, may deduct VAT, urban maintenance and construction tax, education surcharge, local education surcharge and corporate income tax in three years on the basis of the actual number of people to be employed. Third, enterprises recruiting retired soldiers can either apply the preferential tax policies stipulated in this circular, or other preferential tax incentives for supporting employment. Enterprises may choose to apply the most favorable policies, but shall not enjoy both policies at one time. ■

POLICY 29

MOF and SAT jointly published the *Circular on the Relevant Tax Policies for Further Supporting and Promoting the Business Startup and Employment of Key Groups of People*

On February 2, MOF and SAT jointly published the *Circular on the Relevant Tax Policies for Further Supporting and Promoting the Business Startup and Employment of Key Groups of People*, which provided the following. First, the documented poor people and the people holding an *Employment and Business Startup Certificate,* or an *Employment and Unemployment Registration Certificate* who engage in self-employed business may, starting from the month of the registration of individual industrial and commercial business, deduct payable VAT, urban maintenance and construction tax, education surcharge, local education surcharge and personal income tax in the current year by up to 12,000 RMB per year in three years. Second, the enterprises that recruit, sign plus one-year labor contract with, and pay social insurance premiums for the documented poor people and the people registered as jobless for more than half a year at the public job service organization of the human resources and social security department and holding an Employment and Business Startup Certificate or an *Employment and Unemployment Registration Certificate* may deduct, starting from the month of signing the labor contract and paying social insurance premiums, VAT, urban maintenance and construction tax, education surcharge, local education surcharge and corporate income tax in three years on the basis of the actual number of people to be employed. ■

POLICY 30

MOF and SAT jointly published the *Circular on Clarifying the Policies for Exempting VAT for Elderly-care Agencies*

On February 2, MOF and SAT jointly published the *Circular on Clarifying the Policies for Exempting*

VAT for Elderly-care Agencies, which provided the following. First, from February 1, 2019 to December 31, 2020, the VAT exemption policy stipulated in the *Regulations on the Transitional Policy for the Trial Replacement of Business Tax with VAT* will be applied to the medical institutions entrusted by other medical institutions to provide the services listed in the *National Standard Medical Service Price Items* at a price level no higher than the guided price set by the competent price authorities and the relevant health authorities above the prefecture (city) level. Second, from February 1, 2019 to December 31, 2020, the interest-free lending of funds between units within the enterprise group (including enterprise groups) is exempted from VAT. Third, the premium income obtained before the receipt of approval documents from insurance regulators by insurance companies that provide refundable life insurance with a term of more than one year shall belong to the premium income as prescribed in the Regulations. After being included in the list of business tax exemption published by MOF and SAT or after the completion of procedures for tax exemption filing, the part of the business tax that has not been deducted or refunded before may be offset against the VAT payable in the following months. ■

POLICY 31 Three departments jointly published the *Circular on the 2019 Plan of Tax-free Imports of Seeds and Provenances*

Source: MOF

On February 12, MOF, GAC and SAT jointly published the *Circular on the 2019 Plan of Tax-free Imports of Seeds and Provenances*, which provided the following. First, the import of seeds (seedlings), breeding stock (poultry), fish seeds (fry) and wild fauna and flora provenance will continue to be exempted from import VAT during the 13th Five-Year Plan period. Second, MOA 2019 Plan for tax-free import of seeds (seedlings), breeding stock (poultry) and fish seeds (fry) as well as the State Forestry and Grassland Administration's 2019 plan of tax-free import of seeds (seedlings) and wild fauna and flora provenance have been endorsed. ■

POLICY 32 Four departments jointly published the *Circular on Adjusting and Improving the Implementation Mechanism for Government Procurement of Energy-efficient Products and Environmental Labeling Products*

On February 13, MOF, NDRC, MEE and SAMR jointly published the *Circular on Adjusting and Improving the Implementation Mechanism for Government Procurement of Energy-efficient Products and Environmental Labeling Products*, which provided the following. First, the government procurement of energy-efficient products and environmental labeling products is administered on the basis of the list of items. Second, priority procurement and compulsory procurement will be conducted based on the list of items and certification. Third, gradually expand the scope of certification bodies for energy-efficient products and environmental labeling products. Fourth, establish an information release platform for the certification results of energy-efficient products and environmental labeling products, and publish information on relevant certification bodies and certified products. Fifth, the purchasers may propose higher procurement requirements for resource conservation and environmental protection, and give preferential treatment to the eligible certified products. ■

POLICY 33

MOF published the *Circular on the Relevant Matters Concerning the Reporting of Local Government Treasury Information in 2019*

On February 14, MOF published the *Circular on the Relevant Matters Concerning the Reporting of Local Government Treasury Information in 2019*, which provided the following. First, on the monthly report of local treasury information, it should reflect the treasury balance at the beginning of the year, the accumulated amount of inflows and outflows of the treasury funds in the current year, and the treasury balance at the end of the period. Second, with regard to the analytical note of the monthly operation of treasury, it should focus on the structural analysis of the treasury funds, quantitative measurement of the main items that affect the changes in the treasury funds, and analysis of the causes of the monthly and yearly changes in the local treasury funds and problems that merit attention. Third, on the quarterly performance analysis of treasury funds, the study shall take into account the local economic and fiscal performance, analyze comprehensively the program made in accelerating the implementation of expenditure budget and promoting the revitalization of the stock of fiscal funds, and propose follow-up measures for proper management of treasury funds. ■

POLICY 34

MOF published *the Circular on Improving the Annual Reporting Work of Accounting Firms in 2018*

On February 19, MOF published the *Circular on Improving the Annual Reporting Work of Accounting Firms in 2018*, which provided the following. First, the annual reporting of the accounting firms includes a brief description of the current reporting; information on the licensing conditions of accounting firms; business operation in 2018; development of international operation of accounting firms and establishment of branches abroad; performance of anti-money laundering and anti-terrorism financing obligations of accounting firms. Second, the annual reporting of the branches of accounting firms includes a brief description of the current reporting; relevant information on the licensing conditions of the branches; and the business operation in 2018. ■

POLICY 35

MOF and SAT jointly published the *Circular on the Property Tax and Stamp Tax Policy for the Apartment of College Students*

On February 20, MOF and SAT jointly published the *Circular on the Property Tax and Stamp Tax*

Policy for the Apartment of College Students, which provided the following. First, the college student apartments are exempted from property tax. Second, the lease contract for the college student apartments signed with college students is exempted from stamp tax. Third, the enterprises that enjoy the tax exemption policy stipulated in this circular shall make tax exemption declaration according to the regulations, and keep the proof of the property ownership, the relevant materials showing the original value of the property, the proof of use of the property, and the lease contract for future reference. ■

POLICY 36 MOF and SAT jointly published the *Circular on the Vehicle and Vessel Tax Policy for State Comprehensive Fire Rescue Vehicles*

On February 20, MOF and SAT jointly published the *Circular on the Vehicle and Vessel Tax Policy for State Comprehensive Fire Rescue Vehicles*, which provided the following. The state comprehensive fire rescue vehicles that change their number plates from military ones to emergency rescue ones will be exempted from the vehicle and vessel tax in the year of the change of number plates. ■

POLICY 37 CPC Central Committee and the State Council published the *Several Opinions on Prioritizing the Development of Agriculture and Rural Areas and Improving the Work Related to Rural Areas, Agriculture and Farmers*

On February 20, the CPC Central Committee and the State Council published the *Several Opinions on Prioritizing the Development of Agriculture and Rural Areas and Improving the Work Related to Rural Areas, Agriculture and Farmers*, which provided the following. First, complete the task of poverty alleviation; focus on the extremely poor areas; make efforts to address the outstanding problems; and consolidate and expand the outcomes of poverty alleviation. Second, stabilize grain output; complete the task of the development of high-standard farmland; adjust and optimize agricultural structure; accelerate efforts to make breakthroughs in key and core agricultural technologies; and implement strategies to ensure the supply of important agricultural products. Third, carry out the three-year movement to improve the rural living environment; implement village infrastructure construction projects; enhance rural public service levels; strengthen rural pollution control and ecological and environmental protection; and improve the planning of rural areas. Fourth, accelerate the development of rural industries with special characteristics; vigorously develop the modern processing industry for agricultural products; develop new service industry in rural areas; implement the digital

Source: MOF

rural strategy; promote the migration of rural labor for employment; support rural innovation and entrepreneurship. Fifth, consolidate and improve the basic rural operation system; deepen the reform of the rural land system; further promote the reform of the rural collective property rights system; and improve the agricultural support and protection system. Sixth, strengthen the capacity of rural governance; promote cultural progress in rural areas; and continue to promote the construction of safe rural areas. Seventh, strengthen the leadership role of the rural grass-root Party organizations; give play to the role of various types of organizations at the village level; strengthen the service functions of village-level organizations; and improve the funding mechanism for the operation of village-level organizations. Eighth, strengthen the institutional guarantee for the rural revitalization; firmly establish the policy orientation of the priority development of agriculture and rural areas; cultivate the work teams that understand agriculture and love the countryside and farmers; and give play to the principal role of farmers. ■

POLICY 38 MOF published the *Circular on Intensifying Efforts to Transfer the Long-Used Construction-in-Progress Projects of Administrative Institutions to Fixed Assets*

On February 25, MOF published the *Circular on Intensifying Efforts to Transfer the Long-Used Construction-in-Progress Projects of Administrative Institutions to Fixed Assets*, which provided the following. First, speed up to go through the procedures to transfer the completed projects with mature conditions to fixed assets. After a project is completed and accepted, the procedures for asset delivery shall be handled in a timely manner; the payment shall generally be made within 2 months after the project is completed and accepted, or no more than 3 months if the project is of large scale. Second, take the initiative to complete the basic work of the preparation of financial final accounts. After the capital construction project is completed and put into use or is qualified for trial operation, the financial final accounts should be prepared within 3 months. The competent authorities of the project shall firstly review the financial final accounts of the project before they grant the approval, and the projects that meet the conditions for approval shall be approved within 6 months. Third, actively intensify efforts to transfer the long-used construction-in-progress projects to fixed assets. The project agencies should further standardize and strengthen project management and comprehensively clean up the accounting accounts. Fourth, incorporate the information regarding the transfer of long-used construction-in-progress projects to fixed assets into the progress report on the work of financial final accounts of the central capital construction projects. Fifth, incorporate into the annual asset report the information regarding the transfer of long-used construction-in-progress projects to fixed assets. ■

POLICY 39 MOF, SAT and the Central Publicity Department jointly published the *Circular on Continued Implementation of Several Tax Policies for the Conversion of Commercial Cultural Institutions into Enterprises in the Reform of Cultural System*

On February 26, MOF, SAT and the Central Publicity Department jointly published the *Circular on Continued Implementation of Several Tax Policies for the Conversion of Commercial Cultural*

Institutions into Enterprises in the Reform of Cultural System, which provided the following. First, the commercial cultural institutions converted into enterprises will be exempted from the corporate income tax in five years from the date of the registration after conversion. Enterprises that have completed the conversion before December 31, 2018 may continue to be exempted from the corporate income tax for five years starting from January 1, 2019. Second, if the cultural institutions financed by the finance authorities are converted into enterprises, property tax will be exempted for their self-use property for five years starting from the date of the registration after conversion. Enterprises that have completed the conversion before December 31, 2018 will continue to be exempted from property tax for their self-use property for five years starting from January 1, 2019. Third, the cultural enterprises which are set up by separating the publishing, printing and other relevant commercial assets from Party newspapers and journals will be exempted from VAT on their income derived from the publication of Party newspapers and Party journals starting from the date of registration. Fourth, the corporate income tax, VAT, urban maintenance and construction tax, deed tax and stamp tax involved in the evaluation of asset value appreciation and asset transfer during the conversion of commercial cultural institutions may continue to enjoy relevant preferential tax policies in line with the existing regulations. ■

POLICY 40

MOF, SAT and PBoC jointly published the *Circular on Further Strengthening the Management of Service Fees for Agents that Withhold, Collect and Levy Taxes*

On February 27, MOF, SAT and PBoC jointly published the *Circular on Further Strengthening the Management of Service Fees for Agents that Withhold, Collect and Levy Taxes*, which provided the following. First, budget management. The services fees for agents withholding, collecting and levying taxes shall be included in budget management, and be arranged by the finance authorities through budgetary expenditures; such service fees will be settled on an annual basis; if the relationship with the agents that withhold, collect and levy taxes is terminated within a year, the application for service fees shall be submitted to the tax authorities within 3 months after the termination for the tax authorities to handle the settlement of the service fees; the tax authorities at all levels shall, in accordance with the procedures and requirements, include the application from the agents for service fees into the departmental budget for the next year; MOF will approve the fund-using plan in a timely manner according to the approved budget of services fees. Second, accounting management. The tax authorities at all levels shall, in accordance with the relevant regulations on accounting of administrative institutions, make timely, comprehensive and complete accounting of service fees; the tax authorities at all levels shall, in accordance with the requirements of finance authorities on preparing and reviewing final accounts, prepare the final accounts of service fees in a truthful, accurate, comprehensive and timely manner, and do a good job in the review of final accounts. Third, payment management. The tax authorities shall not pay service fees to the agents, whether they are units or individuals, that fail to withhold, collect and levy taxes in accordance with laws and regulations; no service fees shall be paid for the entrusted levying of taxes on other's behalf among tax authorities; the service fee income earned by the agents shall be separately accounted for and included in the income of the agents for funding the expenses related to office supplies, personnel costs, IT development, consumables, transportation expenses, etc.. Fourth, supervision and management. Except as otherwise stipulated by laws and administrative regulations, tax authorities at all levels may not directly withhold the service fees from taxes or remove the service fees from the treasury. The treasury at all levels shall not handle the removal of the above-mentioned service fees from the treasury. ■

41

MOF and SAT published the *Circular on the Continued Implementation of the VAT Policy for Supporting the Development of Cultural Enterprises*

Source: MOF

On March 1, MOF and SAT published the *Circular on the Continued Implementation of the VAT Policy for Supporting the Development of Cultural Enterprises,* which provided the following. First, for the film group companies (including member companies) authorized by the film authorities (including at the central, provincial, prefecture and county levels) to engage in film production, distribution and screening as well as film studios and other film companies, their income obtained from the sales of the copies of films (including digital copies), the transfer of film copyrights (including transfer and licensing), the release of films and the screening of films in rural areas will be exempted from VAT. Second, the basic cable TV viewing maintenance fees charged by radio and television operating service companies and the basic viewing fees of rural cable TV will be exempted from VAT. ■

42

MOF published the *Implementation Guidelines on Promoting the Well-regulated Development of PPP*

On March 8, MOF published the *Implementation Guidelines on Promoting the Well-regulated Development of PPP,* which provided the following. First, the finance authorities at all levels should further raise their awareness, follow the principle of "well-regulated operation, strict supervision, openness and transparency, integrity and compliance", effectively prevent and control the hidden debt risks of local governments, resolutely fight the battle against major risks, and solidly advance the well-regulated development of PPP. Second, the well-regulated PPP projects should meet certain conditions, and the new government-paid projects should also comply with the relevant prudential requirements. Third, the finance authorities at all levels should put well-regulated operation first, implement the well-regulated PPP projects in strict accordance with requirements, and must not carry out any prescribed behaviors. Fourth, the finance authorities at all levels should work with relevant authorities to take multiple measures, with a view to strengthening well-regulated management and classified guidance and increasing policy support for key areas and key projects. Fifth, the finance authorities at all levels should take the initiative to accelerate the establishment of a well-coordinated and effective working mechanism. ■

43 MOF published the *Circular on the Open Selection and Appointment of Consulting Experts for Revising the Law of the People's Republic of China on Certified Public Accountants*

On March 12, MOF published the *Circular on the Open Selection and Appointment of Consulting Experts for Revising the Law of the People's Republic of China on Certified Public Accountants,* which provided the following. First, the consulting experts to be selected and appointed should comply with laws and regulations, conscientiously fulfill duties and responsibilities, and possess professional competence. Second, the rights of consulting experts mainly include: attending the plenary meetings and group meetings of consulting experts and expressing opinions and suggestions on the topics discussed at the meetings; participating in relevant research activities on the revision of the CPA Law; and presenting comments and suggestions on the key and difficult issues arising from the revision of the CPA Law. The obligations of consulting experts mainly include: attending the plenary meetings and group meetings of consulting experts on time; cooperating with research activities and other related work in the process of revising the CPA Law; undertaking the confidentiality obligations as required, and promptly informing their changes in work and contact information. ■

44 MOF published the *Circular on Improving the Management of the Central Government's Special Funds for the Development of Financial Inclusion in 2019*

On March 12, MOF published the *Circular on Improving the Management of the Central Government's Special Funds for the Development of Financial Inclusion in 2019,* which provided the following. First, increase subsidies and incentives for the guarantee loans to business startup and earnestly implement the policy of providing targeted subsidies for rural financial institutions. Second, starting from 2019, the incentive policy for the increase of agriculture-related loans of county-level financial institutions will cease to be implemented. Starting from 2019, the central government will no longer earmark incentive funds for PPP projects. Third, the Inspector's Office of MOF should attach great importance to the management of special funds for financial inclusion, consolidate the foundation of management, and ensure the authenticity of data. The provincial finance departments shall, in conjunction with the relevant authorities, organize the monitoring and analysis of guarantee loans for business startup, strengthen the precise management of guarantee loans for business startup, and further promote the well-regulated development of guarantee loans for business startup. Encourage all localities to explore and innovate according to local conditions, further leverage fiscal and financial policies, effectively guide financial resources to "support small businesses and help micro businesses", ease the difficulties of private and small and micro enterprises in accessing affordable financing, and promote the optimization of economic structure and high-quality development. ■

POLICY 45

MOF and the State Council Leading Group Office of Poverty Alleviation and Development published the *Circular on Improving the Pilot Program on the Consolidation of Agricultural-related Funds in Poor Counties in 2019*

Source: MOF

On March 13, MOF and the State Council Leading Group Office of Poverty Alleviation and Development published the *Circular on Improving the Pilot Program on the Consolidation of Agricultural-related Funds in Poor Counties in 2019,* which provided the following. First, all provinces should supervise and guide poor counties to earmark the consolidated funds for agricultural production and development and rural infrastructure construction and prioritize the industrial development projects that help poor people to continuously increase income, consistent with the poverty reduction plan, annual poverty reduction task and the current poverty reduction standard. Second, all localities must address the problem of not firmly supporting or even resisting the consolidation of funds, and resolutely expose the typical cases and seriously hold the persons involved accountable. Third, all provinces must conscientiously guide poor counties to prepare annual consolidation plans according to requirements and effectively increase the proportion of substantive consolidation, in line with the county-level poverty reduction plans and the annual poverty reduction task. Fourth, effectively require provincial-level governments to assume the overall responsibilities, strengthen the accountability of major players, and enhance inspection, audit, performance evaluation and supervision. ■

POLICY 46

MOF and SAT jointly published the *Announcement on the Standards for Determining the Residence Time of Individuals without Domicile in China*

On March 16, MOF and SAT jointly published the *Announcement on the Standards for Determining the Residence Time of Individuals without Domicile in China,* which provided the following. First, for individuals without domicile who have resided in China for over 183 days or more in a tax year, if the cumulative number of days of residing in China was over 183 days or more in the previous six years, and there was no single departure from China for more than 30 days in any of the previous six years, their income derived from China and overseas in the tax year shall be subject to individual income tax; if the cumulative number of days of residing in China in any of the previous six years was less than 183 days or a single departure exceeded 30 days, their income of the tax year from outside China and paid by overseas units or individuals will be exempted from individual income tax. Second, for individuals without domicile, the number of residing days in China within one tax year is calculated as the cumulative number of days that individuals have stayed in China. If the duration of stay in China is 24 hours on a given day, the day shall be counted into the number of days of residing in China. If the duration of stay in China is less than 24 hours on a given day, the day shall not be counted into the number of days of residing in China. ■

47 MOF and SAT jointly published the *Circular on the Individual Income Tax Preferential Policies for The Guangdong-Hong Kong-Macao Greater Bay Area*

On March 16, MOF and SAT jointly published the *Circular on the Individual Income Tax Preferential Policies for The Guangdong-Hong Kong-Macao Greater Bay Area,* which provided the following. First, Guangdong Province and Shenzhen City, in light of the difference between the Mainland and Hong Kong Special Administrative Region on SAR individual income tax bearing, may provide subsidies for the overseas (including Hong Kong SAR, Macao SAR and Taiwan) high-end talents and urgently-needed talents working in the Greater Bay Area. These subsidies are exempted from individual income tax. Second, the identification and subsidy methods for the overseas high-end talents and urgently-needed talents working in the Greater Bay Area shall be implemented in accordance with the relevant regulations of Guangdong Province and Shenzhen City. Third, the applicable scope of this Circular includes nine cities in the Pearl River Delta: Guangzhou, Shenzhen, Zhuhai, Foshan, Huizhou, Dongguan, Zhongshan, Jiangmen and Zhaoqing. ■

48 MOF and SAT jointly published the *Circular on the Individual Income Tax Policies for Non-Resident Individuals and Individuals without Domicile*

On March 17, MOF and SAT jointly published the *Circular on the Individual Income Tax Policies for Non-Resident Individuals and Individuals without Domicile,* which provided the following. First, the non-resident individuals who have resided in China for no more than 90 days in a tax year shall calculate and pay individual income tax only for their wage and salary incomes derived from their working period in China and paid or borne by their employers in China. Second, in a tax year, non-resident individuals who have more than 90 but less than 183 cumulative days of residing in China shall calculate and pay individual income tax for their wage and salary incomes derived from their working period in China; wage and salary incomes derived from their working period outside China are not subject to individual income tax. Third, when individuals without domicile are resident individuals and have resided in China for less than six consecutive years of accumulated domestic residence of 183 days per year, if relevant preferential conditions are met, all their wage and salary incomes, except for the portion derived from their working period outside China and paid or borne by units and individuals outside China, shall be subject to individual income tax. Fourth, after six consecutive years of continuous domestic residence of 183 days or more in China per year, resident individuals without domicile who do not meet the relevant preferential conditions, shall calculate and pay individual income tax for all their wages and salary incomes derived from within and outside China. ■

POLICY 49 MOF published the *Decision on Revising the Registration Procedures for Certified Public Accountants*

On March 19, MOF published the *Decision on Revising the Registration Procedures for Certified Public Accountants,* which provided the following. First, the Article 6 is revised as: applicants applying for registration should submit, through the accounting firms at which they work, the application form for CPA registration to the provincial CPA Associations in the provinces/cities where the accounting firms are located. Second, the Article 7 is revised as: applicants and the accounting firms at which the applicants work shall be responsible for the authenticity of the content of application materials. Third, the Article 9 is revised as: the provincial CPA Associations shall review the application materials submitted by applicants. If the application materials are incomplete or do not conform to the statutory form, they shall inform, on the spot or within 5 working days, the applicants about the materials and contents that need to be supplemented. If the application materials are complete and conform to the statutory form, the application should be processed readily. Fourth, one more paragraph is added to the Article 16 as the second paragraph: those who are deregistered or have their CPC certificate revoked due to item (4) of the preceding paragraph will be warned by the provincial finance departments and be made public. Fifth, one more article is added as the Article 17: if the applicants and the accounting firms at which they work present false application materials, the provincial finance departments shall issue a warning to the applicants and the chief partners (the chief accountants) of the accounting firms and make the case public. ■

POLICY 50 MOF and MOHRSS jointly published the *Circular on Adjusting the Basic Pensions for Retired Persons in 2019*

Source: MOF

On March 20, MOF and MOHRSS jointly published the *Circular on Adjusting the Basic Pensions for Retired Persons in 2019,* which provided the following. First, the overall adjustment level is set at around 5% of the monthly basic pension for retirees in 2018. Second, continue to adopt a combined policy of fixed-sum adjustment and linkage adjustment, and appropriately tilt to unify the adjustment measures for retirees of enterprises and government institutions. Third, adjust the funds required for basic pensions. Basic pension insurance for enterprise employees will be funded by the basic pension insurance fund for enterprise employees, and the basic pension insurance for government institution employees will be funded by the basic pension insurance fund for government institution employees. Fourth, all regions should attach great importance to the adjusting work, strengthen leadership, well organize the implementation, enhance publicity and explanation, properly guide the public opinion, and ensure that all work is carried out smoothly. In accordance with the unified deployment of the State Council and in line with the local conditions, specific implementation plans shall be formulated and submitted to MOHRSS and MOF for approval before May 31, 2019. ■

51 MOF, SAT and GAC jointly published the *Announcement on Policies for Deepening the VAT Reform*

On March 21, MOF, SAT and GAC jointly published the *Announcement on Policies for Deepening the VAT Reform,* which provided the following. First, VAT general taxpayers (hereinafter referred to as taxpayers) who make VAT taxable sales or import goods will see their VAT rate fall to 13% if the original 16% rate is applied; and see their VAT rate fall to 9% if the original 10% rate is applied. Second, if the taxpayers purchase agricultural products and the original 10% deduction rate is applied, the deduction rate will be adjusted to 9%. If the taxpayers purchase agricultural products for production or for entrusted processing of goods with a 13% tax rate, the input tax amount will be calculated according to the 10% deduction rate. Third, the export goods service with the original 16% tax rate and the export tax rebate rate of 16% will see the export tax rebate rate adjusted to 13%; the export goods and cross-border taxable activites with the original export tax rate of 10% and the export tax rebate rate of 10% will see the export tax rebate rate adjusted to 9%. Fourth, the original 13% tax refund rate for goods purchased by overseas passengers will fall to 11%; the original 9% tax refund rate for goods purchased by overseas passengers will fall to 8%. Fifth, starting from April 1, 2019, the input tax of taxpayers acquiring real estate or real estate construction projects will no longer be deductible in two years. Sixth, the taxpayers who purchase domestic passenger transportation services will be allowed to deduct the input tax from the output tax. Seventh, from April 1, 2019 to December 31, 2021, taxpayers in the producer and consumer services industries will be allowed to deduct the taxable amount by an extra 10% of the current deductible input tax. Eighth, the trial of the tax refund system for the un-deducted input tax at the end of the VAT period will be carried out starting from April 1, 2019. ■

52 MOF and MOA jointly published the *Circular on Improving the Demonstration Program for Developing Townships with Strong Agricultural Industries in 2019*

On March 25, MOF and MOA jointly published the *Circular on Improving the Demonstration Program for Developing Townships with Strong Agricultural Industries in 2019,* which provided the following. First, focus on the main business and promote cluster development; encourage innovation-led and integrated development; promote participation by various parties and coordinated advancement. Second, strengthen the leading agricultural industry, foster major players for industrial integration, develop innovative mechanisms for linked interests, establish and improve the systems and mechanisms, and eradicate poverty through enhanced industrial development. Third, the central government will provide appropriate support for the demonstration program for developing townships with strong agricultural industries through financial incentives and other means. Fourth, the towns applying for the program should meet the following conditions: strong support of local governments; solid foundation of leading industries; strong demonstration impact of industrial integration; scientific and reasonable planning; and sound mechanism for close interaction with the agricultural industry. Fifth, observe relevant requirements; strengthen organizational leadership; strengthen coordination and cooperation; strengthen supervision and management; and enchance the work on stock-taking and publicity. ■

53 MOF, MIIT, MOST, and NDRC jointly published the *Circular on Further Improving the Government Subsidy Policy for the Promotion and Application of New Energy Vehicles*

Source: MOF

On March 26, MOF, MIIT, MOST, and NDRC jointly published the *Circular on Further Improving the Government Subsidy Policy for the Promotion and Application of New Energy Vehicles*, which provided the following. First, appropriately raise the threshold of technical indicators, keep the upper limit of technical indicators unchanged, focus on supporting high-quality products with high technology level, and encourage enterprises to pay attention to safety and consistency. Second, reduce the subsidy standards for new energy passenger cars, new energy buses and new energy trucks, promote the survival of the fittest in the industry, and prevent severe fluctuations of the market. Third, starting from 2019, a portion of funds will be pre-allocated to vehicles with operating mileage requirements after the completion of sales. After the mileage requirements are met, subsidies can be applied for in accordance with procedures. Fourth, starting from 2019, models that meet the requirements of the Circular but have not yet met the technical conditions for subsidies are also included in the recommended model list. Fifth, further strengthen the safety and consistency oversight, and require the competent authorities to speed up the establishment of a mechanism for product safety monitoring and "consistency" random inspection. ■

54 MOF and MOA jointly published the *Circular on Improving the Implementation of the 2019 Promotion Project for the Green, Circular, Quality and Efficient Agriculture with Special Features*

On March 28, MOF and MOA jointly published the *Circular on Improving the Implementation of the 2019 Promotion Project for the Green, Circular, Quality and Efficient Agriculture with Special Features,* which provided the following. First, the promotion project for the green, circular, quality and efficient agriculture with special features will be under the central planning, provincial responsibility and county implementation. Second, encourage the provinces to develop innovative institutional mechanisms and policy systems, make coordinated use of funds to support agricultural production and development as well as agricultural resources and ecological protection, encourage industrial and commercial capital to participate in the development of the green and quality agricultural products with special features, and guide financial institutions to support project implementation. Third, the provincial finance departments should strengthen financial support and policy supervision. The financial divisions of the provincial agricultural departments should step up organization and policy coordination. The divisions for rural industrial development should do a good job in project implementation, study and refine specific measures, and guide and urge local governments to improve project implementation. Fourth, provincial agricultural departments and finance departments should enhance daily supervision and guidance, improve management and assessment mechanisms, and accelerate the implementation of projects. ■

55 MOF and the National Natural Science Foundation of China (NSFC) jointly published the *Circular on Further Improving the Management of Projects and Funds by NSFC*

On April 1, MOF and the National Natural Science Foundation of China (NSFC) jointly published the *Circular on Further Improving the Management of Projects and Funds by NSFC,* which provided the following. First, when developing the budget, the projects supported by fixed-sum subsidies only need to provide basic calculation explanations without details; cost-compensated projects only need to provide necessary explanations of the calculation process. Second, except for the equipment fees of the direct expenses of NSFC project, the budget adjustment rights of other subjects will all be delegated to the dependent units. Third, for the cost-compensated projects, after the expiry of subsidy period, the dependent units should promptly measure the accounts and assets and independently select qualified third-party institutions to complete the financial audit which will serve as the basis for financial acceptance. Fourth, the cost-compensated NSFC projects are required to go through project and financial acceptance procedures to be completed by a group of NSFC experts. ■

56 MOF, GAC and SAT jointly published the *Circular on Adjusting the Volume of Imported Natural Gas in the Tax Rebate Policy for Some Projects*

On April 4, MOF, GAC and SAT jointly published the *Circular on Adjusting the Volume of Imported Natural Gas in the Tax Rebate Policy for Some Projects,* which provided the following. First, starting from January 1, 2019, the Zhejiang LNG Project's import volume that enjoys favorable policy will be adjusted to 7 million tons/year, and the import volume that enjoys favorable policy for the Tangshan LNG project, the Tianjin LNG project, the Guangxi LNG project and the Tianjin floating LNG project will be adjusted to 6 million tons/year. Second, the import volume that enjoys favorable policy in 2018 for the Zhejiang LNG project, the Tangshan LNG project, the Tianjin floating LNG project and the Shanghai LNG project are 5.472 million tons, 5.466 million tons, 3.535 million tons and 3.985 million tons respectively. ■

57 MOF, SAT and the State Council Leading Group Office of Poverty Alleviation and Development jointly published the *Announcement on the Pre-tax Deduction Policy for the Income Tax of Enterprise Poverty Alleviation Donations*

On April 8, MOF, SAT and the State Council Leading Group Office of Poverty Alleviation and Development jointly published the *Announcement on the Pre-tax Deduction Policy for the Income Tax of Enterprise Poverty Alleviation Donations,* which provided the following. First, from January 1, 2019 to December 31, 2022, the poverty alleviation donations made by enterprise to the targeted

Source: MOF

poor regions through public welfare organizations or governments at or above the county level (including county level) and their constituent departments and directly affiliated institutions shall be deducted when the taxable corporate income is calculated. Second, for the enterprise that spends on both poverty alleviation donations and other public welfare donations at the same time, when the annual deduction limit for public welfare donation expenditures is calculated, the poverty alleviation donation expenditures that meet the above-mentioned conditions will not be counted. Third, the part of the enterprise's poverty alleviation donations that occurred during the period from January 1, 2015 to December 31, 2018 and has not been deducted from the taxable income may implement the above-mentioned corporate income tax policy. ■

POLICY 58

MOF and MOA jointly published the *Circular on Further Strengthening the Supervision and Discipline of Agricultural Machinery Purchase Subsidy Policy*

On April 8, MOF and MOA jointly published the *Circular on Further Strengthening the Supervision and Discipline of Agricultural Machinery Purchase Subsidy Policy*, which provided the following. First, establish and improve the joint supervision mechanism of agricultural machinery and finance authorities under the leadership of the government, and enhance the supervisory accountability of sub-provincial agricultural machinery and financial authorities. Second, crackdown on fraudulent claims of subsidies and strictly punish such behaviors in accordance with regulations. Third, strengthen the analysis of the implementation of funds in counties (cities) within the province, and urge the areas that are slow with budget implementation to accelerate the use of funds. Improve the allocation of funds among counties (cities) in the second half of the year and guide the counties (cities) to prioritize the use of carryover funds. Require sub-county level agriculture machinery authorities to complete a formal review within 30 working days (excluding the publicity time) after receiving the purchaser's subsidy application and send it to the finance authorities of the same level. ■

POLICY 59

MOF and MOA jointly published the *Circular on Improving the Implementation of the Program for Agricultural Production and Development in 2019*

On April 9, MOF and MOA jointly published the *Circular on Improving the Implementation of the Program for Agricultural Production and Development in 2019*, which provided the following. First, implement the quality-driven agriculture development strategy, improve the funding system for implementing the rural revitalization strategy, develop innovative mechnisms and approaches for investing and using funds, and further improve the benefits of fund use. Second, further innovate and improve the mechanism for fund management and use, consolidate the government special transfer payment for agriculture, and fully implement the management model of "major special programs + task list". Third, develop provincial implementation plans as soon as possible and clarify the implementation conditions, subsidy recipients, subsidy standards, implementation requirements and regulatory measures. MOF and MOA will comprehensively establish a project performance evaluation system. On the basis of the task list and performance targets assigned to provinces, project performance evaluation will be organized in a timely manner and a result-oriented incentive mechanism will be established to reward the good performers and punish the bad ones. ■

POLICY 60 MOF published the *Circular on Printing and Distributing the No. 1101 Auditing Standard for Chinese Certified Public Accountants - Overall Objectives of Certified Public Accountants and General Requirements for Audit Work and Other 18 Auditing Standards*

On April 9, MOF published the *Circular on Printing and Distributing the No. 1101 Auditing Standard for Chinese Certified Public Accountants - Overall Objectives of Certified Public Accountants and General Requirements for Audit Work and Other 18 Auditing Standards*, which provided the following. First, the Chinese Institute of Certified Public Accountants has revised 18 Auditing Standards, including the No. 1101 Auditing Standard for Chinese Certified Public Accountants - Overall Objectives of Certified Public Accountants and General Requirements for Audit Work, which will come into force on July 1, 2019. Second, after the entry into force of this batch of auditing standards, the corresponding 18 auditing standards in the Circular of the Ministry of Finance on Printing and Distributing the No. 1101 Auditing Standard for Chinese Certified Public Accountants - Overall Objectives of Certified Public Accountants and General Requirements for Audit Work and Other 38 Auditing Standards as well as in the Circular of the Ministry of Finance on Printing and Distributing the No. 1504 Auditing Standard for Chinese Certified Public Accountants - Communication of Key Audit Matters in Audit Reports and Other 12 Standards will be repealed at the same time. ■

Source: MOF

POLICY 61 MOF and SAT jointly published the *Circular on Extending the Preferential Policy of VAT, Real Estate Tax and Urban Land Use Tax for Heating Suppliers*

On April 10, MOF and SAT jointly published the *Circular on Extending the Preferential Policy of*

VAT, Real Estate Tax and Urban Land Use Tax for Heating Suppliers, which provided the following. First, from January 1, 2019 to the end of the heating period in 2020, the income obtained by heating suppliers by providing heating to residents will be exempted from the value-added tax. Second, from January 1, 2019 to December 31, 2020, heating suppliers that charge heating fees to residents will be exempted from real estate tax and urban land use tax for the factories and land used for providing heating services; other factories and land of heating suppliers shall be subject to real estate tax and urban land use tax in accordance with regulations. ■

POLICY 62

MOF and SAT jointly published the *Circular on Matters Concerning the Pre-tax Deduction Policy for the Corporate Income Tax of the Risk Reserve Fund and Futures Investor Protection Fund of the Shanghai International Energy Trading Center*

On April 10, MOF and SAT jointly published *the Circular on Matters Concerning the Pre-tax Deduction Policy for the Corporate Income Tax of the Risk Reserve Fund and Futures Investor Protection Fund of the Shanghai International Energy Trading Center,* which provided the following. First, for the risk reserve fund paid with 20% of service fees charged to members, the balance of the risk reserve fund, if within the prescribed quota, may be deducted on a pre-tax basis from the corporate income tax. Second, for the Futures Investor Protection Fund paid with 2% of service fees charged to members of the futures companies, the total amount of the fund, if within the prescribed quota, may be deducted on a pre-tax basis from the corporate income tax. Third, if the above-mentioned reserve fund and protection fund are liquidated or rebated, the corporate income tax shall be reinstated as required. ■

POLICY 63

MOF published the *Circular on Printing and Distributing the Interim Measures for the Record-filing of Overseas Accounting Firm's Audit over the Financial Reports of Overseas Institution's Bond Issuance in the National Interbank Bond Market*

On April 11, MOF published the *Circular on Printing and Distributing the Interim Measures for the Record-filing of Overseas Accounting Firm's Audit over the Financial Reports of Overseas Institution's Bond Issuance in the National Interbank Bond Market,* which provided the following. First, if the overseas accounting firm, entrusted by an overseas institution, is to audit the financial reports of overseas institution's bond issuance in the National Interbank Bond market, the overseas accounting firm shall comply with the relevant provisions and be subject to the supervision of MOF. Second, the overseas accounting firm that engages in the financial reporting and auditing business related to bond issuance by overseas institution shall make its first record-filing to MOF no later than 20 business days before the overseas institution submits the application for bond issuance, and shall make annual record-filing to MOF before May 31 of each year during the duration of the bonds. Third, when the overseas accounting firm makes the first record-filing, it shall submit the form concerning the overseas accounting firm's engagement in the financial reporting and auditing business for bond issuance by overseas institutions as well as the relevant documents relating to the business permit granted by the country or region where the overseas accounting firm is located. Fourth, when an overseas accounting firm makes an annual record-filing, it shall submit the form concerning the overseas accounting firm's engagement in the financial reporting and auditing business for bond issuance by overseas institutions. ■

POLICY 64

MOF and MOA jointly published the *Circular on Carrying out the Rural "Toilet Revolution" in Villages and Advancing the Work on Fiscal Rewards and Subsidies*

On April 12, MOF and MOA jointly published the *Circular on Carrying out the Rural "Toilet Revolution" in Villages and Advancing the Work on Fiscal Rewards and Subsidies,* which provided the following. First, the principle of rewards and subsidies. Promote gradual coverage in the whole village; enable farmers to play the principal part and the government to provide guidance; allow the local government to play the main role and the central government to provide support; enhance coordination across regions and offer differentiated subsidies. Second, procedures for rewards and subsidies. Data submission and review; fund allocation and disbursement; the scope of use of funds; and the submission of the plan for rewards and subsidies. Third, related requirements. All localities should, in accordance with the requirements of "provincial responsibility and county implementation", effectively balance the sources of funds such as subsidies from the higher-level government, the local general public budget and the land value-added income; and enhance the financial support for whole-village coverage. The central government will continue to support the treatment of rural household garbage and sewage, the utilization of livestock and poultry manures and the construction of toilets in tourist scenic spots through existing channels, and encourage local governments to strengthen coordination with the whole-village coverage in terms of project layout, fundraising and functional coordination. Local agricultural and rural departments at all levels should, in conjunction with relevant departments, timely collect and accurately monitor the dynamic information of rural toilet reform work, strictly verify relevant data, and ensure the authenticity, accuracy and completeness of the basic data. It is necessary to publicly disclose the use of reward and subsidy funds in various forms. The fund allocation plan for the rewards and subsidies to administrative villages shall be publicized on the official website of the relevant departments at the county level. The distribution of funds to households shall be publicized in the local village, subject to the supervision of the society and the masses, and enhance the transparency of the use of funds. The finance departments at all levels should, in conjunction with the agricultural and rural affairs departments, observe the requirements of the full implementation of budget performance management, establish and improve the whole-process budget performance management mechanism, improve ex-ante performance evaluation, set performance targets in a scientific and appropriate way, undertake performance monitoring and self-assessment against performance targets, make timely evaluation of key performance targets, strengthen the use of performance results, and publicize performance information. The payment of the central fiscal reward and subsidy funds shall be implemented in accordance with the relevant provisions of the centralized treasury payment. ■

POLICY 65

MOF, SAT and CSRC jointly published the *Circular on the Tax Policy for the Pilot Issuance of Chinese Depositary Receipts by Innovative Enterprises*

Source: MOF

On April 12, MOF, SAT and CSRC jointly published the *Circular on the Tax Policy for the Pilot Issuance of Chinese Depositary Receipts by Innovative Enterprises,* which provided the following. First, personal income tax policy. From the starting date of the pilot, the income earned by individual investors from the price difference in the transfer of the CDR of innovative enterprises will be temporarily exempted from personal income tax within three years (36 months, the same below); the dividend income earned by individual investors by holding the CDR of innovative enterprises will be applicable for the differentiated personal income tax policy of dividend income within three years. Second, the corporate income tax policy. For the income earned by the enterprise investors from the price difference in the transfer of the CDR of innovative enterprises and the dividend income earned through holding the CDR of innovative enterprises, the corporate income tax shall be exempted according to the policy governing the income earned from the price difference in the transfer of stock and the dividend income earned through holding stock. The income earned by public-equity investment fund (closed securities investment fund and open-end securities investment fund) from the price difference in the transfer of the CDR of innovative enterprises and the dividend income earned through holding the CDR of innovative enterprises shall not be levied with corporate income tax according to the tax policy governing the public-equity investment fund. The income accumulated by Qualified Foreign Institutional Investors (QFII) and RMB Qualified Foreign Institutional Investors (RQFII) from the price difference in the transfer of the CDR of innovative enterprises and the dividend income accumulated through holding the CDR of innovative enterprises shall be deemed as the income from the transfer of equity assets and the dividend income and be exempted from corporate income tax. Third, the VAT policy. The income earned by individual investors from the price difference in the transfer of the CDR of innovative enterprises shall be temporarily exempted from VAT. The income earned by institutional investors from the price difference in the transfer of the CDR of innovative enterprises shall be exempted from VAT according to the financial product transfer policy. From the starting date of the pilot, the income earned by public-equity investment fund managers (closed securities investment fund and open-end securities investment fund) from the price difference in the transfer of the CDR of innovative enterprises shall be temporarily exempted from VAT within three years. The income earned by the QFII and RQFII from the price difference in the transfer of the CDR of innovative enterprises by entrusting domestic companies to conduct the transfer shall be temporarily exempted from VAT. Fourth, the stamp duty policy. Within three years from the starting date of the pilot, for the CDR of innovative enterprises transferred on the Shanghai Stock Exchange and the Shenzhen Stock Exchange, the transferor shall pay the stamp duty on securities transactions at a rate of 1‰ of the actual transaction value. ■

66 MOF published the *Circular on Printing and Distributing the Measures for the Management of the Funds for the Service Industry Development*

On April 16, MOF published the *Circular on issuing the Measures for the Management of the Funds for the Service Industry Development,* which provided the following. In order to support the accelerated development of the service industry, the central government set up the funds for the development of the service industry. To strengthen fund management and improve the efficiency of fund use, the Measures for the Management of the Funds for Service Industry Development were revised in accordance with relevant national laws, regulations, and budget management requirements. ■

67 MOF and SAT jointly published the *Announcement on the Income Tax Policy for Railway Bond Interest Income*

On April 17, MOF and SAT jointly published the *Announcement on the Income Tax Policy for Railway Bond Interest Income,* which provided the following. First, the corporate income tax levied on the interest income earned by the enterprise investors through holding the railway bonds issued from 2019 to 2023 will be halved. Second, the interest income earned by individual investors through holding the railway bonds issued from 2019 to 2023 will be included into the taxable income at a rate to be reduced by 50% when the personal income tax is calculated. The taxes will be withheld and paid by the redemption agency when interest payments are made to individual investors. Third, railway bonds refer to bonds issued and repaid by the China Railway Corporation, including the China railway construction bills, medium-term notes, short-term financing bonds and other debt financing instruments. ■

68 MOF and MNR jointly published the *Circular on Further Clarifying the Matters Concerning the Collection and Administration of Mining Rights Transfer Income*

On April 18, MOF and MNR jointly published the *Circular on Further Clarifying the Matters Concerning the Collection and Administration of Mining Rights Transfer Income,* which provided the following. First, before the issuance of the document No. 35 of Cai Zong [2017], the capital occupation fees to be paid by mining rights owners who should pay for exploration. Mining rights in installments shall continue to be paid in accordance with the original mining rights transfer contract or installment payment plan under the subject of mining rights transfer income, and shall be divided according to the prescribed proportion. Second, if non-profit mining enterprises that undertake special functions explicitly required by laws and regulations or the State Council find it difficult to pay the mining rights transfer income, the payment may be deferred for a certain period of time with the approval of MOF and the Ministry of Natural Resources. Third, mining rights transfer income late payment fees shall be paid under the subject of mining rights transfer income, and be divided according to the prescribed proportion. ■

69 MOF and MOHURD jointly publi-shed the *Circular on the Special Fund Budget for the Urban Subsidized Housing Project Supported by the Central Government in 2019*

On April 15, MOF and MOHURD jointly published the *Circular on the Special Fund Budget for the Urban Subsidized Housing Project Supported by the Central Government in 2019,* which provided the following. First, the special funds are used to provide rental subsidies for eligible households and to support urban shantytown renovation projects. Second, within 30 days after receiving special funds, the special funds will be allocated to the finance authorities at or above the county level. Third, after receiving the special funds, the city and county finance authorities shall implement special management and conduct separate accounting, and use the funds to provide rental subsidies for eligible households and to support urban shantytown renovation projects in accordance with regulations. Fourth, step up performance monitoring to ensure to achieve performance targets on schedule. ■

70 MOF, SAT and the State Council Leading Group Office of Poverty Alleviation and Development jointly published the *Announcement on the VAT Exemption Policy for Donations for Poverty Alleviation*

On April 19, MOF, SAT and the State Council Leading Group Office of Poverty Alleviation and Development jointly published the *Announcement on the VAT Exemption Policy for Donations for Poverty Alleviation,* which provided the following. First, from January 1, 2019 to December 31, 2022, institutional or individual businesses which donate the self-produced, commissioned or purchased goods indirectly through public welfare social organizations, people's governments at or above the county level and their constituent departments and directly affiliated institutions, or directly to units and individuals in poverty-stricken areas, shall be exempted from VAT. Second, the above VAT policy can be retroactively applied to the donation that occurred from January 1, 2015 to December 31, 2018. Third, the VAT that should be exempted according to the above provisions but has already been collected before the publication of this announcement can offset against the taxpayer's VAT payable in the following months or be refunded. If special VAT invoice has been issued to the purchaser, the special invoice shall be recovered to enable the application of the tax exemption. If the special invoice cannot be recovered, tax exemption will not be allowed. Fourth, local poverty alleviation offices and tax departments should strengthen communication and clarify the specific scope of local "targeted poverty alleviation areas" to ensure the effective implementation of policies. ■

71 MOF published the *Debt Sustainability Framework for Participating Countries of the Belt and Road Initiative*

On April 25, MOF published the *Debt Sustainability Framework for Participating Countries of the Belt and Road Initiative.* Based on the debt sustainability analysis framework of IMF and World Bank for low-income countries, this framework is a debt sustainability analysis tool that takes into account the reality of BRI countries and encourages the financial institutions in China and BRI countries as well as international institutions to use it on a voluntary basis. The release of the framework not only

Source: MOF

demonstrates China's positive and open attitude on debt sustainability, but also reflects China's emphasis on the actual national conditions and development needs of the low-income BRI countries. It will help make the decision-making of investment and financing more scientific, strengthen debt management capabilities of relevant countries, and promote high-quality development of BRI. ■

POLICY 72 MOF, SAT, NDRC, and MEE jointly published the *Announcement on the Corporate Income Tax Policy for the Third-Party Enterprises Engaging in Pollution Prevention and Control*

On April 26, MOF, SAT, NDRC, and MEE jointly published the *Announcement on the Corporate Income Tax Policy for the Third-Party Enterprises Engaging in Pollution Prevention and Control,* which provided the following. First, a corporate income tax rate at 15% is applicable to the eligible third-party enterprises engaging in pollution prevention and control. Second, third-party enterprises referred in this announcement shall simultaneously satisfy the following conditions. It includes legally registered resident enterprises in China (excluding Hong Kong SAR, Macao SAR and Taiwan), more than one year of continuous practice in operating environmental pollution control facilities and the ability to ensure normal functioning of facilities, and the annual operating income from providing environmental protection facilities services accounting for no less than 60% of the total income. Third, third-party enterprises shall judge whether they meet the above-mentioned conditions on their own. If they meet the conditions, they may declare to enjoy the tax breaks and keep the relevant materials for future reference. As the tax department carries out the follow-up management according to law, it may seek verification of the ecological environment department which may entrust professional institutions to carry out relevant verification work. ■

POLICY 73 MOF and SAT jointly published the *Announcement on the Issues Concerning the Corporate Income Tax Policy of Perpetual Bonds*

On April 26, MOF and SAT jointly published the *Announcement on the Issues Concerning the Corporate Income Tax Policy of Perpetual Bonds,* which provided the following. First, corporate income tax policies for dividends can be applied to the perpetual bonds issued by enterprises. Second, eligible perpetual bonds issued by enterprises may also apply to the corporate income tax policy for bond interest. Third, the eligible perpetual bonds refer to the perpetual bonds that meet 5 conditions, among them, the invested enterprises have the obligation to repay the principal; the bonds have clearly agreed interest rate and frequency of interest payment; and the bonds have certain investment terms. Fourth, enterprises that issue perpetual bonds should disclose to the investors their applicable tax treatment methods in the issuance documents at such issuance markets as the stock exchange and the inter-bank bond market. Fifth, enterprises that issue perpetual bonds shall not change the tax treatment method for each perpetual bond product once the method is determined. If the tax treatment method adopted by the enterprises for perpetual bonds is inconsistent with the accounting method, the issuer and the investor shall make corresponding tax adjustments when conducting tax treatment. ■

POLICY 74 MOF and SAT jointly published the *Announcement on Expanding the Application Scope of the Preferential Policy of Accelerated Depreciation for Fixed Assets*

On April 29, MOF and SAT jointly published the *Announcement on Expanding the Application Scope of the Preferential Policy of Accelerated Depreciation for Fixed Assets,* which provided the following. First, the industry scope for accelerated depreciation of fixed assets is extended to all manufacturing industries. Second, the manufacturing industry is defined according to the Industry Classification and *Code of National Economy of NBS (GB/T 4754-2017)*. Third, the manufacturing enterprises that have not enjoyed the preferential policy of accelerated depreciation of fixed assets before the publication of this announcement may enjoy such preferential treatment in the monthly (quarterly) prepayment declaration after the publication of this announcement or enjoy the preferential treatment in the 2019 annual tax calculation and payment. ■

POLICY 75 MOF and SAT jointly published the *Announcement on the Continued Implementation of the Preferential Tax Policy for Rural Safe Drinking Water Project*

On May 8, MOF and SAT jointly published the *Announcement on the Continued Implementation of the Preferential Tax Policy for Rural Safe Drinking Water Project,* which provided the following. First, the drinking water project operation and management unit will be exempted from deed tax if it obtains land use rights for the construction of drinking water project. Second, the property right transfer document signed by the drinking water project operation and management unit for obtaining the land use rights for the construction of the drinking water project as well as the construction project contract signed with the construction unit will be exempted from stamp duty. Third, the property and land used by the drinking water project operation and management unit for production and office will be exempted from property tax and urban land use tax. Fourth, the sales revenue of tap water obtained from the drinking water project operation and management unit providing rural residents with running water will be exempted from VAT. Fifth, for the income obtained by the drinking water project operation

Source: MOF

and management unit from the investment and operation of the new drinking water projects stipulated in the *Catalogue of Preferential Corporate Income Tax for Public Infrastructure Projects,* starting from the tax year of the first production and operation income obtained from the project, the corporate income tax will be exempted from the first year to the third year and be halved from the fourth year to the sixth year. ■

POLICY 76

Four departments jointly published the *Circular on Supporting the Promotion and Application of New Energy Buses*

On May 8, MOF, MIIT, MOT and NDRC jointly published the *Circular on Supporting the Promotion and Application of New Energy Buses,* which provided the following. First, appropriately raise the threshold of technical indicators for new energy buses, in order to support high-quality products with high technical level. Second, the localities may continue to provide subsidies for the purchase of new energy buses and allow the purchase of new energy buses to be exempted from vehicle purchase tax and vehicle and vessel tax. Third, give full play to the central public finance for the infrastructure subsidies, innovate supporting methods, attract private capital, accelerate the construction of new energy bus charging infrastructure, and meet the needs of vehicle use. Fourth, the transportation, finance, industry and information, development and reform departments of all provinces (autonomous regions and municipalities) should formulate implementation plans for new energy bus promotion and application and clarify the goals and timetable for new energy bus applications. Fifth, issue a notice before the funds are disbursed and make them public after disbursement. Set up and make public the reporting hotline or online reporting platform to receive the scrutiny of the public. ■

POLICY 77

MOF and SAT jointly published the *Announcement on the Preferential Tax Policies for Public Rental Housing*

Source: MOF

On May 9, MOF and SAT jointly published the *Announcement on the Preferential Tax Policies for Public Rental Housing, which provided the following.* First, the land used during the construction of public rental housing and the land occupied after the construction of public rental housing will be exempted from urban land use tax. For the public rental housing built in other housing projects, the urban land use tax involved in the construction and management of public rental housing will be exempted according to the proportion of the public rental housing floor area to the total floor area. Second, the public rental housing management units will be exempted from the stamp duty involved in the construction and management of public rental housing. For the public rental housing built in other housing projects, the stamp duty involved in the construction and management of public rental housing will be exempted according to the proportion of the public rental housing floor area to the total floor area. Third, the public rental housing management unit that purchases houses to be used as public rental housing will be exempted from deed tax and stamp duty; the lessor and lessee of the public rental housing will be exempted from the stamp duty involved in the signing of a lease agreement. Fourth, for the transfer of old houses to be used as public rental housing by enterprises, public institutions and social organizations, if the appreciation amount does not exceed 20% of the deduction amount, land appreciation tax will be exempted. Fifth, for the donation of houses to be used as public rental housing by enterprises, public institutions and social organizations consistent with tax laws and regulations, the portion of the public welfare donation expenditure that does not exceed 12% of the total annual profit is allowed to be deducted when calculating the taxable income, and the portion exceeding 12% of the total annual profit is allowed to be deducted when calculating the taxable income in the following three years. For the donation of houses to be used as public rental housing by individuals consistent with tax laws and regulations, the portion of the public welfare donation that does not exceed 30% of the declared taxable income is allowed to be deducted from the taxable income. Sixth, the housing rental subsidies received by the eligible families covered by the urban housing security scheme will be exempted from personal income tax. Seventh, public rental housing is exempted from property tax. The rental income from the operation of public rental housing is exempted from VAT. The public rental housing management unit shall keep separate accounting for the rental income of public rental housing, otherwise, it shall not enjoy the preferential policies of VAT and property tax exemption. ■

POLICY 78 The central government disbursed 1.985 billion RMB to support local government's implementation of the 2019 National Training Program for primary, secondary school and kindergarten teachers

According to the news published by MOF on May 13, to thoroughly implement the *Village Teacher Support Program (2015-2020),* the central government recently disbursed 1.985 billion RMB of special funds for the 2019 National Training Program for primary, secondary school and kindergarten teachers, so as to continue to support the central and western provinces to strengthen the training of teachers of primary and secondary schools and kindergartens in rural areas through methods such as off-the-job training, training in rural areas, online training and visits to prestigious schools. In 2019, factors such as "extremely poverty-stricken counties" and "the number of extremely poverty-stricken villages" are added to the allocation of funds to increase the support to the extremely poor areas. At the same time, all provincial education and finance departments are required to reasonably arrange budgets, scientifically allocate funds and prioritize the training of teachers and headmasters for extremely poor counties that are geographically connected, state-designated poverty-stricken counties, and "three regions and three prefectures". ■

POLICY 79 The Customs Tariff Commission of the State Council published an announcement on raising the tariff rate on certain goods imported from the United States

On May 13, the Customs Tariff Commission of the State Council published an announcement on raising the tariff rate on certain goods imported from the United States, which provided the following. On May 9, 2019, the U.S. government announced that starting from May 10, 2019, the tariff rate imposed on 200 billion USD worth of imports from China will be raised from 10% to 25%. The above measures of the United States have led to an escalation of Sino-U.S. economic and trade frictions, violated the consensus between China and the United States on resolving trade differences through consultations, hurt the interests of both sides, and failed to meet the general expectations of the international community. According to the *Foreign Trade Law of the People's Republic of China,* the *Import and Export Tariff Regulations of the People's Republic of China* and the other laws and regulations and the basic principles of international law, the Customs Tariff Commission decided that starting from 0:00 on June 1, 2019, the tariff rate on certain goods imported from the United States will be raised. ■

POLICY 80 MOF published a circular on promoting the integration of agricultural and commercial enterprises to improve the supply chain of agricultural products

On May 14, MOF published a circular on promoting the integration of agricultural and commercial enterprises to improve the supply chain of agricultural products, which provided the following. First, the central government's financial support is mainly aimed to make up for market failures, improve the basic and public work, leverage the central government's funds to guide private capital, and support the weak links and key areas of the agricultural product supply chain system. The proportion of central government funds that support post-production processing facilities and cold chain logistics of agricultural products shall be no less than 70%. Second, the provinces (autonomous regions and municipalities) that have secured the central government support may each receive 200 million RMB. The funds will be arranged in two years. In 2019, each province (autonomous region and municipality) will receive 100 million RMB. In 2020, the remaining funds will be allocated according to the performance. Third, support enterprises and units that meet the requirements, encourage the management under the form of "menu-style, full disclosure, traceability and performance accountability", increase the use of performance evaluation results, and base the provision of rewards more on ex-post performance evaluation results. ■

POLICY 81 MOF published a circular on the development of the IPR service system in 2019

On May 15, MOF published a circular on the development of the IPR service system in 2019, which provided the following. First, provide guidance for the establishment of an industry IPR alliance and an early warning and joint response mechanism for major IPR risks, and deepen the coordinated use of industry IPR. Second, optimize the patent subsidy policy, and vigorously implement the patent quality improvement project; implement the high-value patent cultivation plan, and build a number of key patent pools that support industrial development and international competitiveness. Third, support enterprises and institutions to implement national standards for IPR management, improve the trademark and brand management system, and accelerate the development of enterprises with strong IPR. Fourth, increase the IPR-pledged financing line, broaden the scope of IPR collaterals for loans, and explore a new model of mixed pledge of patent and trademark; improve the risk sharing and compensation mechanism of IPR-pledged financing and give play to the role of IPR insurance. Fifth, build a public service platform for IPR operation in a certain area by leveraging the patent or trademark examination and collaboration center, IPR operation center, and IPR legal, evaluation and consulting service providers in industrial parks. ■

POLICY 82 MOF published a circular on allocating the budget for the subsidies for urban and rural compulsory education in 2019

On May 15, MOF published a circular on allocating the budget for the subsidies for urban and rural compulsory education in 2019, which provided the following. First, starting from the fall semester of 2019, the non-boarding students among the documented poor students in compulsory education stage, the undocumented disabled students from poor families, students from rural families covered by subsistence allowance scheme, and students from extremely poor rural areas will be included in the scope of the recipients of living allowances. Second, starting from the spring semester of 2019, the funds required for the long-term mechanism for the safety of rural public school buildings will be shared by the central and local finance departments in accordance with a certain proportion. Third, appropriate incentives will be given to the provinces with good performance of implementation. Fourth, starting from July 1, 2018, the salary subsidy standard for special-post teachers will be raised. The annual per capita subsidy standard will be raised from 31,600 RMB to 35,200 RMB in central regions, and from 34,600 RMB to 38,200 RMB in western regions. Fifth, the nutrition and dietary subsidy standard for students of rural compulsory education in poverty-stricken areas which was previously separately formulated by the central government and local government will be unified into a national basic standard as 4 RMB per day per student. Sixth, all provincial-level education and finance departments should give full play to the provincial-level coordination, urge and guide local governments to do a good job in compulsory education, strive to "control school dropout", put the meeting of basic needs in the first place, and improve the targeted assistance to students. Seventh, the provincial education and finance departments, in consideration of the central government's fiscal subsidy standard, may adjust the provincial performance targets. ■

POLICY 83 MOF published a circular on the 2018 pilot program for the preparation of government financial reports

On May 21, MOF published a circular on the 2018 pilot program for the preparation of government financial reports, which provided the following. First, the pilot central departments and the finance authorities of pilot areas should set up the leading groups and their offices for pilot work, and establish a relatively stable working team comprised of competent officials from relevant authorities. Second, the pilot central departments and the finance authorities of pilot areas should strengthen internal control and create a control mechanism connecting to accounting with operation. Third, personnel with junior qualifications in accounting or with college degree and a corresponding level or above in accounting are, in principle, required for the preparation of government financial reports. Fourth, regulate accounting practice according to relevant accounting standards and requirements for the preparation of government financial reports. Fifth, carefully summarize the experience in the process of report preparation, and study and improve the preparation method. Sixth, ensure standardized methodology, complete content, reliable data and in-depth analysis. ■

84

MOF and SAT jointly published an announcement on the corporate income tax policy for enterprises in integrated circuit design and software industry

On May 22, MOF and SAT jointly published an announcement on the corporate income tax policy for enterprises in integrated circuit design and software industry, which provided the following. IC design companies and software companies that are legally established and meet the required criteria will be exempted from corporate income tax in the first two years if they are profitable before December 31, 2018, and enjoy 50% reduction of corporate income tax at a statutory tax rate of 25% from the third year to fifth year until the expiration of the policy. ■

85

The State Council published the *Implementation Plan for Deepening the Reform of the Expressway Toll Road System and Removing the Toll Stations at Provincial Borders*

On May 22, the General Office of the State Council published the *Implementation Plan for Deepening the Reform of the Expressway Toll Road System and Removing the Toll Stations at Provincial Borders,* which provided the following. First, develop the overall technical plan, engineering construction plan, operation and service rules, and network security protection system, by deploying the technology of electronic non-stop toll collection supplemented by license plate image recognition and multiple payment methods. Second, expand service functions and encourage ETC to be used in parking lots and other vehicle-related places; speed up the free installation of ETC devices for existing vehicles; improve the settlement system and provide convenient and efficient services. Third, speed up the revision of relevant laws and regulations such as the highway law and toll road management regulations; clean up and regulate the local toll reduction and exemption policy, and introduce specific implementation opinions on the toll reduction and exemption policies such as the free passage of small passenger cars during major holidays and the "green channel" for transportation of fresh agricultural products. Fourth, allow local government bonds to be swapped for the stock of eligible toll road debts as of the end of 2014. ■

86

The State Council determined the measures to advance the market-oriented and law-based debt-to-equity swap

On May 22, Premier Li Keqiang presided over an executive meeting of the State Council, which determined the measures to further promote market-oriented and law-based debt-to-equity swap, which provided the following. First, establish a reasonable pricing mechanism for debt-to-equity swap, improve the due diligence and the measures to enforce due diligence liability of procedures for SOE and implementing agencies, innovate the approaches to debt-to-equity swap, expand the pilot program of debt-to-equity swap, give priority to the implementation of debt-to-equity swap for high-leverage and high-quality enterprises, and promote the signing of more projects. Second, improve the policy and properly solve the problem that the financial asset investment companies and other institutions are running the risks of holding too many debt-to-equity swaps that take up their capital, take multiple measures to support them to replenish capital, allow the qualified exchanges to trade debt-to-equity swap assets, and give play to the important role of financial asset investment companies in debt-to-equity swap. Third, actively attract private forces to participate in market-oriented debt-to-equity swaps, optimize the shareholding structure, and equally protect the rights and interests of private capital in accordance with laws. Support financial asset investment companies to create asset management products and allow insurance fund and pension fund to make investments. Explore the possibility of allowing public-equity asset management products to participate in debt-to-equity swaps in accordance with laws and regulations. Encourage foreign capital to hold shares in the implementing agencies. ■

POLICY 87

MOF published an announcement on the specific policies related to vehicle purchase tax

Source: MOF

On May 24, MOF published an announcement on the specific policies related to vehicle purchase tax, which provided the following. First, subway, light rail and other urban rail transit vehicles, loaders, graders, excavators, bulldozers, as well as cranes, forklifts, electric motorcycles are not taxable vehicles. Second, the actual price paid by taxpayers to sellers for the purchase of taxable vehicles for their own use shall be determined by the price as shown on the purchase invoice and shall exclude the amount of VAT. Third, the taxable price of the taxable vehicle produced and used by taxpayer is determined according to the sales price of taxable vehicles of the same category (i.e. vehicles with the same vehicle configuration serial number) and shall exclude the amount of VAT; if the sales price of taxable vehicles of the same category is not available, the taxable price shall be determined according to the composite assessable price. Fourth, the starting time for the liability of the vehicle purchase tax is based on the time indicated on the vehicle-related invoice obtained by the taxpayer for the purchase of the taxable vehicle. The announcement also stipulates the scope of urban public transport enterprises exempted from vehicle purchase tax, the time when the tax liability for vehicle purchase tax is incurred, and the relevant conditions for tax exemption, tax reduction and tax refund procedures. ■

88

MOF published an announcement on the second batch of the 2017 and the first batch of the 2018 list of eligible public-welfare social organizations that allow for pre-tax deduction of donations

On May 27, MOF published an announcement on the second batch of the 2017 and the first batch of the 2018 list of eligible public-welfare social organizations that would be allowed for pre-tax deduction of donations, which provided the following. First, the second batch of eligible public-welfare social organizations that would be allowed for pre-tax deduction of donations in 2017 includes 7 social organizations, among them, the China Women's Development Foundation, the Practical Aid Foundation, and the Zhang Rugeng Charitable Foundation. Second, the first batch of eligible public-welfare social organizations that would be allowed for pre-tax deduction of donations in 2018 includes 175 social organizations, among them, the National Energy Group Public Welfare Foundation, Aiyou Foundation and Chen Xiangmei Public Welfare Foundation. ■

89

MOF published a circular on further deepening the pilot insurance compensation mechanism for the first (set) major technical equipment

On May 28, MOF published a circular on further deepening the pilot insurance compensation mechanism for the first (set) major technical equipment, which provided the following. First, the first (set) major technical equipment refers to the first (set) or first batch of equipments, systems and core components with major breakthroughs in varieties, specifications or technical parameters after innovation, and with IPR but have not yet earned market profits. Second, the MIIT drafted the Guiding Catalogue for the Promotion and Application of the First (Set) Major Technical Equipment and will adjust it, where appropriate, according to the development of major technical equipment. Third, the first (set) major technical equipment insurance refers to the comprehensive insurance products that are purchased by the equipment manufacturing enterprise in the Catalogue, with benefits shared with the users, for insuring against the quality risks and liability risks of the first (set) major technical equipment. Fourth, the first (set) major technical equipment insurance compensation mechanism gives full play to the decisive role of the market mechanism, with the central government providing appropriate amount of insurance compensation to qualified insured enterprises. Fifth, enterprise that manufactures the equipment in the Catalogue and purchases comprehensive insurance for the first (set) major technical equipment or opts for the international general insurance clause may apply for insurance compensation after the delivery of equipment to users, the official entry into effect of insurance policy, and with premiums in excess of 200,000 RMB. Sixth, the central government will provide insurance compensation to qualified insured enterprises at no more than 3% of the actual insurance rate and 80% of the actual annual insurance premiums. ■

90

MOF published an announcement on the pre-tax deduction policy for insurance companies' service fees and commission expenses

On May 29, MOF published an announcement on the pre-tax deduction policy for insurance companies' service fees and commission expenses, which provided the following. First, for the service fees and commissions incurred by insurance companies in relation to their business activities, the portion not exceeding 18% of the balance from the total annual premiums income netting premiums withdrawal is allowed to be deducted when calculating the taxable income; the excess is allowed to be carried forward to the following years for deduction. Second, other matters related to the pre-tax deduction of service fees and commission expenses incurred by insurance companies will continue to be governed by the relevant provisions of Article 2 to 5 of the *Circular of MOF and SAT on the Pre-tax Deduction Policy for Enterprise Service Fees and Commission Expenses.* Insurance companies should establish a sound management system for service fees and commissions, and keep account of the deduction of service fees and commissions. ■

POLICY 91

The State Council published the *Reform Plan for the Division of Fiscal Mandates and Spending Responsibilities between the Central and Local Governments in the Field of Science and Technology*

On May 31, the General Office of the State Council published the *Reform Plan for the Division of Fiscal Mandates and Spending Responsibilities between the Central and Local Governments in the Field of Science and Technology,* which provided the following. First, scientific and technological research and development. The scientific and technological plans formulated with the use of fiscal funds to support basic research, applied research and technological research and development (special funds, facility, etc.) are recognized as the joint fiscal mandates of central and local governments, with the central and local finance authorities bearing the corresponding spending responsibilities in light of different situations. Second, the construction and development of scientific and technological innovation bases. The subsidies for the construction and development of scientific and technological innovation bases are recognized as the joint fiscal mandates of the central and local governments, with the central and local finance authorities bearing the corresponding spending responsibilities in light of different situations. Third, the development of scientific and technological talents. For the development of high-level scientific and technological talents, the special projects for the development of scientific and technological talents implemented in a unified way according to relevant plans are recognized as the fiscal mandates of either the central government or the local government, with the finance authorities of the same level bearing the spending responsibilities. Fourth, the transfer and application of scientific and technological achievements. The transfer and application of scientific and technological achievements supported by methods such as risk compensation, post-subsidy and venture capital channeling are recognized as the joint fiscal mandates of the central and local governments, with the central and local finance authorities bearing the corresponding spending responsibilities in light of different situations. Fifth, the construction of regional innovation system. The funding of the construction of regional innovation system will be adjusted as the joint fiscal mandates of the central and local governments, with the central and local finance authorities bearing the corresponding spending responsibilities in light of different situations. Sixth, the popularization of science and technology. The supporting funding of the popularization of scientific and technological knowledge, the promotion of scientific methods, the dissemination of scientific ideas, the promotion of scientific spirit, and the improvement of the scientific quality of the whole nation is recognized as the joint fiscal mandates of the central and local governments, with the central and local finance authorities bearing the corresponding spending responsibilities in light of different situations. Seventh, the reform and development of scientific research institutions.

The subsidies for the reform and development of scientific research institutions established with the use of fiscal funds are recognized as the fiscal mandates of either the central government or the local government, with the finance authorities of the same level bearing the spending responsibilities. Eighth, other unlisted items in the field of science and technology. The division of the fiscal mandates and spending responsibilities of the matters related to international scientific and technological exchanges and cooperation is to be implemented in accordance with the reform plan of the diplomatic field. ■

POLICY 92

The State Council published the *Reform Plan for the Division of Fiscal Mandates and Spending Responsibilities between the Central and Local Governments in the Field of Education*

Source: MOF

On June 4, the General Office of the State Council published the *Reform Plan for the Division of Fiscal Mandates and Spending Responsibilities between the Central and Local Governments in the Field of Education,* which provided the following. First, compulsory education. Compulsory education is generally a joint fiscal mandate between the central and local governments, and is refined according to specific matters. Among them, for the funds required for financing the recurring matters related to the daily operation of schools, the safety of school buildings, and the study and life of students, the proportion for sharing the financing burden between the central and local governments is clearly set out in accordance with national basic standards, with the central government's portion financed by the transfer payment for joint fiscal mandate; for matters involving phased tasks and special work, the required funds are financed by the local finance authorities with transfer payment support from the central government. Second, student financial aid. Student financial aid is a relatively independent and complete policy system, covering pre-school education, general high school education, vocational education, higher education, etc.. It is generally recognized as the joint fiscal mandate between the central and local governments, and is refined according to specific matters. Third, other education. For pre-school education, general high school education, vocational education, higher education and other education, the funding is primarily financed by government, with reasonable burden-sharing with students and fund-raising through other channels. It is generally recognized as the joint fiscal mandate between the central and local governments, and the required fiscal subsidies are generally shared between the central and local finance authorities in accordance with administrative affiliation, with the central government supporting local government through transfer payment. Fourth, supporting measures. Strengthen organizational leadership and implement spending responsibilities; improve budget management and enhance fund efficiency; clarify local powers and responsibilities and strengthen provincial-level coordination; revise and improve systems, and promote rule-based operations; and jointly promote reforms to form positive interactions. ■

POLICY 93

MOF published a circular on the application of government procurement policies to support poverty alleviation

Source: MOF

On June 5, MOF published a circular on the application of government procurement policies to support poverty alleviation, which provided the following. First, fully understand the importance of using government procurement policies to support the fight against poverty. Second, encourage the use of priority procurement and reserve procurement to purchase agricultural products and by-products of poor areas. When the budget units at all levels purchase agricultural products, the agricultural products and by-products of poor areas should be given the priority provided that other things are being equal. All competent budget units should make effective coordination, determine and reserve a certain proportion of the agricultural products and by-products purchased by the budget units of the department for the agricultural products and by-products of poor areas. Third, encourage the priority purchase of property management services provided by property management companies staffed by documented poor people. Where budget units at all levels use fiscal funds to purchase property management services, those who have the conditions should give priority to purchase the property management services provided by property management companies registered in the 832 national-level poverty-stricken counties and staffed by documented poor people. Fourth, establish sound safeguard measures. MOF and the Leading Group Office of Poverty Alleviation and Development of the State Council, together with relevant departments, will formulate the implementation plan for priority procurement of agricultural products and by-products of poor areas, set up an online sales platform for agricultural products and by-products of poor areas, and provide efficient and convenient marketing channels for agricultural products and by-products of poor areas. ■

POLICY 94

MOF published a supplementary circular on the *Interim Administrative Measures for Subsidizing Local Funds with Vehicle Purchase Tax Revenues*

On June 10, MOF published a supplementary circular on the *Interim Administrative Measures for Subsidizing Local Funds with Vehicle Purchase Tax Revenues,* which provided the following. First, for the highway projects of Liangshan Prefecture, Nujiang Prefecture and Linxia Prefecture, the subsidies for national-level expressways are 50% of the project construction costs, the subsidies for ordinary national-level highways are 100% of the project construction costs, and the subsidies for village-level hard-surface roads are 700,000 RMB/km. Second, for the toll road projects built with PPP model, the subsidies from introduced capital, and the investment subsidies sourced from the Vehicle Purchase Tax revenue, are subject to the upper limit of the project subsidy standard of the local government toll road projects. Third, for the areas without special policies, the subsidy standard for non-toll ordinary national-level highway projects shall not exceed the project construction costs, and the subsidy standard for ordinary national-level highway projects shall not exceed that for the local national-level highway project. Fourth, the port railway projects undergoing double-track transformation and electrification are included into the scope of subsidies, with the subsidy standard referring to the single-track railway and the upper subsidy limit subject to no more than 20% of the total project investment. Fifth, the purchase of emergency materials and the development of information system for the storage center of regional road traffic emergency equipment and materials are included in the scope of subsidies funded by vehicle purchase tax revenues. Sixth, the road construction of state-owned forest farms is included in the scope of subsidies funded by vehicle purchase tax revenues. Seventh, the construction of hard-surface roads in border villages is included in the scope of subsidies funded by vehicle purchase tax revenues. Eighth, subsidy standard for road disaster recovery and repair projects is implemented according to the disaster classification and level. Ninth, the vehicle purchase tax revenues used for rural road construction projects must be distributed and managed in strict accordance with regulations, and the restrictive provisions regarding the mandatory assessment of poor counties and the intended use of special funds will be removed to further support the needs of poor counties on consolidating agriculture-related funds. Tenth, strengthen budget performance management. Eleventh, the standards above are to be timely adjusted and refined according to the decisions of the CPC and the State Council and the changes of costs. ■

POLICY 95 MOF published a circular on strengthening the use of funds for the renovation of dilapidated rural houses to help implement the task of poverty reduction

On June 10, MOF published a circular on strengthening the use of funds for the renovation of dilapidated rural houses to help implement the task of poverty reduction, which provided the following. First, implement the responsibility for funding the renovation of rural dilapidated houses. The renovation of rural dilapidated houses is the joint fiscal mandate of the central and local governments, with the local government assuming the principal responsibility, the provincial (autonomous region and municipality) government assuming the overall responsibility, the city (prefecture) and county government working on the implementation, and the central government providing guidance and subsidies. The central fiscal subsidy funds shall be strictly used in accordance with the regulations for the renovation of dilapidated houses of such targeted groups as documented poor households, the construction of rural collective public rental housing and other basic housing projects for the rural poor people who meet the policy criteria. Second, increase the support for the renovation of rural dilapidated houses in extremely poor areas. The central government will separately increase subsidies for the renovation of rural dilapidated houses in extremely poor areas such as the "three regions and three prefectures". The finance and housing authorities of all provinces (autonomous regions and municipalities) shall timely allocate the central fiscal subsidy funds in accordance with the requirements, and make coordinated arrangements for local fiscal subsidy funds, giving priority to the extremely poor areas such as the "three regions and three prefectures". Third, continue to support the consolidation of agriculture-related funds in poverty-stricken counties. The increase of central fiscal funds for renovation of rural dilapidated houses allocated by the relevant provinces (autonomous regions and municipalities) to poor counties shall be no smaller than the average increase of such funds, and shall be allocated in tranches without projects specified for the use of funds or requirements unrelated to poverty reduction. Fourth, continuously strengthen the standardized management of funds for the renovation of rural dilapidated houses. The local finance and housing authorities shall implement the regulations related to the management of central fiscal funds for renovation of rural dilapidated houses and the requirements for the regulation of poverty reduction funds, regulate the management of the use of central fiscal funds for renovation of rural dilapidated houses, and disburse the funds in full and on time in accordance with regulations. The information regarding the allocation and payment of funds should be promptly entered into the dynamic monitoring platform for poverty reduction funds. ■

POLICY 96

The CPC Central Committee and the State Council published the *Circular on Improving the Work of Local Government Special Bond Issuance and Project Supporting Financing*

Source: MOF

On June 10, the General Office of the CPC Central Committee and the General Office of the State Council published the *Circular on Improving the Work of Local Government Special Bond Issuance and Project Supporting Financing*, which provided the following. First, the overall requirements and basic principles. With the guidance of the Xi Jinping Thought on Socialism with Chinese Characteristics for a New Era, adhere to the basic principles of maintaining appropriate issuance, keeping effective coordination, highlighting key points, preventing and controlling risks, and stabilizing expectations, and resolutely prevent and resolve major risks. Second, support the financing of special bond projects. Reasonably clarify the criteria of financial support for special bond projects; accurately focus on key areas and major projects; actively encourage financial institutions to provide financing support; allow special bonds to be used as eligible capital for major projects; and ensure the fulfillment of debt repayment obligations. Third, further improve the management of special bonds and supporting measures. Vigorously enhance the promotion of special bond projects; ensure the match between special bond project financing and solvency capacity; strengthen credit rating and differential pricing; make local government bond issuance pricing more market-based; diversify the local government bond investor base; reasonably increase long-term special bond maturity; and speed up the issuance and use of special bonds. Fourth, promote major project financing in accordance with laws and regulations. Support the market-oriented financing of major projects; reasonably ensure the follow-up financing of necessary ongoing projects; and raise capital for major projects through multiple channels. Fifth, strengthen organization. Strictly implement work responsibilities; strengthen departmental cooperation on supervision; promote bond project disclosure; establish a positive incentive mechanism; provide waiver from liability in accordance with laws; and strengthen follow-up evaluation and supervision. ■

97

MOF published a circular on the release of the optimized and adjusted list for the national scientific and technological resource sharing service platforms

On June 11, MOF published a circular on the release of the optimized and adjusted list for the national scientific and technological resource sharing service platforms, which provided the following. First, to regulate and manage the national scientific and technological resource sharing service platforms, improve the scientific and technological resources sharing service system, and promote the open sharing of scientific and technological resource to the society, MOST and MOF optimized and adjusted the original national platform. Through the recommendation by government departments and consultation with experts, 20 national scientific data centers such as the National High Energy Physics Science Data Center and 30 national centers for biological germplasm and experimental materials such as the National Center for Important Wild Plant Germplasm Resources are created. Second, relevant departments should further strengthen the management of national platforms, formulate a five-year development and operation plan for the national platforms, further clarify the functional positioning and objectives of the national platforms, sort out the systemic structure of scientific and technological resources in this field, channel the scientific and technological resources in relevant fields to the national platforms, strengthen the development and application of scientific and technological resources, and enhance the efficiency of the use of scientific and technological resources and the innovation capacity. Improve the infrastructure needed for the storage, management and security of scientific and technological resources, improve the network security assurance system, innovate the operational and management mechanism, strengthen the administration of evaluation and assessment, carry out international exchanges and cooperation, give full play to the main responsibility of legal entities, and provide high-quality scientific and technological resources sharing services for scientific research, technological progress and social development. ■

98

MOF published a circular on the central fiscal support for the 2019 "Maker China" SMEs Innovation and Entrepreneurship Contest

On June 11, MOF published a circular on the central fiscal support for the 2019 "Maker China" SMEs Innovation and Entrepreneurship Contest, which provided the following. First, the objectives. Actively leverage the central government's fiscal funds to support local governments to use the "Maker China" Contest as a platform to effectively connect with businesses, foster an enabling social atmosphere, further stimulate the vitality of SMEs, and promote the healthy development of SMEs. Second, the funding arrangement. In 2019, the central government will use the special fund for SMEs development and provide rewards and subsidies to support the local promotion of the "Maker China" Contest. In terms of the use of funds, the central government's rewards and subsidies will be disbursed to the provincial-level finance departments and be used in coordination with the SMEs authorities at the same level. Third, the working mechanism. MIIT will provide guidance for and conduct performance monitoring of local contests. MOF, together with MIIT, will conduct performance evaluation on the overall use of rewards and subsidies, and the evaluation results will serve as an important basis for future budgetary arrangements of rewards and subsidies. ■

POLICY 99

MOF published the *Opinions on Promoting the Sustainable and Healthy Development of Private Hospitals*

On June 12, MOF published the *Opinions on Promoting the Sustainable and Healthy Development of Private Hospitals,* which provided the following. First, increase government support for private hospitals. Expand the space for establishing private hospitals; increase the supply of land; promote government procurement of services; and implement tax incentives. Second, streamline administration, delegate powers and simplify the access approval services. Improve the efficiency of access approval; standardize review and evaluation; further relax planning restrictions; and allow record-filing management of pilot clinics. Third, cooperation between public hospitals and private hospitals. Enable the third-tier public hospitals to play a leading role; explore a variety of cooperation models for medical institutions; and expand talent services. Fourth, optimize operational and management services. Optimize testing services; optimize the professional title evaluation; improve clinical services and academic capacity; and step up training efforts. Fifth, improve the medical insurance support policy. Optimize medical insurance management services; support the development of "Internet + health" by private hospitals; and support the development of commercial health insurance. Sixth, improve the comprehensive supervision system. Implement departmental supervision responsibilities; strengthen medical quality and safety management; establish and improve credit system; and give play to the self-discipline functions of industry organizations. ■

POLICY 100

MOF and MOA jointly published the *Measures for the Performance Management of Agriculture-related Transfer Payment Funds*

On June 18, MOF and MOA jointly published the *Measures for the Performance Management of Agriculture-related Transfer Payment Funds,* which provided the following. First, the general principles. Agriculture-related transfer payments refer to agricultural production and development funds, subsidy funds for agricultural resource and ecological protection, animal epidemic prevention subsidies, and farmland construction subsidies. The performance management of agriculture-related transfer payment funds should follow the principles of scientific norms, result orientation, promotion of integration, and tiered management. Second, performance target setting, review and monitoring. The performance targets of agriculture-related transfer payment funds are divided into overall performance targets and regional performance targets. The performance targets should clearly reflect the expected output and effect of agricultural-related transfer payments, correspond to the number of tasks, match the amount of funds, and be refined in terms of quantity, quality, timeliness, cost, economic, social and ecological effects, sustainable impact, satisfaction level and other aspects. The agricultural and rural affairs authorities at all levels are responsible for designing the performance indicators according to the performance targets. Third, performance evaluation and results application. The overall performance evaluation work is organized and implemented by MOF in conjunction with MOA. The regional performance evaluation is overseen by the provincial finance departments and the agricultural and rural affairs departments. In principle, performance evaluation is conducted on an annual basis. Interim performance evaluation can be carried out in light of the needs of work. The provincial finance departments and the agricultural and rural affairs departments are responsible for the authenticity of the provincial self-assessment results and materials related to performance evaluation. Fourth, organization and implementation. The provincial finance departments, along with the agricultural and rural affairs authorities, in light of the local circumstances, the annual implementation plan of the agriculture-related transfer payment (task list), the performance targets and the performance evaluation results of the previous year, and the budget released in advance, should study the design of regional performance targets for agriculture-related transfer payment funds in the current year, submit the targets to MOF and MOA by the end of January in each year, and copy them to the local regulatory bureaus of MOF. Fifth, the supplementary provisions. The provincial finance departments and the agricultural and rural affairs departments shall formulate implementation rules in accordance with the Measures, submit them to MOF and MOA for record-keeping, and send a copy to the local regulatory bureaus of MOF. If the agriculture-related transfer payment funds are used to support the poverty-stricken counties to carry out the pilot consolidation of agriculture-related funds, the budget performance management would be implemented in accordance with the relevant regulations during the period of poverty alleviation. ■

POLICY 101 MOF, SAMR and FDA jointly issued the *Interim Measures for the Administration of Subsidy Funds for Food and Drug Supervision*

On June 19, MOF, SAMR and FDA jointly issued the *Interim Measures for the Administration of Subsidy Funds for Food and Drug Supervision,* which provided the following. First, the subsidy funds for food and drug supervision mentioned in the Measures refer to the subsidy funds arranged by the central government's special transfer payment in support of the market supervision by local governments, the food and drug supervision and management by drug regulatory authorities, and the capacity building. Second, the implementation period of the subsidy funds is 5 years. Whether to continue and extend the time limit shall be determined according to the relevant provisions of the State Council and the circumstances of food and drug supervision. Third, MOF is responsible for reviewing the proposal for the allocation of subsidy funds, preparing and approving the subsidy fund budget, organizing the whole process of budget performance management, and guiding local efforts to strengthen the management of subsidy funds. Fourth, the subsidy funds are mainly used for expenses such as food and drug supervision and management, spot check and inspection, as well as expenditures of equipment purchase, operation and maintenance, and personnel development related to food and drug supervision capacity building. Fifth, the subsidy funds are allocated by the factor method. The distribution factors include basic factors, business factors, performance factors and financial factors. Sixth, MOF will release the estimated amount of subsidy funds for the next year to the provincial finance departments before October 31 of each year, and disburse to the provincial finance departments within 90 days after the approval of budget by NPC. Seventh, the provincial market supervision departments and drug regulatory departments would set their own performance targets for their administrative region. After review by the finance departments at the same level, they would report the targets to MOF and the central competent authorities before the end of March in each year, and send a copy to the local regulatory bureaus of MOF. Eighth, local finance, market supervision, and drug regulatory authorities at all levels should make overall arrangements for the use of relevant funds allocated from the same level and the higher level. Ninth, the local finance authorities at all levels should cooperate with the market supervision and drug regulatory authorities, as well as the specific users of subsidy funds at the same level to strengthen the management of fund usage and regulate budget execution. ■

POLICY 102

MOF published a supplementary circular on the *Interim Measures for the Administration of Special Funds for Renewable Energy Development*

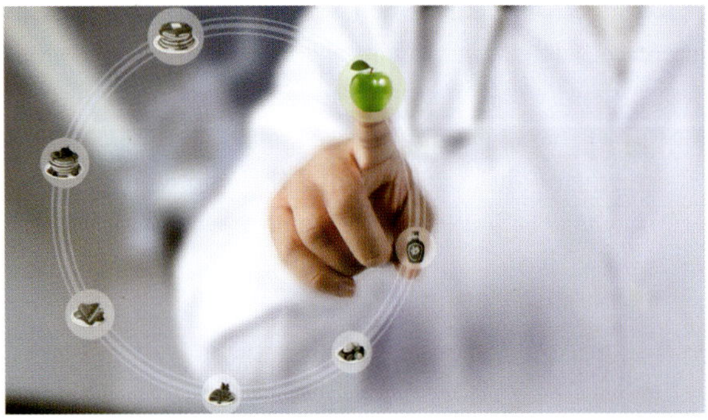

Source: MOF

On June 20, MOF published a supplementary circular on the *Interim Measures for the Administration of Special Funds for Renewable Energy Development,* which provided the following. First, the implementation period of special funds for renewable energy development is from 2019 to 2023. Among them, the central fiscal subsidies for the efficiency enhancement and expansion of rural hydropower projects during the 13th Five-Year Plan period will be ended after the expiry of the policy in 2020. Second, special funds for renewable energy development would support the efficiency enhancement and expansion of rural hydropower projects. The efficiency enhancement and expansion of rural hydropower projects will be funded on the basis of actual results, and rewards will be provided for the increase of the installed capacity of power station (including the new ecological retrofitting) during the 13th Five-Year Plan period. Third, special funds for renewable energy development will support the exploitation and utilization of unconventional natural gas such as coal-bed methane (mine gas), shale gas and tight gas. In 2018, the subsidy standard is 0.3 RMB/cubic meter. Starting from 2019, subsidies are no longer provided according to the fixed standard. In accordance with the principle of "more subsidies for greater output", if the mining and utilization volume exceeds that of the previous year, tiered rewards and subsidies will be provided according to the excess degree; correspondingly, if the mining and utilization volume falls short of that of the previous year, rewards and subsidies will be deducted according to the degree of shortfall. At the same time, for the increment of unconventional natural gas produced during the heating season, special subsidies for the winter season will be provided. Fourth, the rewards and subsidies will be pre-allocated and post-settled, with MOF releasing budget in advance and disbursing funds to central and local enterprises according to the data provided by the NEA, the local regulatory bureaus of MOF, central enterprises and local governments. ■

POLICY 103

MOF and MNR jointly published a circular on the issuance of the *Measures for the Administration of Budget for Land Reserve Projects (Trial)*

On June 21, MOF and MNR jointly published a circular on the issuance of the *Measures for the Administration of Budget for Land Reserve Projects (Trial),* which provided the following. First, the first batch of pilot areas of MOF include 7 provinces (cities) of Beijing, Tianjin, Hebei, Henan, Shandong (including Qingdao), Zhejiang (including Ningbo) and Xiamen, and the scope of the pilot program could be gradually expanded based on situation in the following years. Pilot areas can select cities and counties (districts) on their own to carry out pilot projects. Other regions that meet the conditions are encouraged to select cities and counties (districts) to carry out pilot projects. Second, when allocating the special debt limits, provinces may properly offer preferential treatment to the cities and counties (districts) that carry out pilot projects. Third, the cities and counties (districts) that carry out pilot projects should strengthen their staffing and make overall arrangements for the funding to ensure the smooth implementation of the pilot work. Fourth, the pilot areas should regularly evaluate the performance of the pilot work. Significant matters shall be reported to MOF and MNR in a timely manner. ■

POLICY 104

MOF and MOA jointly published the *Measures for the Administration of Farmland Development Subsidy Funds*

On June 21, MOF and MOA jointly published the *Measures for the Administration of Farmland Development Subsidy Funds,* which provided the following. First, the general principles. Farmland development subsidy funds refer to the funds for transfer payment with joint finance mandates for the development of farmland-related projects to support the stabilization and optimization of farmland layout and comprehensively improve farmland quality. The implementation period of farmland development subsidy funds is up to 2022. After the end of the period, MOF and MOA will conduct an assessment according to the relevant provisions of the State Council and the needs of farmland development, and make adjustments on the basis of the results of the assessment. Second, the scope of the expenditure of funds. The scope of the expenditure of farmland development subsidy funds includes: project material expenses, equipment purchase expenses and construction expenditure, project pre-construction expenses, project bidding and tendering expenses, project supervision expenses and necessary project management expenses. Farmland development subsidy funds shall not be used for the construction of office buildings and halls or make up for budgetary expenditure gaps and other expenditures unrelated to farmland development. Third, allocation and disbursement of funds. Farmland development subsidy funds are allocated according to the factor method. The factors of fund allocation mainly include basic resource factors, work performance factors and other factors, among which the basic resource factors account for 70%, the work performance factors account for 20%, and other factors account for 10%. Before March 15 of each year, MOA will propose the allocation of farmland development subsidy funds among provinces and send a letter to MOF. Within 30 days after the approval of the budget by NPC, MOF will release the budget for farmland development subsidy funds and copy it to MOA and the relevant regulatory bureaus of MOF. Fourth, the use and management of funds. The farmland development subsidy funds enforce the management model of "special program + task list". Local governments may, in light of the local conditions, mobilize farmland development funds from different channels for the development of high-standard farmland. Fifth, the supervision, inspection and performance evaluation. The competent finance and agricultural and rural affairs authorities at all levels shall strengthen the supervision and inspection over the allocation and management of farmland development subsidy funds, and promptly rectify the identified problems. The performance evaluation system is adopted for the management of farmland development subsidy funds, and the evaluation results serve as an important basis for the allocation of farmland development subsidy funds. Sixth, the supplementary provisions. The provincial finance authorities shall, in conjunction with the agricultural and rural affairs authorities, formulate implementation rules in accordance with the Measures and the actual conditions of the region, submit the implementation rules to MOF and MOA, and send a copy to the local regulatory bureaus of MOF. ■

POLICY 105 MOF and NFSRA jointly published the opinions on the in-depth implementation of the Quality Grain Project

Source: MOF

On June 24, MOF and NFSRA jointly issued the opinions on the in-depth implementation of the Quality Grain Project, which provided the following. First, strengthen the overall requirements and innovate the implementation method of the Quality Grain Project. Give full play to the role of incentives and promote the "five linkages" of quality production, quality purchase, quality storage, quality processing and quality selling. All localities should further refine the three-year implementation plan and set detailed tasks for demonstration counties (cities), demonstration enterprises and related projects, in line with the target of achieving full coverage of the post-production services in all the major grain-producing counties, expanding the coverage of the grain quality and safety inspection and monitoring system to 60%, and raising the percentage of quality grain by 30%. Second, highlight demands and optimize the layout and function of the post-production services system. Scientifically arrange the post-production services centers and strive to provide full coverage for major grain-producing counties, in light of regional grain output, production concentration, and service scope. Third, expand functions and improve the capacity of food quality and safety inspection and monitoring. Allow the existing institutions affiliated to the food and strategic reserves authorities to play their principal role supplemented by the key food enterprises and related universities, in order to improve the network of inspection and monitoring institutions at the national, provincial, city and county levels. Fourth, highlight brand promotion and play a leading role in the "China Good Grain and Oil" campaign. Select demonstration counties (cities) and demonstration enterprises on a merit basis, with due consideration to the major grain-producing counties and grain-and-oil producing counties with special features. Support demonstration enterprises to form a community of shared interests with the model of "company + cooperative + base + farmers", carry out the order-based purchase, build planting and processing bases, increase the production of high-quality grain and oil products, and enable farmers to continue to increase their income. Fifth, conduct meticulous organization and build synergy to ensure effective implementation. The finance authorities shall, under the leadership of government at all levels, coordinate the multiple tasks of project planning, enforcement organization, operation, and supervision and assessment. ■

POLICY 106 MOF and SAT jointly published an announcement on subjecting individual's relevant income to the taxable income items of individual income tax

On June 25, MOF and SAT jointly published an announcement on subjecting individual's relevant income to the taxable income items of individual income tax, which provided the following. First, individual's income obtained from providing guarantees for units or other individuals is subject to individual income tax under the "accidental income". Second, if the owner of housing property donates housing property rights to others, the recipients' income obtained from such donation is subject to individual income tax under the "accidental income". Third, in the business promotion, advertising and other activities of enterprises, the gifts (including online red envelopes) randomly offered to individuals outside enterprises, the gifts offered to individuals outside enterprises during annual meetings, symposiums, celebrations and other activities, as well as the personal income obtained from gifts are subject to individual income tax under the "accidental income", except for such gifts as coupons and vouchers with price discount offered by enterprises. Fourth, for the individual pension income obtained from tax-deferred commercial pension insurance, 25% of such income is exempted from tax, and the remaining 75% is subject to individual income tax at a rate of 10%. The tax is included under the item of and shall be reported with full payment at the location where the insurer sells the tax-deferred pension insurance after the withholding of taxes by the insurer. Fifth, this announcement is implemented starting from January 1, 2019. ■

POLICY 107

MOF, SAMR and NMPA jointly published a circular on the release of 2019 budget of subsidies for food and drug supervision

Source: MOF

On June 28, MOF, SAMR and NMPA jointly published a circular on the release of 2019 budget of subsidies for food and drug supervision, which provided the following. First, according to the *2019 Government Revenue and Expenditure Classification*, the relevant departments should include the subsidy funds under "201 General Public Service Expenditure" of 2019 government revenue and expenditure classification. Second, in order to improve the efficiency of fund use, local finance authorities at all levels should, in conjunction with market regulation and medical products regulatory authorities, consider local circumstances and make coordinated arrangement of central and local fiscal subsidies, with a focus on supporting food and drug supervision and management, as well as related capacity building. At the same time, it is necessary to strengthen the management of subsidy funds and improve the efficiency of the use of subsidy funds. Third, in order to further strengthen the budget performance management, it is important to effectively improve the efficiency of the use of fiscal funds and ensure that the annual performance targets are achieved on schedule. The market regulation and medical products regulatory authorities of all provinces, autonomous regions and municipalities are responsible for assessing the completion of performance targets in their jurisdiction. SAMR and NMPA will then examine the assessment results. ■

POLICY 108 MOF and SAT jointly published a circular on the continued implementation of the preferential vehicle purchase tax policies

On June 28, MOF and SAT jointly published a circular on the continued implementation of the preferential vehicle purchase tax policies, which provided the following. First, the purchase of one domestically produced car for self-use by students returning from studying abroad with foreign currency and the import of one car by foreign experts with long residence in China is exempted from vehicle purchase tax. The designated model of vehicles with fixed devices produced by the designated manufacturer and used by flood control authorities and forest fire control authorities to command, inspect, dispatch, report (alert) and contact are exempted from vehicle purchase tax. Second, from January 1, 2018 to December 31, 2020, the purchase of new energy vehicles is exempted from vehicle purchase tax. Third, from July 1, 2018 to June 30, 2021, the vehicle purchase tax will be halved for the purchase of trailers. Fourth, mobile medical vehicles of the "Mother Health Express" project of China Women Development Foundation are exempted from vehicle purchase tax. Fifth, the newly purchased vehicles of the Beijing 2022 Winter Olympics and Winter Paralympics Games Organizing Committee are exempted from vehicle purchase tax. Sixth, the vehicles with local motor vehicle license plates but previously used by public security forces and armed police gold, forest and hydropower units (except for the vehicles used by public security fire units and armed police forest units to carry out fire fighting and rescue mission) are offered one-time exemption from vehicle purchase tax. ■

POLICY 109 MOF published a circular on the issuance of the *Measures for the Administration of Subsidy Funds for Urban Pipe Network and Sewage Treatment*

On July 2, MOF published a circular on the issuance of the *Measures for the Administration of Subsidy Funds for Urban Pipe Network and Sewage Treatment,* which provided the following. In order to regulate and strengthen the management of subsidy funds for urban pipe network and sewage treatment and improve the efficiency of the use of fiscal funds, these measures are formulated. The subsidy funds for urban pipe network and sewage treatment referred to in these Measures are the transfer payment funds arranged by the central finance authorities to support the construction of urban pipe network, intensive use of urban underground space, construction of urban sewage treatment facilities, urban drainage and flood control, and water ecological restoration. The subsidy funds are earmarked for special purposes and managed separately, under the administration of MOF and MOHURD. MOF is responsible for formulating the expenditure standards and allocation factors of subsidy funds. According to the funding arrangements proposed by the Ministry of Housing and Urban-Rural Development, MOF determines the annual scale and allocation plan of subsidy funds, allocates the funds, organizes budget performance management, and guides local efforts to strengthen fund management. MOHURD is responsible for formulating relevant program or implementation plan, proposing funding arrangements, and guiding and supervising local implementation. ■

POLICY 110

MOF and five other ministries jointly published an announcement on the preferential tax policies for community and family-based services such as elderly care, childcare, and domestic services

On July 4, MOF, SAT,NDRC, MCA, MOFCOM, NHC jointly published an announcement on the preferential tax policies for community and family-based services such as elderly care, childcare and, domestic services, which provided the following. First, institutions that provide elderly care, childcare, and domestic services for community shall enjoy preferential tax and fee policies. Second, the housing property and land owned or acquired through lease by institutions to provide elderly care, childcare, and domestic services are exempted from property tax and urban land use tax. Third, the community mentioned in this announcement refers to the social life community composed of people living in a certain geographical area, including urban communities and rural communities. Fourth, income from the provision of domestic services by eligible domestic service companies is exempted from VAT. Fifth, the finance and tax collection authorities may establish information sharing and work coordination mechanisms with civil affairs, health, and commercial service authorities according to their working needs. Civil affairs, health and commercial service authorities should actively cooperate to ensure that preferential policies are well implemented. Sixth, this announcement will be implemented from June 1, 2019 to December 31, 2025. ■

POLICY 111

MOF and four other ministries jointly published a circular on the issuance of the *Interim Measures for the Administration of Duty-Free Shops at Departure Ports*

On July 4, MOF, MOFCOM, MCT, GAC, SAT jointly published a circular on the issuance of the *Interim Measures for the Administration of Duty-Free Shops at Departure Ports hereafter"the Measures"*, which provided the following. In order to regulate the management of duty-free shops at departure ports and promote the healthy and orderly development of duty-free shops at departure ports, the Measures is formulated in accordance with relevant laws and regulations and the policy of duty-free shops at departure ports in China. The Measures also apply to the establishment application, approval, bidding, operation, supervision and other matters related to the departure duty-free shops within the borders of the People's Republic of China. The sales target of duty-free goods is passengers who have already completed the departure procedures and are about to board plane, ship and bus to the overseas territory and passengers in outbound transportation vehicles. The state implements franchise operation for duty-free shops at departure ports. The state plans the overall layout and construction of duty-free shops. The location of duty-free shops should be determined on the basis of the flow of inbound and outbound passengers, taking into account regional distributional factors and meeting the requirements of resource conservation, environmental protection, orderly competition, avoidance of waste and convenience for supervision. ■

POLICY 112

MOF and MOE jointly published a circular on adjusting the scholarship and financial aid policy for vocational colleges

On July 5, MOF and MOE jointly published a circular on adjusting the scholarship and financial aid policy for vocational colleges, which provided the following. First, expand the coverage of scholarships and financial aids for higher vocational colleges and raise the subsidy standard. The number of national scholarships in higher vocational colleges will be raised. Starting in 2019, the number of national scholarship awards for undergraduate students will be increased from 50,000 to 60,000. The increased scholarship will all be awarded to the outstanding full-time higher vocational college students, with 8,000 RMB per student per year. The coverage of National Encouragement Scholarships in higher vocational colleges will also be expanded. Starting in 2019, the coverage of National Encouragement Scholarship for higher vocational college students will be increased by 10%, i.e., from 3% to 3.3%, and the reward standard will be 5,000 RMB per student per year. The coverage of national financial aid for students in higher vocational colleges will be expanded and the subsidy standards will be raised. Starting from the spring semester of 2019, the coverage of national financial aids for students in higher vocational colleges will be increased by 10%, and the average subsidy standard will be raised from 3,000 RMB per year to 3,300 RMB. The average subsidy of financial aids for general undergraduate students will be increased from 3,000 RMB to 3,300 RMB per student per year. Second, establish a national scholarship for secondary vocational education. Starting in 2019, a national scholarship for secondary vocational education will be established to reward the outstanding full-time students in secondary vocational schools (including technical schools). Each year, 20,000 people will be awarded the scholarship, with 6,000 RMB per student per year. Third, effectively strengthen the implementation. All relevant departments and schools must conscientiously understand the spirit of the policy and improve implementation so that more students can enjoy greater state financial support, with the priority being given to students from families with financial difficulties. It is also important to coordinate the central government's transfer payment funds with local funds, and urge relevant departments and schools at the sub-provincial levels to improve the awarding of scholarships and provision of financial aids for the spring semester of 2019. ■

POLICY 113 MOF and NDRC jointly published a circular on exempting the governmental funds and administrative fees for relocation for poverty alleviation

On July 5, MOF and NDRC jointly published a circular on exempting the governmental funds and administrative fees for relocation for poverty alleviation, which provided the following. First, exempt urban infrastructure supporting fees and real estate registration fees for relocation for poverty alleviation. Exempt the air defense basement construction fees for the relocation projects with the purpose of poverty alleviation if geological conditions do not allow for the construction of air defense basement. Second, the information of relocation projects, project implementing agencies, population to be relocated and resettlement housing will be determined by the competent departments of the relocation work. Third, if resettlement housing is constructed in the development of commercial housing, the governmental funds and administrative fees due to be exempted will be calculated

Source: MOF

according to the proportion of the floor area of the resettlement housing to the total floor area. Fourth, after the exemption of the above-mentioned governmental funds and administrative fees, the funding required for the performance of managerial duties by relevant departments and units shall be financed by the government budget at the same level. Fifth, this circular will be effective from July 1, 2019. The governments of all provinces, autonomous regions, and municipalities may use this circular as a reference for the relocation projects implemented during the period from January 1, 2016 to June 30, 2019. ■

POLICY 114 MOF and SAT jointly published a circular on the tax policies of some national reserve commodities

On July 5, MOF and SAT jointly published a circular on the tax policies of some national reserve commodities, which provided the following. First, the commodity reserve management companies and their financial account books are exempted from stamp duties; the purchase and sales contract entered into during the commodity reserve business process is exempted from stamp duties, and the stamp duties payable by other parties to the contract should be levied according to the regulations. Second, the real estate and land used for the commodity reserve business by the commodity reserve management companies and their directly affiliated warehouses are exempted from property tax and urban land use tax. Third, the commodity reserve management companies and their directly affiliated warehouses mentioned in this announcement refer to the commodity reserve enterprises that take up the task of stockpiling five commodities of grain (including soybean), edible oil, cotton, sugar and meat, with authorization from the relevant government departments above the county level and government funding or subsidies for reserve. Fourth, the authorized commodity reserve management companies and their directly affiliated warehouses include the China Grain Reserves Group Co., Ltd. and its subsidiaries as well as the China Merchandise Reserve Management Center Co., Ltd. and National Sugar Reserve and National Meat Reserve. Fifth, the enterprises enjoying the tax exemption policy stipulated in this announcement shall apply for tax exemption in accordance with the regulations, and keep the information such as the certificate of the property right, the original value of the real estate, the business of the commodity reserve, and the reserve construction plan for future reference. Sixth, the implementation time of this announcement is from January 1, 2019 to December 31, 2021. The taxes that should have been exempted but paid after January 1, 2019 may be deducted from the payable taxes of the enterprise or be refunded. ■

POLICY 115 MOF published a circular on carrying out the pilot program of providing central rewards and subsidies for the promotion of insurance for agricultural products with special local advantages

On July 5, MOF published a circular on carrying out the pilot program of providing central rewards and subsidies for the promotion of insurance for agricultural products with special local advantages, which provided the following. First, on the basis of independent operation and voluntary application, the central government will provide rewards and subsidies that are equivalent to a certain proportion of insurance premiums for the eligible insurance of agricultural products with special local advantages conducive to the development of small-scale farmers and new agri-business operations.

Second, the reward and subsidy policy adheres to the principle of "local responsibility, incentive orientation, poverty reduction and step-by-step implementation". The central rewards and subsidies will reflect regional differences, encourage local governments to give priority support to poor areas, and gradually expand the scope of implementation on the basis of piloting experience. Third, the insurance products applying for the rewards and subsidies should be no more than two in number, and meet the relevant conditions. Fourth, for the insurance premiums included in the pilot scope, on top of the at least 35% of the provincial and sub-provincial fiscal subsidies, the central government will subsidize 30% of the premium of the central and western regions and 25% of the premium of the eastern regions. Fifth, the application report for the 2019 rewards and subsidies should be submitted to MOF before June 30, 2019. Sixth, in conjunction with the relevant departments and in accordance with the provisions of this circular, MOF will timely adjust and improve the agricultural insurance policy, formulate detailed implementation rules for the pilot program, clarify the types of eligible insurance products, and do a good job in harmonizing with other agricultural insurance premium subsidy policies. Seventh, this circular is effective since January 1, 2019, and the pilot period is tentatively scheduled for one year. ■

POLICY 116

MOA and MOF jointly published a circular on supporting the cultivation of new agricultural business entities

On July 9, the MOA and MOF jointly published a circular on supporting the cultivation of new agricultural business entities, which provided the following. First, significance. Accelerating the cultivation of new agricultural business entities is of great significance for promoting agricultural supply-side structural reform, guiding the moderate-scale operation of agriculture, boosting farmers' employment and income, and enhancing the momentum of agricultural and rural development. Second, overall requirements. Guided by the Xi Jinping Thought on Socialism with Chinese Characteristics for a New Era, the new agricultural business entities will be encouraged to enhance key development capabilities, stimulate internal vitality, and better play a leading role in driving small holder farmers to enter the market for higher income and building modern agriculture. Third, supportive measures. Support the initial processing of agricultural products, improve the quality and safety of products, and strengthen the branding of high-quality specialty products. Fourth, recipients of support and the approach of support. With the farmers' cooperatives, family farms, and agricultural industrialization complexes as the recipients of support, localities may consider local conditions and use the moderate-scale operating funds in the central agricultural production development funds and their own financial resources to provide support. Fifth, safeguard measures. Strengthen policy organization and leadership, improve the mechanism of interest linkage, innovate fund supervision approaches, and increase publicity and guidance. ■

POLICY 117

MOF and MWR jointly published the *Measures for the Administration of Water Resource Development Funds*

On July 10, MOF and MWR jointly published the *Measures for the Administration of Water Resources Development Funds, which provided the following. To strengthen the management of water resource development funds,* improve the rule-based, safe and effective use of funds, and promote the reform and development of water resources, these Measures are formulated in accordance with relevant laws and regulations. The water resource development funds mentioned in these Measures refer to the central government transfer payment funds used to support water resource development and reform. These Measures are applicable to the allocation, use, management and supervision of water resource development funds. The water resource development fund policy will be implemented until 2023. Before the expiration, MOF and the Ministry of Water Resources will assess whether to continue the implementation and extend the time limit. Before the preparation of the annual budget or during budget execution, MOF and the Ministry of Water Resources will carry out relevant assessment according to the policy implementation and the needs of the work, and improve the fund management policy on the basis of the assessment results. The water resource development fund is managed by MOF and MWR. The management follows the principles of scientific norms, openness and transparency, overall consideration, highlighted key points, performance management, and strengthened supervision. ■

POLICY 118

MOF and MOA jointly published a circular on the issuance of the *Interim Measures for the Disposal of Property Formed through the Acceptance of Direct State Fiscal Subsidy during the Dissolution and Liquidation of Farmers' Professional Cooperatives*

Source: MOF

On July 12, MOF and MOA jointly published a circular on the issuance of the *Interim Measures for the Disposal of Property Formed through the Acceptance of Direct State Fiscal Subsidy during the Dissolution and Liquidation of Farmers' Professional Cooperatives*, which provided the following. To support the healthy development of farmers' professional cooperatives and regulate their dissolution and liquidation, these Measures are formulated. These Measures are applicable to the disposal of property formed through the acceptance of direct state fiscal subsidy during the dissolution and liquidation of farmers' professional cooperatives. During the dissolution and liquidation of farmers' professional cooperatives, if there is surplus property after paying off the debt, the liquidation group shall calculate the total amount of property formed through the acceptance of direct state fiscal subsidy. Where such property is to be transferred, the liquidation group shall show the transfer situation in the liquidation plan, report the liquidation plan to the county-level agricultural department and the finance department for the record, and at the same time, prepare for the handover of the relevant financial accounts and original documents. The relevant government departments at or above the county level that are responsible for subsidizing and allocating funds for farmers' professional cooperatives shall, according to their duties, strengthen the guidance and supervision of the disposal of property formed through the acceptance of direct state fiscal subsidy. ■

POLICY 119 MOF published a circular on the release of the special subsidy fund budget for the local development of the national film industry in 2019

On July 12, MOF published a circular on the release of the special subsidy fund budget for the local development of the national film industry in 2019, which provided the following. In order to support the development of the film industry, MOF issued a circular requiring the improvement of work related to budget preparation and fund arrangement. First, guide cinemas to screen domestic films. In accordance with the "Double Hundred" policy, cinemas will be guided to screen domestically produced films with cultural characteristics and artistic innovation, in order to boost the development of the film market and to strive for 55% of the share of the total box office for domestic films. Second, support pilot projects in the county and township cinemas in the central and western regions, develop the film market in a balanced manner, promote the sustainable development of the film industry, and complete the construction of 707 cinemas. Third, improve the ethnic-minority-language translation capacity of films, and complete the translation of 885 films into ethnic minority languages in this year. ■

POLICY 120 MOF, the National Offices Administration, and the CPC Offices Administration published a circular on regulating the collection and payment of travel and meal expenses and intra-city transportation expenses

On July 18, MOF, the National Offices Administration, and the CPC Offices Administration published a circular on regulating the collection and payment of travel and meal expenses and intra-city transportation expenses, which provided the following. First, the central department officials who are on business trips shall receive meal stipends according to regulations. Except for the one working meal that needs to be provided by the reception unit, the other meal expenses shall be paid by the traveling officials themselves. Second, employees who are on business trips shall receive intra-city transportation stipends according to regulations. If the reception unit that assists in providing transportation has charging standard, the traveling officials shall pay according to the standard, and the amount shall not exceed the daily transportation expense standard; if there is no charging standard, each person shall pay 50% of the daily transportation expense standard every half day. Third, if the reception unit assists in arranging meals and providing transportation, the traveling officials should ask for receipts or tax invoices , which would be kept for future reference and would not serve as the basis for reimbursement. Fourth, the reception unit should collect the relevant fees of the traveling officials according to the regulations, and provide receipts or tax invoices in a timely manner. Fifth, all departments in various regions should urge the reception units to further improve the internal management system and reasonably set the charging standards in accordance with the Eight-point regulations and relevant provisions of the official hospitality arrangement of Party and government organs. Sixth, all localities should, in light of the local conditions, formulate regulations governing the meal and intra-city transportation expenses of traveling officials. The central departments may, in accordance with the requirements of this circular, formulate their own specific operational regulations for the payment and reimbursement of meal and intra-city transportation expenses. Seventh, this circular will come into force on August 1, 2019. ■

121 MOF, SAT and CSRC jointly published an announcement on the continuous implementation of differentiated personal income tax policy for dividends from companies listed on the National Equities Exchange and Quotation (NEEQ)

On July 19, MOF, SAT and CSRC jointly published an announcement on the continuous implementation of differentiated personal income tax policy for dividends from companies listed on the NEEQ, which provided the following. First, individuals who hold shares of listed companies for more than one year are allowed a temporary exemption of personal income tax for their dividend income. Second, when listed company distributes dividends, if individuals hold shares for less than one year since the equity registration closing date and have not transferred the shares, the company shall not withhold the personal income tax; when individuals transfer the shares, the securities registration and settlement company shall calculate the amount of payable tax according to the shareholding period. Third, when individuals transfer shares, the shareholding period shall be calculated according to the principle of first-in-first-out, i.e., the shares first obtained in the securities account will be regarded as the first transfer. Fourth, the dividend income obtained by securities investment fund from listed companies shall be subject to personal income tax in accordance with the provisions of this announcement. Fifth, the shares held by individuals in listed companies as mentioned in this announcement include the shares obtained before the listing on the NEEQ, the shares obtained through the transfer on the NEEQ, and the shares obtained through judicial seizure. Sixth, the transfer of shares referred to in this announcement applies to the transfer of shares through the NEEQ and the judicial seizure of shares. Seventh, the dividend income obtained by individuals and securities investment fund from the NEEQ-listed companies previously listed on the STAQ and the NET and the NEEQ-delisted companies will be subject to personal income tax in accordance with this announcement. Eighth, the term "year" in this announcement refers to the natural year, i.e., the one-year holding means the continuous shareholding from the certain month of the last year to the previous date of the same day of the same month of the current year. Ninth, finance, taxation, securities supervision and other departments should strengthen coordination, work together, and do a good job in all aspects of policy implementation. Tenth, this announcement will be implemented from July 1, 2019 to June 30, 2024. The dividend income of listed companies, two-net companies, and delisted companies that distribute dividends, with the stock registration date being from July 1, 2019 to June 20, 2024, shall be governed by the provisions of this announcement. Eleventh, the *Circular of the Ministry of Finance, the State Administration of Taxation, and the China Securities Regulatory Commission on Matters Related to the Implementation of Differentiated Personal Income Tax Policy for Dividends from Companies Listed on the National Equities Exchange and Quotation* and the Fourth Article of the *Circular of the Ministry of Finance, the State Administration of Taxation, and the China Securities Regulatory Commission on Matters Related to the Differentiated Personal Income Tax Policy for Dividends from Listed Companies* are abolished. ■

122 MOF published a circular on the *issuance of the No. 1 Interpretation of the Government Accounting Standards System*

On July 23, MOF published a circular on the *issuance of the No. 1 Interpretation of the Government Accounting Standards System,* which provided the following. This circular is formulated to further improve the government accounting standards system and ensure the effective implementation of the government accounting standards system. First, the implementation of the accounting system of the government-sponsored institutions in enterprise group. Government-sponsored institutions that are included in the scope of departmental budget preparation in an enterprise group shall conduct accounting in accordance with the government accounting standards system. Second, the accounting treatment of long-term equity investment in government-sponsored institutions. The government-sponsored institutions shall adopt the equity method in the accounting of long-term equity investment. During the period of holding the investment, it should be based on the net profit attributable to the parent company and the changes in other owners' equity in the consolidated financial statements of the invested entity. Third, the accounting treatment of the temporarily collected non-fiscal funds at the end of the year. Before the end of the year, departments should thoroughly clean up the temporary funds, confirm the relevant budget revenue and expenditure, and ensure that the budget accounting information can fully reflect the implementation of the department's budget revenue and expenditure for the current year. Fourth, the accounting treatment of fixed assets that are centrally managed by relevant departments but are held and used by other departments. The department that holds and uses the asset should be the accounting recognition entity and should conduct accounting for the asset. Fifth, the financial treatment of the department's free transfer of assets. If the book value of the transferred assets is zero on the transferor's book or if the book balance is nominal, the department shall include the relevant taxes and expenses incurred by it in the transfer process into the current expenses, and shall not include them in the initial cost of the transferred assets. Sixth, the accounting scope of the "business activity expenses" and "department management expenses". According to the regulations, administrative departments shall not use the "department management expenses", and all their expenses incurred to fulfill functional objectives and perform duties shall be included in the "business activity expenses". Seventh, the scope of accounting for "subsidized housing". The subsidized housing here mainly refers to the housing that is fully or partially owned by the local government housing security department, included in the urban housing security plan and annual plan, and provided to eligible recipients. Eighth, the application of accounting subjects for the funds of third-party payment platform accounts. The balances of third-party payment platform accounts such as Alipay and WeChat Pay that have not been transferred to bank deposits should be accounted for under the "Other Money Funds". Ninth, the disclosure of detailed information about the subject and income as well as expense subjects. On the basis of detailed accounting of the debtor's corresponding receivables, the department shall disclose the receivables according to the debtor's classification in the notes to the financial statements. Tenth, the accounting treatment of the house sales income. The central administrative departments shall, starting from January 1, 2019, including the house sales income and its interest income attributable to the department in the departmental budget management. Eleventh, the accounting treatment of the special maintenance funds for houses centrally managed by the department. The department shall conduct accounting treatment of the special maintenance funds for the houses centrally managed by it, in accordance with the provisions related to the accounting of house sales income in this Interpretation. Twelfth, this Interpretation takes effect on January 1, 2019. ■

POLICY 123 MOF published a circular on the issuance of the *Measures for the Accountability of Finance Departments in the Mismanagement of Poverty Alleviation Funds*

On July 24, MOF published a circular on the issuance of the *Measures for the Accountability of*

Finance Departments in the Mismanagement of Poverty Alleviation Funds, which provided the following. These Measures are formulated to further strengthen and standardize the management of finance departments' poverty alleviation funds, ensure the safety of funds, and improve the efficiency of capital use. First, the general rule. These measures are applicable to all levels of finance departments and their staff that should be held accountable for mismanaging poverty alleviation funds in violation of regulations. Second, the cases and forms of accountability. The forms of accountability to the finance department include: make rectification, adjust relevant accounting records, recover relevant poverty alleviation funds, return illegal income within a time limit, and give warnings to or make public censure of the agency. Third, the transfer procedure. Where the finance department at the same level has no right to deal with the persons who should be held accountable according to the law, the case shall be transferred to the competent department for handling. Fourth, the supplementary rule. Local finance departments at all levels may, in light of the local conditions, formulate specific implementing measures. These Measures shall be implemented 30 days after the date of promulgation. ■

POLICY 124 The CAC, NDRC, MIIT and MOF jointly published the Announcement on *Measures for Cloud Computing Service Security Assessment*

On July 24, CAC, NDRC, MIIT and MOF jointly published the Announcement on *Measures for Cloud Computing Service Security Assessment,* which provided the following. To improve the security of cloud computing services purchased and used by Party and government agencies as well as key information infrastructure operators, these Measures are formulated. The cloud computing service security assessment combines ex-ante assessment with continuous supervision to ensure the security of the application. In accordance with relevant laws, regulations and policies, and with reference to relevant national network security standards, the assessment leverages the role of professional technical institutions and experts, carries out objective evaluation and strict supervision of the security and controllability of the cloud computing service platforms, and provides a reference for Party and government agencies and key information infrastructure operators when they purchase cloud computing services. CAC, along with NDRC, MIIT, and MOF established a coordination mechanism for cloud computing service security assessment, in order to review the policy documents related to cloud computing service security assessment, approve the cloud computing service security assessment results, and coordinate the handling of important matters about cloud computing service security assessment. ■

POLICY 125 MOF published a circular on the release of the 2019 budget for the central natural disaster relief funds

On July 24, MOF published a circular on the release of the 2019 budget for the central natural disaster relief funds, which provided the following. According to the relevant stipulations of the central fiscal subsidy policy for geological disaster relief, 30 million RMB of the budget for the central natural disaster relief funds is now released to support Guizhou Province in dealing with the landslide relief of Shuicheng Mountain in Liupanshui City. The proceeds of the disbursed funds

Source: MOF

shall be included in the "1100260 other transfer payment income from common fiscal mandates" of 2019 government revenue and expenditure classification, and the expenditure of the funds is included in the "224 disaster prevention and emergency management expenditure" of 2019 government revenue and expenditure classification. The above-mentioned funds are pre-allocated funds. MOF will carry out the settlement on the basis of the subsequently verified disaster situation, and the relevant requirements for performance evaluation will be notified separately when it comes to settlement. Guizhou Province is required to strictly manage and use the assistance funds in accordance with relevant regulations, and fully carry out search and rescue and disaster emergency response to ensure the safety of people's lives and property. ■

POLICY 126

MOF published a circular on the issuance of the *Measures for the Administration of Central Special Lottery Public Welfare Funds for Supporting Local Public Welfare Undertakings*

On July 29, MOF published a circular on the issuance of the *Measures for the Administration of Central Special Lottery Public Welfare Funds for Supporting Local Public Welfare Undertakings,* which provided the following. these Measures are formulated to regulate and strengthen the administration of central special lottery public welfare funds to support local public welfare undertakings, and improve the effectiveness of the use of funds. The public welfare funds are included in the budget management of governmental funds. Funds for public welfare undertakings should tilt toward the public welfare projects that "shore up the weak links" as well as toward the industries faced with difficulties and disadvantaged groups of people, in order to support the weak areas in local public welfare undertakings. MOF is responsible for proposing to the State Council suggestions on the allocation of funds for local public welfare undertakings and compiling the annual budget for such funds based on the comments of the State Council. The provincial finance department may adopt factor method, project method, or a combination of the two, in proposing the fund allocation plan, in accordance with the transfer payment budget, the direction of the use of funds and the principle of allocation determined by MOF and in line with the local reality of public welfare undertakings. The competent provincial departments for public welfare undertakings shall, in coordination with the finance department, manage the funds for public welfare undertakings, do a good job in organization and implementation, and strictly follow the approved budget. ■

127 Five ministries jointly published a circular on the implementation of the pilot city program for leveraging public finance in support of the comprehensive reform of financial services for private sector and small and micro-sized enterprises

On July 29, MOF, MOST, MIIT,PBOC, CBIRC jointly published a circular on the implementation of the pilot city program for leveraging public finance in support of the comprehensive reform of financial services for private sector and small and micro-sized enterprises, which provided the following. First, follow the guidance of the Xi Jinping Thought on Socialism with Chinese Characteristics for a New Era, conscientiously implement the decisions of the Party Central Committee and the State Council on supporting the development of private sector and small and micro-sized enterprises, aim at promoting the high-quality development of financial services for private sector and small and micro-sized enterprises, leverage the role of public financial resources, and support local government in creating pilot cities for comprehensive reform of financial services in line with local conditions. Second, the basic principles are as follows: local ownership and central guidance; sound mechanism and market-oriented operation; innovation and experience accumulation; and performance-based reward and punishment. Third, starting from 2019, the central government will allocate around 2 billion RMB of funds through the special funds for financial inclusion to support a certain number of pilot cities. The pilot cities should generally be the prefecture-level cities, districts and counties of provincial capital cities, and new development areas. For the provinces and autonomous regions with less than 10 prefecture-level jurisdictions as well as the 5 cities with independent planning status, 1 pilot city will be selected each year; for other provinces, autonomous regions and the 4 directly under the central government, two pilot cities will be selected each year. The work for performance target setting and evaluation of pilot cities will be shared by various authorities: the branch of the PBoC and the banking and insurance regulatory authorities are responsible for the overall financial services in support of private sector and small and micro-sized enterprises and the indicators related to comprehensive financial services and innovation, while the specific measurement and scores are determined by both sides through consultation; the finance authorities and the local financial regulatory authorities are responsible for the indicators related to financing guarantee and risk compensation mechanism; the science and technology authorities and the industry and information technology authorities are responsible for the indicators related to local financial development; and the local regulatory authorities of MOF are responsible for the regulated use of the central fiscal incentive funds. These authorities should regularly hold joint meetings to strengthen communication and information sharing and build an effective and efficient working mechanism. ■

128 MOF published a circular on promoting fair competition in government procurement to optimize the business environment

On July 30, MOF published a circular on promoting fair competition in government procurement to optimize the business environment, which provided the following. First, comprehensively sort through the regulations and practices that hinder fair competition in the field of government procurement, and ensure the right of all market players to participate in government procurement activities on an equal footing. Second, strictly implement the fair competition review system. All regions and departments, when formulating government procurement rules involving market entities, shall strictly implement the fair competition review system, fully listen to the opinions of market players and relevant industry associations, evaluate the impact on market competition, and prevent the exclusion and restriction of market competition. Third, strengthen the management of government procurement. Optimize the procurement procedures, refine the implementation requirements of procurement activities, standardize the collection and refund of deposits, timely pay for procurement, and improve the indemnity and compensation mechanisms for suppliers. Fourth, accelerate the application of electronic government procurement, improve the online transaction function of the e-government procurement platform, and expedite the implementation of the "Internet + government procurement" initiative. Fifth, further enhance the transparency of government procurement. Strengthen the transparency of government procurement and promote the disclosure of procurement intentions. Sixth, improve the government procurement challenging and complaining mechanism as well as the administrative ruling mechanism. Unblock the channels for suppliers to voice their queries and complaints and enforce administrative penalties in accordance with the law. ■

POLICY 129

Six ministries jointly published a circular on matters related to the central fiscal subsidy for the social insurance of some veterans

Source: MOF

On July 31, MOF, MVA, MOHRSS, NHSA, MCA and SAT jointly published a circular on matters related to the central fiscal subsidy for the social insurance of some veterans, which provided the following. First, the scope of government subsidies. Veterans who have retired from active service through government arranged employment scheme and have not participated in the basic pension insurance and basic medical insurance schemes or have stopped premiums payment before the implementation of this *Circular* may make up for the premiums payment for no more than their years of military service. Premiums for participation in the basic pension insurance and basic medical insurance scheme are to be shared by their employers and veterans. Second, the scope and standards of the central fiscal subsidies. For the government subsidy funds required for the employers' payment for the veterans' basic endowment insurance premiums, the central finance authorities will subsidize the major military human resource supplying provinces in central and western China, non-major military human resource supplying provinces in central and western China, major military human resource supplying provinces in eastern China and non-major military human resource supplying provinces in eastern China at a rate of 50%, 40%, 30% and 20% respectively. Third, the pre-allocation and settlement of central fiscal subsidy funds. The central fiscal subsidy funds are allocated first and settled later. Starting from 2019, the central government will allocate subsidy funds according to the progress of local work, and settle the remaining subsidy funds in 2022. Fourth, the management of the use of subsidies. The local finance departments shall make overall use of the subsidy funds arranged by the central and local governments, do a good job in making up for the payment of veterans' basic pension insurance premiums, and effectively safeguard the rights of veterans in pension insurance. Fifth, supervision and inspection. MVA, MOHRSS, and MOF will conduct special inspections on the use of the central fiscal subsidy funds by provinces (autonomous regions and municipalities). Sixth, work requirements. All relevant departments in all localities must perform their duties and cooperate closely, and complete the payment of basic pension insurance premiums for veterans by the end of 2021. The finance department shall promptly allocate subsidies for the payment of basic pension insurance and basic medical insurance premiums, provide adequate funding, and strengthen fund management with relevant departments, in order to ensure the safe, regulated and efficient use of funds. ■

POLICY 130 MOF, the National Health Commission, and NHSA jointly published a circular on the comprehensive implementation of the reform of electronic bills for healthcare expenses

On August 1, MOF, the National Health Commission, and NHSA jointly published a circular on the comprehensive implementation of the reform of electronic bills for healthcare expenses, which provided the following. First, the comprehensive implementation of the reform of electronic bills for healthcare expenses. Unify the formats of bills for healthcare expenses across the country, and officially launch the nationally unified bills. The finance departments of all regions should provide funding support for the reform of electronic bills for healthcare expenses; the health departments of all regions should urge local medical and health institutions to do a good job in the reform of electronic bills for healthcare expenses; the healthcare security departments in all regions should promote information exchange with the finance departments in accordance with the requirements of building the nationally unified healthcare security information system; the local medical and health institutions should retrofit information system, and adjust business processes. To standardize the reimbursement and filing of electronic bills for healthcare expenses, the reimbursement agencies shall promptly report information such as the status of account, the time of account entry, and the amount of funds to the finance department. Second, standardize the nationally unified data entry of electronic bills for healthcare expenses. To standardize the data entry of outpatient fee bills, medical and health institutions, when issuing outpatient fee bills, shall enter data according to the required sequence by filling in all the charging items first and then entering the specific details contained in each item. To standardize the data entry of inpatient fee bills, medical and health institutions, when issuing inpatient fee bills, shall enter data according to the required sequence by filling in all the charging items first and then entering the specific details contained in each item. Local regions may add other information they see fit in line with local reality. Third, further strengthen safeguard measures. Do a good job in implementation and promote the upgrading and transformation of relevant systems; enhance communication and exchange with medical and health institutions, medical expense payers and reimbursement agencies; strengthen publicity work, and make full use of media, internet and other channels to enhance public awareness of electronic bills for healthcare expenses. ■

POLICY 131

MOF published a circular on the issuance of the *Interim Measures for the Administration of the Monitoring of the Central Department's Budget Performance*

Source: MOF

On August 1, MOF published a circular on the issuance of the *Interim Measures for the Administration of the Monitoring of the Central Department's Budget Performance,* which provided the following. First, the general principles. These measures are formulated to strengthen the monitoring of the central department's budget performance, improve the efficiency of budget execution and the effectiveness of fund use. Performance monitoring is organized by MOF and implemented by the central departments at different levels. Second, the division of responsibilities. The main responsibilities of MOF include the overall organization and guidance of performance monitoring of central departments, development of measures for performance monitoring management, monitoring the performance of key areas according to work needs, and urging the application of performance monitoring results; the central departments are responsible for implementing budget performance monitoring and their main responsibilities include taking the lead in organizing the budget performance monitoring at the departmental level and conducting daily monitoring of budget performance. Third, the scope and content of monitoring. The scope of central department's performance monitoring covers all project expenditures of the central department's general public budget, governmental fund budget and state-owned capital operation budget; the content of performance monitoring mainly includes the completion of performance targets, budget fund implementation, extended monitoring of key policies and major project performance, etc. Fourth, the monitoring methods and processes. Performance monitoring adopts the target comparison method. By combining quantitative analysis and qualitative analysis, this method compares performance target realization with the expected performance target, and analyzes and assesses target completion, budget execution, organization and fund management. Performance monitoring includes timeliness, compliance, and effectiveness monitoring. Performance monitoring is the continuous management of the entire process, which is carried out through a combination of daily monitoring by the central departments and regular monitoring by MOF. Fifth, the application of results. The performance monitoring results are used as reference for future budget arrangement and policy formulation, and the effectiveness of performance monitoring is part of the assessment of central department's budget performance management work. If deviation of performance target implementation and management loopholes are found in performance monitoring, timely measures should be taken to correct them. Sixth, the supplementary rules. The central departments may, in accordance with these measures, formulate specific management measures or implementation rules for budget performance monitoring and report to MOF for the record-keeping. These Measures shall be implemented starting from the date of issuance. ■

132 MOF and SAT jointly published a circular on the addition of tourism industry projects to the *Hengqin New Area Preferential Corporate Income Tax Catalogue*

On August 16, MOF and SAT jointly published a circular on the addition of tourism industry projects to the Hengqin New Area Preferential Corporate Income Tax Catalogue, which provided the following. First, add relevant tourism industry projects to the *Hengqin New Area Preferential Corporate Income Tax Catalogue*. The encouraged industrial enterprises that enjoy the preferential corporate income tax policy at a reduced rate of 15% in the Hengqin New Area shall implement the policy in accordance with the *Hengqin New Area Preferential Corporate Income Tax Catalogue (2019 Edition)*. Second, other matters related to the reduced corporate income tax rate of 15% for the encouraged industrial enterprises in the Hengqin New Area shall continue to be governed by the *Circular of MOF and SAT on the Preferential Corporate Income Tax Policy and Catalogue for the Guangdong Hengqin New Area, Fujian Pingtan Comprehensive Experimental Zone, and Shenzhen Qianhai Shenzhen-Hong Kong Modern Service Industry Cooperation Zone*. Third, the implementation period of this circular will be from January 1, 2019 to December 31, 2020. ■

133 Three departments jointly published a circular on the issuance of the *Implementation Plan for the Government Procurement of Agricultural Products and By-products in Poor Areas*

On August 19, MOF, State Council Leading Group Office of Poverty Alleviation and Development, and the All China Federation of Supply and Marketing Cooperatives jointly published a circular on the issuance of the *Implementation Plan for the Government Procurement of Agricultural Products and By-products in Poor Areas*, which provided the following. First, the overall requirements. Thoroughly implement the important instructions of General Secretary Xi Jinping on poverty alleviation, adhere to the basic strategy of targeted poverty alleviation, set the goal of promoting the sales of agricultural products and by-products in poverty-stricken areas and increasing the income of poverty-stricken households, and fully deploy government procurement policies to encourage budget units at all levels to buy agricultural and by-products in poverty-stricken areas through preferential procurement and reserved procurement in order to support the fight against poverty. Second, mission and goals. Establish an online sales platform for agricultural products and by-products in poverty-stricken areas integrating "transaction, services and supervision" before the end of October 2019; compile a catalogue of key poverty alleviation product suppliers in the state-designated poverty-stricken counties before the end of October 2019; starting from 2020, each budget unit will fully launch the procurement of agricultural products and by-products in poverty-stricken areas through the online sales platform. MOF and State Council Leading Group Office of Poverty Alleviation and Development will use the online sales platform to regularly collect data and report on the progress of procurement. Third, the key work is to strengthen the supply of agricultural products and by-products in poverty-stricken areas, build a sales platform for agricultural products and by-products in poverty-stricken areas, and guide budget units to purchase agricultural products and by-products in poverty-stricken areas. Fourth, the working mechanism includes the organizational guarantee mechanism, the interest linkage mechanism, the publicity and guidance mechanism, the incentive mechanism, and the supervision and reporting mechanism. Fifth, the implementation steps. Before September 15, 2019, the provincial poverty alleviation departments shall submit the *Recommended*

List of Key Poverty Alleviation Product Suppliers in Poor Counties filled out by poor counties in their jurisdiction and the reviewed *Suggested List of Key Poverty Alleviation Product Suppliers in Poor Counties* to the State Council Leading Group Office of Poverty Alleviation and Development; before the end of October 2019, the online sales platform will be put into operation, the consumption for poverty alleviation database system will be launched, and pilot demonstration will be started in some areas. From 2020, budget units at all levels will start in full scale start the procurement of agricultural products and by-products in poverty-stricken areas. ■

POLICY 134

MOF and the Organization Department of the CPC Central Committee jointly published a circular on the cessation of requirements for the annual record-filing of training plan and the reporting of implementation progress

On August 19, MOF and the Organization Department of the CPC Central Committee jointly published a circular on the cessation of requirements for the annual record-filing of training plan and the reporting of implementation progress, which provided the following. In order to implement the documents of the CPC Central Committee and the State Council on improving the fund management of research projects supported by public finance and promote the "streamlining of administration, delegations of powers and improving of services", the relevant matters concerning the annual record-filing of training plan and the reporting of implementation progress are announced as follows: First, starting from August 1, 2019, Article 7 and 21 of the *Measures for the Administration of Training Expenses of Central and State Agencies* will be suspended. Second, all departments must conscientiously implement the *Regulations of Party and Government Organs on Promoting Saving and Opposing Waste* and regulations on training expense management, improve the training plan preparation and approval system, strictly implement the plan, standardize the management of training expenses, strengthen supervision and inspection, and improve the effectiveness of the use of fiscal funds. ■

POLICY 135

The Customs Tariff Commission of the State Council published an announcement on imposing additional tariffs on some imported goods (the third batch) from the United States

Source: MOF

On August 23, the Customs Tariff Commission of the State Council published an announcement on imposing additional tariffs on some imported goods (the third batch) from the United States, and decided to increase tariffs on 5078 tax items of products worth around 75 billion USD imported from the U.S. First, starting from 12:01 on September 1, 2019, an additional tariff of 10% is imposed on

270 items listed in the first part of Annex 1, an additional tariff of 10% is imposed on 646 items listed in the second part of Annex 1, an additional tariff of 5% is imposed on 64 items listed in the third part of Annex 1, and an additional tariff of 5% is imposed on 737 items listed in the fourth part of Annex 1. Second, starting from 12:01 on December 15, 2019, an additional tariff of 10% is imposed on 749 items listed in the first part of Annex 2, an additional tariff of 10% is imposed on 163 items listed in the second part of Annex 2, an additional tariff of 5% is imposed on 634 items listed in the third part of Annex 2, and an additional tariff of 5% is imposed on 1815 items listed in the fourth part of Annex 2. Third, for the imported U.S. goods listed in the annexes, the corresponding tariffs shall be levied on the basis of the current applicable tariff rate. The current bonded, tax reduction and exemption policies shall remain unchanged, and the tariffs imposed shall not be reduced. Fourth, the calculation of relevant import taxes: additional customs tariff (duty) = customs duty-paid price × increased tariff rate; total tariff (duty) = the amount of duty payable at the current applicable tax rate + the amount of tariff; the VAT and consumption tax on import links are calculated in accordance with relevant laws and regulations. ■

POLICY 136 The Customs Tariff Commission of the State Council published an announcement on re-imposing tariffs on automobiles and parts originating from the U.S.

On August 23, the Customs Tariff Commission of the State Council published an announcement on re-imposing tariffs on automobiles and parts originating from U.S., and decided to re-impose tariffs on automobiles and auto parts originating from U.S. Starting from 12:01 on December 15, 2019, for the 28 items listed in Annex 1 of *the Announcement of the State Council Customs Tariff Commission on the Suspension of Tariffs on Automobiles and Parts Originating from the U.S.*, an additional tariff of 25% is re-imposed as per *the Announcement of the State Council Customs Tariff Commission on Imposing an Additional Tariff on 50 Billion USD of Imported Goods Originating from the U.S.* For the 116 items listed in Annex 2 of the [2018] No. 10 Announcement of State Council Customs Tariff Commission, an additional tariff of 25% is re-imposed as per *the Announcement of State Council Customs Tariff Commission on Imposing Additional Tariffs on 16 Billion USD of Imported Goods Originating from the U.S.*; for the 67 items listed in Annex 3 of the [2018] No. 10 Announcement of State Council Customs Tariff Commission, an additional tariff of 5% is re-imposed as per *the Announcement of State Council Customs Tariff Commission on Imposing Additional Tariffs on 60 Billion USD of Imported Goods Originating from the U.S.* ■

POLICY 137 MOF published a circular on the issuance of guidelines for the disclosure standards of grass-root government affairs in the field of fiscal budget and final accounts

On August 26, MOF published a circular on the issuance of guidelines for the disclosure standards of grass-root government affairs in the field of fiscal budget and final accounts, which provided the following. First, strengthen organizational leadership. Local finance departments and budget departments must conscientiously implement the decisions of the Party Central Committee and the State Council on the disclosure of fiscal budget and final accounts, strengthen organizational leadership, and do a good job in relevant work. Second, items of disclosure and catalogue of standards. The second-tier items of the disclosure of grass-root government affairs in the field of fiscal budget and final accounts are divided into four categories, including government budget, government final accounts, departmental budget, and departmental final accounts. The catalogue of standards sets out the content (elements) of disclosure and requirements, as well as the basis, time limit, subject, channels, matters, methods and levels of disclosure. Third, the specific work requirements. The principle of the disclosure of budget and final accounts is to make disclosure a norm and non-disclosure an exception, and disclose the budget and final accounts according to the law. The government budget and final accounts shall be disclosed to the public within 20 days after the approval by the people's congress at the corresponding level or its standing committee. The departmental budget and final accounts shall be disclosed to the public within 20 days after the approval by the finance department of the government at the corresponding level. The local finance departments at all levels shall set up a unified platform (or column) at the portal website of government or finance department for the disclosure of budget and final accounts, and publicize the government budget and final accounts and departmental budget and final accounts on the platform (or column). Local finance departments and budget departments shall establish and improve the confidential review mechanism for the disclosure of budget and final accounts, and conduct strict examinations in accordance with the *Law of the People's Republic of China on the Protection of State Secrets* and the *Regulations of the People's Republic of China on the Disclosure of Government Information*. ■

POLICY 138

MOF and MOE jointly published a circular on the issuance of the *Measures for the Administration of Subsidy Funds for the Improvement and Capacity Enhancement of the Weak Links in Compulsory Education*

On August 29, MOF and MOE jointly published a circular on the issuance of the *Measures for the Administration of Subsidy Funds for the Improvement and Capacity Enhancement of the Weak Links in Compulsory Education*, which provided the following. To standardize and strengthen the administration of subsidy funds for the improvement and capacity enhancement of the weak links in compulsory education, and improve the effectiveness of the use of funds, the Measures are formulated in accordance with the relevant laws and regulations. The administration of subsidy funds follows the principle of "central-guided, provincial-coordinated, priority-oriented, performance-focused, rule-based and transparent, and strong supervision". The subsidy funds mainly go to: orderly increase the supply of educational resources and eliminate "large classes" through the construction, renovation, expansion and repair of necessary school buildings; strengthen the construction of dormitory, canteen, toilet and sports ground in township boarding schools and provide necessary bathing, water drinking and heating facilities and equipments for students according to the basic schooling standards determined by the provincial people's government; set up functional classrooms and equip them with necessary facilities to meet the basic educational and teaching needs of small-scale village schools; improve the school internet-based teaching environment with broadband connection and provide quality digital educational resources for small-scale village schools to support the pilot program of "internet + education". The subsidy funds are jointly managed by MOF and MOE. MOE is responsible for reviewing relevant local materials and data, providing basic data needed for fund calculation, and proposing the plan for the calculation of funding needs. MOF, in accordance with the relevant provisions of budget management, will work with MOE to study and determine the budgeted amount of subsidy funds for relevant provinces. The provincial finance and education departments shall clarify the responsibilities of fund arrangement, use and management at the provincial and sub-provincial levels, and effectively strengthen fund management. ■

POLICY 139 MOF, SAT, MNR, MOA and MEE jointly published an announcement on the issuance of the *Measures for the Implementation of the Law of the People's Republic of China on Farmland Occupation Tax*

On August 30, MOF, SAT, MNR, MOA and MEE jointly published an announcement on the issuance of the *Measures for the Implementation of the Law of the People's Republic of China on Farmland Occupation Tax,* which provided the following. These Measures are formulated to implement the *Law of the People's Republic of China on Farmland Occupation Tax.* In the case of the approved occupation of farmland, the taxpayer shall be the owner of construction land indicated in the farmland conversion approval document. If the owner of construction land is not indicated in the farmland conversion approval document, the taxpayer shall be the land use applicant. If the land use applicant happens to be the people's government, the land reserve center, the competent department of natural resources or other departments and units entrusted by the government at the same level shall perform the obligation for the declaration and payment of farmland occupation tax. In case of the unapproved occupation of farmland, the taxpayer shall be the actual land user. Information on the conversion of farmland and temporary land occupation provided to the tax authorities by the relevant natural resources, agriculture, rural areas, water conservancy, and ecological environment departments of the local people's government at or above the county level shall include: farmland conversion information, information on the converted but unsupplied construction land in urban and village towns, information on approved temporary land occupation, information on the change of original land use purpose, information on unapproved but occupied farmland, land damage information, soil pollution information, land reclamation information, and information on the licensing of pasture use and aquaculture. The people's governments of all provinces, autonomous regions and municipalities shall establish and improve the coordination and information exchange mechanism for the farmland occupation tax departments in the region. The Measures will come into force on September 1, 2019. ■

POLICY 140 MCA and MOF jointly published a circular on determining the fourth batch of pilot areas supported by the central finance authorities in carrying out home and community-based elderly care services

On August 30, MCA and MOF jointly published a circular on determining the fourth batch of pilot areas supported by the central finance authorities in carrying out home and community-based elderly care services, which provided the following. According to the *Circular of the Ministry of Civil Affairs and the Ministry of Finance on Central Finance Authorities Supporting the Pilot Work of Home and Community-based Elderly Care Services* and the *Circular of the General Office of the Ministry of Civil Affairs and the General Office of the Ministry of Finance on the Application for the Fourth Batch of Pilot Work of Home and Community-based Elderly Care Services,* on the basis of the application and recommendation of localities, and with the review of experts, MCA and MOF determined that 54 cities (districts), such as Beijing Chaoyang District, are included in the fourth batch of pilot areas supported by the central finance authorities in carrying out home and community-based elderly care services. The civil affairs departments (bureaus) and finance departments (bureaus) of all provinces, autonomous regions and municipalities as well as the Civil Affairs Bureau and Finance Bureau of the Xinjiang Production and Construction Corps shall strictly supervise and urge the pilot areas to carry out pilot work in accordance with the above-mentioned documents and in light of local conditions, so as to ensure that good outcomes are achieved. MCA and MOF will organize the evaluation and acceptance of the pilot work in a timely manner, and disqualify the underperforming areas from the pilot program. ■

POLICY 141

MOF and SAT jointly published an announcement on the continued implementation of the VAT policy for border area tea

On September 2, MOF and SAT jointly published an announcement on the continued implementation of the VAT policy for border area tea, which provided the following. First, from January 1, 2019 to December 31, 2020, the sales of border area tea by border-tea-producing enterprises and border-tea-distribution enterprises will be exempted from VAT. The border area tea mentioned in this announcement refers to the pressed tea and square tea (horse tea) that uses dark tea, old green tea, black tea powder and green tea as the main raw materials, and is specifically sold to the ethnic-minority border areas after fermentation, steaming, pressurization or crushing and frying. Second, the VAT that should be exempted according to the above provisions but is already paid before the announcement may be deducted from the taxpayer's VAT payable in the following months or be refunded. If special VAT invoice has been issued to the purchaser, the special invoice shall be recovered before tax exemption. If the special invoice cannot be recovered, tax exemption shall not be granted. ■

POLICY 142

MOF, MCA, MOHURD, and the China Disabled Persons' Federation jointly published a circular on the revision of the measures for the administration of central fiscal subsidies for helping people living with difficulties and other subsidy funds

On September 3, MOF, MCA, MOHURD, and the China Disabled Persons' Federation jointly published a circular on the revision of the measures for the administration of central fiscal subsidies for helping people living with difficulties and other subsidy funds, which provided the following. To further enhance the management of central fiscal subsidy funds for helping people living with difficulties, renovation of rural dilapidated houses, and helping people with disabilities, clarify the implementation timeframe and the weight of distribution factors for such funds, and budget performance management, it has now been decided to revise the relevant provisions of the *Circular of MCA and MOF on Printing and Distributing the Measures for the Administration of the Central Government's Subsidy Funds for Helping People Living with Difficulties, the Circular of the Ministry of Finance and the Ministry of Housing and Urban-Rural Development on Publishing and Publishing*

Source: MOF

the Measures for the Administration of the Central Government's Subsidy Funds for Renovation of Rural Dilapidated Houses, and the Circular of the Ministry of Finance and the China Disabled Persons' Federation on Printing and Publishing the Measures for the Administration of the Central Government's Subsidy Funds for the Development of Disabled Persons. ■

POLICY 143

MOF and MOA jointly published a circular on supporting the work of stabilizing pig production and ensuring market supply

On September 4, MOF and MOA jointly published a circular on supporting the work of stabilizing pig production and ensuring market supply, which provided the following. In order to implement the requirements of the Party Central Committee and the State Council on stabilizing pig production and ensuring market supply, the central finance authorities decided to take further measures to promote pig production, ensuring market supply, and maintain economic stability. First, effectively implement the policy of subsidizing the mandatory culling of pigs affected by African swine fever. Further improve the method for disbursing subsidy funds. The funds will be disbursed semi-annually rather than annually. After the release of the central and provincial fiscal funds, counties and cities should speed up the disbursement of subsidy funds and strive to disburse the subsidy funds in three months, so as to help alleviate the financing pressure on farms (farming households). Second, improve the temporary interest subsidy policy for pig breeding farms and large-scale pig farms. The implementation period of the *Circular of the General Office of the Ministry of Agriculture and Rural Affairs and the General Office of the Ministry of Finance on Subsidizing the Loan Interest for Boar Stud Farms and Large-scale Pig Farms* is extended to December 31, 2020. During the extension period, the scope of loan interest subsidy will be appropriately expanded to ease the financing pressure of pig farms and stabilize the production capacity of pigs. Third, increase the incentives for counties that sell large quantity of pigs outside the county. In 2019, the central government appropriately increased the scale of reward funds for counties that sell large quantity of pigs outside the county, and encouraged localities to fast convert the potential for increasing production into actual production capacity. Fourth, increase the insurance coverage of pig-breeding. Temporarily increase the insurance coverage of sows and growing-finishing pigs, increase the amount of insurance for fertile sows from 1000-1200 RMB to 1,500 RMB, and increase the amount of insurance for growing-finishing pigs from 500-600 RMB to 800 RMB. Fifth, support the implementation of the policy of subsidizing quality pig breeds. The subsidy targets sow farms (farming households) that carry out artificial insemination with the semen of quality pig breeds. The annual subsidy for each sow is no more than 40 RMB. Sixth, strengthen provincial fiscal coordination. All provincial-level finance authorities must strictly follow the requirements, effectively increase the support for stabilizing the production and supply of pigs, and support the work related to the prevention and control of African swine fever, pig production, and market supply. ■

POLICY 144

MOF and SAT jointly published an announcement on clarifying the tax refund policy for un-deducted input tax at the end of VAT period for some advanced manufacturing enterprises

On September 4, MOF and SAT jointly published an announcement on clarifying the tax refund policy for un-deducted input tax at the end of VAT period for some advanced manufacturing enterprises, which provided the following. In order to further promote the high-quality development of the manufacturing industry, the policy related to the VAT refund for some taxpayers in the manufacturing industry is announced as follows. First, starting from June 1, 2019, taxpayers in advanced manufacturing industry who simultaneously meet the following conditions may apply to the competent tax authorities for refund of un-deducted input tax for the period from July 2019 and beyond: the amount of un-deducted input tax is greater than zero; the tax credit rating is Grade A or Grade B; no fraudulent claim for refund of un-deducted input tax and export tax rebate or issuance of false VAT invoice 36 months prior to the application for tax refund; no case of being fined twice or more times by tax authorities for tax evasion 36 months prior to the application for tax refund; and no case of enjoying the policy of "instant tax refund after taxation" and "taxation first, refund later" since April 1, 2019. Second, the taxpayers in the advanced manufacturing industry mentioned in this announcement refer to the taxpayers whose sales of non-metallic mineral products, general equipment, special equipment and computers, communications and other electronic equipment in accordance with the *National Economic Industry Classification* account for over 50% of total sales. Third, the amount of un-deducted input tax mentioned in this announcement refers to the newly added un-deducted input tax compared with March 31, 2019. Fourth, the amount of un-deducted input tax allowed to be refunded for some taxpayers in the advanced manufacturing industry is calculated according to the following formula: the amount of un-deducted input tax allowed to be refunded = the amount of un-deducted input tax × input component ratio. Fifth, other provisions governing the application for refund of un-deducted input tax for some taxpayers in the advanced manufacturing industry shall be implemented in accordance with the *Announcement of the Ministry of Finance, the State Administration of Taxation and the General Administration of Customs on Policies Related to Value-Added Tax Reform*. Sixth, provisions governing the application for refund of un-deducted input tax for taxpayers other than those in the advanced manufacturing industry would continue to follow the No. 39 Announcement. Seventh, the taxpayers who meet the requirements of the No. 39 Announcement and this Announcement shall submit an application for tax refund to the competent tax authority. ■

POLICY 145

The Customs Tariff Commission of the State Council published an announcement on the first batch of lists of U.S. products to be excluded from the first round of additional tariffs on U.S. products

On September 11, the Customs Tariff Commission of the State Council published an announcement on the first batch of lists of U.S. products to be excluded from the first round of additional tariffs on U.S. products, which provided the following. According to the *Announcement of the Customs Tariff Commission of the State Council on the Trial Implementation of Exclusion from Additional Tariffs on U.S. Products,* the Customs Tariff Commission reviewed the valid applications submitted by applicants and decided to exclude some U.S. products from the first round of additional tariffs on U.S. products in accordance with due procedures. These exclusions will be implemented under two separate lists. For the products under List 1, no additional tariffs enacted in retaliation for the U.S. action under Section 301 will be imposed from September 17, 2019 until September 16, 2020 (one year). The paid tariffs will be refunded, and importers should apply to the customs authorities for the refund of tariffs previously paid within six months after the publication date of these exclusions. For the products under List 2, no additional tariffs enacted in retaliation for the U.S. action under Section 301 will be imposed from September 17, 2019 until September 16, 2020 (one year). The paid tariffs will not be refunded. The Customs Tariff Commission will continue to exclude U.S products from additional tariffs and issue additional batches of tariff exclusions in due course. ■

POLICY 146

MOF published a circular on the 2019 nationwide supervision and inspection of government procurement agencies

On September 11, MOF published a circular on the 2019 nationwide supervision and inspection of government procurement agencies, which provided the following. In order to thoroughly implement the requirements of the *Plan for Deepening the Reform of Government Procurement System,* strengthen and improve the supervision and management of government procurement according to law, regulate the practice of government procurement agencies, and further optimize the government procurement business environment, MOF decided to carry out the nationwide supervision and inspection of government procurement agencies starting from October 2019. First, the scope of inspection. The finance authorities will randomly select government procurement agencies from the list of government procurement agencies that have completed online registration on the Chinese Government Procurement Web and the sub-webs of government procurement of provinces, and carry out inspection over 25 government procurement agencies in the 4 provinces and municipalities of Beijing, Liaoning, Shandong and Guangdong. Second, the content and time of inspection. The inspection covers the whole process of government procurement activities, including entrusted procurement, documentation, import approval, change of method, information announcement, review process, successful bidding, deposit, contract management and challenge response. The inspection time is starting from October 2019 and includes the self-inspection phase, the written review phase, the on-site inspection phase, the penalization phase, and the summary reporting phase. Third, the work requirements. The finance authorities will fully implement the requirements of "random selection of subjects and inspectors and public disclosure" and conduct supervision and inspection of the annual practice of the government procurement agencies in 2018 in accordance with the principle of "vertical coordination, unified standards, tiered inspection and law-based penalization". ■

POLICY 147

MOF and SAT jointly published an announcement on the policy of pre-tax deduction of the financial enterprises' loan loss reserves for agriculture-related loans and SME loans

On September 16, MOF and SAT jointly published an announcement on the policy of pre-tax deduction of the financial enterprises' loan loss reserves for agriculture-related loans and SME loans, which provided the following. First, financial enterprises' agriculture-related loans and SME loans may be classified into special-mention loans, sub-standard loans, doubtful loans and loans according

Source: MOF

to the *Guidelines for Loan Risk Classification,* and loan loss reserves may be provisioned at a ratio of 2%, 25%, 50% and 100% accordingly and be deducted from the taxable income. Second, the agriculture-related loans mentioned in this Announcement refer to the loans provided to rural households, rural enterprises and various rural organizations as set out in the *Special Statistical System for Agriculture-related Loans.* Among them, loans provided to rural households refer to all loans extended by financial enterprises to rural households; loans provided to rural enterprises and various rural organizations refer to all loans extended by financial enterprises to enterprises and various organizations registered in rural areas. Third, the SME loans mentioned in this Announcement refer to the loans extended by financial enterprises to enterprises whose annual sales and total assets are less than 200 million RMB. Fourth, the eligible loss incurred by financial enterprises for agriculture-related loans and SME loans should be first offset against the loan loss reserves that have been deducted before taxation. The shortfall can be deducted when taxable income is calculated. Fifth, this Announcement will be implemented from January 1, 2019 to December 31, 2023. ■

POLICY 148

MOF and SAT jointly published an announcement on the policy of pre-tax deduction of the financial enterprises' loan loss reserves from corporate income tax

On September 16, MOF and SAT jointly published an announcement on the policy of pre-tax deduction of the financial enterprises' loan loss reserves from corporate income tax, which provided the following. First, the scope of loan assets eligible for provisioning of loan loss reserves before taxation includes loans, bank card overdraft, and other risk assets with loan characteristics as well as foreign loans for which financial enterprises make on-lending and bear the responsibility for repayment. Second, the formula for calculating the financial enterprises' loan loss reserves eligible for pre-tax deduction of the current year is "the loan loss reserves eligible for pre-tax deduction of the current year = the balance of the loan assets allowed for the provisioning of loan loss reserves at the end of the year × 1% – the balance of the loan loss reserves deducted before taxation as of the end of the previous year". Third, the financial enterprises' entrusted loans, agency loans, treasury bonds investment, dividends receivable, central bank reserves, debt claims and equities divested from financial enterprises, subsidized interest receivables, central bank payments and other assets that do not bear risks and losses, as well as the risk assets other than those listed in the first article of this Announcement shall not have their loan loss reserves deducted before taxation. Fourth, the eligible loan loss incurred by financial enterprises should be offset against the loan loss reserves that have been deducted before taxation. The shortfall can be deducted when taxable income is calculated. Fifth, the Articles 1 to 4 of this Announcement shall not apply if the policy of pre-tax deduction of the financial enterprises' loan loss reserves for agriculture-related loans and SME loans is implemented in accordance with the *Announcement of the Ministry of Finance and the State*

Administration of Taxation on the Policy Related to the Pre-tax Deduction of the Financial Enterprises' Loan Loss Reserves for Agriculture-related Loans and SME Loans. Sixth, this Announcement will be implemented from January 1, 2019 to December 31, 2023. ■

POLICY 149 Five ministries jointly published a circular on the comprehensive implementation of the transfer of some state-owned capital to replenish the social security fund

On September 20, MOF, MHRSS, SASAC, SAT and CSRC jointly published a circular on the comprehensive implementation of the transfer of some state-owned capital to replenish the social security fund, which provided the following. First, the central and local transfer of some state-owned capital to replenish social security fund will be fully launched in 2019. Second, shareholders of the state-owned capital should do a good job in the equity transfer of relevant enterprises, and urge enterprises to go through relevant procedures in a timely manner. Third, the people's government of all provinces (autonomous regions and municipalities) shall take overall responsibility for the transfer in their jurisdiction, strengthen organizational work, and formulate specific implementation measures in light of actual conditions to ensure that the transfer tasks are completed as required. Fourth, to push forward the transfer in an active, steady, regulated and orderly way, the *Operational Measures on Transferring Some State-owned Capital to Replenish the Social Security Fund* has been formulated and will be effective from the date of issuance of this circular. ■

POLICY 150 MOF published a circular on revising and publishing the format of consolidated financial statements (2019 version)

On September 27, MOF published a circular on revising and publishing the format of consolidated financial statements (2019 version), which provided the following. In order to resolve the practical problems in the preparation of consolidated financial statements, in light of the *Accounting Standards for Business Enterprises No.21—Leases* that was implemented in phases starting from January 1, 2019, and in view of the implementation of the Accounting Standards for Business Enterprises, MOF revised the format of the consolidated financial statements. *The Circular of the Ministry of Finance on Revising and Publishing the Format of the 2018 Consolidated Financial Statements* shall be repealed at the same time. The main changes in the format of consolidated financial statements are as follows: first, in line with the new lease standards and new financial standards, the "right-of-use assets" and "lease liabilities" have been added to the original consolidated balance sheet, and "where: the gains from the financial assets measured at amortized cost are derecognised" is added to "investment gains" under the original consolidated financial statement. Second, in light of some items adjusted in accordance with the implementation of the Accounting Standards for Business Enterprises, the "notes receivable and accounts receivable" in the original consolidated balance sheet was split into "notes receivable", "accounts receivable" and "accounts receivable financing", and "notes payable and accounts payable" was split into "notes payable" and "accounts payable". The presentation of the "asset impairment loss" and "credit impairment losses" in the original consolidated income statement was adjusted to delete the "net increase in financial assets held for trading purposes" and "cash received from bonds" in the original consolidated cash flow statement, and "special reserves" was added to the original consolidated balance sheet and the consolidated statement of changes in owner's equity. ■

POLICY 151

MOF and SAT jointly published an announcement on clarifying the extra VAT deduction policy for the consumer services industry

On September 30, MOF and SAT jointly published an announcement on clarifying the extra VAT deduction policy for the consumer services industry, which provided the following. First, from October 1, 2019 to December 31, 2021, the taxpayers of the consumer services industry are allowed an extra 15% deduction of deductible input tax against the amount of tax payable. Second, the taxpayers of consumer services industry mentioned in this announcement refer to the taxpayers whose sales from consumer service provision account for more than 50% of the total sales. The specific scope of consumer services is in line with the Notes on Sales Services, Intangible Assets and Real Estate. For taxpayers established before September 30, 2019, if their sales from October 2018 to September 2019 meet the above-mentioned requirements (or the sales of the actual operating period if the operating period is less than 12 months), the extra 15% deduction policy shall apply starting from October 1, 2019. For taxpayers established after October 1, 2019, if the sales of the three months since the date of establishment meet the above-mentioned requirements, the extra 15% deduction policy shall apply starting from the date of registration as general taxpayers. After the application of the extra 15% deduction policy by taxpayers, the policy shall not be adjusted during the year, and whether the policy is still applicable in the following years will be determined on the basis of the sales of the previous year. Third, the taxpayers of the consumer services industry shall calculate the amount of extra deduction for the current period according to the 15% of the current deductible input tax amount. The input tax that cannot be deducted from the output tax in accordance with the current regulations shall not be calculated for the extra deduction; if the input tax amount has been calculated at the extra 15% and transferred out as input tax amount in accordance with regulations, the amount of extra deduction shall be reduced accordingly during the period of transfer. Fourth, other matters for taxpayers to apply the extra deduction policy shall follow the relevant provisions of the *Announcement on the Policies Related to the Deepening of Value-Added Tax Reform.* ■

POLICY 152

MOF published a circular on further increasing the delegation of powers to promote the commercialization of scientific and technological findings

On October 11, MOF published a circular on further increasing the delegation of powers to promote the commercialization of scientific and technological findings, which provided the following. First, increase the delegation of powers and simplify the administrative procedures. Central-level research and development institutions and institutions of higher learning may independently transfer, license or invest with their scientific and technological findings, and are not required to report to the competent authorities and MOF for approval or filing except for those involving state secrets, national security and key core technologies; the competent authorities in charge of the central-level research and development institutions and institutions of higher learning will be mandated to deal with the matters related to the transfer, free transfer or overseas investment of state-owned shares formed through the investment with the scientific and technological findings , and will not be required to report to MOF

Source: MOF

for approval or filing; the competent authorities in charge of the central-level research and development institutions and institutions of higher learning will be mandated to deal with the matters related to the registration of the property rights of state-owned assets formed through enterprises established with the investment with the scientific and technological findings , and will not be required to report to MOF for approval or filing. Second, optimize the evaluation management and clarify the attribution of income. Central-level research and development institutions and institutions of higher learning may independently decide whether to conduct asset evaluation when they transfer, license or invest with scientific and technological findings; the income from the commercialization of scientific and technological findings by central-level research and development institutions and institutions of higher learning shall be retained by themselves, incorporated into their departmental budget, and not to be turned over to the state treasury. Third, enhance accountability and strengthen supervision and management. Central-level research and development institutions and institutions of higher learning should strengthen the management of scientific and technological findings and regulate the procedures for the commercialization of scientific and technological findings; the competent authorities in charge of central-level research and development institutions and institutions of higher learning should take the main responsibility for the management of state-owned assets related to the commercialization of scientific and technological findings, and strengthen the management of state-owned equities formed through investment with scientific and technological findings; the finance authorities shall strengthen supervision over the management of state-owned assets related to the commercialization of scientific and technological findings. Fourth, encourage local exploration and support reform and innovation. Local finance authorities should take supporting the transfer and commercialization of scientific and technological findings and promoting scientific and technological innovation as an important responsibility; encourage local innovation and exploration of management models that conform to the characteristics of scientific and technological findings as state-owned assets, give full play to the supporting role of state-owned assets in the commercialization of scientific and technological findings, and support local efforts in the commercialization of scientific and technological findings. ■

POLICY 153

MOF, MOA, CBIRC, and the State Administration for Forestry and Grassland jointly published a circular on the issuance of the *Guiding Opinions on Accelerating the Quality Development of Agricultural Insurance*

On October 12, MOF, MOA, CBIRC, and the State Administration for Forestry and Grassland jointly published a circular on the issuance of the *Guiding Opinions on Accelerating the Quality Development of Agricultural Insurance,* which provided the following. First, the overall requirements. Guided by the Xi Jinping Thought on Socialism with Chinese Characteristics for a New Era, and consistent with the basic principles of government guidance, market operation, voluntary participation and coordinated promotion, the main goal is to build by 2022 a well-functioning and sound multi-level agricultural insurance system that is compatible with the development stage, meets the farmers' risk protection needs, and features the central and local division of labor. By 2030, agricultural insurance will continue to improve its quality and efficiency, get upgraded, and basically reach the advanced international level, resulting in multi-win outcomes with efficient subsidies, sound industry safeguards, concrete benefits for farmers and sustainable institutional development. Second, improve the service ability of agricultural insurance. Expand the coverage of agricultural insurance, improve the level of agricultural insurance protection, broaden the scope of agricultural insurance services, and implement measures to deliver real benefits to people. Third, optimize the operation mechanism of agricultural insurance. Clarify the boundary between government and market, improve the disaster risk dispersion mechanism, clean up and regulate the agricultural insurance market, and encourage the exploration and development of "agricultural insurance+". Fourth, strengthen the construction of agricultural insurance infrastructure. Improve insurance clauses and rate formulation mechanism, strengthen the sharing of agricultural insurance information, optimize the layout of insurance institutions, and improve the risk prevention mechanism. Fifth, improve organization and implementation. Strengthen synergy and coordination, increase policy support, and foster a sound market environment. ■

POLICY 154

MOF and MOST jointly published a circular on the issuance of the *Measures for the Administration of the Central Funds for Guiding the Local Scientific and Technological Development*

On October 14, MOF and MOST jointly published a circular on the issuance of the *Measures for the Administration of the Central Funds for Guiding the Local Scientific and Technological Development,* which provided the following. To regulate the administration of central funds for guiding the local scientific and technological development, improve the effectiveness of the use of guiding funds, and promote scientific and technological innovation, these Measures are formulated in accordance with relevant state regulations. The term "guiding funds" as mentioned in these Measures refers to the transfer payment funds from the central government to support and guide local government in implementing national innovation-driven development strategies and policies on scientific and technological reform and development, optimize regional environment for scientific and technological innovation, and enhance regional capability for scientific and technological innovation. The guiding funds are jointly managed by MOF and MOST. MOST is responsible for reviewing related local materials and data, providing basic data needed for funding estimation, and proposing funding demand measurement plans and allocation recommendations. MOF, in accordance with the relevant provisions of budget management, will work with MOST to study and determine the amount of guiding funds for each province. The management of guiding funds follows the principle of "central guidance, provincial coordination, streamlining administration, delegating power, stimulating vitality, focusing on priorities and highlighting performance". The guiding funds are to support basic research in free exploration, construction of science and technology innovation bases, and development of the system for commercialization of scientific and technological findings and regional innovation. Local governments are encouraged to use multiple means of funding, such as direct subsidy, ex post subsidy, replacing subsidy with rewards, etc. ■

155 MOF and MOE jointly published a circular on the issuance of the *Measures for the Administration of Subsidy Funds for Urban and Rural Compulsory Education*

On October 15, MOF and MOE jointly published a circular on the issuance of the *Measures for the Administration of Subsidy Funds for Urban and Rural Compulsory Education,* which provided the following. To strengthen the management of urban and rural compulsory education subsidies, improve the efficiency of fund use, and promote the balanced development of compulsory education, these Measures are formulated. The term "subsidy funds for urban and rural compulsory education" as mentioned in these Measures refers to the transfer payment funds used by the central government to support the development of compulsory education in urban and rural areas. The management of subsidy funds follows the principle of "unified approach for urban and rural areas, emphasis on rural areas, coordinated arrangement, highlighting of priorities, being objective and fair, being standardized and transparent, focus on performance and strong supervision". At this stage, the subsidies are to mainly support: implementing the funding guarantee mechanism for urban and rural compulsory education; implementing the special post program for school teachers in rural compulsory education, providing wage subsidies to the special-post teachers, and settling the subsidy funds according to the regulations; and implementing the nutrition improvement plan for rural compulsory education students. MOF and MOE shall, in accordance with the relevant decisions and arrangements of the Party Central Committee and the State Council and in view of the reform and development of compulsory education and the adequacy of financial resources, may adjust the relevant subsidy standards, distribution factors and calculation formulas in a timely manner, and report to the State Council for approval before implementation. The provincial finance and education authorities shall submit the application materials for the subsidies of the current year to MOF and MOE before the end of February each year. ■

156 MOF and the four other ministries jointly published a circular on the issuance of the measures for the administration of five subsidy funds for basic public health services

On October 16, MOF, NHC, NHSA, and NATCM jointly published a circular on the issuance of the measures for the administration of five subsidy funds for basic public health services, which provided the following. To regulate and strengthen the central government's transfer payment funds to local government and improve the effectiveness of fund use, in line with the regulations and policy requirements of the *Budget Law of the People's Republic of China* and the *Circular of the General Office of the State Council on Printing and Distributing the Reform Plan for the Division of Central and Local Fiscal Powers and Expenditure Responsibilities in the Area of Healthcare,* as well as the MOF regulations on budget management of transfer payment funds, the *Measures for the Administration of Subsidy Funds for Basic Public Health Service,* the *Measures for the Administration of Medical Service and Support Capacity Enhancement Funds,* the *Measures for the Administration of Basic Drug System Subsidy Funds,* the *Measures for the Administration of Family Planning Transfer Payment Funds,* and the *Measures for the Administration of Subsidy Funds for Major Infectious Disease Prevention and Control* are now revised. ■

157 MOF published a circular on the 2019 subsidy budget for central special lottery public welfare fund to support the pilot reform of home and community-based elderly care services

On October 18, MOF published a circular on the 2019 subsidy budget for central special lottery public welfare fund to support the pilot reform of home and community-based elderly care services, which provided the following. The central fiscal subsidy funds released this time are used to support the expenditures on the development of home and community-based elderly care services by the pilot areas in accordance with the requirements of the *Circular of the Ministry of Civil Affairs and the Ministry of Finance on Supporting the Pilot Reform of Home and Community-based Elderly Care Services with Central Public Finance.* The finance authorities of the pilot areas should work closely with the civil affairs authorities to ensure that the central government subsidy funds are allocated to the pilot areas in full and on time. In order to further strengthen the performance management of funds and effectively improve the efficiency of the use of fiscal funds, in accordance with the relevant requirements of the *Interim Measures for the Management of the Performance Targets of Central-to-Local Special Transfer Payments,* and with reference to the requirements of the pilot reform work and the amount of subsidy funds, performance targets will be scientifically and reasonably determined, the *Regional Performance Target Form for Central-to-Local Special Transfer Payments* will be filled out, and reports will be submitted to MOF and MCA within 60 days of receiving the subsidy funds and be copied to the local regulatory bureaus of MOF as the basis for performance monitoring and performance evaluation. ■

158 MOF published a circular on the issuance of the *Administrative Measures for the Registration of State-owned Financial Capital Property Rights (Trial)*

On October 21, MOF published a circular on the issuance of the *Administrative Measures for the Registration of State-owned Financial Capital Property Rights (Trial),* which provided the following. To strengthen the registration and management of state-owned financial capital property rights, reflect the changes and distribution of state-owned financial capital in a timely, comprehensive and accurate manner, realize the dynamic and thorough regulation over the changes of state-owned property rights, and prevent the loss of state-owned assets, these Measures are formulated in accordance with the *Guiding Opinions of the CPC Central Committee and the State Council on Improving the Management of State-Owned Financial Capital* and the *Administrative Measures for the Registration of the Property Rights of the State-owned Assets of Enterprises.* Financial institutions established within or outside the territory of the People's Republic of China that possess state-owned financial capital shall register property rights in accordance with the provisions of these Measures. Enterprises inside and outside China over which state-holding financial institutional wield actual control as well as enterprises invested by the afore-mentioned enterprises shall be included in the scope of property rights registration. The authorities for the registration and management of state-owned financial capital property rights are finance authorities at the same level. The registration of state-owned financial capital property rights shall follow the principle of unified regulation and tiered management and be conducted by the finance authorities at or above the county level. ■

POLICY 159

MOF and SAT jointly published an announcement on the tax policy for civil aircraft engines, new regional aircrafts and large passenger aircrafts

Source: MOF

On October 22, MOF and SAT jointly published an announcement on the tax policy for civil aircraft engines, new regional aircrafts and large passenger aircrafts, which provided the following. From January 1, 2018 to December 31, 2023, the un-deducted input VAT at the end of the VAT period from taxpayers' engagement in the R&D projects of large-scale civil passenger aircraft engines and the medium-high power civil turboshaft and turboprop engines shall be refunded; the real estate and land for scientific research, production and office used by the above-mentioned taxpayers and their wholly-owned subsidiary for the R&D projects of large-scale civil passenger aircraft engines and the medium-high power civil turboshaft and turboprop engines shall be exempted from property tax and urban land use tax. From January 1, 2019 to December 31, 2020, the taxpayers that manufacture and sell new regional aircrafts shall pay VAT at a reduced rate of 5% and their un-deducted input VAT at the end of the VAT period from their manufacturing and selling of new regional aircrafts shall be refunded. From January 1, 2019 to December 31, 2020, the un-deducted input VAT at the end of the VAT period from taxpayers' engagement in the R&D projects of large-scale civil passenger aircrafts shall be refunded; the real estate and land for scientific research, production and office used by the above-mentioned taxpayers and their wholly-owned subsidiary shall be exempted from property tax and urban land use tax. The un-deducted input VAT at the end of the VAT period that meets the provisions of this announcement may be refunded lump sum when refund application is first made. Taxpayers who enjoy the exemption from property tax and urban land use tax policy stipulated in this announcement shall apply for tax exemption in accordance with the regulations, and keep the documents related to property ownership, original value of property, and purpose of land use for future reference. The tax that should have been exempted or reduced in accordance with the provisions of this announcement but is already paid by the taxpayers shall be deducted from the tax payable or be refunded. ■

POLICY 160

MOF published a circular on the issuance of the *Measures for the Administration of the Funds for the Prevention and Control of Significant Geologic Hazards*

On October 28, MOF published a circular on the issuance of the *Measures for the Administration of the Funds for the Prevention and Control of Significant Geologic Hazards,* which provided the following. The funds for the prevention and control of significant geologic hazards refer to the subsidy funds arranged by the central government to support local government in fulfilling the responsibility of geologic hazard prevention and control, improving the capacity of geologic hazard prevention and control, and increasing input and efforts in geologic hazard prevention and control. The funds are mainly used for comprehensive prevention of significant geologic hazards and post-hazard project management. The scope of expenditure of the funds for the prevention and control of significant geologic hazards includes investigation, monitoring, early warning and comprehensive management. ■

POLICY 161

MOF published a circular on the issuance of the *Measures for the Administration of the Special Funds for Development of Financial Inclusion*

On October 28, MOF published a circular on the issuance of the *Measures for the Administration of the Special Funds for Development of Financial Inclusion,* which provided the following. To implement the *Plan for Promoting Development of Financial Inclusion (2016-2020),* accelerate the establishment of inclusive financial services and safeguard system, strengthen the administration of the special funds for development of financial inclusion, these Measures are formulated in accordance with the relevant provisions of the *Budget Law of the People's Republic of China* and the *Opinions of the State Council on Reforming and Perfecting the Central-to-Local Transfer Payment System.* MOF is responsible for the budget management and release of special funds, and will organize the budget supervision and performance management of the use of funds. The provincial finance authorities are responsible for the disbursement, review, supervision and budget performance management of the special funds, and are responsible for the compliance and effectiveness of the use of funds. ■

POLICY 162

MOF published the guiding opinions on strengthening the implementation of the nationally unified accounting system

Source: MOF

On October 31, MOF published the guiding opinions on strengthening the implementation of the nationally unified accounting system, which provided the following. First, fully acknowledge the importance of strengthening the implementation of the nationally unified accounting system. The nationally unified accounting system established according to the accounting law is an important standard for generating accounting information and an important basis for regulating accounting behavior and accounting order. Second, the overall requirement. Be guided by the Xi Jinping Thought on Socialism with Chinese Characteristics for a New Era. Third, the major measures. Maintain the unity of the nationally unified accounting system; supervise the implementation of the accounting responsibilities of all units; strengthen internal control; effectively improve the audit quality of accounting firms; strengthen the daily supervision of the implementation of the nationally unified accounting system; strengthen publicity training; enhance the accounting ethics; and strengthen organization and leadership. ■

163 MOF and SAT jointly published an announcement on the VAT policy for the comprehensive utilization of resources

On October 31, MOF and SAT jointly published an announcement on the VAT policy for the comprehensive utilization of resources, which provided the following. First, starting from September 1, 2019, taxpayers may enjoy the instant VAT rebate at a rate of 70% for their sales of self-produced products with comprehensive use of phosphogypsum resources. Second, starting from September 1, 2019, the tax rebate rate of the 3.12 "Waste Glass" item in the *Catalogue of Preferential VAT Treatment for Products and Labor Service with Comprehensive Utilization of Resources* attached to the Caishui [2015] No. 78 Document will be adjusted to 70%. Third, in the Item 1, Article 2 of the Circular of MOF and SAT on the *VAT Policy for New Wall Materials* (Caishui [2015] No. 73) and the Item 2, Article 2 of the Caishui [2015] No. 78 Document, the "Prohibited and Restricted Items in the *Guiding Catalogue for Industrial Structural Adjustment*" was revised to "Phased-out and Restricted Items in the Guiding Catalogue for Industrial Structural Adjustment". Fourth, the "highly-polluting products with high environmental risks" mentioned in the Item 2, Article 2 of the Caishui [2015] No. 73 Document and the Item 3, Article 2 of the Caishui [2015] No. 78 Document refer to the products marked with the characteristics of "GHW/GHF" in the Comprehensive List of Environmental Protection, with the exception for the products with comprehensive utilization of resources produced and sold by the taxpayers that meet the terms and conditions of the exception clause of "GHW/GHF". ■

164 The State Council determined relevant preferential tax policies to reduce burden on taxpayers

On November 20, Premier Li Keqiang presided over an executive meeting of the State Council to listen to the report on personal income tax reform and determine relevant preferential tax policies to reduce burden on taxpayers; plan the deepening of the reform of medical and health system to further promote the centralized procurement and use of medicines; and pass the *Urban Maintenance and Construction Tax Law of the People's Republic of China (Draft)*. The meeting decided that in order to further reduce burden on taxpayers, especially low and middle-income groups, taxpayers with a comprehensive income of less than 120,000 RMB or a low amount of annual tax payment will be exempted from the tax calculation and filing obligations. The meeting called for strengthening the interpretation of relevant policies, streamlining operational procedures, optimizing tax services, and facilitating tax payment according to law. The meeting also decided that in order to promote the development of the maritime transport industry and meet the fast growing domestic demand for seafood, and with reference to international practices, from January 1, 2019 to the end of 2023, ocean-going crew members who have sailed for more than 183 days in a tax year will have their taxable personal income calculated at 50% of their wage and salary income. ■

POLICY 165

Three Ministries jointly published a circular on the preferential tax policies for imported exhibits sold during the second China International Import Expo

On November 5, MOF, GAC and SAT jointly published a circular on the preferential tax policies for imported exhibits sold during the second China International Import Expo, which provided the following. First, a reasonable quantity of imported exhibits sold during the second China International Import Expo from November 5, 2019 to November 10, 2019 will be exempted from import tariffs and import VAT, and enjoy consumption tax levied at 70% of the payable amount. Second, the sales income of the participating enterprises listed in the Annex that are entitled to the above-mentioned preferential tax policies shall not exceed the limit. The sales income of other participating enterprises that are entitled to preferential tax policies shall not exceed 20,000 USD. Third, for the exhibits of which the sales income exceeds the limit of preferential tax policies and could not be returned outbound, the existing tax policy shall apply and tariffs shall be imposed. ■

POLICY 166

MOF published a circular on the advance release of the 2020 transfer payment to the old revolutionary base areas

Source: MOF

On November 5, MOF published a circular on the advance release of the 2020 transfer payment to the old revolutionary base areas, which provided the following. In order to improve the budget integrity and speed up the expenditure progress, the 2020 transfer payment to the old revolutionary base areas in relevant provinces (autonomous regions and municipalities) are now released in advance. These subsidy funds are included under the "1100228 transfer payment revenue of old revolutionary base areas" of the 2020 government revenue and expenditure classification. After the start of the 2020 budget year, the funds will be disbursed and used in accordance with the procedures. The relevant provinces (autonomous regions and municipalities) are required to do a good job in budget preparation, indicators and program arrangement, fund disbursement and other related works in accordance with the *Circular of the MOF on the Relevant Matters Concerning the Advance Notification of Transfer Payment Indicators* and the *Supplementary Circular of the MOF on the Advance Release of Transfer Payment Indicators.*

POLICY 167

MOF published a circular on the advance release of the 2020 transfer payment budget to the border areas

On November 6, MOF published a circular on the advance release of the 2020 transfer payment budget to the border areas, which provided the following. In order to improve the budget integrity and speed up the expenditure progress, the 2020 transfer payment to the border areas in relevant provinces (autonomous regions and cities with independent planning status) are now released in advance. These subsidy funds are included under the "1100230 transfer payment revenue of border areas" of the 2020 government revenue and expenditure classification, and will be disbursed and used in accordance with the procedures after the start of the 2020 budget year. The relevant provinces (autonomous regions and cities with independent planning status) are required to do a good job in budget preparation, indicators and project arrangement, fund disbursement and other related works in accordance with the *Circular of the MOF on the Relevant Matters Concerning the Advance Notification of Transfer Payment Indicators* and the *Supplementary Circular of the MOF on the Advance Release of Transfer Payment Indicators*. At the same time, they are required to follow the requirements of the *Measures for the Administration of Transfer Payment Funds to the Border Areas* to strengthen fund management and effectively improve the effectiveness of fund use. ■

POLICY 168 MOF published a circular on the advance release of the 2020 transfer payment budget to ethnic minority areas

Source: MOF

On November 11, MOF published a circular on the advance release of the 2020 transfer payment budget to ethnic minority areas, which provided the following. In order to improve the budget integrity and speed up the expenditure progress, the 2020 transfer payment budget is now released in advance to the ethnic minority areas in relevant provinces (autonomous regions and municipalities), and will be used in accordance with the procedures after the start of the 2020 budget year. The relevant provinces (autonomous regions and municipalities) shall, in accordance with the *Circular of the MOF on the Relevant Issues Concerning the Advance Notification of Transfer Payment Indicators* and the *Supplementary Circular of the MOF on the Advance Release of Transfer Payment Indicators*, do a good job in budget preparation, indicators arrangement and disbursement of funds. At the same time, in light of the state of the sub-provincial fiscal system and the distribution of financial resources within the administrative region, it is important to increase support for financially difficult areas and use the transfer payment funds to meet basic public service expenditures such as compulsory education, health care and social security, in order to actively improve people's livelihood and promote social harmony. ■

POLICY 169 MOF and the State Council Leading Group Office of Poverty Alleviation and Development jointly published a circular on adjusting the *Score Sheet for the Performance Evaluation Indicators of Government Special Poverty Alleviation Funds*

On November 13, MOF and the State Council Leading Group Office of Poverty Alleviation and Development jointly published a circular on adjusting the *Score Sheet for the Performance Evaluation Indicators of Government Special Poverty Alleviation Funds,* which provided the following. To further enhance the guiding and stimulating effects of performance evaluation on the management of the use of government special poverty alleviation funds, the Annex 2 of the *Score Sheet for the Performance Evaluation Indicators of Government Special Poverty Alleviation Funds* attached to the *Measures for the Performance Evaluation of Government Special Poverty Alleviation Funds* is adjusted. The adjusted *Score Sheet for the Performance Evaluation Indicators of Government Special Poverty Alleviation Funds* is now issued, please follow the guidance. This circular shall be implemented as of the date of issuance. If the relevant provisions of the *Measures for the Performance Evaluation of Government Special Poverty Alleviation Funds* are inconsistent with this Circular, this Circular shall prevail. ■

POLICY 170 MOF released in advance 113.6 billion RMB of the 2020 special poverty alleviation funds to support the fight against poverty

On November 18, MOF published a message stating that the central government has recently released in advance 113.6 billion RMB of the 2020 central special poverty alleviation funds to 28 provinces (autonomous regions and municipalities), accounting for about 90% of the 126.1 billion RMB of central special poverty alleviation funds in 2019. Among them, 14.4 billion RMB was specifically arranged to support the extremely poor areas in the "three regions and three prefectures" and directed in a detailed manner to specific regions and prefectures. ■

POLICY 171 Two ministries clarified the measures for the administration of agriculture-related transfer payment funds

On November 19, MOF and MOA jointly published a supplementary circular on the measures for the administration of agriculture-related transfer payment funds, which provided the following. First, the implementation period. The implementation period for the agricultural production and development funds, the subsidy funds for agricultural resources and ecological protection, and the subsidy funds for animal epidemic prevention will last until 2023. Before the expiration, MOF will work with MOA to determine whether to continue with the implementation. Second, the allocation of funds. The agricultural production and development funds, the subsidy funds for agricultural resources and ecological protection, and the subsidy funds for animal epidemic prevention will be allocated adopting the factor method in light of the nature of the tasks and the targets of spending. The cities with independent planning status focused on the management of programs, which have had fewer tasks, or assumed some pilot tasks and other tasks to be funded according to results, may adopt the fixed-sum method for allocation according to their needs. ■

172 Three ministries jointly published an announcement on the continued implementation of the VAT policy for R&D institutions' procurement of equipment

On November 25, MOF, MOC and SAT jointly published an announcement on the continued implementation of the VAT policy for R&D institutions' procurement of equipment, which provided the following. In order to encourage scientific research and technological development, as well as promote scientific and technological progress, VAT will continue to be fully refunded for the procurement of domestically made equipment by domestic R&D institutions and foreign R&D centers. The approved domestic R&D institutions and foreign R&D centers shall not enjoy the tax refund policy in the event of the major tax-related violations of laws. Specific measures for the administration of tax refund shall be formulated separately by SAT in conjunction with MOF. ■

173 Three ministries jointly published an announcement on the preferential tax policies for the Beijing 2022 Winter Olympic Games and Winter Paralympic Games

On November 26, MOF, SAT and GAC jointly published an announcement on the preferential tax policies for the Beijing 2022 Winter Olympic Games and Winter Paralympic Games, which provided the following. First, income related to the Beijing Winter Olympic Games gained by the non-resident enterprises among the associated entities of the International Olympic Committee will be exempted from corporate income tax. Second, income related to the Beijing Winter Olympic Games earned by the Olympic Broadcasting Service Company, Olympic Channel Service Company, International Olympic Committee Television and Market Development Service Company, Olympic Culture and Heritage Fund, and Official Timekeeping Company will be exempted from VAT. Third, designated goods or services provided by the sponsors, suppliers, franchisors and subcontractors of international sponsorship programs, global supply programs, and global franchise programs in accordance with the agreement for the Organizing Committee of the Beijing 2022 Winter Olympic Games and Paralympic Games will be exempted from VAT and consumption tax. Fourth, the various contracts signed by the relevant entities of the International Olympic Committee and the Organizing Committee of the Beijing Winter Olympic Games will be exempted from stamp duties. ■

174 MOF issued 5 billion RMB of government bonds in Hong Kong SAR

On November 27, MOF issued 5 billion RMB of government bonds in Hong Kong SAR. In the total 5 billion RMB debt, 3.5 billion RMB were two-year term with a yield of 2.726% and 1.5 billion RMB is for a five-year term with a yield of 2.8%. The bid-winning prices are 100.34 RMB and 100.98 RMB respectively. ■

175

MOF issued 6 billion USD of dollar-denominated sovereign bonds in Hong Kong SAR

On November 27, MOF issued 6 billion USD of unrated dollar-denominated sovereign bonds in Hong Kong SAR. Among them, 1.5 billion USD is for a three-year term with a yield of 1.929%; 2 billion USD is for a five-year term with a yield of 1.996%; 2 billion USD is for a ten-year term with a yield of 2.238%; and 500 million USD is for a twenty-year term with a yield of 2.881%. This is the single largest dollar-denominated sovereign bond issuance by the Chinese government. The size of issuance increased significantly compared to the previous year, and the bonds were enthusiastically subscribed by investors, with the order reaching 3.6 times the scale of the issuance. ■

176

MOF released in advance 1 trillion RMB of quota for the additional special debts in 2020

On November 27, MOF announced that MOF had recently released in advance 1 trillion RMB of quota for the additional special debts in 2020, accounting for 47% of the 2.15 trillion RMB of the additional special debts for the year of 2019, and the quota was within the range authorized by laws. At the same time, all localities are required to break down the special bond quota as soon as possible to specific projects, and do a good job in the issuance and use of the special bonds, to ensure that the bonds be early issued and early used, so that early next year there would be tangible results in increased work, which would soon become an effective driving force to boost the economy. ■

177

Three ministries jointly published a circular on the issuance of the *Guiding Opinions on Doing a Good Job in the Post-Disaster Recovery and Reconstruction of Major Natural Disasters*

On November 28, NDRC, MOF, and the Ministry of Emergency Management jointly published a circular on the issuance of the *Guiding Opinions on Doing a Good Job in the Post-Disaster Recovery and Reconstruction of Major Natural Disasters,* which provided the following. First, the general requirements. Implement the principal responsibilities of all levels of people's governments in the province where the disaster occurred, and solidly complete the post-disaster recovery and reconstruction tasks after major natural disasters. Second, move forward post-disaster recovery and reconstruction in an orderly way. Establish a post-disaster recovery and reconstruction guidance and coordination group in accordance with the procedures, and organize the preparation or provide guidance for the preparation of post-disaster recovery and reconstruction plan by local government. Third, strengthen the principal role of local government. The provincial people's government of the province in which the disasters occurred need to effectively connect with the relevant central ministries and scientifically formulate the implementation plans. Fourth, strengthen safeguard measures. Establish and properly use provincial reconstruction funds, and strengthen the coordination of publicity work. ■

178 The State Council published a circular on strengthening the capital management of fixed assets investment projects

Source: MOF

On November 27, the State Council published a circular on strengthening the capital management of fixed assets investment projects, which provided the following. First, further improve the capital system for investment projects. Clarify the scope and nature of the capital system for investment projects, implement itemized capital accounting management of investment projects, and standardize the determination of capital ratios. Second, appropriately adjust the minimum capital ratio of infrastructure projects. For port, coastal and inland waterway projects, the minimum capital ratio has been adjusted from 25% to 20%. Third, encourage the financing of major investment projects in accordance with laws and regulations. For the infrastructure sector and industries encouraged by the state, project legal persons and project investors are encouraged to finance the investment projects through multiple channels such as the issuance of equity financial instruments. Fourth, strictly strengthen management to prevent risks. Funds that do not comply with state regulations such as shareholder borrowings and "debts disguised as stocks" shall not be used as capital for investment projects. ■

179 The Executive meeting of the State Council planned to take further measures to stabilize employment

On December 4, Premier Li Keqiang presided over the executive meeting of the State Council, which planned to take further measures to stabilize employment and called for strong support for flexible employment; decided to improve the employment security system for the disabled, and better promote the employment of the disabled; passed the *Regulations on Ensuring the Payment of Wages for Migrant Workers (Draft)* to address the problem of wage arrears through legal means. The meeting pointed out that more efforts should be made to implement the employment priority policy and further improve the employment promotion measures; promote innovation and entrepreneurship, and lower the conditions for small and micro enterprises when applying for start-up guarantee loans. The local governments may provide one-time funding support for migrant workers who return to their hometown and start business for the first time. The meeting decided to improve the collection of disability benefits and encourage more employers to hire more people with disabilities. The meeting passed the *Regulations on Ensuring the Payment of Wages for Migrant Workers (Draft)*, which clarified the principal responsibilities of employers, the territorial responsibilities of government, and the supervisory responsibilities of government departments, and required that migrant workers' wages be paid in full and on time as agreed. ■

POLICY 180 Four ministries published the *Interim Measures for the Management of Credit Rating Industry*

On November 29, PBoC, NDRC, MOF and CSRC jointly published the *Interim Measures for the Management of Credit Rating Industry*, which provided the following. In order to regulate the credit rating business, protect the legal rights and interests of the parties involved, and promote the healthy development of the credit rating industry, these Measures are formulated. These Measures shall apply to the credit rating business within the territory of the People's Republic of China. NDRC, MOF and CSRC are the regulatory authorities for the credit rating business, and shall supervise and regulate the credit rating business within the scope of their duties. Credit rating agencies engaging in credit rating business shall follow the principles of independence, objectivity, fairness and prudence, operate with integrity, and must not harm the national interests, public interests, and the legitimate rights and interests of market entities.

POLICY 181 MOF published a circular on matters related to effectively strengthening the implementation of local budgets and the security management of fiscal funds

On December 3, MOF published a circular on matters related to effectively strengthening the implementation of local budgets and the security management of fiscal funds, which provided the following. First, strictly regulate the management of fund payment and clearing. Local finance departments and budget units must strictly implement relevant regulations on budget management and centralized treasury payment management, and shall not pay funds according to contracts or agreements that do not comply with laws and regulations. Second, attach great importance to the security of funds deposited by finance departments. Establish and improve the scientific, standardized, fair and transparent fund deposit management mechanism to effectively prevent security risks and integrity risks of fund deposit. Third, continue to strengthen the risk prevention of local treasury cash management. Provincial finance departments that carry out local treasury cash management should attach great importance to the selection of participating banks in treasury cash management and scientifically formulate the scoring system. ■

POLICY 182 MOF arranged a total of 10 billion RMB of central special lottery public welfare funds during the 13th Five-Year Plan period to support poverty reduction in the old revolutionary base areas

On December 5, MOF announced that MOF had recently released in advance 2.06 billion RMB of central special lottery public welfare funds to support poverty alleviation in the old revolutionary base areas. The funds are mainly used to support the construction of small productive public welfare facilities in poor villages in the old revolutionary base areas. During the 13th Five-Year Plan period, the central government arranged a total of 10 billion RMB of such funds for all the 397 districts and counties in the old revolutionary base areas, and provided further support towards the extremely poor districts and counties in the old revolutionary base areas. ■

183 Three ministries published a circular on adjusting and improving the local sharing mechanism for the refund of un-deducted input VAT and the matters related to budget management

Source: MOF

On December 6, MOF, SAT and PBoC published a circular on adjusting and improving the local sharing mechanism for the refund of un-deducted input VAT and the matters related to budget management, which provided the following. Starting from September 1, 2019, the 50% portion and the 15% portion of the local sharing of the refund of un-deducted input VAT would be borne by the localities where enterprises are located, and the 35% would be borne by the localities according to the proportion of VAT in the local tax sharing. The treasury transfer for the refund of un-deducted input VAT would be launched by the provincial finance authorities and MOF regulatory bureaus respectively and be locally administered by the provincial treasury in accordance with rules. The MOF regulatory bureaus would supervise the implementation of the tax refund policy by means of spot checks. The MOF regulatory bureaus shall submit supervision reports to MOF annually. ■

184 MOF published the Administrative Measures for the Release of Government Procurement Information

On December 10, MOF published the Administrative Measures for the Release of Government Procurement Information, which provided the following. MOF shall guide and coordinate the release of government procurement information across the country, and supervise and administer the release of government procurement information of central budgetary units. The local finance authorities shall supervise and administer the release of government procurement information of local budgetary units. MOF shall supervise and administer the China government procurement website. Provincial (autonomous regions, municipalities, and cities with independent planning status) finance authorities shall supervise and administer the provincial branch of the China government procurement website. ■

185 MOF published a circular on further clarifying the matters related to the capital increase, equity expansion and equity management of state-owned financial enterprises

On December 12, MOF published a circular on further clarifying the matters related to the capital increase, equity expansion and equity management of state-owned financial enterprises, which provided the following. The central and local finance authorities shall supervise and administer the capital increase activities of state-owned financial enterprises in accordance with the principle of unified policy and tiered management. The capital increase of state-owned financial enterprises shall be in line with the corporate development strategy, be based on sound feasibility study, formulate a capital increase plan, and clarify the amount and purpose of capital increase as well as the criteria and methods for the selection of investors. The enterprises receiving capital increase shall conduct a qualification review of the intended investors, and the investors shall meet the relevant qualification requirements of shareholders. ■

POLICY 186 The State Council adopted the Implementation Regulations of the Foreign Investment Law of the People's Republic of China (Draft)

On December 12, Premier Li Keqiang chaired the executive meeting of the State Council and adopted the *Implementation Regulations of the Foreign Investment Law of the People's Republic of China (Draft)*, which laid out concrete measures to promote and protect foreign investment and created a non-discriminatory and fair market environment for Chinese and foreign-funded enterprises, including those funded from Hong Kong, Macao and Taiwan. In addition, the meeting planned to further reduce the comprehensive financing costs for small and micro enterprises. The meeting also required that the upper limit of the single-unit loan quota for small and micro enterprise loans to enjoy preferential weight of risk capital be raised from 5 million RMB to 10 million RMB, and the average guarantee fee rate of government financing guarantee and re-guarantee institutions be gradually reduced to less than 1%, in order to ensure that notable progress be made in addressing the problem of difficult and expensive financing for small and micro enterprises. ■

POLICY 187 The State Council Customs Tariff Commission announced not to put increased tariffs on some goods imported from the U.S. for the time being

According to the news released by the State Council Customs Tariff Commission on December 15, in order to implement the results of the recent consultations between China and the U.S. on economic and trade issues, the State Council Customs Tariff Commission decided not to put 10% and 5% tariffs on some goods imported from the U.S. which were scheduled to be levied with increased tariffs starting from 12:01 on December 15, and to stop imposing tariffs on automobiles and parts originating from the U.S. Except for the above-mentioned measures, other additional tariffs against the U.S. will remain in accordance with regulations, and the work related to the exclusion of some U.S. products from additional tariffs will continue. ■

POLICY 188 The State Council Customs Tariff Commission published the second exclusion list for the first batch of U.S. goods subject to additional tariffs

According to the news released by the State Council Customs Tariff Commission on December

19, in accordance with the *Announcement of the State Council Customs Tariff Commission on the Trial Implementation of Exclusion of U.S. Goods from Additional Tariffs*, with the approval of the State Council, the State Council Customs Tariff Commission published the second exclusion list for the first batch of U.S. goods subject to additional tariffs, and decided that from December 26, 2019 to December 25, 2020, some U.S. goods in the second exclusion list will not be subject to the additional tariffs imposed by China in response to the U.S. measures taken under section 301, and the tariffs already imposed will not be refunded. The rest of the U.S. goods subject to the first batch of additional tariffs will not be excluded for the time being. ■

POLICY 189

Two ministries published an announcement on the policy matters related to the calculation and settlement of personal income tax for comprehensive income

On December 14, MOF and SAT published an announcement on the policy matters related to the calculation and settlement of personal income tax for comprehensive income, which provided the following. For the comprehensive income obtained by resident individuals from January 1, 2019 to December 31, 2020, if the annual comprehensive income does not exceed 120,000 RMB and is subject to calculation and settlement of tax liability, or if the amount of annual tax liability does not exceed 400 RMB, the resident individuals may be exempted from the calculation and settlement of comprehensive income tax. ■

POLICY 190

MOF released in advance the 2020 central-to-local equalization transfer payment budget and other budgets

From December 16 to 19, MOF published a circular on the advance release of budgets. In order to improve budget integrity and speed up expenditures, in accordance with the relevant budget management regulations, the 2020 central-to-local equalization transfer payment budget, the 2020 central-to-local transfer payment budget for resource-depleted cities, the 2020 budget of central special lottery public welfare fund supporting the development of local public welfare undertakings, the 2020 central-to-local transfer payment budget for key ecological function zones, the 2020 expenditure budget for the revenue arrangement from inter-provincial adjustment of land quotas, the 2020 budget for county-level basic financial capacity guarantee mechanism, and the 2020 central-to-local transfer payment budget for the reform of refined oil taxes and fees are now released in advance, and will be disbursed and used in accordance with procedures after the start of the 2020 budget year. ■

POLICY 191

The CPC Central Committee and State Council published the opinions on creating a better development environment to support the reform and development of private enterprises

On December 22, the CPC Central Committee and the State Council published the opinions on creating a better development environment to support the reform and development of private enterprises, which provided the following. First, optimize the market environment for fair competition. Further open up market access for private enterprises and implement a fair and unified market supervision system. Second, improve the targeted and effective policy environment. Improve the system of banking financial institutions serving private enterprises, and improve the direct financing support system for private enterprises. Third, improve the legal environment for equal treatment protection. Improve theequal treatment protection mechanism of law enforcement and justice for private enterprises, and protect the legal property of private enterprises and entrepreneurs. Fourth, encourage and guide the reform and innovation of private enterprises. Support private enterprises to strengthen innovation, and to protect the equal treatment for private enterprises. Fifth, promote the regulated and healthy development of private enterprises. Guide private enterprises to concentrate their efforts on running their businesses and encourage private enterprises to operate in compliance with laws and regulations. Sixth, build close and clean government-business relations. Establish a standardized mechanism for government-enterprise communication, and improve the enterprise related policy-making and implementation mechanism. ■

POLICY 192

The State Council Customs Tariff Commission published a circular on the plan for adjusting 2020 provisional import tariff rates

On December 23, the State Council Customs Tariff Commission published a circular on the plan for adjusting 2020 provisional import tariff rates, which provided the following. First, adjust import tariff rates. Starting from January 1, 2020, provisional import tariff rates will be applied to 859 goods (excluding goods with tariff quotas); starting from July 1, 2020, provisional import tariff rates for 7 information technology products will be removed. Continue to enforce tariff quota management on 8 categories of commodities such as wheat, with the tax rates unchanged. Second, the export tariff rates. Starting from January 1, 2020, export tariffs will continue to be levied on 107 commodities such as ferrochrome. The export tariff rates or the provisional export tariff rates, and the scope of goods subject to tariffs remain unchanged. The above provisions, unless otherwise specified, will be implemented starting from January 1, 2020. ■

POLICY 193

The State Council published the *Opinions on Further Stabilizing Employment*

On December 24, the State Council published the Opinions on Further Stabilizing Employment, which provided the following. First, support enterprises to stabilize job positions. Implement the policy of targeted reduction of required reserve ratio and release funds to primarily support the financing of private enterprises and small and micro enterprises. Second, develop more job opportunities. Increase investment to create jobs, rationally expand effective investment, and appropriately reduce the capital ratio of some infrastructure projects. Third, promote multi-channel employment and entrepreneurship for workers. Lower the conditions for applying for startup guarantee loans of small and micro enterprises. Fourth, carry out large-scale vocational skills training. Vigorously promote vocational skills upgrading and provide vocational training subsidies and living allowances in accordance with regulations. Fifth, provide sound employment and business startup services. Promote full coverage of employment services and strengthen management services. Sixth, provide basic living safety-net. Make timely payment of unemployment insurance benefits for those who meet the conditions for receiving such benefits. ■

POLICY 194 Two ministries published the *Measures for the Administration of Performance Evaluation and Incentives for Renovation of Rural Dilapidated Houses amid Poverty Alleviation*

On December 20, MHURD and MOF published the *Measures for the Administration of Performance Evaluation and Incentives for Renovation of Rural Dilapidated Houses amid Poverty Alleviation*, which provided the following. The performance evaluation for renovation of rural dilapidated houses mainly covers the following three cases: funding arrangements and formulation of policy measures for renovation of rural dilapidated houses, including investment of provincial subsidies and setting of classified subsidy standards; implementation and supervision of projects for renovation of rural dilapidated houses, including quality and safety inspection, technical training, and supervision over the use of subsidy funds; progress of rural dilapidated house renovation projects and the quality and safety of projects, including the completion rate and the renovation effects. MHURD and MOF may evaluate the annual performance of provinces (autonomous regions and municipalities) in renovating rural dilapidated houses. The evaluation results will serve as an important reference for MHURD and MOF to allocate subsidy funds for the renovation of rural dilapidated houses in provinces (autonomous regions and municipalities) in the next year. ■

POLICY 195 MOF published a circular on issuing the *Basic Guidelines for the Cost Accounting of Public Institutions*

On December 25, MOF published a circular on issuing the *Basic Guidelines for the Cost Accounting of Public Institutions*, which provided the following. These guidelines apply to public institutions that implement government accounting standards and carry out cost accounting. The cost accounting should meet the specific cost information needs of internal management and external management. The public institutions shall perform cost accounting on the basis of accrual-based financial accounting data, and the detailed account items setting and auxiliary accounting shall meet the needs of cost accounting. The public institutions may determine the costing cycle based on cost information needs and costing targets, and compile cost reports based on the costing cycle to fully reflect the costing situation. These guidelines will come into effect on January 1, 2021. ■

POLICY 196 National Fiscal Work Conference was held in Beijing

From December 26 to 27, the National Fiscal Work Conference was held in Beijing. The conference, in an effort to earnestly implement the decisions of the Central Economic Work Conference, reviewed fiscal work in 2019 and planned fiscal work in 2020. Finance Minister Liu Kun made a work report at the conference. The conference emphasized that 2020 is the year when a moderately prosperous society in all respects will be fully built and the "13th Five-Year Plan" will be completed. The finance authorities should adhere to the reform and opening up as the driving force, promote high-quality development, resolutely win the three critical battles, do a good job of the "six stabilization", and make coordinated efforts to promote stable growth, advance reform, adjust economic structure, improve people's livelihood, prevent risks, and maintain stability. Proactive fiscal policy must vigorously enhance its quality and effectiveness, pay more attention to structural adjustment, and consolidate and expand the effect of tax and fee cut; we will conscientiously implement the principle of "determining expenditures according to revenues", step up efforts to optimize fiscal expenditure structure, and tighten the belt for government spending; we will make good use of the special bonds of local government, regulate the borrowing and financing of local government, and prevent and resolve the hidden debt risks of local government; we will deepen the reform of fiscal and tax system, accelerate the establishment of a modern fiscal system, and promote social and economic development in a sustainable and healthy manner, so as to ensure the successful building of a moderately prosperous society in all respects and the completion of the "13th Five-Year Plan". ■

POLICY 197 State Council Customs Tariff Commission issued the Circular on *the Import and Export Tariff Rules of the People's Republic of China (2020)*

Source: MOF

On December 30, the State Council Customs Tariff Commission issued the Circular on *the Import and Export Tariff Rules of the People's Republic of China (2020)*, which provided the following. The Import and Export Tariff Rules of the People's Republic of China is a component of the *Import and Export Tariff Regulations*, and mainly include import tariff rules and export tariff rules. The import and export tariff items of the 2020 version of the Tariff Rules are the same as those of the 2019 version; the most-favored nation tariff rate, the provisional import tariff rate, the agreed tariff rate and the preferential tariff rate of the 2020 version of Tariff Rules have been recalibrated on the basis of the 2019 version in accordance with the *Circular of the State Council Customs Tariff Commission on the Plan for Adjusting the Provisional Import Tariff Rates*. Except for the tariff items and rates announced in the 2020 version of Tariff Rules, import and export tariff items and rates that are otherwise governed by laws and administrative regulations shall continue to be implemented in accordance with laws and administrative regulations. ■

198 Six ministries jointly issued *the Master Plan for Improving the Employment Security Fund System for the Disabled and Better Promoting the Employment of the Disabled*

On December 30, NDRC, MOF, MCA, MOHRSS, SAT, and the China Disabled Persons' Federation jointly issued *the Master Plan for Improving the Employment Security Fund System for the Disabled and Better Promoting the Employment of the Disabled*, which provided the following. The method for collection of employment security fund for the disabled is adjusted from a single standard to tiered standard. If the proportion of employment of the disabled at the employer is above 1% (included) but lower than the percentage stipulated by the province (district and city), the fund will be collected at 50% of the payable amount within three years; if the proportion is less than 1%, the fund will be collected at 90% of the payable amount within three years. The finance department is responsible for the daily supervision of the collection and use of the fund. MOF will report to the State Council each year the income and spending of employment security fund for the disabled in the previous year in accordance with the budget management regulations. The provincial, city and county finance departments will, together with the disabled persons' federations at the same level, regularly disclose the above-mentioned information in their jurisdiction to the public and accept public supervision. ■

199 Two ministries jointly issued *the 2019 Report on the Reform and Development of State-owned Cultural Enterprises*

Recently, the Publicity Department of the CPC Central Committee and MOF jointly issued *the 2019 Report on the Reform and Development of State-owned Cultural Enterprises*, which provided the following. The scale and strength of state-owned cultural enterprises have continued to increase. As of the end of 2018, the total assets of state-owned cultural enterprises were 5.3 trillion RMB and the owner's equity was 2.5 trillion RMB, an increase of 15.4% and 11.7% year on year respectively. MOF has cooperated with the Publicity Department of the CPC Central Committee to promote the reform and development of state-owned cultural enterprises for new achievements. First, strengthen the Party's leadership over state-owned cultural enterprises. Require enterprises to include the general requirements of Party building work into their articles of association. Second, improve the state-owned assets supervision system for cultural enterprises. At the central level, the state-owned assets supervision system led by the Publicity Department of the CPC Central Committee, with MOF exercising the responsibilities of capital contributor on behalf of the State Council, is effectively improved. Third, increase support for cultural enterprises. In 2018, MOF arranged 1.5 billion RMB of state-owned capital operating budget to support central cultural enterprises in implementing the national key cultural industry development strategy. Fourth, assist enterprises with operational and institutional innovation. Promote the corporate system reform of central cultural enterprises and key provincial cultural enterprises. Fifth, promote corporate transformation and upgrading. Support state-owned cultural enterprises to facilitate the integration of cultural, scientific and technological, tourism and other related industries and build provincial financial media cloud platform and county-level financial media centers. ■

200 MOF published a circular on issuing the Guidelines for Overseas Accounting Organizations to Apply for the Identification of Competent Regulatory Authorities

On January 2, MOF published a circular on issuing the Guidelines for Overseas Accounting Organizations to Apply for the Identification of Competent Regulatory Authorities, which provided the following. For overseas accounting organizations that meet the requirements set out in *the Guidelines for Registration and Record-filing of Temporary Activities of the Representative Offices of Overseas Non-Governmental Organizations,* if they intend to establish representative offices in China and their scope of business is related to the research, communication and cooperation of international accounting and social auditing, they may request finance authorities to be their competent regulatory authorities. Overseas accounting organizations shall register at the public security authorities within 30 days from the date of issuance of the consent letter by MOF or provincial finance department. ■

FACTS & FIGURES

01 China's manufacturing PMI in December was 49.4%

The data released by the National Bureau of Statistics(NBS) on December 31 showed that China's manufacturing PMI in December was 49.4%, down by 0.6 percentage points from the previous month and was below the critical points, indicating that the manufacturing sector has weakened. By enterprises of different scale, the PMI of large enterprises was 50.1%, down by 0.5 percentage points from the previous month and stayed slightly above the critical points; the PMI of small and medium-sized enterprises was 48.4% and 48.6% respectively, down by 0.7 and 0.6 percentage points from the previous month and stayed below the critical points. In terms of the categorized index, among the five sub-indexes that constitute the manufacturing PMI, the production index and supplier delivery time index are above the critical points, and the new order index, raw material inventory index and employee index are below the critical points. The production index was 50.8%, down by 1.1 percentage points from the previous month but stayed above the critical points, indicating that manufacturing production continued to grow. The new order index was 49.7%, down by 0.7 percentage points from the previous month and remained below the critical points, indicating a decrease in orders for manufacturing companies. The raw material inventory index was 47.1%, down by 0.3 percentage points from the previous month and was below the critical points, indicating a further decline in the main raw material inventory of the manufacturing industry. ■

02 China's non-manufacturing business activity index in December was 53.8%

The data released by the NBS on December 31 showed that China's non-manufacturing business activity index in December was 53.8%, up by 0.4 percentage points from the previous month, indicating that non-manufacturing sector's expansion has accelerated. The service industry business activity index was 52.3%, a slight decrease of 0.1 percentage points from the previous month but still remained above the critical points, signaling that the service industry continued to grow. The index of business activities in the railway transport industry, telecom broadcasting and satellite transmission services, monetary and financial services, insurance industry and other financial industries stayed at a high level above 60.0%, indicating that these industries have achieved rapid growth. The industries of road transport, postal services, catering, capital market services and real estate are in the contraction zone, and the total business volume has decreased. The construction industry business activity index was 62.6%, up by 3.3 percentage points from the previous month, showing that the construction industry activities have accelerated. The new order index was 50.4%, up by 0.3 percentage points from the previous month and stayed above the critical points, indicating that demand growth in the non-manufacturing market has accelerated. ■

03 China's CPI rose by 1.9% year on year in December, 2018

The data released by NBS on January 10 showed that China's CPI rose by 1.9% year on year and stayed flat month on month in December, among which, CPI rose by 1.9% year on year and stayed flat month on month in both urban and rural areas; went up by 2.5% year on year and 1.1% month on month for food and went up by 1.7% year on year and down by 0.2% month on month for non-food; increased by 1.7% year on year and stayed flat month on month for consumer goods; increased by 2.1% year on year and stayed flat month on month for services. ■

CPI in 2019

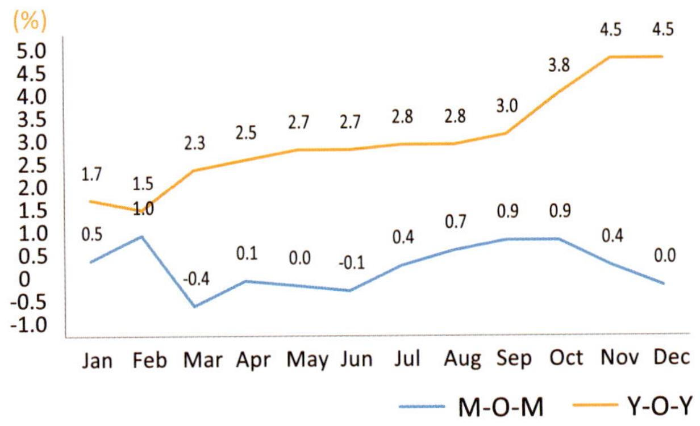

Source: NBS

04 China's PPI rose by 0.9% year on year in December, 2018

The data released by NBS on January 10 showed that China's PPI in December rose by 0.9% year on year, and down by 1.0% month on month. The price of the means of production jumped by 1.0% year on year, and down by 1.3% month on month; specifically, the figure surged by 3.8% year on year in the extractive industry, and down by 3.9% month on month; rose by 0.8% year on year in the raw material industry, and down by 2.5% month on month; went up by 0.8% year on year in the processing industry, and down by 0.6% month on month. In terms of the price of the means of consumption, the figure rose by 0.9% year on year for food, and up by 0.1% month on month; rose by 1.6% year on year for apparel, and up by 0.2% month on month; rose by 0.4% year on year for daily necessities, and down by 0.1% month on month; and went up by 0.2% for durable consumer goods, and stayed flat month on month. ■

05 China's M2 increased by 8.1% year on year in late December, 2018

The data released by PBoC (People's Bank of China) on January 15 showed that in late December 2018, M2 balance was 182.67 trillion RMB, up by 8.1% year on year; M1 balance was 55.17 trillion RMB, up by 1.5% year on year; M0 balance was 7.32 trillion RMB, up by 3.6% year on year. 256.3 billion RMB of cash was injected into circulation in 2018. In late December, the balance of RMB and foreign currency loans totaled 141.75 trillion RMB, up by 12.9% year on year, among them, the balance of RMB loans was 136.3 trillion RMB, up by 13.5% year on year; and the balance of foreign currency loans was 794.8 billion USD, down by 5.2% year on year. ■

06 China's social financing increased by 9.8% year on year in 2018

The data released by PBoC on January 15 showed that China's social financing reached 200.75 trillion RMB in 2018, up by 9.8% year on year. Specifically, the balance of RMB loans to the real economy reached 134.69 trillion RMB, up by 13.2% year on year; the balance of foreign currency-denominated loans to the real economy reached 2.21 trillion RMB, down by 10.7% year on year; the balance of entrusted loans reached 12.36 trillion RMB, down by 11.5% year on year; the balance of trust loans reached 7.85 trillion RMB, down by 8% year on year; the balance of undiscounted bankers' acceptance notes reached 3.81 trillion RMB, down by 14.3% year on year; the balance of corporate bonds stood at 20.13 trillion RMB, up by 9.2% year on year; the balance of local government special bonds reached 7.27 trillion RMB, up by 32.6% year on year; and the balance of domestic stock financing of non-financial enterprises was 7.01 trillion RMB, up by 5.4% year on year. ■

07 China's fiscal revenue and expenditure in 2018

The data released by MOF on January 23 showed that from January to December 2018, the national general public budget revenue was 18.3352 trillion RMB, a year-on-year increase of 6.2%. Among them, the central general public budget revenue was 8.5447 trillion RMB, a year-on-year increase of 5.3%; the local general public budget revenue was 9.7905 trillion RMB, a year-on-year increase of 7%. The tax revenue of the national general public budget revenue was 15.6401 trillion RMB, up by 8.3% year on year; the non-tax revenue was 2.6951 trillion RMB, down by 4.7% year on year. From January to December 2018, the national general public budget expenditure was 22.0906 trillion RMB, a year-on-year increase of 8.7%. Among them, the central general public budget expenditure was 3.2708 trillion RMB, a year-on-year increase of 8.8%; the local general public budget expenditure was 18.8198 trillion RMB, a year-on-year increase of 8.7%. From January to December 2018, the cumulative revenue of the national government fund budget was 7.5405 trillion RMB, a year-on-year increase of 22.6%. Among them, the revenue of the central government fund budget was 403.3 billion RMB, up by 4.2% year on year; the revenue of the local government fund budget was 7.1372 trillion RMB, a year-on-year increase of 23.8%, of which revenue from the transfer of land use rights was 6.5096 trillion RMB, a year-on-year increase of 25%. From January to December 2018, the cumulative expenditure of the national government fund budget was 8.0562 trillion RMB, a year-on-year increase of 32.1%. Among them, the expenditure of the central government fund budget was 308.9 billion RMB, a year-on-year increase of 13.4%; the expenditure of local government fund budget was 7.7473 trillion RMB, a year-on-year increase of 32.9%, of which the expenditure related to land-transfer revenue was 6.9941 trillion RMB, a year-on-year increase of 34.2%. From January to December 2018, the cumulative revenue of national state-owned capital operating budget was 290 billion RMB, a year-on-year increase of 9.8%. Among them, the revenue of the central state-owned capital operating budget was 132.5 billion RMB, a year-on-year increase of 1.6%; the revenue of the local state-owned capital operating budget was 157.5 billion RMB, a year-on-year increase of 17.8%. From January to December 2018, the cumulative expenditure of the national state-owned capital operating budget was 215.9 billion RMB, a year-on-year increase of 6.7%. Among them, the expenditure of the central state-owned capital operating budget was 102.5 billion RMB, a year-on-year increase of 32.4%; the expenditure of the local state-owned capital operating budget was 113.4 billion RMB, down by 9.2% year on year. ■

08 China's local government bond issuance and outstanding debts in 2018

The data released by MOF on January 23 showed that 4.1652 trillion RMB of local government bonds were issued in 2018, among which, 2.2192 trillion RMB were general bonds and 1.946 trillion RMB were special bonds; by the purpose of use, 2.1705 trillion RMB were new bonds, accounting for 99.6% of the new debt limit in 2018, and 1.9947 trillion RMB were swapped bonds and refinanced bonds. As of the end of 2018, nationwide outstanding local government debts amounted to 18.3862 trillion RMB, which is within the limit imposed by NPC. Among them, general debts were 10.9939 trillion RMB, and special debts were 7.3923 trillion RMB; government bonds were 18.0711 trillion RMB, and the stock of government debts that are not in the form of government bonds amounted to 315.1 billion RMB. ■

09 The total profits of industrial enterprises above designated size in China rose by 10.3% year on year in 2018

The data published by NBS on January 28 showed that the profits of industrial enterprises above designated size in China totaled 6.63514 trillion RMB in 2018, up by 10.3% year on year. By types of ownership, the figure stood at 1.85831 trillion RMB for state-holding industrial enterprises, up by 12.6% year on year; 10.22 billion RMB for collective-owned enterprises, down by 1%; 4.69751 trillion RMB for joint-stock enterprises, up by 14.4%; 1.67755 trillion RMB for foreign funded enterprises and enterprises Hong Kong, Macao and Taiwan, up by 1.9%; and 1.7137 trillion RMB for private enterprises, up by 11.9%. The main business income was 102.2 trillion RMB, an increase of 8.5% over the previous year; the main business cost was 85.7 trillion RMB, an increase of 8.3%; the main business income profit rate was 6.49%, an increase of 0.11 percentage points over the previous year. ■

10 The operating income of China's cultural and related enterprises above designated size in 2018 increased by 8.2%

The data released by NBS on January 31 showed that after a survey of over 60,000 cultural and related enterprises above designated size, the operating income of China's cultural and related enterprises above designated size in 2018 reached 8.9257 trillion RMB, representing an increase of 8.2% year on year. By sectors, the operating income of cultural manufacturing sector was 3.8074 trillion RMB, up by 4.0% year on year; the operating income of cultural wholesale and retail sector was 1.6728 trillion RMB, up by 4.5%; the operating income of cultural services sector was 3.4454 trillion RMB, up by 15.4%. By regions, the operating income of cultural and related enterprises above designated size reached 6.8688 trillion RMB in the eastern region, up by 7.7%; 1.2008 trillion RMB in the central region, up by 9.7%; 761.8 billion RMB in the western region, up by 12.2% year on year; and 94.3 billion RMB in the northeastern region, down by 1.3% year on year. ■

11 China's manufacturing PMI in January was 49.5%

The data published by NBS on January 31 showed that China's manufacturing PMI in January was 49.5%, up by 0.1 percentage points month on month. In breakdown of enterprises, PMI was 51.3% for large-sized ones, up by 1.2 percentage points month on month and stayed consistently above the critical points; 47.2% for medium-sized ones and 47.3% for small-sized ones, down by 1.2 percentage points and 1.3 percentage points month on month respectively and stayed below the critical points. In specific terms, the production index and supplier delivery time index were above the critical points while the new order index, the raw material inventory index and the employee index were below the critical points. The comprehensive PMI output index in January was 53.2%, up by 0.6 percentage points month on month. ■

12 China's import and export of goods increased by 8.7% in January

The data released by GAC on February 14 showed that the total value of China's import and export of goods in January 2019 was 2.73 trillion RMB, a year-on-year increase of 8.7%. Among them, exports were 1.5 trillion RMB, up by 13.9%; imports were 1.23 trillion RMB, up by 2.9%; trade surplus was 271.16 billion RMB, an increase of 1.2 times. ■

13 China's CPI rose by 1.7% year on year in January

The data released by National Bureau of Statistics (NBS) on February 15 showed that China's CPI rose by 1.7% year on year in January, among which, CPI rose by 1.8% in urban areas and 1.7% in rural areas; went up by 1.9% for food and by 1.7% for non-food; increased by 1.3% for consumer goods and by 2.4% for services. In month-on-month terms, CPI rose by 0.5%, among which, CPI went up by 0.5% in urban areas and 0.4% in rural areas; rose by 1.6% for food and 0.2% for non-food; increased by 0.4% for consumer goods and 0.6% for services. ■

14 China's M2 increased by 8.4% and M1 increased by 0.4% in January

The data released by PBoC on February 15 showed that China's outstanding M2 at the end of January was 186.59 trillion RMB, up by 8.4% year on year, or 0.3 percentage points higher than the end of last month and 0.2 percentage points lower than the same period of the previous year. The outstanding M1 was 54.56 trillion RMB, a year-on-year increase of 0.4%, or 1.1 percentage points and 14.6 percentage points lower than the end of last month and the same period of last year; the outstanding currency in circulation was 8.75 trillion RMB, a year-on-year increase of 17.2%. The net injection of cash in January was 1.43 trillion RMB. ■

15

China's nationwide sales of lottery totaled 47.955 billion RMB in January 2019

The data published by MOF on February 26 showed that the nationwide sales of lottery totaled 47.955 billion RMB in January, an increase of 9.626 billion RMB, or up by 25.1%. Among them, welfare lottery sales were 21.219 billion RMB, an increase of 1.883 billion RMB, or up by 9.7%. Sports lottery sales were 26.736 billion RMB, an increase of 7.742 billion RMB, or up by 40.8%. The main reason for the rapid growth in lottery sales in January was that the sales of quiz-type sports lottery increased significantly due to the Asian Cup. ■

16

China's manufacturing PMI was 49.2% in February 2019

The data published by NBS on February 28 showed that China's manufacturing PMI was 49.2% in February, down by 0.3 percentage points from the previous month. By enterprises, the PMI of large enterprises was 51.5%, up by 0.2 percentage points from the previous month and continued to remain above the critical points; the PMI of small and medium-sized enterprises was 46.9% and 45.3% respectively, down by 0.3 percentage points and 2.0 percentage points respectively from the previous month and stayed below the critical points. In terms of the classification indexes, among the five indexes that constitute the manufacturing PMI, the new order index was above the critical points, while the production index, raw material inventory index, employee index and supplier delivery time index were below the critical points. ■

17

The central and local budget implementation in 2018

According to the news released by MOF on March 7, China's general public budget revenue in 2018 was 18.335184 trillion RMB, which was 100.1% of the budget, an increase of 6.2% over 2017. The general public budget expenditure was 22.090607 trillion RMB, which was 105.3% of the budget, an increase of 8.7%. With the addition of 101.854 billion RMB of the Central Budget Stabilization Fund, the total expenditure was 22.192461 trillion RMB. When total revenue was measured against expenditure, deficit was 2.38 trillion RMB, which was the same as the budget. The general public budget revenue at the central level was 8.544734 trillion RMB, which was 100.1% of the budget, an increase of 5.3%. The general public budget expenditure at the central level was 10.23818 trillion RMB, which was 99.1% of the budget, an increase of 7.7%. The general public budget revenue at the local level was 16.757849 trillion RMB, and the general public budget expenditure at the local level was 18.819826 trillion RMB, an increase of 8.7%. The government-managed fund revenue was 7.54045 trillion RMB, an increase of 22.6%. The government-managed fund expenditure was 8.056207 trillion RMB, an increase of 32.1%. The state-owned capital operating budget revenue was 289.995 billion RMB, an increase of 9.8%. The national state-owned capital operating budget expenditure was 215.926 billion RMB, an increase of 6.7%. The revenue of social security fund was 7.264922 trillion RMB, an increase of 24.3%, and the expenditure of social security fund was 6.458645 trillion RMB, an increase of 32.7%. ■

18 The change of China's foreign exchange reserves in February

According to the news released by SAFE on March 7, China's foreign exchange reserves at the end of February was 3.0902 trillion USD, up by 2.3 billion USD from the previous month, or an increase of 0.1%. ■

19 China's economic performance was generally stable from January to February

The data published by NBS on March 14 showed that China's economy continued to operate within an appropriate range of growth from January to February, maintaining an overall stable and progressive development trend. From January to February, China's service industry production index increased by 7.3% year on year; nationwide added value of industrial enterprises above designated size increased by 5.3% year on year; investment in fixed assets was 4.4849 trillion RMB, up by 6.1% year on year; retail sales of consumer goods totaled 6.6064 trillion RMB, up by 8.2% year on year; new job creation in urban areas was 1.74 million; the urban surveyed unemployment rate was 5.3%; the urban surveyed unemployment rate in 31 large cities was 5.0%; the consumer price rose by 1.6% year on year; the total import and export was 4.5441 trillion RMB, up by 0.7% year on year, while the figure in December of last year was down by 1.2%. ■

20 China's fiscal revenues and expenditures from January to February 2019

According to the news released by MOF on March 18, China's general public budget revenue was 3.9104 trillion RMB from January to February, a year-on-year increase of 7%, among which, the tax revenue was 3.5114 trillion RMB, a year-on-year increase of 6.6%; the non-tax revenue was 399 billion RMB, a year-on-year increase of 10.8%. The national general public budget expenditure was 3.3314 trillion RMB, a year-on-year increase of 14.6%, among which, the general public budget expenditure of the central level was 407.8 billion RMB, an increase of 15.4% year on year; the general public budget expenditure of the local level was 2.9236 trillion RMB, an increase of 14.5% year on year. The national government fund budget revenue was 945 billion RMB, down by 2.3% year on year, among which, the central government fund budget revenue was 61.2 billion RMB, an increase of 5% year on year; the local government fund budget revenue was 883.8 billion RMB, down by 2.8% year on year. The national government fund budget expenditure was 1.4374 trillion RMB, a year-on-year increase of 1.1 times, among which, the government fund budget expenditure of the central level was 10.7 billion RMB, a year-on-year increase of 1.4 times; the government fund budget expenditure of the local level was 1.4267 trillion RMB, an increase of 1.1 times year on year. ■

Fiscal Revenue in 2019

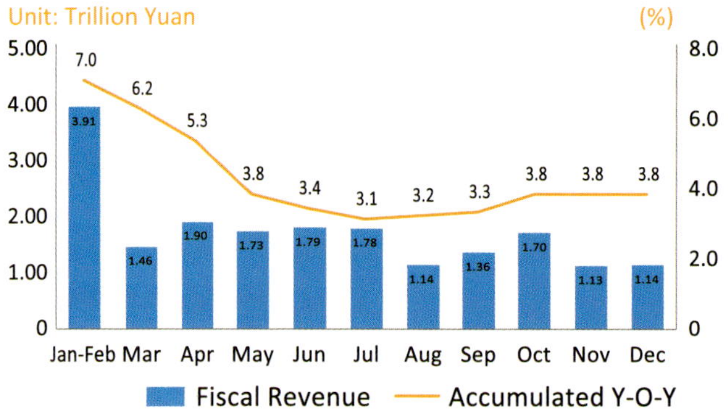

Source: NBS

21 Issuance of local government bonds and outstanding debts in February 2019

According to the news released by MOF on March 20, China issued 364.2 billion RMB of local government bonds in February 2019. Among them, 192.5 billion RMB were general bonds and 171.7 billion RMB were special bonds; by the purpose of use, 327.4 billion RMB were new bonds and 36.8 billion RMB were bonds for swap and refinancing. As of the end of February 2019, the outstanding national local government debts stood at 19.142 trillion RMB, which were within the limits approved by NPC. Among them, the general debts stood at 11.4273 trillion RMB and the special debts at 7.7147 trillion RMB; the government bonds stood at 18.8269 trillion RMB, and the outstanding government debts that are not in the form of government bonds at 315.1 billion RMB. As of the end of February 2019, the average remaining maturity of local government bonds was 4.4 years, including 4.4 years for general bonds and 4.5 years for special bonds; the average interest rate was 3.5%, including 3.49% for general bonds and 3.51% for special bonds. ■

22 The performance of Chinese SOEs from January to February 2019

The data published by MOF on March 26 showed that the gross renenue of SOEs totaled 8.70527 trillion RMB from January to February, up by 6.3% year on year, among which, the figure for central SOEs was 5.20425 trillion RMB, up by 5.0% year on year, and the figure for local SOEs was 3.50102 trillion RMB, up by 8.3% year on year. The operating costs of SOEs totaled 8.42819 trillion RMB, up by 6.5% year on year, among which, the figure for central SOEs was 4.95261 trillion RMB, up by 4.9% year on year, and the figure for local SOEs was 3.47558 trillion RMB, up by 9.0% year on year. The profits of SOEs totaled 452.05 billion RMB, up by 10.0% year on year, among which, the figure for central SOEs was 332.74 billion RMB, up by 14.3% year on year, and the figure for local SOEs was 119.31 billion RMB, down by 0.5% year on year. The after-tax net profits totaled 327.8 billion RMB, up by 10.3% year on year, among which, the figure for central SOEs was 244.53 billion RMB, up by 16.6% year on year, and the figure for local SOEs was 83.27 billion RMB, down by 4.6% year on year. The payable taxes of SOEs totaled 817.46 billion RMB, up by 0.6% year on year, among which, the figure for central SOEs was 605.69 billion RMB, up by 1.5% year on year, and the figure for local

SOEs was 211.77 billion RMB, down by 1.9% year on year. At the end of February, the assets of SOEs totaled 187.97945 trillion RMB, up by 8.5% year on year; the liabilities totaled 121.1418 trillion RMB, up by 8.1% year on year; and the owners' equities totaled 66.83765 trillion RMB, up by 9.2% year on year. ■

23 China's lottery sales in February 2019

The data released by MOF on March 28 showed that nationwide lottery sales in February were 23.412 billion RMB, down by 8.8% year on year. The welfare lottery sales were 11.295 billion RMB, down by 13.9% year on year. The sports lottery sales were 12.117 billion RMB, down by 3.4% year on year. By type, the lotto lottery sales were 11.719 billion RMB, down by 23.1% year on year; the toto lottery sales were 6.651 billion RMB, up by 19.8% year on year; the instant lottery sales were 1.789 billion RMB, down by 0.6% year on year; the video lottery sales were 3.244 billion RMB, up by 6.2% year on year; and the keno lottery sales were 9 million RMB, up by 8.5% year on year. In February, the lotto, the toto, the instant, the video and the keno lottery sales respectively accounted for 50.1%, 28.4%, 7.6%, 13.8% and 0.1% of the total lottery sales. ■

24 China's manufacturing PMI in March 2019 was 50.5%

The data published by NBS on March 31 showed that China's manufacturing PMI in March 2019 was 50.5%, up by 1.3 percentage points from the previous month and returning above the critical points. First, by the scale of enterprises, the PMI of large enterprises was 51.1%, down by 0.4 percentage points month on month and staying higher than the critical points; the PMI of medium-sized and small-sized enterprises was 49.9% and 49.3% respectively, up by 3.0 and 4.0 percentage points month on month respectively. Second, in terms of the classification index, among the five sub-indices that constitute the manufacturing PMI, the production index was 52.7%, up by 3.2 percentage points from the previous month and returning above the critical points, indicating the resumption of business operation after the Spring Festival and the acceleration of manufacturing production; the new order index was 51.6%, up by 1.0 percentage points from the previous month and was above the critical points for two consecutive months, indicating that the demand for manufacturing market continued to grow; the raw material inventory index was 48.4%, up by 2.1 percentage points from the previous month and was still below the critical points, indicating that the main raw material inventory of the manufacturing industry was decreasing, but the decline was narrowed; the employee index was 47.6%, up by 0.1 percentage points from the previous month and was below the critical points, indicating that the decline in the amount of labor used by manufacturing enterprises was narrowed slightly; the supplier delivery time index was 50.2%, up by 0.4 percentage points from the previous month and was above the critical points, indicating that the delivery time of raw material suppliers in manufacturing industry was faster than last month. ■

25 China's CPI in March 2019 increased by 2.3% year on year

The data published by NBS on April 11 showed that China's CPI in March 2019 increased by 2.3% year on year. Among them, the figure rose by 2.3% for cities and 2.3% for rural areas; 4.1% for food prices and 1.8% for non-food prices; 2.4% for consumer goods prices and 2.0% for service prices. In the first quarter, the overall level of CPI increased by 1.8% over the same period of last year. In March, the CPI fell by 0.4% month on month. Among them, the figure fell by 0.4% for cities and 0.3% for rural areas; 0.9% for food prices and 0.2% for non-food prices; 0.1% for consumer goods prices and 0.8% for service prices. ■

26 China's PPI in March 2019 increased by 0.4% year on year

The data published by NBS on April 11 showed that China's PPI in March 2019 increased by 0.4% year on year and rose by 0.1% month on month; the IPI rose by 0.2% year on year and stayed flat month on month. In the first quarter, PPI rose by 0.2% year on year, and IPI rose by 0.1% year on year. ■

PPI in 2019

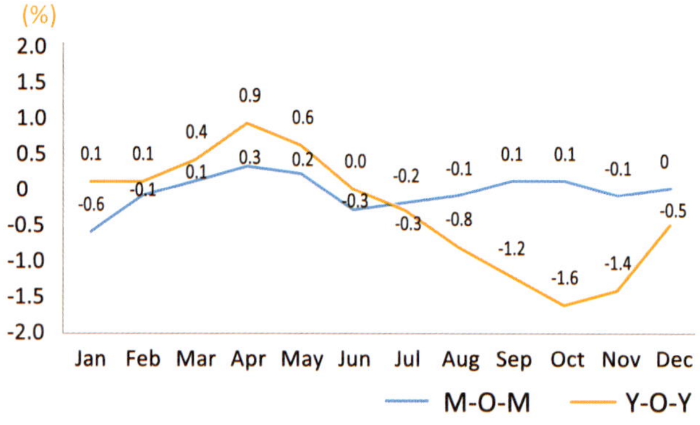

Source: NBS

27 China's fiscal revenues and expenditures in the first quarter of 2019

The data published by MOF on April 16 showed that China's general public budget revenues from January to March 2019 were 5.3656 trillion RMB, a year-on-year increase of 6.2%. Among them, the central general public budget revenues were 2.5338 trillion RMB, a year-on-year increase of 5.4%; the local general public budget revenues were 2.8318 trillion RMB, a year-on-year increase of 6.8%. The tax revenues of general public budget revenues were 4.6706 trillion RMB, up by 5.4% year on year; non-tax revenues were 695 billion RMB, up by 11.8% year on year. China's cumulative general public budget expenditures from January to March were 5.8629 trillion RMB, a year-on-year increase of 15%. Among them, the central general public budget expenditures were 691.9 billion RMB, a year-on-year increase of 14.6%; the local general public budget expenditures were 5.171 trillion RMB, a year-on-year increase of 15%. China's cumulative government fund budget revenues from January to March were 1.43 trillion RMB, down by 6.2% year on year. Among them, the central government fund budget revenues were 100.3 billion RMB, up by 6.1% year on year; the local government fund budget revenues were 1.3297 trillion RMB, down by 7.1% year on year; the state-owned land use rights transfer revenues fell by 9.5%. China's cumulative government fund budget expenditures for the first three months of the year were 1.8881 trillion RMB, a year-on-year increase of 55.9%. Among them, the central government fund budget expenditures were 29.3 billion RMB, an increase of 89% year on year; the local government fund budget expenditures were 1.8588 trillion RMB, an increase of 55.5% year on year; the expenditures funded by state-owned land use rights transfer revenues increased by 45.2%. ■

28 Chinese Residents' income and consumption expenditures in the first quarter of 2019

The data published by NBS on April 17 showed that in the first quarter of 2019, China's per capita disposable income was 8,493 RMB, 8.7% higher than the nominal growth of the same period of the previous year. After adjusting for the price factor, the actual increase was 6.8%. Among them, the per capita disposable income of urban residents was 11,633 RMB, an increase of 7.9%. After adjusting for the price factor, the actual increase was 5.9%. The per capita disposable income of rural residents was 4,600 RMB, an increase of 8.8%. After adjusting for the price factor, the actual increase was 6.9%. In the first quarter of 2019, China's per capita consumption expenditure was 5,538 RMB, an increase of 7.3% over the same period of the previous year. After adjusting for the price factor, the actual increase was 5.4%. Among them, the per capita consumption expenditure of urban residents was 7,160 RMB, an increase of 6.1%. After adjusting for the price factor, the actual increase was 4.1%; the per capita consumption expenditure of rural residents was 3,525 RMB, an increase of 8.7%. After adjusting for the price factor, the actual increase was 6.8%. ■

29 Value-added of industrial enterprises above a designated size increased by 8.5% year on year in China

The data published by NBS on April 17 showed that the value-added of industrial enterprises above a designated size increased by 8.5% year on year in March 2019 and increased by 1% month on month. In the first quarter, the value-added of industrial enterprises above a designated size increased by 6.5% year on year. In terms of three categories, the value-added of the mining industry increased by 4.6% year on year in March, 4.3 percentage points higher than that in January and February; the value-added of the manufacturing industry increased by 9.0%, an acceleration of 3.4 percentage points; the value-added of the electricity, thermal, gas and water production and supply industry grew by 7.7%, accelerating by 0.9 percentage points. In terms of ownership types, the value-added of state-owned and holding companies increased by 4.7% year on year in March; the value-added of joint-stock enterprises increased by 10.0%; the value-added of foreign-invested enterprises as well as enterprises funded from Hong Kong, Macao and Taiwan increased by 4.2%; the value-added of private enterprises increased by 14.2%. In terms of sectors, 40 of the 41 major sectors in March maintained a year-on-year increase in value-added. In terms of regions, the value-added of the eastern region increased by 10.3% year on year in March, the central region increased by 9.6%, the western region increased by 7.5%, and the northeast region increased by 8.0%. In terms of products, the value-added of the 414 of the 605 products in March maintained year-on-year increase. ■

30 Local government bond issuance and outstanding debts in March 2019

The data published by MOF on April 18 showed that China issued 624.5 billion RMB of local government bonds in March 2019. Among them, general bonds were 233.5 billion RMB and special bonds were 391 billion RMB; in terms of the use of bonds, new bonds were 488.6 billion RMB (including new general bonds of 130.4 billion RMB and new special bonds of 358.2 billion RMB), swapped bonds and refinanced bonds amounted to 135.9 billion RMB. As of the end of March 2019, the local government debt balance was 19.6194 trillion RMB, within the limits approved by NPC. Among them, the general debts were 11.5559 trillion RMB, the special debt was 8.0635 trillion RMB; the government bonds was 19.3043 trillion RMB, the outstanding government debts that are not in the form of government bonds was 315.1 billion RMB. The average remaining maturity of local government bonds is 4.5 years, including 4.4 years for general bonds and 4.6 years for special bonds; the average interest rate is 3.5%, including 3.5% for general bonds and 3.51% for special bonds. ■

31 China's nationwide lottery sales in March 2019

The data released by MOF on April 23 showed that nationwide lottery sales in March 2019 were 34.951 billion RMB, a decrease of 5.236 billion RMB over the same period of last year, and down by 13.0% year on year. The welfare lottery sales were 16.546 billion RMB, a decrease of 3.249 billion RMB over the same period of last year, and down by 16.4% year on year. The sports lottery sales were 18.404 billion RMB, a decrease of 1.988 billion RMB over the same period of last year, down by 9.7% year on year. From January to March, cumulative lottery sales were 106.317 billion RMB, an increase of 2.142 billion RMB over the same period of last year, and up by 2.1% year on year, among them, the welfare lottery sales were 49.06 billion RMB, a decrease of 3.189 billion RMB over the same period of last year, down by 6.1% year on year; and sports lottery sales were 57.257 billion RMB, an increase of 5.33 billion RMB over the same period of last year, and up by 10.3% year on year. ■

32 Performance of Chinese SOEs from January to March

The data released by MOF on April 24 showed that the total operating income of SOEs was 13.99431 trillion RMB from January to March, a year-on-year increase of 8.9%. The total operating cost was 13.5208 trillion RMB, a year-on-year increase of 9.2%, among them, the sales expenses, management expenses, research and development expenses and financial expenses increased by 3.4%, 12.6%, 23.3% and 11.5% respectively. The total profit was 819.77 billion RMB, a year-on-year increase of 15.6%. The net profit after tax was 603.56 billion RMB, an increase of 18.6%, and the net profit attributable to owners of the parent company was 380.03 billion RMB. The tax payable was 1.20854 trillion RMB, a year-on-year increase of 3.5%. At the end of March, the total assets of state-owned enterprises were 190.26962 trillion RMB, up by 9.0% year on year; the total liabilities were 122.57053 trillion RMB, up by 8.8% year on year; the owners' equity was 67.69909 trillion RMB, up by 9.3% year on year. The ratio of profit to cost and expense was 6.1%, an increase of 0.3 percentage points. At the end of March, the asset-liability ratio of SOEs was 64.4%, a decrease of 0.1 percentage points. ■

33 The total profits of major industrial enterprises in China from January to March

The data published by NBS on April 27 showed that the profits of major industrial enterprises in China totaled 1.2972 trillion RMB from January to March, down by 3.3% year on year and registering a fall of 10.7 percentage points narrower compared with the period from January to February. By types of ownership, the figure stood at 414.62 billion RMB for state-holding industrial enterprises, down by 13.4% year on year; 917.09 billion RMB for joint-stock enterprises, down by 1.0%; 318.22 billion RMB for foreign enterprises and enterprises Hong Kong, Macao and Taiwan, down by 7.9%; and 325.98 billion RMB for private enterprises, up by 7.0%. By sectors, the figure stood at 122.88 billion RMB for the mining sector, down by 3.4% year on year ; 1.05779 trillion RMB for the manufacturing sector, down by 4.2%; and 116.54 billion RMB for the electricity, thermal, gas and water production and supply sector, up by 5.7%. ■

34 The operating income of China's major cultural and related enterprises in the first quarter

The data released by NBS on April 30 showed that the operating income of China's major cultural and related enterprises in the first quarter reached 1.9799 trillion RMB, representing an increase of 8.3% year on year. 8 of the 9 cultural and related industries posted an increase in their operating income. By sectors, the operating income of cultural manufacturing sector was 840 billion RMB, up by 5.2% year on year; the operating income of cultural wholesale and retail sector was 358.8 billion RMB, up by 5.8%; the operating income of cultural services sector was 781.2 billion RMB, up by 13.2%. By areas, the operating income of core cultural areas reached 1.1592 trillion RMB, up by 12.0% year on year; and the operating income of cultural related areas reached 820.7 billion RMB, up by 3.5%. By regions, the operating income of major cultural and related enterprises reached 1.5125 trillion RMB in the eastern region, up by 7.3% year on year; 270.4 billion RMB in the central region, up by 10.7%; 177.9 billion RMB in the western region, up by 15.2% year on year; and 19.2 billion RMB in the northeastern region, down by 1.2% year on year, accounting for 76.4%, 13.7%, 9.0% and 1.0% of the national total respectively. ■

35 China's fiscal revenues and expenditures in April

The data released by MOF on May 8 showed that the national general public budget revenue was 7.2651 trillion RMB from January to April, a year-on-year increase of 5.3%. Among them, the central general public budget revenue was 3.4667 trillion RMB, a year-on-year increase of 4.3%;

the local general public budget revenue was 3.7984 trillion RMB, an increase of 6.1% year on year. The tax revenue of the national general public budget revenue was 6.3692 trillion RMB, a year-on-year increase of 4.6%; the non-tax revenue was 895.9 billion RMB, a year-on-year increase of 10.3%. The national general public budget expenditure was 7.5667 trillion RMB, a year-on-year increase of 15.2%. Among them, the central general public budget expenditure was 1.03 trillion RMB, an increase of 14.9% year on year; the local general public budget expenditure was 6.5367 trillion RMB, an increase of 15.2% year on year. The national government fund budget revenue was 1.9563 trillion RMB, down by 4.8% year on year. Among them, the central government fund budget revenue was 126.1 billion RMB, an increase of 3.8% year on year; the local government fund budget revenue was 1.8302 trillion RMB, down by 5.4% year on year. The national government fund budget expenditure was 2.2421 trillion RMB, a year-on-year increase of 38.3%. Among them, the central government fund budget expenditure was 36.5 billion RMB, a year-on-year increase of 100%; the local government fund budget expenditure was 2.2056 trillion RMB, an increase of 37.6% year on year. ■

Fiscal Expenditure in 2019

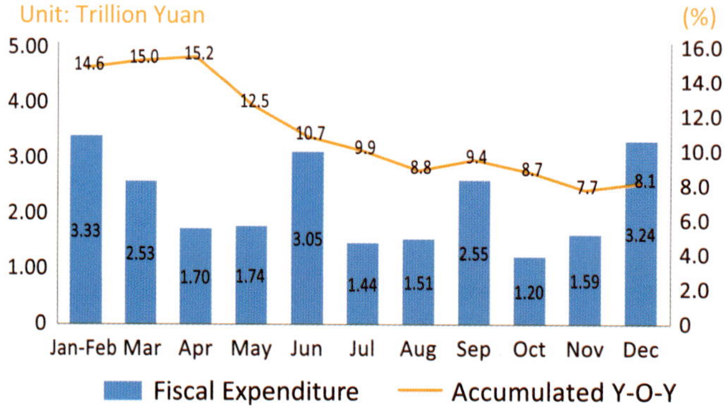

Source: NBS

36

China's CPI in April rose by 2.5% year on year

The data released by NBS on May 9 showed that China's CPI rose by 2.5% year on year in April, among which, CPI rose by 2.5% year on year in urban areas and 2.6% year on year in rural areas; went up by 6.1% year on year for food and 1.7% year on year for non-food; increased by 2.9% year on year for consumer goods and 2.0% year on year for services. ■

37

China's PPI in April rose by 0.9% year on year

The data released by NBS on May 9 showed that China's PPI in April rose by 0.9% year on year and up by 0.3% month on month; IPI rose by 0.4% year on year and down by 0.1% month on month. Among the PPI, the price of production materials rose by 0.9% year on year; the price of living materials rose by 0.9% year on year. Among IPI, the price of construction materials and non-metals rose by 5.1% year on year, the price of ferrous metal materials rose by 3.1%, the price of fuels rose by 1.6%, the price of chemical raw materials fell by 2.8%, and the price of non-ferrous metal materials and wires fell by 1.6%. ■

38 Total retail sales of consumer goods increased by 7.2% in April

The data published by NBS on May 15 showed that the total retail sales of consumer goods in April reached 3.0586 trillion RMB, a nominal increase of 7.2% year on year. Among them, the retail sales of consumer goods by sellers above a designated size reached 1.112 trillion RMB, an increase of 2.0%. In terms of the location of the business units, the retail sales of consumer goods in urban areas reached 2.6259 trillion RMB, up by 7.1% year on year; the retail sales of consumer goods in rural areas reached 432.7 billion RMB, up by 7.8%. From January to April, the retail sales of consumer goods in urban areas reached 10.9661 trillion RMB, up by 7.9% year on year; the retail sales of consumer goods in rural areas reached 1.8715 trillion RMB, up by 8.9%. In terms of the types of consumption, catering revenues were 328.1 billion RMB, up by 8.5% year on year; retail sales of goods were 2.730.5 trillion RMB, up by 7.0%. From January to April, the catering revenues were 1.3925 trillion RMB, a year-on-year increase of 9.3%; the retail sales of goods reached 11.4451 trillion RMB, an increase of 7.9%. ■

39 Value-added of industrial enterprises above a designated size increased by 5.4% in April

The data published by NBS on May 15 showed that the value-added of industrial enterprises above a designated size increased by 5.4% year on year in April 2019 and fell by 3.1 percentage points compared with the figure in March. On month-on-month terms, the value-added of industrial enterprises above a designated size rose by 0.37% over March. From January to April, the value-added of industrial enterprises above a designated size increased by 6.2% year on year. In terms of three categories, the value-added of the mining industry increased by 2.9% year on year in April, 1.7 percentage points lower than that in March; the value-added of the manufacturing industry increased by 5.3%, a fall of 3.7 percentage points; the value-added of the electricity, thermal, gas and water production and supply industry grew by 9.5%, accelerating by 1.8 percentage points. In terms of ownership types, the value-added of state-owned and holding companies increased by 6.0% year on year in April; the value-added of joint-stock enterprises increased by 6.3%; the value-added of foreign-invested enterprises as well as enterprises funded from Hong Kong, Macao and Taiwan increased by 2.5%; the value-added of private enterprises increased by 5.1%. In terms of regions, the value-added of the eastern region increased by 2.5% in April, the central region increased by 7.7%, the western region increased by 4.0%, and the northeast region decreased by 0.1%. ■

40 China's lottery sales in April 2019 fell by 13.7% year on year

The data released by MOF on May 21 showed that nationwide lottery sales in April were 35.988 billion RMB, down by 5.717 billion RMB or 13.7%. The welfare lottery sales were 16.285 billion RMB, down by 3.424 billion RMB or 17.4%. The sports lottery sales were 19.703 billion RMB, down by 2.293 billion RMB or 10.4%. From January to April, the nationwide lottery sales were 142.305 billion RMB, down by 3.575 billion RMB or 2.5%. The welfare lottery sales were 65.346 billion RMB, down by 6.613 billion RMB or 9.2%. The sports lottery sales were 76.96 billion RMB, up by 3.038 billion RMB or 4.1%. ■

41 Total operating incomes of SOEs in China from January to April increased by 8.3% over the same period of last year

The data published by MOF on May 27 showed that the total operating incomes of SOEs in China from January to April reached 18.9023 trillion RMB, an increase of 8.3% over the same period of last year. Among them, the figure for central SOEs was 10.97842 trillion RMB, up by 6.7% year on year; the figure for local SOEs was 7.92388 trillion RMB, up by 10.5% year on year. The total operating costs reached 18.23466 trillion RMB, an increase of 8.5% year on year. Among them, the figure for central SOEs was 10.41162 trillion RMB, up by 6.8% year on year; the figure for local SOEs was 7.82304 trillion RMB, up by 10.8% year on year. The total profits reached 1.12447 trillion RMB, a year-on-year increase of 12.6%. Among them, the figure for central SOEs was 774.94 billion RMB, up by 11.8% year on year; the figure for local SOEs was 349.53 billion RMB, up by 14.4% year on year. The net profits after tax of SOEs reached 831.90 billion RMB, a year-on-year increase of 15.6%. The payable taxes of SOEs reached 1.55398 trillion RMB, a year-on-year increase of 1.7%. ■

42 China's industrial enterprises above designated size achieved a total profit of 1.81294 trillion RMB from January to April

The data published by NBS on May 27 showed that China's industrial enterprises above designated size achieved a total profit of 1.81294 trillion RMB from January to April, down by 3.4% year on year. By types of enterprises, the figure for state-owned and controlled enterprises was 570.43 billion RMB, a year-on-year decrease of 9.7%; the figure for joint-stock enterprises was 1.28733 trillion RMB, a year-on-year decrease of 1.0%; the figure for foreign invested enterprises and enterprises funded from Hong Kong, Macao and Taiwan was 445.52 billion RMB, a year-on-year decrease of 8.3%; the figure for private enterprises was 459.71 billion RMB, a year-on-year increase of 4.1%. In terms of three major categories, the figure for the mining industry was 173.26 billion RMB, a year-on-year decrease of 0.7%; the figure for manufacturing industry was 1.48364 trillion RMB, down by 4.7% year on year; the figure for electricity, heat, gas and water production and supply industries was 156.04 billion RMB, up by 8.0% year on year. ■

43 China's PMI in May was 49.4%

The data published by NBS on May 31 showed that China's PMI in May was 49.4%, down by 0.7 percentage points month on month. In breakdown of enterprises, PMI was 50.3% for large-sized ones, down by 0.5 percentage points month on month; 48.8% for medium-sized ones, down by 0.3 percentage points month on month; and 47.8% for small-sized ones, down by 2.0 percentage points month on month. In specific terms, the production index was 51.7%, down by 0.4 percentage points month on month; the new order index was 49.8%, down by 1.6 percentage points month on month; the raw material inventory index was 47.4%, up by 0.2 percentage points month on month; the employee index was 47.0%, down by 0.2 percentage points month on month; and the supplier delivery time index was 50.9%, up by 1.0 percentage points month on month. ■

44 China's CPI rose by 2.7% year on year in May

The data published by NBS on June 12 showed that China's CPI rose by 2.7% year on year in May. In breakdown, the figure rose by 2.7% year on year in urban areas, and 2.8% year on year in rural areas; increased by 7.7% year on year for food prices and 1.6% year on year for non-food prices; rose by 3.2% year on year for consumer goods, and 1.9% year on year for services. The data also showed that China's CPI in May was flat month on month. Among them, the figure was flat month on month in urban areas, and rose by 0.1% month on month in rural areas; increased by 0.2% month on month for food prices and stayed flat for non-food prices; rose by 0.1% month on month for consumer goods and fell by 0.1% month on month for services. ■

45 China's PPI rose by 0.6% year on year in May

The data published by NBS on June 12 showed that China's PPI in May rose by 0.6% year on year and 0.2% month on month. In terms of the year-on-year changes, the price of production materials rose by 0.6% year on year. Among them, the price of mining industry rose by 6.1%, the price of raw material industry fell by 0.6%, and the price of processing industry rose by 0.5%. The price of living materials rose by 0.9%. Among them, the food price rose by 2.2%, the apparel price rose by 1.5%, the price of general daily goods rose by 0.4%, and the price of consumer durables fell by 0.8%. In terms of month-on-month changes, the price of production materials rose by 0.2% month on month. Among them, the price of mining industry rose by 1.9%, the price of raw material industry went up by 0.2%, and the price of processing industry stayed flat. The price of living materials rose by 0.1%. Among them, the food price rose by 0.4%, the apparel price stayed flat, the price of general daily goods rose by 0.1%, and the price of consumer durables fell by 0.2%. ■

46 China's general public budget revenue registered a year-on-year increase of 3.8% from January to May

According to the news released by MOF on June 14, China's general public budget revenue was 8.9919 trillion RMB from January to May, a year-on-year increase of 3.8%. In breakdown, the general public budget revenue of the central level was 4.3397 trillion RMB, an increase of 3.6% year on year; the general public budget revenue of the local level was 4.6522 trillion RMB, an increase of 3.9% year on year. The tax revenue was 7.8493 trillion RMB, a year-on-year increase of 2.2%; the non-tax revenue was 1.1426 trillion RMB, a year-on-year increase of 16.1%. In terms of general public budget expenditures, China's general public budget expenditure was 9.3023 trillion RMB from January to May, a year-on-year increase of 12.5%. Among them, the general public budget expenditure of the central level was 1.3439 trillion RMB, an increase of 12.5% year on year; the general public budget expenditure of the local level was 7.9584 trillion RMB, an increase of 12.5% year on year. In terms of government fund budget revenue and expenditure, China's government fund budget revenue was 2.4744 trillion RMB, down by 3.8% year on year; and the government fund budget expenditure was 2.7857 trillion RMB, a year-on-year increase of 32.8%. ■

47 China issued 304.3 billion RMB of local government bonds in May

According to the news released by MOF on June 17, China issued 304.3 billion RMB of local government bonds in May. Among them, 146.4 billion RMB were general bonds and 157.9 billion RMB were special bonds; according to the purpose of use, 165.7 billion RMB were new bonds, 138.6 billion RMB were swapped bonds and refinanced bonds. The average maturity of local government bonds is 12.0 years, including 10.4 years for new bonds and 13.9 years for refinanced bonds. As of the end of May 2019, the outstanding nationwide local government debts were 19.8953 trillion RMB, which was controlled within the limit approved by NPC. Among them, the general debts were 11.671 trillion RMB, and the special debts were 8.2243 trillion RMB; the government bonds were 19.5802 trillion RMB, and the stock of government debts that are not in the form of government bonds amounted to 315.1 billion RMB. The average remaining maturity of local government bonds is 4.5 years, including 4.5 years for general bonds and 4.6 years for special bonds; the average interest rate is 3.52%, including 3.51% for general bonds and 3.52% for special bonds. ■

48 Total operating income of SOEs in China from January to May increased by 7.7% year on year

The data published by MOF on June 21 showed that the total operating income of SOEs in China from January to May was 23.773 trillion RMB, a year-on-year increase of 7.7%; the total operating cost was 22.92401 trillion RMB, a year-on-year increase of 7.8%; the total profit was 1.3929 trillion RMB, a year-on-year increase of 8.7%; net profit after tax was 1.02808 trillion RMB, up by 9.3% year on year; tax payable was 1.90431 trillion RMB, up by 1.2% year on year. The data also showed that at the end of May, the total assets of SOEs were 192.86409 trillion RMB, up by 8.8% year on year; the total liabilities were 124.36378 trillion RMB, up by 8.5% year on year; and the total owner's equities were 68.50031 trillion RMB, up by 9.3% year on year. ■

49 China's lottery sales totaled 35.523 billion RMB in May

The data released by MOF on June 25 showed that nationwide lottery sales in May were 35.523 billion RMB, down by 12.7% year on year. The welfare lottery sales were 16.493 billion RMB, down by 15.7% year on year. The sports lottery sales were 19.03 billion RMB, down by 10.0% year on year. By type, the lotto lottery sales were 19.035 billion RMB, down by 22.9% year on year; the toto lottery sales were 9.55 billion RMB, down by 5.7% year on year; the instant lottery sales were 2.602 billion RMB, up by 42.5% year on year; the video lottery sales were 4.321 billion RMB, up by 6.8% year on year; and the keno lottery sales were 15 million RMB, up by 47.8% year on year. ■

50 The total profits of major industrial enterprises in China fell by 2.3% year on year from January to May

The data published by NBS on June 27 showed that the profits of major industrial enterprises in China totaled 2.37902 trillion RMB from January to May, down by 2.3% year on year. By types of ownership, the figure stood at 734.23 billion RMB for state-holding enterprises, down by 9.7% year on year; 1.69931 trillion RMB for joint-stock enterprises, up by 0.4%; 577.58 billion RMB for foreign invested enterprises and enterprises funded from Hong Kong, Macao and Taiwan, down by 8.3%; and 607.27 billion RMB for private enterprises, up by 6.6%. ■

51 China's manufacturing PMI in June was 49.4%

The data published by NBS on June 30 showed that China's manufacturing PMI in June was 49.4%, staying flat month on month. In specific terms, the production index was 51.3%, down by 0.4 percentage points month on month; the new order index was 49.6%, down by 0.2 percentage points month on month; the raw material inventory index was 48.2%, up by 0.8 percentage points month on month; the employee index was 46.9%, down by 0.1 percentage points month on month; and the supplier delivery time index was 50.2%, down by 0.7 percentage points month on month. ■

52 China's PPI in June was flat year on year

The data published by NBS on July 10 showed that China's PPI in June was flat year on year, and went down by 0.3% from the previous month. In terms of the changes in the prices of production materials, the prices of production materials fell by 0.3% year on year and by 0.4% month on month. Among them, the price of mining industry rose by 4.5% year on year and fell by 0.1% month on month; the price of raw material industry fell by 2.1% year on year and 1.0% month on month; the processing industry price was flat year on year, and went down by 0.2% from the previous month. In terms of the changes in the price of living materials, the price of living materials rose by 0.9% year on year, which was flat month on month. Among them, food prices rose by 2.2% year on year and stayed flat month on month; apparel prices rose by 1.6% year on year, and stayed flat from the previous month; general daily goods prices rose by 0.5% year on year and up by 0.1% month on month. ■

53 Consumer prices in China rose by 2.7% year on year in June

The data published by NBS on July 10 showed that consumer prices in China rose by 2.7% year on year in June. Among them, the prices in both urban and rural areas rose by 2.7%; food prices rose by 8.3%, non-food prices rose by 1.4%; consumer goods prices rose by 3.2%, and service prices rose by 1.8%. China's consumer prices in June fell by 0.1% from the previous month. Among them, prices in urban areas fell by 0.1%, and prices in rural areas fell by 0.2%; food prices fell by 0.3%, non-food prices fell by 0.1%; consumer goods prices fell by 0.2%, and service prices rose by 0.1%. ■

54 General public budget revenue of China registered a year-on-year increase of 3.4% in the first half of the year

The data published by MOF on July 16 showed that the general public budget revenue of China in the first half of the year was 10.7846 trillion RMB, a year-on-year increase of 3.4%. Among them, the central general public budget revenue was 5.1589 trillion RMB, a year-on-year increase of 3.4%; the local general public budget revenue was 5.6257 trillion RMB, a year-on-year increase of 3.3%. The national tax revenue was 9.2424 trillion RMB, a year-on-year increase of 0.9%; non-tax revenue was 1.5422 trillion RMB, a year-on-year increase of 21.4%. In the first half of the year, China's general public budget expenditure was 12.3538 trillion RMB, a year-on-year increase of 10.7%. Among them, the central general public budget expenditure was 1.689 trillion RMB, a year-on-year increase of 9.9%; the local general public budget expenditure was 10.6648 trillion RMB, a year-on-year increase of 10.8%. ■

55 China's GDP grew by 6.3% year on year in the first half of the year

The data published by NBS on July 15 showed that China's GDP in the first half of the year was 45.0933 trillion RMB, a year-on-year increase of 6.3%. On the quarterly basis, the figure for the first quarter increased by 6.4% year on year, and increased by 6.2% for the second quarter. In terms of industries, the added value of the primary industry was 2.3207 trillion RMB, up by 3.0% year on year; the added value of the secondary industry was 17.9984 trillion RMB, up by 5.8% year on year; the added value of the tertiary industry was 24.7743 trillion RMB, up by 7.0% year on year. Market sales increased steadily. In the first half of the year, the total retail sales of consumer goods reached 19.521 trillion RMB, an increase of 8.4% year on year, and the growth rate was 0.1 percentage points higher than that in the first quarter. The investment growth was basically stable. In the first half of the year, the fixed asset investment (excluding farmer household) was 29.91 trillion RMB, a year-on-year increase of 5.8%, and the growth rate was 0.2 percentage points higher than that from January to May and 0.5 percentage points lower than that in the first quarter. The growth rate of imports and exports increased slightly. The total import and export of goods in the first half of the year was 14.6675 trillion RMB, a year-on-year increase of 3.9%, and the growth rate was 0.2 percentage points higher than that in the first quarter. ■

GDP in 2019

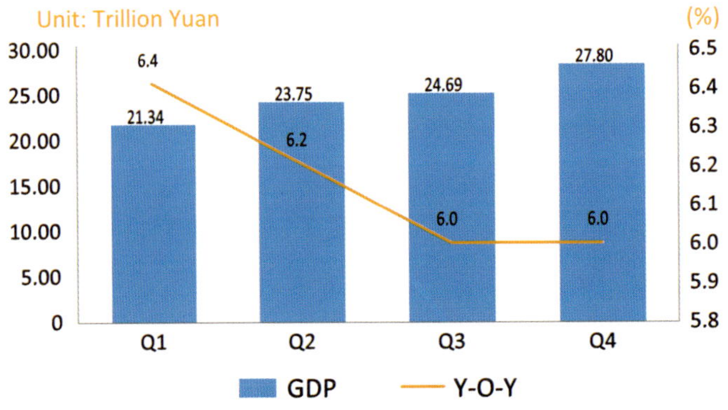

Source: NBS

56 Total operating income of SOEs in China registered an increase of 7.8% year on year from January to June

The data published by MOF on July 22 showed that the total operating income of SOEs in China from January to June was 29.4921 trillion RMB, an increase of 7.8% year on year. Among them, the total operating income of central SOEs was 17.09464 trillion RMB, an increase of 6.2% year on year; the total operating income of local SOEs was 12.39746 trillion RMB, an increase of 10.0% year on year. The total operating cost of SOEs in China from January to June was 28.44518 trillion RMB, an increase of 8.0% year on year. Among them, the total operating cost of central SOEs was 16.23422 trillion RMB, an increase of 6.3% year on year; the total operating cost of local SOEs was 12.21096 trillion RMB, an increase of 10.3% year on year. The total profit of SOEs in China from January to June was 1.82004 trillion RMB, an increase of 7.2% year on year. Among them, the total profit of central SOEs was 1.21753 trillion RMB, an increase of 8.8% year on year; the total profit of local SOEs was 602.51 billion RMB, an increase of 4.1% year on year. ■

57 China issued 899.6 billion RMB of local bonds in June

The data published by MOF on July 19 showed that 899.6 billion RMB of local bonds were issued in June. Among them, 317.8 billion RMB were general bonds and 581.8 billion RMB were special bonds. According to the purpose, 717 billion RMB were new bonds, and 182.6 billion RMB were swapped bonds and refinanced bonds. From January to June, China issued 2.8372 trillion RMB of local government bonds. Among them, 1.2858 trillion RMB were general bonds and 1.5514 trillion RMB were special bonds. According to the purpose, 2.1765 trillion RMB were new bonds and 660.7 billion RMB were swapped bonds and refinanced bonds. After deliberation and approval at the 2nd Meeting of the 13th National People's Congress, the nationwide local government bond limit in 2019 is 24.07743 trillion RMB. Among them, the general debt limit is 13.308922 trillion RMB, and the special debt limit is 10.768508 trillion RMB. As of the end of June 2019, the nationwide local government debt balance was 20.5477 trillion RMB, which was controlled within the limit approved by NPC. Among them, the general debt was 11.8397 trillion RMB, the special debt was 8.708 trillion RMB; the government bonds were 20.2326 trillion RMB, and the outstanding government debts that are not in the form of government bonds was 315.1 billion RMB. ■

58 Total profit of China's major industrial enterprises went down by 2.4% year on year from January to June

The data published by NBS on July 27 showed that the total profit of China's major industrial enterprises from January to June reached 2.984 trillion RMB, down by 2.4% year on year. Among them, the total profit of mining industry was 283.86 billion RMB, up by 4.2% year on year; the total profit of manufacturing industry was 2.46083 trillion RMB, down by 4.1% year on year; the total profit of electricity, heating, gas and water production and supply industry was 239.31 billion RMB, up by 9.0% year on year. Among the major industrial enterprises, the total profit of state holding enterprises was 936.88 billion RMB, down by 8.7% year on year; the total profit of joint-stock enterprises was 2.13906 trillion RMB, up by 0.2% year on year; the total profit of foreign invested enterprises and enterprises funded from Hong Kong, Macao and Taiwan was 718.62 billion RMB, down by 8.4% year on year; the total profit of private enterprises was 743.07 billion RMB, up by 6.0% year on year. ■

59 China's manufacturing PMI in July was 49.7%

The data published by NBS on July 31 showed that China's manufacturing PMI in July was 49.7%, up by 0.3 percentage points from the previous month, indicating the rebound of prosperity. By enterprise scale, the PMI of large enterprises was 50.7%, up by 0.8 percentage points over the previous month, rising to the expansion range; the PMI of small and medium-sized enterprises was 48.7% and 48.2% respectively, down by 0.4 and 0.1 percentage points from the previous month, staying below the critical points. Specifically, among the five sub-indices that constitute the manufacturing PMI, the production index and supplier delivery time index were above the critical points, and the new order index, raw material inventory index and employee index were below the critical points. The production index was 52.1%, up by 0.8 percentage points from the previous month and was above the critical points, indicating that the overall expansion of manufacturing production had accelerated; the new order index was 49.8%, up by 0.2 percentage points from the previous month and was below the critical points, indicating that the decline in orders for manufactured products had narrowed; the raw material inventory index was 48.0%, down by 0.2 percentage points from the previous month and was below the critical points, indicating that the main raw material inventory of the manufacturing industry had decreased; the employee index was 47.1%, up by 0.2 percentage points from the previous month and was below the critical points, indicating that the manufacturing industry's employment prosperity level had rebounded slightly; the supplier delivery time index was 50.1%, down by 0.1 percentage points over the previous month and was above the critical points, indicating that the manufacturing raw material supplier's delivery time had slightly accelerated. ■

60 China's Economic Development New Driver Index in 2018 grew by 28.7% year on year

The data published by NBS on July 31 showed that with year 2014 as the baseline of 100, China's Economic Development New Driver Index from 2015-2018 was 123.5, 156.7, 210.1 and 270.3 respectively, an increase of 23.5%, 26.9%, 34.1% and 28.7% year on year, suggesting a sustained and rapid growth momentum. In 2018, the five sub-indices achieved different degree of increase. First, the cyber economy index. In 2018, the cyber economy index was 605.4, a year-on-year increase of 67.2%, contributing to 80.8% of the overall index growth. Second, the innovation drive index. In 2018, the innovation drive index was 174.4, a year-on-year increase of 21.8%, contributing to 10.3% of the overall index growth. Third, the transformation and upgrading index. In 2018, the transformation and upgrading index was 143.9, an increase of 8.8% year on year, contributing to 3.9% of the overall index growth. Fourth, the economic vitality index. The economic vitality index for 2018 was 292.0, an increase of 2.7% year on year, contributing to 2.6% of the overall index growth. Fifth, the knowledge capability index. In 2018, the knowledge capability index was 135.9, an increase of 5.8% over the previous year, contributing to 2.4% of the overall index growth. ■

61 Value-added of industrial enterprises above the designated size increased by 4.8% year on year in China in July

The data published by NBS on August 14 showed that the value-added of industrial enterprises above the designated size increased by 4.8% year on year in July and increased by 0.19% month on month. From January to July, the value-added of industrial enterprises above a designated size increased by 5.8% year on year. In terms of three categories, the value-added of the mining industry increased by 6.6% year on year in July, 0.7 percentage points lower than that in June; the value-added of the manufacturing industry increased by 4.5%, down by 1.7 percentage points; the value-added of the electricity, thermal, gas and water production and supply industry grew by 6.9%, accelerating by 0.3 percentage points. In terms of ownership types, the value-added of state-owned and holding companies increased by 3.7% year on year in July; the value-added of joint-stock enterprises increased by 6.1%; the value-added of foreign-invested enterprises as well as enterprises invested by Hong Kong, Macao and Taiwan decreased by 0.2%; the value-added of private enterprises increased by 7.3%. In terms of sectors, 36 of the 41 major sectors in July maintained a year-on-year increase in value-added. In terms of regions, the value-added of the eastern region increased by 3.0% in July, the central region increased by 7.2%, the western region increased by 7.1%, and the northeast region increased by 2.9%. In terms of products, the value-added of the 336 of the 605 products in July maintained a year-on-year increase. ■

62 China's general public budget revenue from January to July registered an increase of 3.1% year on year

The data published by MOF on August 16 showed that China's general public budget revenue from January to July was 12.5623 trillion RMB, an increase of 3.1% year on year. Among them, the central general public budget revenue was 6.0411 trillion RMB, an increase of 3.3% year on year; the local general public budget revenue was 6.5212 trillion RMB, an increase of 3% year on year. The tax revenue of the national general public budget revenue was 10.8046 trillion RMB, a year-on-year increase of 0.3%; the non-tax revenue was 1.7577 trillion RMB, a year-on-year increase of 24.8%. From January to July, the general public budget expenditure was 13.7963 trillion RMB, a year-on-year increase of 9.9%. Among them, the central general public budget expenditure was 1.9608 trillion RMB, a year-on-year increase of 9.5%; the local general public budget expenditure was 11.8355 trillion RMB, a year-on-year increase of 10%. China's governmental fund budget revenue from January to July was 3.8691 trillion RMB, a year-on-year increase of 5.5%. Among them, the central governmental fund budget revenue was 227.7 billion RMB, an increase of 3.1% year on year; the local governmental fund budget revenue was 3.6414 trillion RMB, an increase of 5.6% year on year. From January to July, the governmental fund budget expenditure was 4.4446 trillion RMB, a year-on-year increase of 33.8%. Among them, the central governmental fund budget expenditure was 130.9 billion RMB, a year-on-year increase of 43.1%; the local governmental fund budget expenditure was 4.3137 trillion RMB, an increase of 33.5% year on year. ■

63 Total operating income of SOEs registered a year-on-year increase of 7.7% from January to July

The data published by MOF on August 26 showed that the main economic indicators of state-owned enterprises (SOEs) in China continued to grow from January to July. The tax payable increased at a low rate, and the tax and fee cut policies have paid off. From January to July, the total operating income of SOEs was 34.47 trillion RMB, a year-on-year increase of 7.7%. Among them, the total operating income of central SOEs was 19.9482 trillion RMB, a year-on-year increase of 6.2%; the total operating income of local SOEs was 14.5218 trillion RMB, a year-on-year increase of 10.0%. From January to July, the total operating cost of SOEs was 33.25265 trillion RMB, a year-on-year increase of 7.9%. Among them, the total operating cost of central SOEs was 18.95165 trillion RMB, a year-on-year increase of 6.3%; the total operating cost of local SOEs was 14.301 trillion RMB, a year-on-year increase of 10.2%. From January to July, the total profit of SOEs was 2.13662 trillion RMB, a year-on-year increase of 7.3%. Among them, the total profit of central SOEs was 1.4119 trillion RMB, a year-on-year increase of 7.7%; the total profit of local SOEs was 724.72 billion RMB, a year-on-year increase of 6.6%. From January to July, the tax payable of SOEs was 2.66456 trillion RMB, a year-on-year increase of 0.5%. Among them, the tax payable of central SOEs was 1.90709 trillion RMB, a year-on-year increase of 0.8%; the tax payable of local SOEs was 757.47 billion RMB, down by 0.1% year on year. From January to July, the ratio of profits to cost was 6.5%, which was basically flat from the same period of last year. Among them, the ratio of profits to cost of central SOEs was 7.6%, an increase of 0.1 percentage points; the ratio of profits to cost and expense of local SOEs was 5.1%, down by 0.2 percentage points. At the end of July, the asset-liability ratio of SOEs was 64.4%, a decrease of 0.2 percentage points. Among them, the asset-liability ratio of central SOEs was 67.5%, down by 0.3 percentage points; the asset-liability ratio of local SOEs was 62.1%, down by 0.1 percentage points. ■

64 Total profits of major industrial enterprises went down by 1.7% year on year from January to July

The data published by NBS on August 27 showed that the profits of major industrial enterprises in China totaled 3.4977 trillion RMB from January to July, down by 1.7% year on year. By sectors, the figure stood at 335.44 billion RMB for the mining sector, up by 4.2%; 2.87737 trillion RMB for the manufacturing sector, down by 3.4%; and 284.89 billion RMB for the electricity, thermal, gas and water production and supply sector, up by 10.6%. By types of ownership, the figure stood at 1.08374 trillion RMB for stated-holding enterprises, down by 8.1% year on year; 2.5033 trillion RMB for joint-stock enterprises, up by 0.6%; 850.24 billion RMB for foreign invested enterprises, and enterprises funded from Hong Kong, Macao and Taiwan, down by 6.9%; and 884.91 billion RMB for private enterprises, up by 7.0%. ■

65 China's lottery sales totaled 32.734 billion RMB in July

The data released by MOF on August 30 showed that nationwide lottery sales in July were 32.734 billion RMB, down by 40.1% year on year. The welfare lottery sales were 15.046 billion RMB, down by 21.3% year on year. The sports lottery sales were 17.688 billion RMB, down by 50.2% year on year. By type, the lotto lottery sales were 19.115 billion RMB, down by 18.3% year on year; the toto lottery sales were 8.189 billion RMB, down by 68.1% year on year; the instant lottery sales were 2.206 billion RMB, up by 40.8% year on year; the video lottery sales were 3.208 billion RMB, down by 18.8% year on year; and the keno lottery sales were 16 million RMB, up by 48.5% year on year. ■

66 China's manufacturing PMI in August was 49.5%

The data released by NBS on August 31 showed that China's manufacturing PMI in August was 49.5%, a slight decrease of 0.2 percentage points from the previous month. By enterprise scale, the PMI of large enterprises was 50.4%, 0.3 percentage points lower than that of the previous month and remained in the expansionary range; the PMI of medium-sized enterprises was 48.2%, 0.5 percentage points lower than that of the previous month and stayed below the critical points; the PMI of small enterprises was 48.6%, up by 0.4 percentage points from the previous month and stayed below the critical points. Among the five sub-indices that constitute the manufacturing PMI, the production index and supplier delivery time index were above the critical points, and the new order index, raw material inventory index and employee index were below the critical points. Among them, the production index was 51.9%, down by 0.2 percentage points from the previous month and was above the critical points, indicating the overall expansion of manufacturing production; the new order index was 49.7%, down by 0.1 percentage points from the previous month and was below the critical points, indicating the fall of order for manufactured products; the raw material inventory index was 47.5%, down by 0.5 percentage points from the previous month and was below the critical points, indicating the decline of the inventory of major raw materials in the manufacturing industry; the employee index was 46.9%, down by 0.2 percentage points from the previous month and was below the critical points, indicating the decrease of employment in the manufacturing industry; the supplier delivery time index was 50.3%, up by 0.2 percentage points from the previous month and was above the critical points, indicating the faster delivery of raw material suppliers for manufacturing industry. ■

67 China's government procurement in 2018 reached 3.58614 trillion RMB

The data published by MOF on September 6 showed that China's government procurement in 2018 reached 3.58614 trillion RMB, an increase of 11.7% over the previous year, accounting for 10.5% and 4% of the national fiscal expenditure and GDP respectively. The scale of the procurement of goods and engineering grew steadily, and the scale of the procurement of services increased rapidly. The procurement of goods was 806.53 billion RMB, accounting for 22.5% of the nationwide government procurement, an increase of 0.8%; the procurement of engineering was 1.57142 trillion RMB, accounting for 43.8% of the nationwide government procurement, an increase of 3.3%; the procurement of services was 1.20819 trillion RMB, accounting for 33.7% of the nationwide government procurement, an increase of 35.7%. The proportion of centralized procurement continued to decline, and the proportion of decentralized procurement continued to rise. The government centralized procurement was 1.57678 trillion RMB, accounting for 44% of the nationwide government procurement; the departmental centralized procurement was 521.11

billion RMB, accounting for 14.5% of the nationwide government procurement; the decentralized procurement was 1.48825 trillion RMB, accounting for 41.5% of the nationwide government procurement. The open-tendering procurement still dominates, and the scale of procurement from a single source has declined. The proportion of the open-tendering procurement was 70.5%, the invitation-to-tender procurement was 1.1%, the competitive-negotiation procurement was 3.6%, the competitive-consultation procurement was 8.3%, the inquiry procurement was 2.3%, and the single-source procurement was 11.8%. ■

68

Consumer prices in China rose by 2.8% year on year in August

The data published by NBS on September 10 showed that consumer prices in China rose by 2.8% year on year in August. Among them, the prices went up by 2.8% in urban areas and rose by 3.1% in rural areas; food prices rose by 10.0%, non-food prices rose by 1.1%; consumer goods prices rose by 3.6%, and service prices rose by 1.6%. China's consumer prices in August rose by 0.7% from the previous month. Among them, prices in urban areas increased by 0.6%, and prices in rural areas rose by 1.0%; food prices rose by 3.2%, non-food prices rose by 0.1%; consumer goods prices rose by 1.1%, and service prices rose by 0.2%. ■

69

China's general public budget revenue from January to August registered a year-on-year increase of 3.2%

The data published by MOF on September 17 showed that China's general public budget revenue from January to August was 13.7061 trillion RMB, a year-on-year increase of 3.2%. Among them, the central general public budget revenue was 6.5901 trillion RMB, a year-on-year increase of 3.5%; the local general public budget revenue was 7.116 trillion RMB, a year-on-year increase of 2.8%. The national tax revenue was 11.7134 trillion RMB, down by 0.1% year on year; non-tax revenue was 1.9927 trillion RMB, up by 27.3% year on year. From January to August, the general public budget expenditure was 15.3069 trillion RMB, a year-on-year increase of 8.8%. Among them, the central general public budget expenditure was 2.2185 trillion RMB, an increase of 8.6% year on year; the local general public budget expenditure was 13.0884 trillion RMB, an increase of 8.8% year on year. China's governmental fund budget revenue from January to August was 4.5987 trillion RMB, a year-on-year increase of 6.4%. Among them, the central governmental fund budget revenue was 281.3 billion RMB, a year-on-year increase of 1.1%; the local governmental fund budget revenue was 4.3174 trillion RMB, a year-on-year increase of 6.7%. From January to August, governmental fund budget expenditure was 5.2745 trillion RMB, a year-on-year increase of 30.8%. Among them, the central governmental fund budget expenditure was 161.5 billion RMB, a year-on-year increase of 18.6%; the local governmental fund budget expenditure was 5.113 trillion RMB, a year-on-year increase of 31.2%. ■

70

China issued 569.5 billion RMB of local government bonds in August

The data published by MOF on September 18 showed that 569.5 billion RMB of local government bonds were issued in August, among which, 163.2 billion RMB were general bonds and 406.3 billion RMB were special bonds; 342.1 billion RMB were new bonds and 227.4 billion RMB were swapped bonds and refinanced bonds. From January to August, 3.9626 trillion RMB of local government bonds were issued, among which, 1.611 trillion RMB were general bonds and 2.3516 trillion RMB were special bonds; 2.8951 trillion RMB were new bonds and 1.0675 trillion RMB were swapped bonds and refinanced bonds. With the review and approval of the Second Meeting of the 13th National People's Congress, the limit of Chinese local government bonds in 2019 is 24.07743 trillion RMB. Among them, the general debt limit is 13.308922 trillion RMB, and the special debt limit is 10.768508 trillion RMB. As of the end of August 2019, the outstanding local government debt in China was 21.4139 trillion RMB, which was controlled within the limit approved by NPC. Among them, the general debt was 11.9622 trillion RMB, the special debt was 9.4517 trillion RMB; the government bonds were 21.0231 trillion RMB, and the outstanding government debts that are not in the form of government bonds was 390.8 billion RMB. ■

71

The total operating income of SOEs registered a year-on-year increase of 7.4% from January to August

The data released by MOF on September 25 showed that the main economic indicators of SOEs in China from January to August continued to grow, and the asset-liability ratio continued to fall. From January to August, the total operating income of SOEs was 39.4884 trillion RMB, a year-on-year increase of 7.4%. Among them, the total operating income of central SOEs was 22.85993 trillion RMB, a year-on-year increase of 5.8%; the total operating income of local SOEs was 16.62847 trillion RMB, a year-on-year increase of 9.7%. From January to August, the total operating cost of SOEs was 38.11799 trillion RMB, a year-on-year increase of 7.7%. Among them, the total operating cost of central SOEs was 21.72953 trillion RMB, a year-on-year increase of 6.0%; the total operating cost of local SOEs was 16.38846 trillion RMB, a year-on-year increase of 10.0%. From January to August, the total profit of SOEs was 2.40931 trillion RMB, a year-on-year increase of 6.1%. Among them, the total profit of central SOEs was 1.59929 trillion RMB, a year-on-year increase of 6.6%; the total profit of local SOEs was 810.02 billion RMB, a year-on-year increase of 5.1%. From January to August, the tax payable of SOEs was 3.00598 trillion RMB, a year-on-year decrease of 0.3%. Among them, the tax payable of central SOEs was 2.15564 trillion RMB, down by 0.4% year on year; the tax payable of local SOEs was 850.34 billion RMB, an increase of 0.1% year on year. From January to August, the profit to cost ratio of SOEs was 6.4%, down by 0.1 percentage points. Among them, the profit to cost ratio of central SOEs was 7.5%, which was the same as that of the same period of previous year; the profit to cost ratio of local SOEs was 5.0%, down by 0.2 percentage points. At the end of August, the asset-liability ratio of SOEs was 64.4%, down by 0.1 percentage points. Among them, the asset-liability ratio of central SOEs was 67.5%, down by 0.2 percentage points; the asset-liability ratio of local SOEs was 62.2%, which was the same as that of the same period of previous year. ■

72 China's lottery sales totaled 34.081 billion RMB in August

The data released by MOF on September 27 showed that nationwide lottery sales in August were 34.081 billion RMB, down by 18.5% year on year. The welfare lottery sales were 14.606 billion RMB, down by 17.9% year on year. The sports lottery sales were 19.476 billion RMB, down by 19.0% year on year. By type, the lotto lottery sales were 18.799 billion RMB, down by 15.4% year on year; the toto lottery sales were 10.222 billion RMB, down by 27.8% year on year; the instant lottery sales were 2.191 billion RMB, up by 40.1% year on year; the video lottery sales were 2.854 billion RMB, down by 26.0% year on year; and the keno lottery sales were 15 million RMB, down by 2.8% year on year. ■

73 China's manufacturing PMI in September was 49.8%

The data published by NBS on September 30 showed that China's manufacturing PMI in September was 49.8%, up by 0.3 percentage points from the previous month. By the scale of enterprises, the PMI of large enterprises was 50.8%, up by 0.4 percentage points from the previous month, and continued to remain in the expansionary range; the PMI of small and medium-sized enterprises was 48.6% and 48.8% respectively, up by 0.4 and 0.2 percentage points. Among the five sub-indices that constitute the manufacturing PMI, the production index, the new order index and the supplier delivery time index were above the critical points, and the raw material inventory index and the employee index were below the critical points. The production index was 52.3%, up by 0.4 percentage points from the previous month and was above the critical points, indicating that the expansion of the manufacturing industry had accelerated; the new order index was 50.5%, up by 0.8 percentage points from the previous month and rose above the critical points, indicating that the order of manufactured products had increased; the raw material inventory index was 47.6%, a slight increase of 0.1 percentage points from the previous month and was below the critical points, indicating that the decline in the main raw material inventory of the manufacturing industry had slightly narrowed; the employee index was 47.0%, a slight increase of 0.1 percentage points from the previous month and was below the critical points, indicating that the employment by the manufacturing industry had fallen by a small margin; the supplier delivery time index was 50.5%, up by 0.2 percentage points from the previous month and was above the critical points, indicating that the delivery time of raw material suppliers in the manufacturing industry had accelerated. ■

PMI in 2019

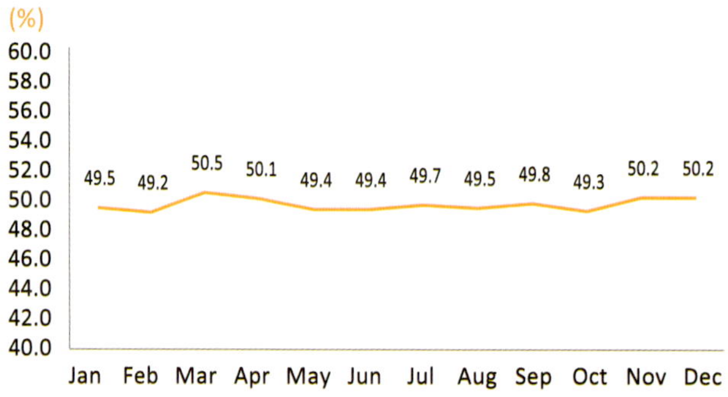

Source: NBS

74 Changes in the market prices of important production materials in the circulation sector in late September 2019

The data published by NBS on October 9 showed that compared with the mid-September of 2019, the prices of 18 products have increased, the prices of 22 products have decreased, and the prices of 10 products have stayed flat in the late-September of 2019. The first category is ferrous metals, in which rebar prices rose by 0.1%, wire prices fell by 0.1%, ordinary mid-plate prices fell by 0.2%, hot-rolled ordinary sheet prices fell by 0.6%, seamless steel pipe prices fell by 0.5%, and steel angle prices rose by 0.1%. The second category is non-ferrous metals, in which the price of electrolytic copper fell by 0.6%, the price of aluminum ingots fell by 1.3%, the price of lead ingots fell by 0.8%, and the price of zinc ingots fell by 2.0%. The third category is chemical products, in which sulfuric acid prices fell by 2.3%, caustic soda prices rose by 5.8%, methanol prices rose by 5.7%, pure benzene prices fell by 0.8%, styrene prices fell by 2.9%, and polyethylene prices rose by 0.4%, polypropylene prices rose by 0.7%, PVC prices fell by 0.6%, butadiene rubber prices rose by 10.1%, and polyester filament prices fell by 1.6%. The fourth category is oil and gas. Among them, the prices of liquefied natural gas fell by 0.7%, the prices of liquefied petroleum gas decreased by 0.7%, the prices of gasoline (95#National VI) rose by 1.2%, the prices of gasoline (92#National VI) rose by 1.5%, the prices of diesel were flat, and the prices of paraffin were flat. The fifth category is coal, in which the prices of anthracite, ordinary mixed coal, Shanxi mixed coal, Shanxi quality mixed coal, Datong mixed coal, coking coal and coke were all flat. The sixth category is non-metallic building materials, in which the prices of composite Portland cement increased by 1.3%, the prices of ordinary Portland cement rose by 1.5%, and the prices of float flat glass rose by 1.0%. The seventh category is agricultural products, in which rice prices rose by 0.1%, wheat prices rose by 0.1%, corn prices fell by 1.7%, cotton prices fell by 0.3%, hog prices rose by 0.7%, soybean prices fell by 2.5%, soybean meal prices rose by 0.5%, and peanut prices were flat. The eighth category is agricultural production materials, in which urea prices fell by 1.2%, compound fertilizer prices fell by 0.6%, and pesticide prices rose by 1.2%. The ninth category is forest products, in which the prices of wood-based panels fell by 0.4%, the prices of pulp fell by 0.1%, and the prices of corrugated paper rose by 0.4%. ■

75 China's CPI rose by 3.0% year on year in September

The data released by NBS on October 15 showed that China's CPI rose by 3.0% year on year in September. Among them, CPI rose by 2.8% in urban areas and 3.6% in rural areas; went up by 11.2% for food and 1.0% for non-food; rose by 4.0% for consumer goods and 1.3% for services. From January to September, the average CPI rose by 2.5% over the same period of last year. In September, CPI rose by 0.9% month on month. Among them, CPI rose by 0.7% in urban areas and 1.3% in rural areas; went up by 3.5% for food and 0.2% for non-food; rose by 1.5% for consumer goods and fell by 0.1% for services. ■

76 China's PPI fell by 1.2% year on year in September

The data released by NBS on October 15 showed that China's PPI in September fell by 1.2% year on year, and rose by 0.1% month on month; IPI fell by 1.7% year on year and rose by 0.2% month on month. From January to September, the average PPI was flat from the same period of last year and the average IPI fell by 0.3%. ■

77 China issued 219.6 billion RMB of local government bonds in September

The data published by MOF on October 24 showed that 219.6 billion RMB of local government bonds were issued in September, among which, 56.6 billion RMB were general bonds and 163 billion RMB were special bonds; 141.6 billion RMB were new bonds and 78 billion RMB were swapped bonds and refinanced bonds. From January to September, 4.1822 trillion RMB of local government bonds were issued, among which, 1.6676 trillion RMB were general bonds and 2.5146 trillion RMB were special bonds; 3.0367 trillion RMB were new bonds and 1.1455 trillion RMB were swapped bonds and refinanced bonds. With the review and approval of the Second Meeting of the 13th National People's Congress, the limit of Chinese local government bonds in 2019 is 24.07743 trillion RMB. Among them, the general debt limit is 13.308922 trillion RMB, and the special debt limit is 10.768508 trillion RMB. ■

78 Value-added of industrial enterprises above designated size increased by 5.8% year on year in China in September

The data published by NBS on October 18 showed that the value-added of industrial enterprises above designated size increased by 5.8% year on year in September and increased by 0.72% month on month. From January to September, the value-added of industrial enterprises above designated size increased by 5.6% year on year. In terms of three categories, the value-added of the mining industry increased by 8.1% year on year in September, 4.4 percentage points higher than that in August; the value-added of the manufacturing industry increased by 5.6%, up by 1.3 percentage points; the value-added of the electricity, thermal, gas and water production and supply industry grew by 5.9%, staying flat from August. In terms of ownership types, the value-added of state-owned and holding companies increased by 4.9% year on year in September; the value-added of joint-stock enterprises increased by 6.9%; the value-added of foreign-invested enterprises as well as enterprises funded from Hong Kong, Macao and Taiwan increased by 2.9%; the value-added of private enterprises increased by 6.7%. In terms of sectors, 35 of the 41 major sectors in September maintained a year-on-year increase in value-added. In terms of regions, the value-added of the eastern region increased by 5.2% in September, the central region increased by 7.5%, the western region increased by 8.2%, and the northeast region increased by 3.6%. In terms of products, the value-added of the 321 of the 605 products in September maintained a year-on-year increase. ■

79 Total operating revenue of SOEs registered a year-on-year increase of 7.1% from January to September

The data published by MOF on October 25 showed that the major economic indicators of state-owned enterprises (SOEs) in China continued to grow from January to September, and their taxes and fees payable continued to decline. From January to September, the total operating revenue of SOEs was 44.89088 trillion RMB, a year-on-year increase of 7.1%. Among them, the total revenue of central SOEs was 26.01326 trillion RMB, a year-on-year increase of 5.5%; the total revenue of local SOEs was 18.87762 trillion RMB, a year-on-year increase of 9.2%. From January to September, the total operating cost of SOEs was 43.38484 trillion RMB, a year-on-year increase of 7.3%. Among them, the total cost of central SOEs was 24.76454 trillion RMB, a year-on-year increase of 5.8%; the total cost of local SOEs was 18.6203 trillion RMB, a year-on-year increase of 9.5%. From January to September, the total profit of SOEs was 2.7163 trillion RMB, a year-on-year increase of 6.6%. Among them, the total profit of central SOEs was 1.79416 trillion RMB, a year-on-year increase of 6.8%; the total profit of local SOEs was 922.14 billion RMB, a year-on-year increase of 6.3%. From January to September, the taxes and fees payable of SOEs were 3.39148 trillion RMB, a year-on-year decrease of 0.5%. Among them, the taxes and fees payable of central SOEs were 2.43341 trillion RMB, down by 0.5% year on year; the taxes and fees payable of local SOEs were 958.07 billion RMB, down by 0.5% year on year. From January to September, the ratio of profit to cost & expenses of SOEs was 6.3%, which was the same as that of the same period of the previous year. Among them, the ratio of profit to cost & expenses of central SOEs was 7.4%, an increase of 0.1 percentage points; the ratio of profit to cost & expenses of local SOEs was 5.0%, down by 0.2 percentage points. At the end of September, the asset-liability ratio of SOEs was 64.4%, a decrease of 0.1 percentage points. Among them, the asset-liability ratio of central SOEs was 67.4%, down by 0.2 percentage points; the asset-liability ratio of local SOEs was 62.2%, an increase of 0.1 percentage points. ■

80 Total profit of industrial enterprises above designated size in China fell by 2.1% year on year from January to September

The data published by NBS on October 27 showed that the total profit of industrial enterprises above designated size in China was 4.59335 trillion RMB from January to September, down by 2.1% year on year. Among them, the total profit of mining industry was 427.94 billion RMB, a year-on-year increase of 3.1%; the total profit of manufacturing industry was 3.79042 trillion RMB, down by 3.9% year on year; the total profit of electricity, heating, gas and water production and supply industry was 374.99 billion RMB, a year-on-year increase 12.3%. Among the industrial enterprises above designated size, the total profit of state-owned and holding enterprises was 936.88 billion RMB, down by 8.7% year on year; the total profit of joint-stock enterprises was 2.13906 trillion RMB, a year-on-year increase of 0.2%; the total profit of foreign invested enterprises and enterprises funded from Hong Kong, Macao and Taiwan was 718.62 billion RMB, a year-on-year decline of 8.4%; the total profit of private enterprises was 743.07 billion RMB, a year-on-year increase of 6.0%. ■

81 Operating income of major enterprises in cultural and related industries registered a year-on-year increase of 7.6% in the first three quarters of 2019

The data published by NBS on October 31 showed that in the first three quarters of 2019, the operating income of major enterprises in cultural and related industries reached 6.2187 trillion RMB, a year-on-year increase of 7.6%. By industry categories, 8 of the 9 cultural and related industries achieved growth in operating income. By the specific types of industries, the operating income of cultural manufacturing industry was 2.6569 trillion RMB, up by 4.2% year on year; the operating income of cultural wholesale and retail industry was 998.3 billion RMB, up by 5.4% year on year; the operating income of cultural service industry was 2.5636 trillion RMB, up by 12.4% year on year. By specific sectors, the operating income in the core cultural sector was 3.7065 trillion RMB, a year-on-year increase of 10.8%; the operating income of cultural related sector was 2.5122 trillion RMB, a year-on-year increase of 3.3%. By regions, the operating income of major enterprises in cultural and related industries in the eastern region was 4.7017 trillion RMB, a year-on-year increase of 6.7%, accounting for 75.6% of the national total; the figure for the central, western and northeastern region was 884.1 billion RMB, 572.7 billion RMB and 60.2 billion RMB respectively, up by 9.4%, up by 13.8%, and down by 1.2% respectively, accounting for 14.2%, 9.2% and 1.0% of the national total. ■

82 China's PPI fell by 1.6% in October year on year

The data published by NBS on November 9 showed that China's PPI fell by 1.6% in October year on year and rose by 0.1% month on month. In terms of the year-on-year changes, the price of production materials decreased by 2.6%, among them, the price of mining industry decreased by 1.9%, the price of raw material industry decreased by 5.6%, and the price of processing industry decreased by 1.5%; the price of consumer service materials rose by 1.4%, among them, food price rose by 4.4%, apparel price rose by 0.6%, price of daily necessities rose by 0.4%, and price of durable consumer goods fell by 1.8%. In terms of the month-on-month changes, the price of production materials was flat, among which, the price of mining industry rose by 0.2%, the price of raw materials industry was flat, and the price of processing industry fell by 0.1%; the price of consumer service materials rose by 0.3%, among which, food price rose by 1.1%, apparel price was flat, price of daily necessities fell by 0.2%, and price of durable consumer goods fell by 0.1%. ■

83 China's CPI rose by 3.8% year on year in October

The data published by NBS on November 9 showed that China's CPI rose by 3.8% year on year in October. Among them, the price of urban areas rose by 3.5% year on year, the price of rural areas rose by 4.6% year on year; food price rose by 15.5% year on year, non-food price rose by 0.9% year on year; consumer goods price rose by 5.2% year on year, and service price rose by 1.4% year on year. China's CPI rose by 0.9% month on month in October. Among them, the price of urban areas rose by 0.8% month on month, the price of rural areas rose by 1.2% month on month; food price rose by 3.6% month on month, non-food price rose by 0.2% month on month; consumer price rose by 1.4% month on month, and service price was flat. ■

84 China's lottery sales totaled 36.399 billion RMB in September

The data released by MOF on November 14 showed that nationwide lottery sales in September were

36.399 billion RMB, down by 13.0% year on year. The Welfare Lottery sales were 15.692 billion RMB, down by 12.0% year on year. The Sports Lottery sales were 20.707 billion RMB, down by 13.8% year on year. By type, the Lotto Lottery sales were 19.324 billion RMB, down by 9.8% year on year; the Toto Lottery sales were 11.425 billion RMB, down by 21.7% year on year; the Instant Lottery sales were 2.526 billion RMB, up by 29.5% year on year; the Video Lottery sales were 3.109 billion RMB, down by 19.6% year on year; and the Keno Lottery sales were 15 million RMB, up by 50.2% year on year.

85 China's general public budget revenue from January to October registered a year-on-year increase of 3.8%

The data released by MOF on November 19 showed that China's general public budget revenue was 16.7704 trillion RMB from January to October, a year-on-year increase of 3.8%. Among them, the central general public budget revenue was 8.0662 trillion RMB, a year-on-year increase of 4.4%; the local general public budget revenue was 8.7042 trillion RMB, a year-on-year increase of 3.3%. The tax revenue of the national general public budget revenue was 14.1514 trillion RMB, a year-on-year increase of 0.4%; the non-tax revenue was 2.619 trillion RMB, a year-on-year increase of 27.1%. The national general public budget expenditure was 19.0587 trillion RMB from January to October, a year-on-year increase of 8.7%. Among them, the central general public budget expenditure was 2.7577 trillion RMB, an increase of 9.0% year on year; the local general public budget expenditure was 16.301 trillion RMB, an increase of 8.7% year on year. From January to October, the national governmental fund budget revenue was 6.0206 trillion RMB, an increase of 8.7% year on year. By central and local governments, the central governmental fund budget revenue was 346.6 billion RMB, up by 2.7% year on year; the local governmental fund budget revenue was 5.674 trillion RMB, up by 9.1% year on year. From January to October, the national governmental fund budget expenditure was 6.8647 trillion RMB, a year-on-year increase of 22.6%. By central and local governments, the central governmental fund budget expenditure was 202 billion RMB, down by 10.1% year on year; the local governmental fund budget expenditure was 6.6627 trillion RMB, a year-on-year increase of 24%. ■

86 Total operating income of SOEs registered a year-on-year increase of 6.5% from January to October

The data published by MOF on November 27 showed that the major economic indicators of SOEs in China maintained an upward trend from January to October while their taxes and fees payable continued to decline. From January to October, the total operating income of SOEs was 50.12905 trillion RMB, a year-on-year increase of 6.5%. Among them, the total income of central SOEs was 29.00245 trillion RMB, a year-on-year increase of 5.4%; the total income of local SOEs was 21.1266 trillion RMB, a year-on-year increase of 8.1%. From January to October, the total operating cost of SOEs was 48.49386 trillion RMB, a year-on-year increase of 6.7%. Among them, the total cost of central SOEs was 27.66145 trillion RMB, an increase of 5.5% year on year; the total cost of local SOEs was 20.83241 trillion RMB, an increase of 8.3% year on year. From January to October, the total profit of SOEs was 2.9394 trillion RMB, a year-on-year increase of 5.4%. Among them, the total profit of central SOEs was 1.94176 trillion RMB, a year-on-year increase of 7.5%; the total profit of local SOEs was 997.64 billion RMB, a year-on-year increase of 1.6%. ■

87

China issued 96.46 billion RMB of local government bonds in October

The data published by MOF on November 27 showed that China issued 96.46 billion RMB of local government bonds in October. Among them, 79.576 billion RMB were general bonds and 16.884 billion RMB were special bonds. By purposes, no new bonds were issued, and 96.46 billion RMB were swapped bonds and refinanced bonds. From January to October, China issued 4.2787 trillion RMB of local government bonds. Among them, 1.7472 trillion RMB were general bonds, 2.5315 trillion RMB were special bonds. By purposes, there were 3.0367 trillion RMB new bonds, 1.242 trillion yuan swapped bonds and refinanced bonds. In 2019, the national local government debt limit was 24.07743 trillion RMB. Among them, the general debt limit was 13.308922 trillion yuan, while special the debt limit was 10.768508 trillion RMB. ■

88

China's manufacturing PMI in November was 50.2%

The data published by NBS on November 30 showed that China's manufacturing PMI in November was 50.2%, an increase of 0.9% month on month. By the scale of enterprises, the PMI of large enterprises was 50.9%, an increase of 1.0% from the previous month; the PMI of medium-sized enterprises was 49.5%, an increase of 0.5% from the previous month; the PMI of small enterprises was 49.4%, an increase of 1.5% from the previous month. In terms of the specific indexes, the production index was 52.6%, an increase of 1.8% from the previous month; the new order index was 51.3%, an increase of 1.7% from the previous month; the raw material inventory index was 47.8%, an increase of 0.4% from the previous month; the employment index was 47.3%, flat from the previous month; and the supplier delivery time index was 50.5%, up by 0.4% from the previous month. ■

89

99% of the annual issuance tasks of local bonds were completed from January to November

The data published by MOF on December 4 showed that from January to November, 4.3244 trillion RMB of local bonds were issued, completing 99% of the annual issuance tasks, among which, 3.0354 trillion RMB were new bonds, 1.1461 trillion RMB were refinanced bonds, and 142.9 billion RMB were swapped bonds. Among the new bonds, 905.7 billion RMB were general bonds and 2.1297 trillion RMB were special bonds. ■

90

China's PPI in November fell by 1.4% year on year

The data published by NBS on December 10 showed that China's PPI in November fell by 1.4% year on year and 0.1% month on month. In terms of the year-on-year changes, the prices of means of production fell by 2.5% year on year, of which the prices of extractive industries fell by 1.4% year on year, the prices of raw materials industries fell by 5.0% year on year, and the prices of processing industries fell by 1.6% year on year; the prices of means of consumption rose by 1.6% year on year, of which food prices rose by 5.4% year on year, apparel prices rose by 0.3% year on year, prices of daily necessity goods rose by 0.1% year on year, and the prices of durable consumer goods fell by 2.1% year on year. In terms of the month-on-month changes, the prices of means of production fell by 0.2% month on month, among them, the prices of extractive industries fell by 0.8% month on month, the prices of raw materials industries fell by 0.4% month on month, and the prices of processing industries fell by 0.1% month on month. The prices of means of consumption rose by 0.3% month on month, among them, the food prices rose 1.1% month on month, apparel prices remained flat, the prices of daily necessity goods fell by 0.3% month on month, and the prices of durable consumer goods fell by 0.2% month on month. ■

91 China's CPI in November rose by 4.5% year on year

The data published by NBS on December 10 showed that China's CPI in November rose by 4.5% year on year. Among them, prices in urban areas rose by 4.2% year on year, and prices in rural areas rose by 5.5% year on year; food prices rose by 19.1% year on year, and non-food prices rose by 1.0% year on year; consumer goods prices rose by 6.5% year on year, and services prices rose by 1.2% year on year. China's CPI in November rose by 0.4% month on month. Among them, prices in urban areas rose by 0.3% month on month, and prices in rural areas rose by 0.5% month on month; food prices rose by 1.8% month on month, and non-food prices were flat; consumer goods prices rose by 0.8% month on month, and services prices fell by 0.4% month on month. ■

92 China's total retail sales of consumer goods in November registered a nominal increase of 8.0% year on year

The data published by NBS on December 16 showed that China's total retail sales of consumer goods in November were 3.8094 trillion RMB, a nominal increase of 8.0% year on year. From January to November, the total retail sales of consumer goods were 37.2872 trillion RMB, a year-on-year increase of 8.0%. By regions, the retail sales of consumer goods in urban areas in November were 3.2345 trillion RMB, a year-on-year increase of 7.9%; the retail sales of consumer goods in rural areas were 574.8 billion RMB, a year-on-year increase of 9.1%. From January to November, the retail sales of consumer goods in urban areas were 31.8614 trillion RMB, a year-on-year increase of 7.9%; the retail sales of consumer goods in rural areas were 5.4259 trillion RMB, a year-on-year increase of 9.0%. By consumption type, the catering revenues in November were 496.4 billion RMB, a year-on-year increase of 9.7%; the revenues of retail sales of goods were 3.313 trillion RMB, a year-on-year increase of 7.8%. From January to November, catering revenues were 4.1896 trillion RMB, a year-on-year increase of 9.4%; the revenues of retail sales of goods were 33.0976 trillion RMB, a year-on-year increase of 7.9%. ■

93 China's general public budget revenues from January to November registered a year-on-year increase of 3.8%

The data published by MOF on December 17 showed that China's general public budget revenues from January to November were 17.8967 trillion RMB, a year-on-year increase of 3.8%. Among them, the central general public budget revenues were 8.6116 trillion RMB, a year-on-year increase of 4.8%; the local general public budget revenues were 9.2851 trillion RMB, a year-on-year increase of 3%. Tax revenues from general public budget revenues were 14.9699 trillion RMB, a year-on-year increase of 0.5%; non-tax revenues were 2.9268 trillion RMB, a year-on-year increase of 25.4%. China's general public budget expenditures from January to November were 20.6463 trillion RMB, a year-on-year increase of 7.7%. Among them, the central general public budget expenditures were 3.0444 trillion RMB, a year-on-year increase of 8.3%; the local general public budget expenditures were 17.6019 trillion RMB, a year-on-year increase of 7.6%. China's governmental fund budget revenues from January to November were 6.808 trillion RMB, a year-on-year increase of 9.5%. In terms of the central and local levels, the revenues of the central governmental fund budget were 371.5 billion RMB, a year-on-year increase of 2.2%; the revenues of the local governmental fund budget were 6.4365 trillion RMB, a year-on-year increase of 10%. China's governmental fund budget expenditures from January to November were 7.5976 trillion RMB, a year-on-year increase of 19%. In terms of the central and local levels, the central governmental fund budget expenditures were 231.2 billion RMB, a year-on-year decrease of 2.7%; the local governmental fund budget expenditures were 7.3664 trillion RMB, a year-on-year increase of 19.9%. ■

94 Total operating income of SOEs registered a year-on-year increase of 6.4% from January to November

The data published by MOF on December 23 showed that from January to November, total operating income of SOEs was 55.74553 trillion RMB, a year-on-year increase of 6.4%. Among them, the total operating income of central SOEs was 32.16491 trillion RMB, an increase of 5.3% year on year; the total operating income of local SOEs was 23.58062 trillion RMB, an increase of 7.9% year on year. From January to November, the total operating cost of SOEs was 53.98583 trillion RMB, a year-on-year increase of 6.6%. Among them, the total operating cost of central SOEs was 30.73401 trillion RMB, an increase of 5.4% year on year; the total operating cost of local SOEs was 23.25182 trillion RMB, an increase of 8.2% year on year. From January to November, the total profit of SOEs was 3.1981 trillion RMB, a year-on-year increase of 5.3%. Among them, the total profit of central SOEs was 2.09312 trillion RMB, a year-on-year increase of 7.7%; the total profit of local SOEs was 1.10498 trillion RMB, a year-on-year increase of 1.0%. ■

95 China issued 45.789 billion RMB of local government bonds in November

The data published by MOF on December 26 showed that China issued 45.789 billion RMB of local government bonds in November. Among them, 23.065 billion RMB were general bonds, and 22.724 billion RMB were special bonds. According to the purpose of usage, no new bonds were issued and

45.789 billion RMB were swapped bonds and refinanced bonds. China issued 4.3244 trillion RMB of local government bonds from January to November. Among them, 1.7702 trillion RMB were general bonds, and 2.5542 trillion RMB were special bonds. According to the purpose of usage, 3.0367 trillion RMB were new bonds, and 1.2877 trillion RMB were swapped bonds and refinanced bonds. As of the end of November 2019, the nationwide outstanding local government debts were 21.3333 trillion RMB. Among them, general debts were 11.879 trillion RMB, special debts were 9.4543 trillion RMB; government bonds were 21.1143 trillion RMB, and government debts in the form of non-government bonds were 219 billion RMB. ■

96 Total profits of major industrial enterprises went down by 2.1% year on year in China from January to November

The data published by NBS on December 27 showed that the profits of major industrial enterprises in China totaled 5.61007 trillion RMB from January to November, down by 2.1% year on year. By sectors, the figure was 517.4 billion RMB for the mining sector, up by 1.0%; 4.62834 trillion RMB for the manufacturing sector, down by 4.1%; and 464.33 billion RMB for the electricity, thermal, gas and water production and supply sector, up by 17.7%. By types of ownership, the figure stood at 1.60366 trillion RMB for state-holding enterprises, down by 11.2% year on year; 4.04823 trillion RMB for joint-stock enterprises, down by 1.6%; 1.41112 trillion RMB for foreign invested enterprises and enterprises funded from Hong Kong, Macao and Taiwan, down by 3.3%; and 1.58933 trillion RMB for private enterprises, up by 6.5%. ■

97 China's manufacturing PMI was 50.2% in December 2019

The data published by NBS on December 31 showed that China's manufacturing PMI was 50.2% in February, which was flat from the previous month. By enterprises, the PMI of large enterprises was 50.6%, down by 0.3 percentage points from the previous month; the PMI of medium-sized enterprises was 51.4%, up by 1.9 percentage points from the previous month; and the PMI of small-sized enterprises was 47.2%, down by 2.2 percentage points from the previous month. In terms of the classified indexes, the production index was 53.2%, up by 0.6 percentage points from the previous month; the new orders index was 51.2%, a decrease of 0.1 percentage points from the previous month; the raw material inventory index was 47.2%, down by 0.6 percentage points from the previous month; the employment index was 47.3%, the same as last month; and the supplier delivery time index was 51.1%, an increase of 0.6 percentage points from the previous month. ■

MOF EVENTS

01

On January 9, Vice Finance Minister Cheng Lihua met with David Cruickshank, Chairman of Deloitte's global organization. The two sides exchanged views on the outcomes of the reform and development of China's accounting industry and the priority tasks for the future. ■

02

On January 17, Finance Minister Liu Kun met with Olaf Scholz, Federal Minister of Finance and Vice Chancellor of Germany, at the Diaoyutai State Guesthouse. The two sides exchanged views on the second China-Germany High-Level Financial Dialogue, China-Germany financial cooperation, and fiscal policies of the two countries. ■

Source: MOF

03

From January 17 to 18, Vice Finance Minister Zou Jiayi attended and addressed the G20 Finance and Central Bank Deputies' Meeting in Tokyo, Japan. The meeting discussed topics such as global economic risks and challenges, growth framework, infrastructure investment, international financial architecture and international tax cooperation. Before the meeting, Zou Jiayi also attended and addressed the BRICS Finance and Central Bank Deputies' Meeting. ■

Source: MOF

04

On January 18, Liu He, Member of the Political Bureau of the CPC Central Committee and Vice Premier of the State Council co-chaired the Second China-Germany High-Level Financial Dialogue in Beijing with Olaf Scholz, Deputy Chancellor and Finance Minister of Germany. Vice Finance Minister Liao Min attended the Dialogue and made a speech on the topic of macroeconomic situation and global economic governance. ■

Source: MOF

05

On January 18, Vice Finance Minister Liu Wei visited the Shanghai Stock Exchange, Shanghai Futures Exchange and other financial institutions to conduct research on the development of the sci-tech innovation board and presided over the symposium on state-owned financial capital management to fully listen to the suggestions of relevant government departments and financial institutions. ■

06

From January 29 to 30, Vice Finance Minister Zou Jiayi made a field visit to Xiong'an New District and Tianjin Municipality to conduct research on the use of resources from multilateral and bilateral development agencies and the implementation of relevant tariff policies in support of local development. ■

07

On February 12, Finance Minister Liu Kun met with David Robert Malpass, the Undersecretary of U.S. Treasury and the nominee for World Bank President of U.S., and exchanged views on relevant issues. ■

08

On February 14, Cheng Lihua, Deputy Head of the State Council Leading Group for Poverty Alleviation and Development and Vice Finance Minister, went to Pingjiang County, Hunan Province to research on targeted poverty alleviation, meeting with the local poor people, and visiting the local government officials involved in the work of poverty alleviation, and listening to the suggestions on rectifying problems identified in the inspection of MOF's poverty alleviation campaign. ■

09

From February 17 to 18, Vice Finance Minister Liu Wei led the officials from the Department of Economic Construction of MOF to conduct a special investigation on the supply and demand of corn in Heilongjiang Province, and chaired a symposium on the analysis of the supply and demand of corn in the three provinces of Northeast China. ■

10

On February 21, Vice Finance Minister Zou Jiayi of China and Vice Finance Minister Hamad bin Suleiman Al-Bazai Saudi Arabia co-chaired the first meeting of Financial Sub-committee of the China-Saudi High-Level Joint Committee. The two sides held in-depth discussions on issues such as macroeconomic situation and policy, global economic governance, and bilateral fiscal, tax and financial cooperation, and reached consensus on mutually beneficial and win-win cooperation. ■

Source: MOF

11

On March 7, Finance Minister Liu Kun, Vice Finance Minister Cheng Lihua and Vice Finance Minister Liu Wei attended the Press Conference of the Second Session of the 13th National People's Congress and answered questions from Chinese and foreign journalists on the "reform of fiscal and tax system and financial issues". ■

12

On March 11, MOF held a symposium on targeted poverty alleviation of Yongsheng County to share information on Yongsheng County's poverty alleviation work and plan the next step forward. Cheng Lihua, Member of the MOF Leadership Party Group, Vice Finance Minister and Deputy Head of the MOF Leading Group for Poverty Alleviation Work, presided over the meeting. Zou Jiayi, Member of the MOF Leadership Party Group, Vice Finance Minister and Deputy Head of the MOF Leading Group for Poverty Alleviation Work, attended the meeting. The representatives of the Finance Department of Yunnan Province, the Government of Lijiang City and the Party Committee of Yongsheng County made presentations on the poverty alleviation work. The MOF's representatives from the Budget Department, the Agriculture Department, the Personnel and Education Department, and the Office of Party Committee participated in the discussions and exchanges of views. ■

13

On March 19, Finance Minister Liu Kun met with H.E. Adriano Afonso Maleiane, Minister of Economy and Finance of Mozambique, and exchanged views on the macroeconomic situations of the two countries and bilateral financial cooperation. ■

Source: MOF

14

On March 19, Finance Minister Liu Kun met with Alikhan Smailov, the First Deputy Prime Minister and Minister of Finance of Kazakhstan, and exchanged views on China-Kazakhstan financial cooperation. ■

15

On March 20, MOF held a video conference on the work of the national fiscal system on poverty alleviation. The conference studied General Secretary Xi Jinping's important speech on poverty alleviation and the spirit of the recent important meetings of the Party Central Committee and the State Council on poverty alleviation, took stock of the 2018 work of fiscal authorities on poverty alleviation, and planned the key tasks of fiscal authorities for poverty alleviation in the next two years. Finance Minister Liu Kun delivered a keynote speech, Vice Finance Minister Liu Wei presided over the conference, and the heads of the finance departments of Xinjiang, Sichuan, Anhui and Shandong provinces also made remarks. ■

16

On March 21, Zou Jiayi, Member of the MOF Leadership Party Group, Vice Finance Minister and Deputy Head of the MOF Leading Group for Targeted Poverty Alleviation, chaired a meeting of the MOF Leading Group for Targeted Poverty Alleviation to study General Secretary Xi Jinping's important speech on poverty alleviation. The meeting reviewed the *2019 Priorities of Targeted Poverty Alleviation of MOF*, and concluded on the work of the next step. Members of the MOF Leading Group for Targeted Poverty Alleviation and the heads of relevant units also attended the meeting. ■

17 On March 24, Finance Minister Liu Kun met with Raymond Thomas Dalio, Chairman of Bridgewater Associates, at the Diaoyutai State Guesthouse. The two sides exchanged views on the global macroeconomic situation and global debt issues. ■

Source: MOF

18 On March 24, Finance Minister Liu Kun attended the 2019 Annual Meeting of the China Development Forum and delivered a speech of *New Measures for Proactive Fiscal Policy.* ■

19 On March 24, Finance Minister Liu Kun met with Joseph Eugene Stiglitz, Nobel Laureate in Economics, at the Diaoyutai State Guesthouse. The two sides exchanged views on China-US economic and trade relations and China's tax reform. ■

Source: MOF

20 On March 25, Finance Minister Liu Kun met with Hon. Margaret Mhango Mwanakatwe, the Special Envoy of Zambian President and Finance Minister. The two sides exchanged views on the macroeconomic situations of the two countries and bilateral financial cooperation. ■

21

On March 25, Finance Minister Liu Kun and the heads or authorized representatives of Asian Infrastructure Investment Bank, Asian Development Bank, Latin American Development Bank, European Bank for Reconstruction and Development, European Investment Bank, Inter-American Development Bank, International Fund for Agricultural Development, and World Bank Group signed the *Memorandum of Understanding on Matters to Establish the Multilateral Cooperation Center for Development Finance* in Beijing. Vice Finance Minister Zou Jiayi presided over the signing ceremony. ■

Source: MOF

22

From March 26 to 27, the 2019 Annual Meeting of Boao Forum for Asia was held in Boao, Hainan. Vice Finance Minister Zou Jiayi attended the sub-forum of Belt and Road: Building Roads for Globalization, and made a keynote speech. ■

23

From April 1 to 2, the 4th Annual Meeting of the Board of Governors of NDB was held in Cape Town, South Africa. Governors or representatives of the members of NDB and representatives of international organizations, business community and civil society attended the meeting. Finance Minister Liu Kun attended the meeting and delivered a speech at the opening ceremony. He also met with South African Finance Minister Tito Titus Mboweni and President of NDB Kundapur Vaman Kamath. During the annual meeting, a seminar on Leveraging International Financial Infrastructure for Sustainable Development was held. Vice Finance Minister Xu Hongcai attended and addressed the seminar on behalf of the Chinese delegation. ■

24

From April 2 to 3, Vice Finance Minister Zou Jiayi attended and chaired the ASEAN+3 Finance and Central Bank Deputies' Meeting in Chiang Rai, Thailand. The meeting discussed topics such as global and regional macroeconomic situation, strategic direction of ASEAN+3 financial cooperation, AMRO, CMIM and Asian Bond Market Initiative. Before the meeting, Zou Jiayi also presided over the Finance and Central Bank Deputies' Meeting of China, Japan and South Korea. ■

Source: MOF

25

On April 9, Finance Minister Liu Kun met with Valdis Dombrovskis, the Executive Vice President of the European Commission, in Brussels, Belgium. The two sides exchanged views on the economic situation and related policies of China and EU, sustainable financing and other issues. ■

Source: MOF

26

From April 9-11, Cheng Lihua, Member of the MOF Leadership Party Group, Vice Finance Minister and Deputy Head of the MOF Leading Group for Poverty Alleviation, visited Guizhou Province to carry out a special research on poverty alleviation and to observe the dynamic monitoring platform for poverty alleviation funds and the performance management of poverty alleviation funds. She also researched the support for relocation of the poor people and the progress of poverty alleviation through industrial development, visited the poor households, hosted a symposium, listened to the suggestions from the Finance Department and relevant poverty-stricken counties, and provided guidance for the role of public finance in poverty alleviation. ■

27

From April 11 to 12, the G20 Finance Ministers and Central Bank Governors' Meeting was held in Washington, DC. The meeting discussed topics such as the global economic situation, high-quality infrastructure, debt sustainability in low-income countries and international taxation. Before the meeting, the BRICS countries held a meeting of finance ministers and central bank governors to exchange views on financial issues such as the membership expansion of NDB and infrastructure cooperation. Finance Minister Liu Kun and Vice Finance Minister Zou Jiayi attended these meetings. ■

Source: MOF

28 From April 11 to 13, during the G20 Finance Ministers and Central Bank Governors' Meeting and the World Bank Spring Meetings in Washington, DC, Finance Minister Liu Kun met with Brazilian Economy Minister Paulo Roberto Nunes Guedes, Italian Finance Minister Giovanni Tria, Luxembourg Finance Minister Pierre Gramegna, Indonesian Finance Minister Sri Mulyani Indrawati, Russian First Deputy Prime Minister and Finance Minister Anton Germanovich Siluanov, South Korean Deputy Prime Minister and Finance Minister Hong Nam-ki, UK Chancellor of the Exchequer The Rt. Hon. Philip Hammond, Singaporean Finance Minister Heng Swee Keat and European Commissioner for Economic and Financial Affairs Pierre Moscovici. ■

29 From April 12 to 13, the World Bank and the IMF held the 99th Development Committee meeting in Washington, DC. Finance Minister Liu Kun attended and addressed the Ministerial Luncheon of the Development Committee, and Vice Finance Minister Zou Jiayi attended and delivered a speech at the Ministerial Meeting of the Development Committee. During the meeting, Finance Minister Liu Kun met with David Robert Malpass, the new president of the World Bank, and exchanged views on issues such as China's cooperation with the World Bank. ■

Source: MOF

30 On April 16, Xu Hongcai, Member of the MOF Leadership Party Group and Vice Finance Minister, presided over the meeting on MOF's proposals of the year 2019 to NPC. The meeting studied the requirements of NPC, CPPCC and the State Council, and planned the work of making and handling proposals in 2019. ■

31 On April 22, Vice Finance Minister Zou Jiayi attended a seminar on "Opportunities for Collaboration on High-quality and Sustainable Infrastructure Interconnectivity" jointly organized by AIIB and the China International Contractors Association. ■

32 On April 23, the meeting on changing the name of MOF's local regulatory bureaus was held in Beijing. Finance Minister Liu Kun attended the meeting and delivered a speech. Zou Jiayi, Member of the MOF Leadership Party Group and Vice Finance Minister, chaired the meeting. ■

33 On April 24, Finance Minister Liu Kun met with the President of the Swiss Confederation and the Head of the Finance Department Ueli Maurer, who was on a state visit to China for the Second Belt and Road Forum for International Cooperation. The two sides had an in-depth exchange of views on bilateral economic situations and financial cooperation. ■

34 On the morning of April 24, Finance Minister Liu Kun met with Farhad Dejpasand, the Minister of Finance and Economic Affairs of Iran, at MOF. The two sides exchanged views on China-Iran bilateral financial cooperation and other issues. ■

35 On the morning of April 24, Finance Minister Liu Kun met with Zainab Shamsuna Ahmed, the Minister of Finance of Nigeria, at MOF. The two sides exchanged views on China-Nigeria bilateral financial cooperation and other issues. ■

36 On April 24, Finance Minister Liu Kun met with IMF's Managing Director Christine Lagarde at MOF. The two sides exchanged views on strengthening future cooperation and signed a MOU on cooperation. Vice Finance Minister Zou Jiayi also attended the activities as mentioned above. ■

Source: MOF

37 On April 25, Finance Minister Liu Kun met with the World Bank's CEO Kristalina Ivanova Georgieva at MOF. The two sides exchanged views on further deepening the cooperation between China and the World Bank. ■

Source: MOF

38 On the morning of April 25, the Thematic Session on Financial Connectivity of the Second Belt and Road Forum for International Cooperation, co-hosted by MOF and PBOC, was held in Beijing. Finance Minister Liu Kun attended and delivered a keynote speech at the session, and Vice Finance Minister Zou Jiayi moderated the discussion. 260 representatives from the ministry of finance of countries such as Russia, Nigeria, Suriname, Vanuatu, UK and Switzerland, international organizations such as IMF, AIIB, World Bank, NDB, IFAD and CAF, financial institutions and business community attended the session. ■

39 On April 26, Vice Finance Minister Zou Jiayi met with the Executive Secretary of the UN Economic Commission for Africa Vera Songwe, who visited China to attend the Second Belt and Road Forum for International Cooperation. The two sides exchanged views on issues such as cooperation

between China and African countries at the World Bank, the Investing in Africa Forum and the debt sustainability framework. ■

40 On May 2, Finance Minister Liu Kun attended and chaired the China, Japan and Korea Finance Ministers and Central Bank Governors' Meeting in Nadi, Fiji. The parties exchanged views on issues such as the macroeconomic situations of the three countries and regional financial cooperation. After the meeting, a joint statement by the finance ministers and central bank governors of the three countries was published. Vice Finance Minister Zou Jiayi also attended the meeting. ■

41 On May 2, Finance Minister Liu Kun, accompanied by Vice Finance Minister Zou Jiayi, chaired the 22nd ASEAN+3 Finance Ministers and Central Bank Governors' Meeting in Nadi, Fiji. The meeting mainly discussed issues such as global and regional macroeconomic situation, future vision and institutional reform of the ASEAN+3 finance process. A joint statement was issued at the end of the meeting. ■

Source: MOF

42 From May 3 to 4, Finance Minister Liu Kun led the Chinese delegation to attend the 52nd Annual Meeting of the ADB Board of Governors in Nadi, Fiji. Governors or representatives of ADB members as well as representatives of relevant international organizations, industrial and commercial enterprises and civil society attended the meeting. The theme of this year's annual meeting was "Prosperity through Unity". Under this theme, the meeting discussed topics such as addressing the growing global uncertainty and mobilizing private sector funds in the international markets full of challenege. ■

43 From May 5 to 6, Liu Kun, the Party Secretary and Minister of the MOF, went to Yongsheng County of Lijiang City and Dali Bai Autonomous Prefecture in Yunnan Province to investigate poverty alleviation and the protection of the Erhai Lake. ■

44 On May 7, the Paris Forum High-Level Conference on Sovereign Debt was held in Paris, France. Vice Finance Minister Zou Jiayi attended the conference. ■

45 On May 13, Zou Jiayi, Member of the MOF Leadership Party Group and Vice Finance Minister, together with Lin Keqing, Vice Mayor of Beijing, attended the inauguration ceremony of the Beijing Regulatory Bureau of MOF. Zou Jiayi also visited the Beijing Regulatory Bureau and had a discussion with all the cadres there. ■

46 On May 15, Zou Jiayi, Vice Finance Minister and Member of the State Council Customs Tariff Committee, attended and addressed the first working meeting of the 7th Expert Advisory Committee of the State Council Tariff Committee. ■

47 On May 20, Vice Finance Minister Cheng Lihua met with Arnold Schilder, the Chairman of the International Auditing and Assurance Standards Board (IAASB). ■

48 On May 23, Finance Minister Liu Kun met with Hon. Prof.Mthuli Ncube, the Zimbabwean Minister of Finance and Economic Development. ■

49 On May 24, the Office of the Customs Tariff Committee of the State Council held a meeting on the exclusion of the listed US products subject to additional tariffs. Vice Finance Minister Zou Jiayi attended the meeting and laid out the work requirements. ■

50 On May 27, Finance Minister Liu Kun met with Takehiko Nakao, President of the Asian Development Bank. ■

51 On May 31, Vice Finance Minister Zou Jiayi met with Kundapur Vaman Kamath, President of the New Development Bank, in Shanghai. ■

Source: MOF

52 On June 4, Finance Minister Liu Kun met with David Lipton, the First Deputy Managing Director of the IMF. ■

53 From June 8 to 9, Finance Minister Liu Kun attended and addressed the G20 Finance Ministers and Central Bank Governors' Meeting in Fukuoka, Japan. Vice Finance Minister Zou Jiayi also attended the meeting. ■

54 From June 8 to 9, during the G20 Finance Ministers and Central Bank Governors' Meeting in Fukuoka, Japan, Finance Minister Liu Kun met with UK Chancellor of the Exchequer The Rt. Hon. Philip Hammond and Argentine Treasury Minister Nicolas Dujovne. ■

55 On June 11, Finance Minister Liu Kun met with World Bank President David Robert Malpass at MOF. ■

Source: MOF

56 On June 21, Finance Minister Liu Kun met with the visiting delegation of the executive directors of Asian Development Bank. ■

57 On June 28, the Joint Meeting of G20 Finance Ministers and Health Ministers was held during the Osaka Summit in Japan. Finance Minister Liu Kun, accompanied by Vice Minister Zou Jiayi, attended the meeting. ■

58 On July 2, Finance Minister Liu Kun met with Lim Guan Eng, Malaysian Finance Minister, at MOF. ■

59 On July 10, Finance Minister Liu Kun and Italian Finance Minister Giovanni Tria co-chaired the first China-Italy Finance Dialogue in Milan, Italy, and attended the China-Italy Financial Forum. Vice Minister Zou Jiayi also attended and addressed the meeting. ■

Source: MOF

60 From July 12 to 13, during the 4th Annual Meeting of the Board of Governors of the Asian Infrastructure Investment Bank, Finance Minister Liu Kun met with European Investment Bank President Werner Hoyer Hong Kong SAR Financial Secretary Paul Chan Mo-po and Luxembourg Finance Minister Pierre Gramegna. ■

61 From July 12 to 13, Finance Minister Liu Kun, as the Chinese Governor, attended the 4th Annual Meeting of the Board of Governors of AIIB. Zou Jiayi, the Vice Finance Minister and the Alternate Governor, also attended the Annual Meeting. ■

62

On August 22, Finance Minister Liu Kun and Russian First Deputy Prime Minister and Finance Minister Anton Germanovich Siluanov co-chaired the 8th China-Russia Finance Ministers Dialogue in Moscow, Russia. Vice Finance Minister Zou Jiayi also attended the Dialogue. ■

Source: MOF

63

On September 10, the 5th Investing in Africa Forum, co-sponsored by MOF, the World Bank, the China Development Bank and the Government of the Republic of Congo, was held in Brazzaville, the Republic of Congo. Vice Finance Minister Xu Hongcai addressed the opening ceremony. ■

64

On September 25, Vice Finance Minister Zou Jiayi and the Indian Secretary for Economic Affairs Atanu Chakraborty co-chaired the 9th China-India Financial Dialogue in New Delhi, India. ■

65

On October 8, Finance Minister Liu Kun met with Bruno Le Maire, Minister of Economy and Finance of France at MOF. The two sides exchanged views on China-France High-level Economic and Financial Dialogue, further opening-up of the financial industry, and China's accession to the WTO *Agreement on Government Procurement.* ■

Source: MOF

66 On October 9, Finance Minister Liu Kun met with Masatsugu Asakawa, the Special Adviser to the Japanese Prime Minister and Finance Minister as well as the Japanese nominee for the President of the Asian Development Bank. ■

Source: MOF

67 On October 11, Vice Finance Minister Yu Weiping met with María Antonieta Alva Luperdi, the Minister of Economy and Finance of Peru, in Lima, Peru. The two sides exchanged views on issues related to China-Peru financial cooperation. ■

68 From October 14 to 15, Vice Finance Minister Yu Weiping attended the 26th APEC Finance Ministers' Meeting in Santiago, Chile. ■

Source: MOF

69 On October 16, Vice Finance Minister Zou Jiayi and Ciro Ferreira Gomes, State Secretary of the Brazilian Ministry of Economy, co-chaired the 8th China-Brazil Financial Subcommittee Meeting in Washington, DC. ■

Source: MOF

70 On October 16, Vice Finance Minister Yu Weiping met with Luis Carranza Ugarte, President of the Latin American Development Bank, in Santiago, Chile. ■

71 From October 17 to 18, Vice Finance Minister Zou Jiayi attended the G20 Finance Ministers and Central Bank Governors' Meeting in Washington, DC. ■

72 On October 19, Vice Finance Minister Zou Jiayi attended the 100th Development Committee Ministerial Meeting in Washington, DC. ■

73 On November 7, Vice Finance Minister Zou Jiayi attended and addressed the Celebration Ceremony for the Successful Issuance of China's euro-denominated sovereign bonds. ■

74 On November 7, Vice Finance Minister Zou Jiayi attended and addressed the Celebration Ceremony on the Successful Issuance of China's Sovereign Bonds in Paris, France. ■

75 On November 14, Vice Finance Minister Xu Hongcai attended the 18th Central Asia Regional Economic Cooperation Program (CAREC) Ministerial Conference in Tashkent, Uzbekistan. ■

Source: MOF

76 On November 18, Vice Finance Minister Cheng Lihua attended the 23rd Greater Mekong Subregion (GMS) Ministerial Conference in Phnom Penh, Cambodia. ■

Source: MOF

77 On November 19, Vice Finance Minister Zou Jiayi attended and addressed the Reception of the 15th Anniversary of China-Belgium Direct Equity Investment Fund in Beijing. ■

78 On November 21, Finance Minister Liu Kun met with Angel Gurria, the Secretary General of OECD. Vice Finance Minister Zou Jiayi also attended the meeting. ■

79 On November 22, Finance Minister Liu Kun met with David Robert Malpass, the World Bank President in Beijing. ■

80 On November 22, Finance Minister Liu Kun met with Kristalina Ivanova Georgieva, Managing Director of IMF. ■

81 On November 26, Finance Minister Liu Kun met with Mihaly Varga, Hungarian Deputy Prime Minister and Minister of Finance. ■

82 On November 29, Vice Finance Minister Xu Hongcai met with Hans Hoogervorst, Chairman of the International Accounting Standards Board. ■

83 On December 3, Finance Minister Liu Kun met with Takehiko Nakao, the President of ADB. Vice Finance Minister Zou Jiayi also attended the meeting. ■

84 From December 6 to 7, Vice Finance Minister Zou Jiayi attended and addressed the G20 Finance and Central Bank Deputies Meeting in Riyadh, Saudi Arabia. ■

85 From December 12 to13, Vice Finance Minister Zou Jiayi attended and chaired the ASEAN+3 Finance and Central Bank Deputies' Meeting in Xiamen. ■

86 On December 17, Vice Finance Minister Zou Jiayi met with Syed Shakeel Shah, Director of the CAREC Institute. ■

LOCAL FINANCE

01 Finance and Audit Bureau of Development Zone of Hohhot City, Inner Mongolia intensified efforts to revitalize the stock of fiscal funds

According to the news released by the Finance and Audit Bureau of Development Zone of Hohhot City on December 29, Inner Mongolia, in accordance with the requirements of the city's finance authorities on strengthening the management of surplus funds and carryover funds, it has strengthened the mechanisms for budget preparation and implementation and clean-up of surplus funds and carryover funds, actively revitalized the stock of fiscal funds, improved the efficiency of the use of fiscal funds, effectively supported the improvement of the quality and efficiency of real economy and promoted the sustained and healthy economic and social development.

First, establish a sound clean-up and management mechanism. Further improve the various fund management methods and establish a mechanism that links the revitalization of the stock of fiscal funds with budget preparation and implementation. At the same time, establish a regular clean-up and management mechanism for the stock of fiscal funds, report the use of the stock of fiscal funds on a monthly basis, reasonably reduce the size of the deposits, ease the pressure on the current stock of fiscal, and speed up the progress of budget expenditures.

Second, strengthen budget management. Effectively strengthen the management of budget preparation, and continuously improve the budget completion rate at the beginning of the year. Improve the project preparatory work in advance, speed up the budget approval and transfer payment disbursement, and strictly control the increase of new stock of fiscal funds. Urge all budget units to speed up project implementation, improve the efficiency of fund use, avoid the formation of surplus funds and carryover funds, and reduce the pressure on the treasury.

Third, deepen the reform of the budget management system and establish a sound budget performance management mechanism. Firmly establish the awareness of performance management, optimize resource allocation and improve the efficiency of using fiscal funds.

Fourth, strengthen fiscal supervision and inspection. Conduct regular supervision and inspection on the project implementing agencies, urge all departments to strictly implement relevant regulations, issue written notice of rectification to the budget units with slow expenditure pace and ineffective progress in revitalizing stock of fiscal funds, and require them to regularly give feedback on the progress of rectification. ■

02 Finance Bureau of Xuhui District, Shanghai actively raised financial resources to move forward the fiscal work of next year

According to the news released by the Finance Bureau of Xuhui District, Shanghai on December 29, the Finance Bureau has actively implemented the requirements of the district committee, adhered to the general principle of making progress while maintaining stability, promoted the high-quality development of economy, worked to build a modern economic system, deepened the reform of the fiscal and tax system, and strengthened the coordination of fiscal funds to promote the economic and social development of the area.

First, focus on science and technology to improve the quality and efficiency of economic growth. In light of the macroeconomic trend and in accordance with the strategic framework of the "Four Xuhui" and the "13th Five-Year Plan" of the whole district, it paid more attention to improve the quality and efficiency of economic development, strengthened the link between industrial funds and industrial policies, further increased investment in science and technology, developed forward-looking plan of technological innovation, promoted the upgrading of industrial structure, supported science and technology enterprises and technological innovation projects, and accelerated the application of artificial intelligence and industrial agglomeration. It further optimized the business environment of private enterprises, broadened the financing channels of enterprises, increased government support by deploying industrial policy funds and government procurement policies, fostered new growth areas, actively collected fiscal revenues, and ensured the smooth and healthy operation of the economy.

Second, focus on improving people's livelihood and enhancing the management of the city district. It prioritized the implementation of major cities and district projects, sped up the improvement of the planning and development of the riverside area, continued to promote the protection of the Hengfu scenic area and the construction of urban road networks, and improved the overall environment of the urban area. It vigorously supported the investment into people's livelihood such as education, health, culture, sports, elderly care and grass-root social governance, implemented projects to improve neighborhood environment, and constantly improved people's livelihood and public services; increased funding support for the weak links of urban management, fully supported the funding of rain and sewage treatment project, promoted the comprehensive management of the residential community, and strengthened the detailed management of urban areas.

Third, remove bottlenecks and deepen fiscal reforms. It fully implemented budget performance management, gradually expanded the scope of performance evaluation, continued to explore policy evaluation, and increased the use of performance evaluation results; it kept track of the progress of budget expenditure, enforced the notification mechanism for the progress of budget implementation, strengthened the supervision and management of key projects, made field visit to the underperforming projects, and improved the efficiency of the use of fiscal funds. ■

03 Finance Bureau of Chongqing Municipality effectively played its role to fight against poverty

According to the news released by the Finance Bureau of Chongqing Municipality on January 7, it has effectively played the role of the government finance authorities by mobilizing financial resources to fight against poverty so as to truly lift the poor out of poverty. First, consolidate the fiscal funds for poverty alleviation. In 2018, the Finance Bureau allocated 4.9 billion RMB of special poverty alleviation funds at or above the municipal level, of which 2.1 billion RMB was from the municipal level, an increase of 4.5% over the previous year. The special poverty alleviation funds were mainly used to support the cultivation and expansion of industries with local characteristics in poverty-stricken areas and improve the basic living and working conditions of the poor. At the same time, it further strengthened the consolidation of agriculture-related funds in poverty-stricken areas and counties, established an incentive mechanism for pilot projects involving the consolidation of agriculture-related funds, and arranged 20 million RMB to reward districts and counties with good performance in carrying out the pilot projects. Second, focus on industrial development and employment to promote poverty alleviation. It arranged 210 million RMB of special funds to support 14 national-level poverty-stricken counties and 1919 poverty-stricken villages to develop village-level collective economy; promoted poverty alleviation through asset incomes, and supported poverty-stricken counties to arrange more than 30 million RMB of agricultural industry development funds annually for poverty alleviation and equity reform; improved the micro-loan policy for poverty alleviation and supported poverty-stricken counties to establish risk compensation fund. As of October 2018, Chongqing has established a risk compensation fund of 700 million RMB with 4.62 billion RMB of cumulative loans. Third, address the shortcomings of the rural living environment. The Finance Bureau of Chongqing strongly supported rural waste control and toilet revolution to improve rural living environment. According to the subsidy standard of no less than 5 million RMB in each pilot district and county, it supported the poverty-stricken districts and counties to carry out rural garbage collection and cleaning pilots, and promoted the establishment of a rural garbage collection and disposal mechanism involving rural households, villages and townships. It provided subsidies for 20 extremely poor townships to carry out municipal demonstration projects for improving rural living environment, 100 demonstration projects for building beautiful and livable villages, and 4 municipal demonstration projects for protecting traditional villages. ■

04 Finance Bureau of Zhangjiajie City of Hunan Province played its role to support the implementation of the rural revitalization strategy

According to the news released by the Finance Department of Hunan Province on January 8, the finance authorities of Zhangjiajie City of Hunan Province has played its role and supported the implementation of the rural revitalization strategy, playing a positive role in boosting rural revitalization. First, give priority to ensure investment in agriculture, rural areas and farmers. The finance authorities at all levels in the city actively played their fiscal role, and prioritized agriculture and rural areas for fiscal expenditure. As of the end of November 2018, the city spent 2.90 billion RMB on agriculture, rural areas and farmers, which was an increase of 24.2% over the final accounts in 2017 and supported the smooth implementation of the city's rural revitalization strategy. Second, lend full support to poverty alleviation. It solidly promoted the consolidation of agriculture-related fiscal funds to boost targeted poverty alleviation. As of the end of November 2018, the finance authorities of Zhangjiajie consolidated 1.207 billion RMB of agriculture-related fiscal funds and spent 1.135 billion RMB, with a fund payment rate of 94.03%. By improving the publicity and disclosure system and improving the departmental coordination mechanism, it improved the supervisory mechanism of poverty alleviation funds and enhanced the efficiency of fund use. Third, prioritize the support for industrial development. Based on the provincial industrial development plan for poverty alleviation, the municipal Finance Bureau vigorously supported the development of the four major industries of giant salamander, vegetable, tea and fruit, and actively developed the industry chain of "tourism + agriculture", forming a new pattern of poverty alleviation with Zhangjiajie characteristics. Fourth, actively cultivate new business entities. It gave play to the role of new business entities and village collective economic organizations in promoting industrial development for poverty alleviation. At present, there are 1,738 farmer professional cooperatives in the city, 1,186 family farms and 162 leading enterprises above the city level. Fifth, support the improvement of the living environment in rural areas. It actively raised funds to be used as rewards for rural environmental improvement, and arranged 1.6 million RMB of budgetary funds at the beginning of 2018 to be used as rewards for rural environmental improvement. In the preparation of the 2019 city-level budget, special funds for rural living environment were set up, and relevant working funds were included in the annual budget to promote the smooth implementation of the rural environmental improvement and continuously improve the quality of rural living environment. ■

05 The Finance Bureau of Jinhua City, Zhejiang Province took a combination of measures to make good use of fiscal funds

According to the news released by the Finance Department of Zhejiang Province on January 15, since 2018, the Finance Bureau of Jinhua City has adhered to the principle of focusing fiscal resources on major matters and taken a combination of measures to add new impetus to the development of the city.

First, increase fiscal spending on key areas. Adjust the expenditure structure and ensure the spending on major and strategic projects to boost economic transformation and development; establish a mechanism for increasing spending on areas related to people's livelihood; promote zero-based budget, compile budget and determine expenditure items and amounts on actual financial resources rather than the budget of the previous year.

Second, reduce administrative costs. Cut the "three public expenses" by 2.5% in 2018; explore the establishment of a regular mechanism for cleaning up carryover and surplus funds to improve the efficiency of the use of fiscal funds.

Third, leverage fiscal funds. Strengthen the consolidation of special funds, classify and sort through the special fiscal funds in 2018, and propose relevant suggestions for improving management.

Fourth, strengthen supervision of the performance of funds. Strengthen the performance review of special funds; improve the special fund exit mechanism and no longer arrange budgets for special funds that have expired or have no termination deadline; strictly monitor the dynamics of funds, establish and improve the monitoring and early warning mechanism, and take disciplinary measures to improve the efficiency of funds. ■

06 The Finance Bureau of Yichun City, Jiangxi Province enhanced the quantity and quality of publicity work

According to the news released by the Finance Department of Jiangxi Province on January 16, the Finance Bureau of Yichun City pursued high-quality development, made notable progress in the publicity of fiscal information, and ranked among the top in the province's fiscal system in terms of information publicity. First, strengthen the organization guarantee and clarify publicity responsibilities. It established the system of information liaison officers in the bureau, encouraged cadres to actively participate in information publicity; strengthened training and arranged special funds to subscribe to financial newspapers and magazines for everyone to learn; clarified the publicity tasks, quantitatively assessed the tasks, and clarified publicity responsibilities. Second, strengthen the institutional building and improve publicity mechanisms. It improved the assessment methods, and specifically revised the *Measures for Administering the Publicity Work of the Finance Bureau of Yichun* and *Measures for Assessing the Publicity Work of the Finance System of Yichun;* to improve the pertinence and effectiveness of the reported information, it strengthened communication with the Finance Department of Jiangxi Province and other departments. Third, strengthen checks and improve information quality. The officer-in-charge of each division is responsible for its publicity work. With a focus on timeliness, the important fiscal policies or important activities were publicized as soon as they were signed by the leaders. Fourth, strengthen supervision and assessment and enhance the publicity drive. It regularly made notifications, included fiscal information publicity work into comprehensive assessment, and strengthened the use of assessment results. ■

07 The Finance Bureau of Xiamen City, Fujian Province promoted effective fiscal management to boost high-quality growth

According to the news released by the Finance Bureau of Xiamen City on January 21, in the year 2018, with the aim of building a modern fiscal system, it has focused on developing mechanisms, improving performance, strengthening supervision, and orderly promoting fiscal reforms in key areas. First, promote steady growth and transformation. It continued to focus on supporting the growth of real economy, gave play to the guiding effects of fiscal policy and capital, accelerated the industrial transformation and upgrading, and achieved steady and quality growth of fiscal revenues. Second, shore up weak links and promote balance. In accordance with the requirements of adhering to the bottom line, highlighting key points, perfecting the system and guiding expectations, it increased spending on areas related to people's livelihood, kept the spending on areas related to people's livelihood as a percentage of the general public budget expenditures at above 70%, and made efforts to address the imbalanced and insufficient development of the social undertakings. Third, improve environment and promote coordination. It raised funds from multiple channels at a low cost to fund urban construction, promoted coordinated regional development, and continuously enhanced the city's sustainability and livability. ■

08 Jiangsu Agriculture Credits Guarantee Company provided over 3.8 billion RMB of policy-based financing guarantee for agricultural development

According to the news released by the Finance Department of Jiangsu Province on January 22, as of the end of 2018, the cumulative amount of guarantees issued by Jiangsu Agriculture Credits Guarantee Company exceeded 3.8 billion RMB and more than 3,000 households were covered, allowing the innovative financial and fiscal policies to be effectively deployed to boost modern agricultural development and rural revitalization. First, make innovative guarantee products accessible to small and micro farmers. In order to enable farmers to access innovative guarantee products, Jiangsu Agriculture Credits Guarantee Company developed a series of credit and guarantee products. Second, reduce financing costs and make the guarantee products affordable for new agribusinesses. Since its inception, Jiangsu Agriculture Credits Guarantee Company has insisted on providing services for the new agribusinesses at a low guarantee rate of 1%, and even adopted more favorable rates in some areas. The overall financing costs of the new agribusinesses supported by Jiangsu Agriculture Credits Guarantee Company are no more than 6.22%, far below the national level of 8%. Third, stay policy-oriented and consolidate the foundation for rural revitalization. Jiangsu Agriculture Credits Guarantee Company insisted on enabling farmers to enjoy the reform dividends as soon as possible and worked to ensure all the agribusinesses are insured to the most possible extent. At present, it has covered all the regions, industries and entities, and focused more on the moderate-scale agribusinesses. As a result, the average guarantee premiums per household have continued to fall. ■

09 Xinxiang City, Henan Province comprehensively enhanced the performance of fiscal funds for poverty alleviation

According to the news released by the Finance Department of Henan Province on January 29, the financial authorities of Xinxiang City thoroughly implemented the decisions and arrangements of the City Party Committee and Government on winning the fight against poverty, strengthened political integrity, enhanced the "four awareness", and proactively fulfilled the responsibilities. First, strengthen the institutional building, comprehensively regulate fund management, and strive to promote the standardized, detailed and institutionalized management of poverty alleviation funds. Second, enhance the safety of funds, effectively improve the level of supervision, implement the "dual track" supervisory system, and continue to step up special inspections. Third, improve institutional mechanisms, improve service quality and efficiency, strengthen organizational leadership, and improve the working mechanism. Fourth, improve work style and conduct, significantly enhance the ability to perform duties, and establish a regular learning assessment mechanism. Fifth, carry out the "five governance and five promotion" activities and focus on major issues such as the innovation of poverty alleviation mechanisms. ■

10 The Finance Bureau of Qujing City, Yunnan Province took six measures to improve Party building and combat corruption

According to the news released by the Finance Department of Yunnan Province on January 30, the Party leadership of the Finance Bureau of Qujing City combined anti-corruption work with fiscal work to fulfill the responsibility of building a clean and corruption-free government. First, put the Party's political building in the first place, enhance political awareness, and ensure that the staff of Qujing's fiscal system are aligned to the Party Central Committee in all aspects. Second, strengthen the responsibility, establish a mechanism for the implementation of responsibility, and form an accountability system that focuses on the implementation. Third, institutionalize the learning and education of Party building studies. Fourth, consolidate the foundation of Party building and enhance the grass-root Party building. Fifth, strengthen supervision and control, regulate the exercise of power, and promote enforcement through effective supervision. Sixth, strengthen the education and management of cadres, enhance the sense of political integrity, further improve work style, conduct, discipline and efficiency, and improve service quality. ■

11 Guangdong Province actively promoted the reform of the management of electronic fiscal notes

According to the news released by the Finance Department of Guangdong Province on February 2, it has issued the *Plan for Implementing the Reform of the Management of Electronic Fiscal Notes in Guangdong Province* to promote the reform of the management of electronic fiscal notes in Guangdong. First, adopt the model of province-wide and centralized deployment, upgrade the system, improve the functions of anti-repetitive reimbursement, offline billing and cloud, and simultaneously expand the supporting hardware, in order to complete the installation of the Guangdong electronic fiscal notes management system. Second, promote online processing of notes for continuing education; advance the reform of electronic notes for expressway tolls funded by government debts; promote the seamless coordination between electronic fiscal notes system and non-tax invoices; and work with the provincial and city medical (social) insurance authorities to study the reimbursement of medical expenses with public funds. Third, adopt a management model featuring centralized deployment and tiered use, comprehensively sort through and consolidate various operational systems, and establish a supervisory and use the model at provincial, city and county levels. Fourth, standardize and regulate the management procedures, coding standards and data standards for electronic fiscal notes and establish a supervisory system for electronic fiscal notes. Fifth, improve the management function of the electronic fiscal notes system and disseminate the reform experience. ■

12 Erdos City of Inner Mongolia Autonomous Region advanced disclosure of budget to promote open and transparent public finance

According to the news released by the Finance Department of Inner Mongolia Autonomous Region on February 3, the Finance Bureau of Erdos City strictly implemented relevant laws and regulations and actively promoted the implementation of a transparent budget in 2018. First, strengthen the institutional building and promote budget disclosure; strengthen organizational guidance and improve the basic work; unify the template and standardize the disclosure of budget; enhance communication and handle difficult problems promptly; strengthen supervision and enhance the accountabilities of all parties. Second, develop a budget disclosure mechanism with a clear division of labor, responsibility and coordination. Third, further improve the basic work for the disclosure of budget and final accounts; explore and formulate a special budget disclosure system; gradually establish an assessment system for the disclosure of budget and final accounts; and develop innovative forms of disclosure. ■

13 Zhejiang Province took the lead in achieving substantive breakthrough in the medium-term fiscal planning and management

According to the news released by the Finance Department of Zhejiang Province on February 12, Zhejiang Province has achieved substantive breakthrough in the medium-term fiscal planning and management. First, achieve the medium-term fiscal planning and management and realize the synergies of policy, capital and work. Second, in light of the five-year national plan and annual plan for economic and social development, consider major changes in the development environment at home and abroad and make sound economic forecasts. Third, focus on the major decisions of the Party Central Committee, the State Council, the Provincial Party Committee and the Provincial Government, and comprehensively sort out and integrate the existing fiscal policies. Fourth, comprehensively balance the five-year general public budget revenues and expenditures according to the 2018-2022 plan for fiscal revenue and expenditure arrangement. ■

14 The Finance Bureau of Xiangyang City, Hubei Province has made every effort to promote the cultural and ethical progress in the bureau

According to the news released by the General Office of the Finance Department of Hubei Province on February 14, the Finance Bureau of Xiangyang City, Hubei Province has made every effort to promote the cultural and ethical progress in the bureau. First, refine the goals, break down the work tasks, and enhance accountability. Second, raise the standards, mobilize all the staff, and enact strict requirements. Third, increase publicity and foster the atmosphere. Fourth, identify role models to promote learning from good examples. Fifth, increase education and training, improve the quality of cadres, and build a strong and professional team of finance cadres. Sixth, serve the overall interests of the city and improve the image of the Finance Bureau of Xiangyang. ■

15 The online supervisory system for the provincial poverty alleviation funds in Fujian functions effectively

According to the news released by the Finance Department of Fujian Province on February 19, the online supervisory system for the provincial poverty alleviation funds has ensured the safe, regulated and effective operation of poverty alleviation funds. First, improve the supervision of poverty alleviation funds. Promote the construction of an online supervisory system for poverty alleviation funds in Fujian Province, in order to promote targeted poverty alleviation through precise supervision. Second, make real-time tracking and monitoring of funds. On one hand, the system would inhibit, to a certain extent, the non-compliant behaviors such as misappropriation of poverty alleviation funds. On the other hand, it would also enable the poverty alleviation fund authorities at all levels to participate in the supervision of poverty alleviation funds in addition to the review and allocation of funds. Third, ensure that every penny is spent on the poor. People can log in to the official website or download APP to have one-stop access to poverty alleviation policies and information on the distribution of poverty alleviation funds to individuals in recent years. ■

16 Finance authorities of Xiamen City efficiently manage public finance to promote high-quality growth

According to the news released by the Finance Bureau of Xiamen City on February 20, the finance authorities of Xiamen City, with the aim of building a modern fiscal system, have moved to build mechanisms, improve performance and strengthen supervision, orderly promoted fiscal reforms in key areas, and continued to deepen budget management reforms in 2018. As a result, fiscal supervision has become more rigorous, and government asset management more regulated. First, lend more support to the development of the real economy, give play to the guiding role of fiscal policy and funds, accelerate the transformation and upgrading of industries, and achieve steady growth in fiscal revenue. Second, ensure the spending on people's livelihood, keep the spending on people's livelihood as a proportion of general public budget expenditures at over 70%, and make efforts to address the imbalanced and inadequate development of social undertakings, in line with the requirements of sticking to the bottom line, highlighting key points, perfecting the system, and guiding expectations. Third, raise funds through multiple channels and at low costs to finance urban construction and operation, promote coordinated regional development, and continuously enhance the city's sustainability and livability. ■

17 The Finance Bureau of Pingdingshan City of Henan Province deepened fiscal reform to support the healthy and sustained economic and social development of the city

According to the news released by the Finance Department of Henan Province on February 26, the Finance Bureau of Pingdingshan City of Henan Province has accelerated the establishment of a modern fiscal system, fully implemented budget performance management, strengthened local government debt management, and maintained the sustained and healthy development of the local economy. First, stay mindful of potential risks and support the fight against the major risks; take a targeted approach to support the fight against poverty; and pursue green development to support the fight against pollution. Second, focus on cultivating high-quality financial resources; support the high-quality development of the manufacturing industry; implement innovation-driven development strategy; and support the implementation of rural revitalization strategy. Third, vigorously develop education and cultural undertakings; improve the social security system; promote the development of health and family planning programs; improve the housing security system; and support the strengthening of comprehensive social governance. Fourth, accelerate the reform of the fiscal and tax system; improve the budget management system; accelerate the performance management; strengthen the administration of budget implementation; continue to strengthen local government debt management. Fifth, implement the principle of economy and frugality, strictly control the operating expenses and the general expenditures of the "three public expenses" of the various government departments, increase the fiscal transfer payments to the grass-root units, strengthen the ability of the financially difficult areas and grass-root government in funding wage payment, government operation and people's livelihood. ■

18 The Finance Bureau of Yueyang City of Hunan Province took concrete measures to play a greater role in the development of Yueyang

According to the news released by the Finance Department of Hunan Province on February 27, the Finance Bureau of Yueyang City of Hunan Province has actively worked to promote steady growth, advance reform, adjust economic structure, improve people's livelihood, and prevent risks, thus playing a greater role in the development of Yueyang City. First, implement the new round of the large-scale reduction of tax and fee of the central government to effectively reduce the burden of companies in terms of taxes and fees and support the development of the real economy. Second, comprehensively evaluate the various income-increasing factors and the impact of income loss in accordance with the province's centralized planning and assessment indicators, realistically determine the 2019 local income budget target under the general public budget, and scientifically break down the tasks. Third, implement the people-centered development philosophy, coordinate economic development with improvement of people's livelihood, strictly manage the "three public expenses", harden the binding constraints of fiscal budget, and ensure that fiscal funds are spent on the key areas. Fourth, stay mindful of the bottom line of "three no" and "three 10%", continue to implement the "stop, slow down and shut down" requirements, and improve the joint review and approval mechanism to resolutely curb the debt increase. Fifth, implement the tax reform plans of the central and provincial governments, and accelerate the construction of the local tax system. Sixth, deeply embed performance into budget management, improve management of performance targets, strengthen performance monitoring, and improve the use of evaluation results. ■

19 Guangxi Zhuang Autonomous Region focused on six areas to promote high-quality economic and social development

According to the news released by the Finance Department of Guangxi Zhuang Autonomous Region on March 4, Guangxi has focused on six areas to promote high-quality economic and social development. First, implement large-scale tax and fee cuts, with a particular focus on reducing the tax burden of the manufacturing industry and small and micro enterprises. Second, support the taxation department to collect and manage taxes according to law, tap the potential for increasing revenue, and make every effort to increase revenue and proportion of tax revenue. Third, support the key areas and key links crucial for reform, development and stability, and highlight the importance of ensuring wage payment, government operation and spending on people's basic livelihood at the grass-root level. Fourth, speed up the establishment of fiscal relations between the autonomous regions and the cities and counties with clear defined fiscal powers and responsibilities, and follow up with the reform of the division of fiscal powers and spending responsibilities in basic public services at the sub-region level. Fifth, track and monitor the fulfillment of performance targets of departments and the expenditure performance targets of projects from the stage of budget preparation, execution and disbursement to supervision, final accounts and evaluation. Sixth, include the bond quota approved by the central government into the budget at the beginning of the year so as to facilitate early arrangements, early issuance, early use and early outcomes in support of the development of various undertakings. ■

20 Kaifeng City of Henan Province will improve the funding mechanism for the key government investment projects

According to the news released by the Finance Department of Henan Province on March 6, the finance authorities of Kaifeng City will improve the funding mechanism for the key government investment projects in 2019. First, reduce general expenditures, better use stock funds, and ensure the funding needs of key projects. Regulate government borrowing and seize the opportunity from the government's issuance of special bonds. Accelerate the allocation of funds and ensure that key projects are started as scheduled. Second, make good use of the special funds for land reserve and renovation of shantytown areas. Accelerate the transformation and reform of investment and financing companies in cities and counties. Regulate the implementation of PPP model to attract private capital. Vigorously promote the model supported by policy finance and development finance. Actively establish funds to support project implementation. Third, strictly manage the funds. Fully implement budget performance management. Strengthen the use of results. ■

21 The Finance Department of Fujian Province took a systemic approach to support urban construction and management

According to the news released by the Finance Department of Fujian Province on March 11, it conscientiously implemented the decisions and plans of the provincial Party committee and government, and supported urban construction and management by strengthening weak links, improving quality, enhancing livability, strengthening management and supporting relevant industries. First, raise funds through multiple channels to support the renovation of shantytowns, the construction of drainage systems, the treatment of polluted and odorous water bodies, and the construction of public parking lots. Second, provide support for water safety, air quality and urban greening as important projects related to people's livelihood. Third, arrange funds every year for the protection of historical buildings and the reparation of old streets. Fourth, promote the holistic and high-level planning, comprehensive policy implementation and high-standard construction to advance urban development. Fifth, promote the sustainable development of urban construction, actively support the transformation and upgrading of urban industries, and push forward the development of headquarters economy, digital economy, modern service industry and high-tech industries. ■

22 The Finance Bureau of Loudi City of Hunan Province took seven steps to promote social and economic development to a higher level

According to the news released by the Finance Department of Hunan Province on March 12, the Finance Bureau of Loudi City will concentrate efforts on fiscal planning from a holistic perspective in 2019 to promote the city's high-quality development with higher efficiency and better effectiveness. First, effectively implement the tax and fee cuts. Improve political consciousness and make the implementation of the tax and fee cuts a litmus stone for testing the "four awareness" and "two safeguards" of finance authorities. Second, deepen the cultivation of financial resources and strengthen tax collection. Select and give priority to supporting the enterprises that are in line with the development direction and possess strong independent innovation capability and development potential. Third, prevent and resolve debt risks and strengthen debt control. Continue to implement the requirements of "stopping, decelerating, shrinking and withdrawing", strengthen the management of government debt limits, and strictly control the scale of government debt. Fourth, optimize the composition of fiscal expenditures and make structural adjustments. Distinguish between priorities and non-priorities, work on "addition, subtraction, multiplication and division", and comprehensively enhance the ability of serving economic development and ensuring people's livelihood. Fifth, implement comprehensive performance management and improve budget performance. Fully include government revenues and expenditures, departmental and unit budget, major policies and projects into performance management. Sixth, improve the financing guarantee system and provide better protection. Focus on supporting small-scale farmers, promote risk sharing, encourage banks to cut fees and cede profits, and fully drive all sources of funds to support small and micro enterprises, "agriculture, rural areas and farmers" and business startups and innovation. Seventh, regulate the fiscal management of cities and counties. Strengthen the supervision and management as well as the guidance for the finances of counties directly under the administration of the province. ■

23 The Finance Bureau of Yichang City enforced the main responsibility in the CPC's comprehensive and Strict Party governance

According to the news released by the Finance Department of Hubei Province on March 20, since 2018, the Finance Bureau of Yichang City has comprehensively implemented the main responsibility in the CPC's comprehensive and strict Party governance. First, strictly control the budgetary arrangement, enhance the accountability of departmental budget management, optimize departmental budget preparation methods, improve budget preparation system, perfect budget preparation model, and strengthen the planning and management of rolling development expenditures. Second, strengthen the management of state-owned assets and SOEs, financial supervision, government-invested projects, shanty town renovation funds, foreign loans, poverty alleviation funds, social security funds and business startup guarantee loans. Third, prevent and resolve government debt risks, and include all government debt-related revenues and expenditures and debt service funds into budget management. Deepen the reform of "streamlining administration and improving services" and fully implement the policy of tax and fee cuts. Strengthen the construction of fiscal information network and explore the construction of an accounting service platform that is "standardized and easy to operate". Fourth, improve the construction of financial and economic systems, improve the specific plans for financial and economic disciplines, deploy systems to manage power, business and people, plug management loopholes, and build a long-term mechanism. Fifth, strengthen internal control and adhere to the right selection and recruitment standards. ■

24 The Finance Bureau of Suzhou City continuously promoted the reform of "streamlining administration and improving services" and earnestly implemented the policy for the development of SMEs

According to the news released by the Finance Department of Anhui Province on March 21, the Finance Bureau of Suzhou City has continuously promoted the reform of "streamlining administration and improving services" and earnestly implemented the policy for the development of SMEs. First, formulate the *Administrative Measures for the Supervision of Government Procurement in Suzhou City* and make clear requirements for setting aside a certain proportion of government procurement budget for SMEs. Second, the finance authorities of all levels have made clear the requirements for implementing policies to promote the development of SMEs when formulating the annual government centralized procurement catalogue and quota standards. Third, work with the public resource transaction management department to implement the requirements of government procurement for the promotion of SMEs during the bidding and procurement process. Fourth, strengthen dynamic supervision of the implementation of the policy of government procurement for the promotion of SMEs, and analyze and understand the situation through quarterly reports on government procurement information. Fifth, strengthen supervision and inspection of the implementation of government procurement policies. If the preferential policies for SMEs are not implemented according to the regulations or if differentiated treatment and discriminatory treatment are accorded to SMEs, rectification within the deadline will be required and punishment will be made according to law. ■

25 The Finance Department of Shan-dong Province established a "1+2" policy system for budget performance management

According to the news released by the Finance Department of Shandong Province on March 25, Shandong Province has established a "1+2" policy system for budget performance management. First, comprehensively strengthen budget performance management from three aspects, and build a comprehensive, full-process and full-coverage budget performance management framework based on the establishment of mechanisms, expansion of scope, focus on key areas and strengthening of weak links. Second, establish and improve a common performance indicator framework combining quantitative and qualitative indicators. With the help of a serial of core performance indicators and standards in different industries and sub-fields, and the indicators with basic public service standards and departmental budget project expenditure standards, the government established a dynamic adjustment mechanism. Third, innovatively establish an incentive and restraint mechanism of "one report, two inclusions, three links and strengthened audit supervision" to strengthen the accountability of those subjects to performance assessment. ■

26 Yunnan Province earnestly implemented relevant documents on granting greater autonomy to scientific research institutions and personnel

According to the news released by the Finance Department of Yunnan Province on March 26, Yunnan Province has earnestly implemented relevant documents on granting greater autonomy to scientific research institutions and personnel. First, delegate the powers for budget adjustment. Project implementing units will be granted the power to independently decide on the "equipment expenses" and "other expenses" in the "direct expenses", if these expenses are adjusted within 20% of the adjustment range, as well as other budget items. Second, simplify budget preparation and reduce unnecessary procedures. Simplify the equipment procurement process of colleges and universities. Provincial universities and research institutes may skip the tendering and bidding procedures and shorten the procurement cycle by using special procurement and on-demand procurement mechanisms for the purchase of equipment and consumables that are urgently needed for scientific research. Third, strengthen the internal management of project implementing units, strengthen the whole-process performance management, and strengthen the fiscal support for the application of science and technology achievements. Fourth, raise the proportion of indirect funding for intellectually intensive scientific research projects, and enforce a differentiated budget implementation assessment mechanism. Repeated and overlapped inspections should be avoided to reduce the interference of scientific research activities and allow for the independent management of horizontal funds. ■

27 Finance Department of Yunnan Province went all out to implement the massive tax and fee cuts

According to the news released by the Finance Department of Yunnan Province on April 1, the Finance Department of Yunnan went all out to implement the policy of large-scale tax and fee cuts. First, improve political consciousness and make arrangements as soon as possible. Second, set up a leading group for the coordination of tax and fee cuts, strengthen leadership over the province's tax and fee cuts, carry out comprehensive coordination and make every effort to advance the province's tax and fee reduction. Third, in accordance with the overall national plan and on the basis of careful analysis and calculation, put forward implementation guidelines of the state-authorized matters and cut the tax by 50% for small-scale taxpayers in the province within the scope of authorization, in order to further reduce the tax burden of small and micro enterprises. Fourth, jointly publish the work plan for implementing the tax and fee cut policy, detail the tasks of the fiscal and taxation departments, clarify the departmental responsibilities, propose the measures for taking forward work, and establish working mechanisms for meetings, liaison officers and publicity. Fifth, enable the provincial finance and taxation departments to work in close cooperation to analyze and measure the inclusive tax relief policy for small and micro enterprises. ■

28 Finance Bureau of Nanchang City, Jiangxi Province took five measures to enhance budget performance management

According to the news released by the Finance Department of Jiangxi Province on April 3, the Finance Bureau of Nanchang City in Jiangxi Province took five measures to enhance budget performance management. First, take the lead in realizing the full coverage of performance management throughout the ex-ante, interim and ex-post process of projects supported by government funds. Second, publish a number of articles related to Nanchang's performance management in important media outlets; make recommendations to MOF in the form of special fiscal reports; and offer lectures to various departments and counties at their invitation. Third, actively maintain daily business communication with the finance departments of Shanghai, Shandong, Guangdong and Jiangxi. Fourth, in the stage of budget performance target management, the Nanchang Finance Bureau invited, for the first time, the Delegates of Nanchang People's Congress and the CPPCC Members to participate in the on-site evaluation of performance targets for "2019 Funds for Nanchang City Flower Arrangement Project" and "2019 Funds for Nanchang City Grass-root Health Organization Service Capacity Building". Fifth, conduct a comprehensive survey of budget performance management work of counties and districts in the first half of 2018, and deliver a research report to the Finance Department of Jiangxi for reference. ■

29 Finance Department of Guangxi Zhuang Autonomous Region worked to keep revenues and expenditures stable and made every effort to complete the annual targets and tasks

According to the news released by the Finance Department of Guangxi Zhuang Autonomous Region on April 4, the finance authorities of Guangxi worked to keep revenues and expenditures stable and made every effort to complete the annual targets and tasks. First, reasonably arrange budget for revenues and expenditures. The budget for revenues should be realistic and scientific, and the budget for expenditures should be balanced with a clear focus. Second, strengthen the analysis and forecast of fiscal and tax revenues, enhance the mobilization of revenues, and ensure the steady transfer of revenues to the treasury. Third, speed up budget approval and disbursement of transfer payment funds and reduce additional expenditures except for emergency expenditures such as disaster relief. Fourth, guide and urge all cities and counties as well as relevant units in districts to actively take effective measures to ensure that the unspent 2018 government bond funds become real expenditures in the first quarter of 2019. ■

30 Qingdao City of Shandong Province actively implemented the requirements of "tightening belt" and further strengthened and standardized the budget management of city departments

According to the news released by the Finance Department of Shandong Province on April 8, the Finance Bureau of Qingdao City has actively implemented the requirements of "tightening belt" and further strengthened and standardized the budget management of city departments. First, the quota of public funds and the budget for the operation and maintenance of official vehicles in 2019 will decrease by 5% from last year. Second, in the implementation process of the budget, the newly added expenditures that need to be funded by the city public finance in the current year should be strictly handled in accordance with regulations. Third, speed up budget implementation and urge project undertaking agencies to make actual expenditures as soon as possible. Fourth, the funds under the city-level general public budget of the current year and the previous years, the special transfer payment funds that have not been used for two consecutive years, as well as the portion of accumulated carryover of government funds that exceeds 30% of the current year's income will be recovered to the overall fiscal budget at the end of year. Fifth, establish a comprehensive, full-process and full-coverage budget performance management system. Sixth, strengthen internal control and management of departments and speed up the establishment of a full-process internal control mechanism for the use of fiscal funds. ■

31 Finance Bureau of Chenzhou City in Hunan Province took five measures to carry out the priority work of 2019

According to the news released by the Finance Department of Hunan Province on April 15, the Finance Bureau of Chenzhou City in Hunan Province adhered to the general principle of making progress while maintaining stability and implemented a more proactive fiscal policy. First, strengthen revenue collection and management with greater efforts. Closely work toward the expected target of fiscal revenue, strengthen coordination with taxation, the central bank and other relevant departments, and strictly enforce the responsibilities for revenue collection and management. Make full use of the tax-related information sharing platform, strengthen the information collection, analysis and application, and improve the comprehensive and long-term management mechanism for taxation. Second, strengthen the cultivation of financial resources through more practical measures. Merge the special funds for open economy, industrial park development, high-quality development of bonded zone, and convention and exhibition industry into a single special fund for open economic development and increase the scale to 100 million RMB which will be specifically used to implement the strategy of "innovation-led growth and opening up". Under the premise of ensuring that government debt is not increasing, issue some new bonds to restart the improved and urgent PPP projects, actively crowd in private funds, and enhance support for infrastructure, agriculture, rural areas, ecological environment and people's livelihood. Third, strengthen financial support with stronger measures. Continue to firmly tighten the belt and cut general expenditures by no less than 5%. Add no new budget in principle, and use departmental special funds to finance necessary expenses added due to temporary work. Enhance coordination and cooperation among departments, increase policy research, and seek greater support for Chenzhou from the central and provincial government when it comes to the division of fiscal powers and expenditure responsibilities, national key ecological function zones, equalization transfer payments, county-level basic funding and targeted poverty alleviation. Fourth, strengthen risk prevention and control with stricter requirements. Urge the counties and districts that have not completed asset verification to speed up the pace, and demarcate the respective debt service responsibilities as soon as possible to clarify the boundary between the government and the financing platform. Focus on the key fields, key regions, key financing platform companies and key financing methods, improve government debt risk emergency response measures, and explore the establishment of an emergency coordination mechanism for debt risk in downtown areas. Fifth, strengthen reform and innovation with better effects. Consolidate and deepen the reforms in the areas of budget management, treasury centralized payment, government procurement, and investment review. Comprehensively clean up and regulate the county-level rewards and subsidies that are financially unbearable for the city government and with poor performance in the use of funds. Substantially reduce and consolidate special funds, require one department to have only one special fund in principle, and strive to consolidate the existing 83 special funds at the city level into less than 40. ■

32 Finance Bureau of Xiamen City adopted more targeted and comprehensive measures to alleviate the financing difficulties of small and micro enterprises

According to the news released by the Finance Bureau of Xiamen City on April 17, the Finance Bureau of Xiamen worked with the relevant departments to fully incentivize banks to provide financing services for micro, small and medium-sized enterprises, effectively alleviating the financing difficulties of micro, small and medium-sized enterprises. First, support micro, small and medium-sized enterprises to repay and renew loans on time. Xiamen Finance Bureau set up the repayment emergency fund for micro, small and micro enterprises, in order to provide interest-free "cross-bridge" loans for enterprises, and help small and micro enterprises with temporary financial difficulties to repay loans on time and obtain liquidity support from banks. Second, establish a risk sharing mechanism of financing for small and micro enterprises. Xiamen Finance Bureau set up a credit risk fund of small and micro enterprises to provide up to 70% of compensation for the principal loss of the eligible banks that offer mortgage-free and guarantee-free credit loans for small and micro enterprises. Third, combine technology with finance to ease the financing difficulties of micro, small and medium-sized enterprises. Xiamen Finance Bureau shared 40% of the principal loss for financial institutions' lending to enterprises and encouraged financial institutions to provide financing services for technology-based SMEs. Fourth, encourage banks to provide financing services for small and micro enterprises. Each year, Finance Bureau of Xiamen, in conjunction with the Xiamen Bureau of Industry and Information Technology, selects and recommends the banking financial institutions that are doing well in providing financial services for small and micro enterprises, and provides 300,000 to 500,000 RMB of rewards for each banking financial institution that offers high-quality lending and financing services to small and micro enterprises. Fifth, leverage fiscal funds to alleviate the financing difficulties. In 2014, the Fund for Science and Technology Findings Application and Industrialization was established. In order to help the technology-based SMEs in Xiamen to address the problem of difficult, expensive and slow financing in their initial stage, it mainly invests in startups that carry out the application of science and technology findings in strategic emerging industries and high-tech fields. ■

33 Finance Bureau of Lu'an City in Anhui Province took five measures to improve the business environment in support of the development of the real economy

According to the news released by the Finance Department of Anhui Province on April 22, the Finance Bureau of Lu'an City of Anhui Province focused on resolving the practical problems encountered by enterprises in their production and operation and was committed to ensuring the smooth "last mile" in serving enterprises and implementing policies. First, increase financial support and promote the transformation and upgrading of the real economy. Second, implement tax and fee reduction to cut the operating costs of enterprises effectively. Third, change the support methods and give full play to the role of market mechanisms. Fourth, strengthen financing guarantees and address the financing difficulty of enterprises. Fifth, strengthen institutional building and constantly regulate the management of special fiscal funds. The Finance Bureau of Lu'an, in conjunction with the Economy and Information Technology Bureau, the Development and Reform Commission, the Commerce Bureau and other departments, issued a number of policies to further clarify the investment direction of fiscal funds, optimize the allocation of funds and the model of fund investment. ■

34 Finance Bureau of Tianjin Municipality promoted the healthy and sustained development of CPA industry in Tianjin

According to the news released by the Finance Bureau of Tianjin Municipality on April 23, the Tianjin CPA industry has made positive progress in optimizing administrative examination and approval, strengthening interim and ex-post supervision, and promoting the opening-up of the accounting services market. First, further improve the convenience of examination and approval services. Continue to encourage the simplification and optimization of public services. Solidly improve the training of CPA talents. Second, strengthen supervision to further build a fair market competition environment. Exercise classified supervision for accounting firms, adopt daily supervision and inspection for different types of accounting firms, and further strengthen internal management and external supervision of accounting firms. Work in coordination with the Development and Reform Commission and guide the Industry Association to carry out the investigation of the intermediary service fees charged by the CPA and asset appraisal industries for administrative examination and approval. Third, strengthen evaluation and further promote the healthy development of the accounting service industry. Improve the comprehensive evaluation of the industry. Plan the record-filing work of accounting firms in 2017. ■

35 Finance Department of Guangxi Zhuang Autonomous Region focused on five areas to advance budget management reform

According to the news released by the Finance Department of Guangxi Zhuang Autonomous Region on April 30, the Guangxi Finance authorities focused its work on the following five aspects. First, increase revenues and cut expenditures, and promote the smooth performance of the public finance. Make reasonable arrangements for revenue and expenditure budgets, strengthen income mobilization and coordination, and improve expenditure efficiency. Second, increase management constraints and improve the budget management system. Improve the budget management system, solidly advance budget execution, and enhance the communication and coordination with the local People's Congress and the coordination with the audit authorities. Third, advance institutional reforms and establish a modern fiscal system. Promote fiscal system reform, improve the transfer payment system and strengthen county-level financial management. Fourth, strengthen debt management and prevent debt risks. Fifth, enhance Party building and create a sound political ecology. ■

36 Finance authorities of Jiangxi Province took practical measures to cut taxes and fees

According to the news released by the Finance Department of Jiangxi Province on May 5, the tax and fee reduction is the top priority of this year's proactive fiscal policy, and the Finance Bureau of Yichun City in Jiangxi Province has focused on building three mechanisms, taking three measures and working on three priorities to ensure effective implementation of the tax and fee reduction. First, build three mechanisms to help implement the policies, specifically, the implementation mechanism, the coordination mechanism and the publicity mechanism. Second, take three measures to help alleviate the funding pressure of market entities, specifically, increase the investment of special funds, exercise leverage to solve the financing difficulty, and make good use of the industrial funds to accelerate development. Third, work on three priorities to ensure the fiscal sustainability, specifically, maintain the stable performance of public finance, spend funds in a frugal manner and stick to the bottom line of "three guarantees". ■

37 Finance Bureau of Linyi City in Shandong Province actively accelerated the implementation of the tax and fee reduction

According to the news released by the Finance Department of Shandong Province on May 6, the Finance Bureau of Linyi City has accelerated the implementation of the tax and fee reduction. First, comprehensively strengthen organization and leadership. Understand the political importance of the work of tax and fee reduction and promptly set up a leading group for tax and fee reduction comprised of the top officials of finance and tax authorities. Second, improve the mechanisms to ensure the orderly operation and smooth coordination of the work. Third, step up publicity and explanation. Improve the policy level and operational capabilities of tax personnel, especially front-office service personnel, while promoting the model of "online publicity + offline counseling". Fourth, optimize services, continue to improve tax convenience, and effectively improve taxpayers' satisfaction. Fifth, conduct strict inspection to ensure effective policy implementation. Enforce strict discipline and ensure that the policy benefits are brought to every taxpayer with the highest standards, the most stringent measures and the greatest efforts. ■

38 Finance authorities of Baotou City in Inner Mongolia Autonomous Region worked on three aspects to improve the business environment

According to the news released by the Finance Department of Inner Mongolia Autonomous Region, the Finance Bureau of Baotou City has worked on three aspects to improve the business environment. First, continue to build a zero-errand procurement platform, actively promote the reform of the treasury electronic payment, and give play to the management function of government investment project pipeline. Second, actively foster and optimize the business environment. Third, promote the "Internet+" model to serve the private economy. Continue to promote government procurement reform and innovation, leverage Internet technology and developed regions' experience in the big data of public finance, enable the big data of Baotou's public finance to serve more users with more content and wider scope while enhancing the ability of Baotou's electronic procurement to provide precision services and management for the private sector, thus make greater contributions to Baotou's economic development, social services and fiscal management. ■

39 Finance and tax authorities of Quanzhou City, Fujian Province enhanced synergy to develop innovative ways of reducing taxes and fees

According to the news released by the Finance Department of Fujian Province on May 13, the finance and tax authorities of Quanzhou City have enhanced synergy to develop innovative ways of reducing taxes and fees. First, make in-depth study and implement the requirements of the Party Central Committee and the State Council on tax and fee cuts, make tax and fee cuts the central task of this year's fiscal and tax work, and integrate tax and fee cuts with comprehensive and strict Party governance, implementation of priority work and enhanced supervision and accountability. Second, the finance and tax authorities, together with nine government agencies including the commission for discipline inspection, the medical insurance bureau and the federation of industry and commerce, signed a cooperation agreement to establish a joint conference mechanism and a joint emergency response mechanism for implementing the tax and fee cuts. Third, create the province's first publicity service center for tax and fee cuts, allow the finance and tax authorities to interpret and explain the tax and fee cut policy, and hold the knowledge contest on tax and fee cut policy in the city. ■

40 Finance Department of Yunnan Province issued the *Opinions on the Full Implementation of Budget Performance Management*

According to the news released by the Finance Department of Yunnan Province on May 14, the CPC Provincial Committee of Yunnan and the Yunnan Provincial People's Government have recently issued the *Opinions on the Full Implementation of Budget Performance Management*, which provided the following. First, establish the awareness about budget performance management and create a comprehensive budget performance management structure and full-process budget performance management chain. Second, improve the management process covering performance pre-assessment, performance target management, performance monitoring, performance evaluation management and application of assessment results, and formulate the system and implementation rules for budget performance management. Third, build a comprehensive process for budget performance management and implement the same platform and standard for budget management and performance management. Fourth, clarify that the governments at all levels and all departments of the province are responsible for the budget performance management, and implement the lifelong accountability system for the responsible persons of major projects. ■

41 Finance Department of Shanxi Province vigorously strengthened the fostering of accounting talents

According to the news released by the Finance Department of Shanxi Province on May 20, the Finance Department of Shanxi Province has comprehensively improved the accounting talent training mechanism. First, increase the training of accounting personnel in administrative institutions, with a focus on strengthening the training of professional ethics, laws and regulations, in order to effectively improve the overall quality of accounting personnel. Second, carry out the assessment of the professional competence of accounting officials in the province in accordance with the requirements of the Shanxi Provincial Party Committee on the "three basic development". Third, develop detailed training programs, adhere to the goal-oriented and problem-oriented principle, and focus on improving the risk prevention and control capabilities, legal awareness and professional ethics of accounting personnel. Fourth, conduct sound accounting qualification exam and professional title review to ensure the quality of accounting personnel. Fifth, leverage information technology to establish the Shanxi Provincial Accounting Management Information System in order to systematically manage the archives of the province's accounting personnel and information on continuing education. Sixth, promote the development of high-end accounting talents to build a pool of professional talents. ■

42 Finance Department of Xinjiang Uygur Autonomous Region actively arranged the budget to support the implementation of the tax and fee cut policy

According to the news released by the Finance Department of Xinjiang Uygur Autonomous Region on May 22, the Finance Department of Xinjiang Uygur Autonomous Region has actively arranged the budget to support the implementation of the tax and fee cut policy. First, increase the mobilization of funds from the budget stabilization fund and transfer the income and balance of the government-managed fund to the general public budget, in order to make up for the shortfall of revenue caused by the implementation of the tax and fee cut policy; collect the non-tax revenue strictly in accordance with regulations; and make efforts to revitalize the stock of funds. Second, exercise economy and strengthen the management of the "three public expenses"; strictly implement the budget approved by the people's congress; and strive to maintain a balanced budget. Third, strictly implement the plan of the central government and the autonomous region on the "three guarantees"; take into account the fall of revenues caused by the tax and fee cuts and coordinate the financial resources of the central government and the autonomous region; further improve the public finance monitoring mechanism, dynamically monitor local fiscal revenues, key expenditures, available financial resources and scale of treasury funds, and pay close attention to the impact of tax and fee cuts on the fiscal performance of the grass-roots government. ■

43 Finance Bureau of Anyang City in Henan Province took five measures to further strengthen budget execution management

According to the news released by the Finance Department of Henan Province on May 27, the

Finance Bureau of Anyang City in Henan Province, having effectively implemented tax and fee cuts, further strengthened budget execution management and promoted the stable fiscal performance of Anyang. First, effectively implement the tax and fee cut policy. Strengthen political responsibility and work initiative of implementing tax and fee cut measures, build up reform synergy, and jointly work with taxation, human resource and other authorities to formulate specific implementation plans for tax and fee cut policy. Second, mobilize fiscal revenues according to laws and regulations. Properly handle the relationship between tax and fee cuts and the mobilization of fiscal revenues, so that what needs to be cut is cut and what needs to be collected is collected. Third, vigorously promote comprehensive tax administration. Study and formulate the priorities and implementation plans for comprehensive tax administration, refine the division of responsibilities among departments, clarify the requirements of a deadline, and develop a working pattern of "coordinated leadership, division of labor and joint management". Fourth, actively optimize the structure of fiscal expenditures. Stay mindful of the need for government to tighten its belt, and cut the general expenditures by no less than 5% except for the prioritized and mandatory expenditures. Fifth, further improve the efficiency of the use of fiscal funds. Strictly implement the evaluation system for budget implementation, track the progress and effectiveness of budget implementation at each budget department (unit), and strengthen the analysis of budget revenues and expenditures, treasury deposits, and carry-over balances. ■

44 Finance Department of Shanxi Province took a mix of measures to further accelerate the implementation of budgetary expenditures

According to the news released by the Finance Department of Shanxi Province on May 28, in order to further accelerate the implementation of budgetary expenditures, the Finance Department of Shanxi Province faced up to the difficulties and took targeted policy measures. First, make budget preparation more scientific and accurate. Require all departments to develop strong project pipelines before budget preparation, shorten the project preparation period, and reduce the cases of "money awaiting projects". Second, release the city and county budgets in advance, approve the departmental budget as soon as possible, and clarify the time limit for expenditures. Third, step up the mobilization and use of funds. In 2019, the Finance Department of Shanxi Province will transfer the government-managed fund that meets the policy requirements to the general budget stabilization fund, and regularly clean up and recover project funds. Fourth, establish and improve the system of assessment, reward and punishment. Fifth, build a long-term mechanism to accelerate the progress of expenditures. The Finance Department of Shanxi is drafting the *Measures for the Administration of Provincial-level Special Funds in Shanxi Province,* which provide detailed requirements on the establishment, adjustment, withdrawal, distribution, preparation and implementation of special funds. ■

45 The Finance Bureau of Changzhou City in Jiangsu Province improved the business environment for SMEs through the Service Platform for Business Startups and Innovation

According to the news released by the Finance Department of Jiangsu Province on June 3, Changzhou City in Jiangsu Province has further optimized and improved the functions of the Service Platform for Business Startups and Innovation, and enhanced the eight sections of "policy services, talent services, financial services, technology services, business startup counseling, market development, management consulting, and procurement", in order to concentrate efforts on the development, align to the first-class service standards, devote every effort to sustain growth, and provide effective services. First, focus on funds and promote "one-stop window" for handling corporate-related funds. With the support of "Internet + Government Services", the Service Platform for Business Startup and Innovation integrated all city-level corporate-related fiscal funds into unified management, and implemented a unified reporting platform, a unified reporting window, and a unified approval process. Second, focus on capital and expand the financing channels for SMEs. As of the end of April 2019, there were 80 online financing products, and 151 registered intermediary service agencies and 54,745 member enterprises on the platform. Third, focus on resources and build a national property rights trading platform. Changzhou has made efforts to build a national Internet trading platform: e-transaction. At the same time, in order to implement the Strategy for Rural Revitalization Changzhou also built a rural property rights trading platform. ■

46 The Finance Department of Guangxi Zhuang Autonomous Region actively supported the development of the automobile industry to promote high-quality and green growth

According to the news released by the Finance Department of Guangxi Zhuang Autonomous Region on June 4, in order to speed up the development of new business models and new growth drivers of the automobile industry, Guangxi Finance authorities, with the aim of building a modern automobile industry with special features of Guangxi, made great efforts to develop new-energy vehicles and accelerate the structural adjustment, transformation and upgrading of the automobile industry. First, focus on strengthening the leading players in the automobile industry. Guangxi finance authorities raised 270 million RMB of funds through various channels and concentrated the resources on vigorously supporting the development of leading enterprises in the automobile industry. Strengthen technological innovation and accelerate the pace of product upgrading, with Shanghai General Motors Wuling (SGMW) as the leading player. Second, strengthen the industrial chain of the automobile industry. Guangxi finance authorities raised 100 million RMB of funds through multiple channels, vigorously supported the lacking or relatively weak links in the auto parts industrial chain, and accelerated the localized production or upgraded the technical level and scale of products. Third, foster clusters of the automobile industry. Guangxi finance authorities raised 2.432 billion RMB of funds through various channels to support the development of modern industrial parks and promote the development of automobile industry clusters. Fourth, cultivate the brand of the automobile industry. Guangxi finance authorities raised 719 million RMB of funds to carry out quality enhancement actions to develop products with famous trademarks and brands in Guangxi. Fifth, promote innovation to remove the "bottlenecks" of the automobile industry. Strengthen technological innovation, new product research and development, and application and commercialization of findings, enhance core competitiveness, and continuously introduce new models for marketable vehicles. Sixth, expand the market and extend the "network" of the automobile industry. Guangxi finance authorities raised 2.376 billion RMB of funds through multiple channels to support the development of the automobile market and enhance the influence of automobile companies. ■

47 The Finance Bureau of Loudi City of Hunan Province adopted multiple measures to make sure it is halfway through the fiscal and taxation targets in the first half of the year

According to the news released by the Finance Department of Hunan Province on June 10, the Finance Bureau of Loudi City has adopted stronger measures, enhanced accountability, and intensified efforts to make sure it is halfway through the fiscal and taxation targets in the first half of the year. First, concentrate efforts on mobilizing fiscal revenues. Give full play to the data analysis and real-time monitoring functions of the comprehensive taxation platform in order to ensure the taxes are fully collected. Second, ensure sound spending. Strictly reduce the general expenditures by no less than 5%, and strengthen the review of the "three public expenses". Third, continue to strengthen the cultivation of financial resources. Establish the expert review mechanism, project monitoring mechanism and dynamic management mechanism for project pipeline, and offer preferential policy and financial support to the enterprises or projects included in the pipeline. Fourth, optimize and improve the business environment. Establish a special fiscal fund management platform, offer preferential policy to enterprises that meet the criteria for financial support, and allow for online project declaration and fund disbursement. Fifth, conduct strict assessments and improve management performance. Improve the incentive mechanism, strengthen performance management, and effectively prevent debt risks. ■

48 The Finance Bureau of Jiangmen City in Guangdong Province accelerated the reform of budget preparation, implementation, supervision and management

According to the news released by the Finance Department of Guangdong Province on June 12, the Finance Bureau of Jiangmen City has accelerated the reform of the city-level budget preparation, implementation, supervision and management. In 2019, Jiangmen City has fully integrated the reform requirements into budget preparation, and 60% of the projects are refined into specific executable projects in advance, in order to make the budget execution smoother. First, carry out the consolidation of projects and streamline the number of projects. Promote the coordinated use of fiscal funds, leverage major departments and platforms, consolidate the dispersed and small projects, and adjust the catalogues of city-level special funds. Second, implement tiered and classified management and establish a "three-item list". With the aim of clarifying powers and responsibilities, the city-level fiscal projects are divided into operational and developmental projects. Operational projects and general developmental projects are mainly funded by the expenses of the departments in performing their functions, therefore, the administration is streamlined, powers are delegated and the approval authority is decentralized to allow the departments to make approval and use the funds on their own. Third, improve the project management process and enhance operability. Reform the budgeting procedures and government procurement processes while enhancing the flexibility and operability of budget execution. ■

49 The Finance Department of Jiangsu Province took an important step towards the centralized and unified management of provincial-level state-owned financial capital

According to the news published by the Finance Department of Jiangsu Province on June 17, it recently issued the *Circular on Implementing the Centralized and Unified Management of Provincial-level State-owned Financial Capital,* in order to make specific arrangements for the centralized management of provincial-level state-owned financial capital. First, highlight key points and conduct comprehensive management, with the scope of management covering all provincial-level state-owned financial capital. The Finance Department of Jiangsu, authorized by the Jiangsu Provincial Government, fulfills the duties of investor in provincial-level state-owned financial capital, and is responsible for the centralized and unified management of provincial-level state-owned financial capital in accordance with the laws. Second, conduct effective and proportionate management, with management methods tailored to management matters. The Finance Department of Jiangsu will formulate a list of management matters, refrain from intervening in the daily operation and management of enterprises, fully delegate and decentralize, and organize the implementation of basic management, budget execution, performance appraisal, salary calculation, and compensation management of responsible persons. Third, ensure sound and sustainable management, with a package of implementation rules to be introduced during the year. Effectively strengthen the design of the supervision system, firmly establish the service awareness, conscientiously implement the requirements of "effectively managing people and money, and building a rule-based firewall", put the implementation rules on the agenda, and ensure full discharge of duties, in order to effectively stimulate and unleash the vitality of state-owned financial institutions and promote the preservation and appreciation of the value of state-owned financial capital. ■

50 The Finance Department of Guangxi Zhuang Autonomous Region took multiple measures to enhance the role of scientific and technological innovation in serving the "agriculture, rural areas and farmers"

According to the news released by the Finance Department of Guangxi Zhuang Autonomous Region on June 18, it attaches great importance to the key role of scientific and technological innovation in serving the "agriculture, rural areas and farmers", and has taken various measures to enhance the service capacity of science and technology in order to promote the development of modern agriculture and boost the income of farmers in the region. First, continue to intensify the research and development efforts in agricultural science and technology projects. Focus on the development of modern agricultural industry, and identify the supporting of "advantageous agriculture with special features" as the key direction of research projects funded by public finance. Second, enhance the ability of science and technology personnel in helping the poor. In 2018, the finance authorities of Guangxi raised a total of 30.307 million RMB to support the selection and appointment of 2,873 science and technology commissioners in poverty-stricken villages. The science and technology commissioners in poverty-stricken villages who carry out public-welfare (free) technology services will be offered work subsidies for rural science and technology work. Third, enhance the role of science and technology in driving the development of agricultural industry. In each year, 34 million RMB of special funds are allocated to support the Guangxi Innovation Team of the National Technology System for Modern Agricultural Industry. Fourth, focus on improving the scientific literacy of farmers. Each year, a special fund of 4.6 million RMB will be arranged to support the Special Action Plan for Improving Scientific Literacy and Revitalizing Villages in Guangxi, in order to support the scientific research personnel to carry out work for enhancing rural scientific literacy at the grassroots level. Fifth, build a complete scientific research service system of the Academy of Agricultural Sciences. Starting from 2015, the finance authorities of Guangxi have arranged a five-year program which allocates 9.9 million RMB per year for the cooperation between the Guangxi Academy of Agricultural Sciences and the Agriculture Department of Guangxi to enhance the coverage of scientific and technological services. ■

51 The Finance Department of Hubei Province streamlined government procurement to deliver better service for enterprises

According to the news released by the Finance Department of Hubei Province on June 17, Wuhan City of Hubei Province has actively responded to the needs of enterprises and continued to optimize the business environment. First, implement a negative list system to create a fair and equitable market environment. Study and release the *Negative List of Wuhan Government Procurement,* which clearly stipulates that in the government procurement activities, purchasers and procurement agencies shall not set such qualification conditions as the supplier's scale, specific administrative regions, industry performances, and awards in the bidding documents, nor shall they illegally restrict the supplier's ownership form, organization form or location, impose differential or discriminatory treatment on suppliers under other unreasonable terms, in order to create a fair and equitable government procurement market environment. Second, cancel the deposits for government procurement bidding and reduce the operating costs of enterprises. Implement the policy of cancelling the deposits for government procurement bidding, and stipulate that purchasers and agencies shall not collect bid deposits for the government procurement bidding activities that use fiscal funds in Wuhan. All procurement agencies are required to comprehensively clean up the bid deposits collected before November 2018 and refund them. Third, standardize the complaint handling procedures and reduce the time limit for reviewing complaints. Reduce the time limit for reviewing complaints from 5 working days to 3 working days after the receipt by finance authorities of written complaints from supplier, and improve the efficiency for handling complaints. Fourth, implement the government procurement credit commitment system and promote the construction of an integrity system. Establish and improve the credit registration system for government procurement bidding suppliers, and incorporate the supplier credit commitment into the credit record of the market player, which may serve as the main basis for interim and ex-post supervision and classified oversight over market entities, in order to promote ethical operation of suppliers. Fifth, promote "Internet + government procurement" and continuously improve service efficiency. Fully draw on the experiences of advanced cities, build and improve an electronic trading platform covering the city's centralized procurement catalogue, and realize the electronic tendering, bidding and bid evaluation of government procurement. Upgrade and improve the Wuhan Government Procurement Information

Release System, set up a disclosure section for government procurement complaints, pilot the parallel online and offline mechanism for government procurement complaints, broaden the online complaint-filing channels for suppliers, and continuously improve the relief mechanism. ■

52 The Finance Department of Jiangxi Province ensured "three guarantees" to accelerate the implementation of policies related to tax and fee cuts

According to the news released by the Finance Department of Jiangxi Province on June 25, the Finance Bureau of Pingxiang City of Jiangxi Province has firmly ensured "three guarantees" and fully implemented all the policies and measures of tax and fee cuts, so that enterprises and general public can truly feel the benefits of the tax and fee cut policy. First, establish mechanisms and strengthen learning to ensure that the work is progressing in an orderly manner. Establish a leading group for the implementation of tax and fee cuts, with the director of the Finance Bureau of Pingxiang as the head, the deputy directors as the deputy heads, and the chiefs of budget, treasury, non-tax management, performance, and discipline inspection and supervision divisions as the members. Clarify the work responsibilities of the relevant functional divisions to promote sound division of labor and coordination. Attach great importance to the study of various policies on tax and fee cuts, and lay a solid foundation for the orderly implementation of tax and fee cuts. Second, carry out extensive publicity work and conduct strict supervision to ensure the implementation of the policy. Further increase the publicity and interpretation of the tax and fee cut policy, and deploy a mix of traditional media, new media and other platforms to carry out various forms of policy publicity activities. Strictly supervise the implementation of the policies by the finance authorities of counties (districts). Third, increase revenues and reduce expenditure, focus on performance, and ensure budget balance. Recognize the importance of "tightening the belt" and provide funding for the supply-side structural reform, the fight of three major battles, the protection and improvement of people's livelihood, and the major decisions of the city Party committee and government, under the premise of sticking to the bottom line of "three guarantees". Strengthen the fiscal budget performance management and continuously expand the channels of financial resources. ■

53 Finance Department of Hunan Province continuously improved accounting management and services for a new era

According to the news released by the Finance Department of Hunan Province on July 1, the Finance Bureau of Xiangtan City, Hunan Province made in-depth research on the new requirements for accounting management under the new context of economic and social development, closely focused on the city's economic and social development and key fiscal work, and achieved notable progress in promoting government accounting reform, strengthening internal control, enhancing the training of accounting personnel, and advancing the development of the industry. First, increase efforts and continue to strengthen internal control management. Second, pay close attention to implementation and do a good job in the implementation of the government accounting standards. Third, standardize management and improve the work of the CPA association. Fourth, strengthen supervision and enhance the management of the book-keeping agencies. Fifth, improve services and strengthen the training of accounting talents. ■

54 Finance Department of Zhejiang Province regulated the exercise of power to promote the integrity of public finance

According to the news released by the Finance Department of Zhejiang Province on July 2, the Finance Bureau of Jinhua City of Zhejiang Province insisted on strict Party governance, continuously strengthened the management of cadres, continued to deepen the fiscal reform, and strived to build clean and corruption-free public finance featuring healthy working atmosphere, efficient performance of funds, and clean and honest cadres, thus injecting the Jinhua elements into the integrity of public finance of Zhejiang and providing financial support for the development of clean and corruption-free Jinhua. First, strengthen the whole-process budget management and fully promote performance management. Second, promote the rule-based exercise of power and actively build sunshine finance. Third, build a clean political ecology and fully promote the integrity of public finance. ■

55 Finance Department of Guangxi took multiple measures to promote lifelong vocational skills training and keep employment stable

According to the news released by the Finance Department of Guangxi on July 9, Guangxi has fully implemented the requirements of the State Council documents on promoting lifelong vocational skills training and achieved remarkable results in supporting large-scale vocational skills training. First, increase investment to meet training needs. The Finance Department of Guangxi raised 1.878 billion RMB of employment subsidies to support vocational skills training programs. Second, improve policy measures and give play to the principal role of enterprises. Guangxi regarded enterprise employee training as the priority of vocational skills training and supported enterprises to carry out vocational skills training on a large scale. Third, focus on poverty alleviation and strengthen the training of poor labor. Support the "Vocational Skills Training Campaign for Tens of Thousands of Villages and Enterprises", respond to the market labor demands and the needs of industrial development, and provide skills training for the rural labor force willing to work and train, with the annual training plan reaching out to 40,000 documented poor people. Fourth, build the training platform to support skills training. Vigorously support the development of highly skilled personnel training bases and skill master studios, support skilled talents to participate in vocational skill competitions, and implement the incentive and reward mechanisms for highly skilled personnel. ■

56 Finance Department of Yunnan achieved notable outcomes in promoting electronic management for treasury centralized payment

According to the news released by the Finance Department of Yunnan Province on July 10, since 2014, Yunnan Province has taken the lead in realizing the all-round, full-process and full-coverage electronic management for fiscal treasury centralized payment and expanded the public service capacity and promoted innovation in social governance. First, promote unified standards to ensure standardized business operation. By optimizing and adjusting the traditional paper-based business review process, proof management and seal management model, Yunnan Finance Department simplified the unnecessary review phases and manual intervention, and replaced them with automated reviewing, checking, reporting and monitoring process. Second, establish rules and policies to prevent and control risks and ensure the safety of fiscal funds. At the beginning of the reform, Yunnan formulated and improved the implementation measures for the electronic management of centralized treasury payment, measures for electronic seal management, measures for electronic certificate management, contingency plan for electronic management and other internal control policies, so that clear rules and policies are followed and powers and responsibilities are clarified. Third, promote efficient information access and improve the efficiency of administrative operations. Through the electronic management of centralized treasury payment, the fiscal funds can be safer and more efficiently managed, so that the timely payment of fiscal funds can be made and effects are maximized at an early date, significantly enhancing the efficiency of payment and administrative performance. Fourth, promote intensive management to improve efficiency and expand public service capabilities. The use of advanced information technology has helped remove the geographical and time constraints and has fundamentally solved the practical difficulties, such as the shortage of bank outlets, premature clearing time and untimely payment. Fifth, promote data aggregation to break down "islands" and advance social governance innovation. By implementing electronic management with unified business norms and data standards, Yunnan Province has integrated the fragmented information "islands" into a unified whole, realizing the simultaneous operation of business flow, capital flow and information flow. ■

57 Finance Bureau of Beijing implemented the reform of "streamlining administration, delegating powers and improving services" and intensified efforts in reforming the electronic fiscal notes

According to the news released by the Finance Bureau of Beijing on July 12, in order to further deepen the reform of "streamlining administration, delegating powers and improving services", the Beijing Finance Bureau, on the basis of the pilot reform of electronic fiscal notes, expanded the coverage of the reform in both the note-using units and the note type. First, adopt five initiatives to promote reform. Strictly implement the requirements of MOF, consider the actual situation in Beijing, introduce a series of policy measures such as the *2019 Implementation Plan for Beijing Electronic Fiscal Notes Management Reform,* and implement reforms at both the municipal and district level. Starting from July 1, 2019, Beijing launched a nationally unified new version of the electronic fiscal notes, and the original notes were discontinued, realizing the integration of management processes, coding standards and data standards for fiscal notes. Second, optimize services and greatly increase the satisfaction level. The finance authorities further strengthened the management of the use of fiscal notes, accelerated the promotion of convenient and standardized electronic notes and machine-made notes, and gradually replaced the manual notes. In the next step, the Beijing Finance Bureau will continue to promote the use of electronic fiscal notes in schools, roadside parking, education exams and comprehensive administrative law enforcement in urban management, and jointly work with the Municipal Health Commission, the Municipal Medical

Administration Bureau, and the Municipal Medical Insurance Bureau in carrying out the pilot program of electronic notes for medical bills, in order to explore experiences that can be replicated and promoted and further give play to the role of pilot programs. ■

58 Finance authorities of Jiangsu Province took five measures to ensure effective implementation of tax and fee cut policy

According to the news released by the Finance Bureau of Taizhou City, Jiangsu Province on July 15, the implementation of larger-scale tax and fee cut policy is an important move to deepen the supply-side structural reform and promote the high-quality development of the economy. Since 2019, the Taizhou Finance Bureau has comprehensively implemented a new round of tax and fee cut policies to ensure that taxpayers and fee-payers in the city can enjoy the benefits of tax and fee reduction. First, strengthen organizational leadership and improve the promotion mechanism. The Taizhou Finance Bureau sets up a leading group to comprehensively coordinate the promotion, deployment, internal and external linkage, consultation, analysis and evaluation, follow-up inspection and supervision of the work related to tax and fee cuts. Second, clarify the division of tasks and responsibilities. Build a long-term and effective work pattern with well-defined responsibilities, clear tasks, efficient operation, and binding constraints. Third, strengthen policy publicity and create a sound atmosphere. Carry out extensive publicity work and make in-depth interpretation of the significance and policy content of the new round of tax and fee cuts, so as to help the taxpayers to get familiar with new policies, master new policies, comply with new policies, and benefit from new policies. Fourth, improve the supporting measures and refine the operational plan. Appropriately lower the minimum tax standard for urban land use tax, define the specific circumstances of the taxpayer's "difficulty" in paying the real estate tax, clarify the application materials, and standardize the processing time limit and workflow for acceptance, review and approval. Fifth, organize supervision and inspection to ensure the implementation of the policies. The Finance Bureau carefully organized and carried out supervision and inspection at city level, timely coordinated the efforts to address the pain points, blocking points and difficulties encountered in the implementation of the tax and fee cut policy, and specifically proposed suggestions for implementing the tax and fee cut policy in greater depth. ■

59 Finance authorities of Henan Province further strengthened budget management and supported the implementation of tax and fee cut policy

According to the news released by the Finance Bureau of Zhengzhou City, Henan Province on July 22, since 2019, the Zhengzhou Finance Bureau has fully played its role, opened up new sources of revenues and reduced expenditures, further strengthened budget management, and supported the implementation of tax and fee cut policy. First, fully implement the tax and fee cut policy. Establish a mechanism where the heads of Bureau and director-level cadres are required to liaise with 16 counties (cities and districts) and visit the counties (cities and districts) to supervise the implementation of tax and fee cut policies, help strengthen budget implementation, advance progress in the disbursement of poverty alleviation funds, and coordinate the resolution of difficulties and problems in budget implementation. Second, correctly handle the relationship between tax and fee reduction and stabilizing growth. While resolutely implementing various tax and fee cut policies, strengthen the collection of revenues, further promote comprehensive tax administration, give full play to the role of the integrated tax administration platform for real estate and construction industry, strengthen the administration of land appreciation tax and deed tax, strictly guard against the evasion and avoidance of small taxes, fully collect all taxes, timely identify and solve problems in revenue mobilization, and ensure that revenues are collected according to law. Third, cut expenditures and reinforce constraints. Reduce general expenditures, and on top of the "more than 5% reduction of general expenditures and further 3% cut of the three public expenses", cut operating expenditures per person by 5%, 10%, 15% and 20% respectively. Fourth, actively raise financial resources to ensure the implementation of key tasks. Raise the scale of the budget stabilization fund and ease the pressure of fiscal balance by increasing the transfer of funds from the governmental fund budget and the state-owned capital operating budget into the general public budget. ■

60

Finance authorities of Shaanxi Province deployed fiscal policies in support of the development of real economy

According to the news released by the Finance Bureau of Tongchuan City, Shaanxi Province on July 23, in the first half of 2019, the Tongchuan Finance Bureau closely focused on the plan of the City Party Committee and Government, continuously freed the mind, vigorously supported the development of real economy, reduced the cost of enterprises, and optimized the business environment, making positive contributions to the city's high-quality economic development. First, deploy supportive fiscal policy to boost enterprise development. Formulate the *Twelve Fiscal, Tax and Financial Measures to Promote Industrial Development* and the *Opinions on Fiscal, Tax and Financial Measures to Support the Development of China (Tongchuan) Commercial Space City* to provide policy support for major industrial projects. Second, reduce the costs of enterprises and offer more growth space for enterprises. Promote policy measures for tax and fee reduction, and implement the policy of reducing Social Insurance Premium Rates. Third, optimize business environment and build a quality fiscal service network. Make scientific integration of windows and strengthen refined management. At the same time, carry out supervision and inspection over the implementation of policy measures, with a focus on the investigation and punishment of the violations of financial and economic laws and problems that increase the burden on enterprises and harm the interests of people. ■

61

Finance authorities of Sichuan Province intensified the mobilization of financial resources to promote high-quality economic development

According to the news released by the Finance Department of Sichuan Province on July 29, in order to effectively deal with the downward pressure on the economy and promote the high-quality development of economy, Chengdu City of Sichuan Province researched and developed 30 measures for the mobilization of financial resources and the 2019 Work Program, and fully promoted industrial development and enterprise growth, thus providing sustainable and strong financial support for accelerating the urban development that fully reflects the new development vision. First, strengthen overall coordination and establish a work promotion mechanism. Establish the Chengdu City Leading Group for Financial Resource Mobilization and include 38 important departments involving finance, tax and financial affairs authorities into the Leading Group; set up a leading group office to organize the policy research of key matters, and supervise and inspect daily work, so as to create an interlinked and coordinated working pattern between different departments. Second, strengthen the orientation to major objectives and ensure that the tasks are implemented. In 2019, the financial resource mobilization work continued to focus on industrial development and enterprise growth, and a series of specific measures were proposed to enhance financial capabilities, promote industrial upgrading, and advance the continuous optimization of financial resources structure. Third, strengthen departmental linkages and effectively improve the effectiveness of work. Carry out special researches involving multiple departments with a focus on the key work of the year, comprehensively sort through the public industrial expenditure policies around the city's major strategy, strengthen the performance management of industrial special fund budget, optimize the special fund catalogue, adjust the special fund arrangement, and further improve the effectiveness of the use of fiscal funds. ■

62 Finance authorities of Hubei Province took four measures to advance the implementation of the tax and fee cut policy

According to the news released by the Finance Department of Hubei Province on July 31, since the implementation of the tax and fee cut policy of the central and Hubei province, the Huangshi City Party Committee and Government have earnestly implemented the policy to good effect. From January to May 2019, the tax and fee cuts in Huangshi City reached 500 million RMB. First, improve political alignment and strengthen organizational support. The Huangshi Party Committee and Government organized a special class study session and conducted a special study at the city government executive meeting. *The Huangshi City Work Program for Tax and Fee Cut* was published, which clarified the work objectives, work responsibilities and deadlines to ensure orderly work progress. Second, develop supporting measures and build a management mechanism. Formulate the *Rules for the Work of Tax and Fee Cut in Huangshi City, Measures for the Responsibility of the Work of Tax and Fee Cut,* and *Measures for the Quick Response to Tax-related Complains of Taxpayers,* further clarify job responsibilities, and enhance work implementation. Third, increase publicity and training to create a sound atmosphere. Publicize tax and fee cut policy through channels such as newspapers, multimedia, bus TV and posters, set up a special section for tax and fee cut policy on the government portal website, and provide policy consultation for businesses, in order to foster an enabling atmosphere for tax and fee cuts. Fourth, highlight the work priorities and increase the intensity of work. In order to comprehensively promote the implementation of the tax and fee cut policy, Huangshi finance authorities strengthened fundraising, and accelerated the progress of fund disbursement. It kept work records, collected feedback, and implemented a list-based management mechanism for tasks such as tax and fee cuts and enterprise services, so as to ensure that policies are well implemented. ■

63 Finance authorities of Zhejiang Province took effective measures to ensure the implementation of tax and fee cut policies

According to the news released by the Finance Department of Zhejiang Province on August 5, since 2019, the Taizhou Finance Bureau has improved its political awareness, acted fast, implemented concrete measures, and enhanced publicity, in order to ensure that all the tax and fee cut policies take effect and allow small-and- micro businesses to reap more benefits. First, establish a comprehensive fiscal and tax coordination mechanism to ensure that the policies are well implemented. Timely establish a fiscal and tax revenue coordination mechanism and a leading group, with the office hosted by the Finance Bureau to coordinate the city's organization of revenue-related work. Establish a coordination mechanism for finance and tax work as well as a special fiscal and tax work taskforce which may serve to put forward suggestions for the reference of Taizhou City Party Committee and Government. Second, build a policy publicity mechanism featuring comprehensive, innovative and targeted publicity of tax and fee cut policies. Compile three service manuals for enterprises, public sector and general public; create the "Finance Knows" program at the Taizhou Traffic Radio Station and publicize fiscal policies in the form of Q&A; carry out knowledge contest for tax and fee cuts in conjunction with the Taizhou City Taxation Bureau, Taizhou Banking and Insurance Supervision Bureau and Taizhou Vocational and Technical College to popularize policies related to tax and fee cuts; organize the first city public finance sports meeting to promote the advocacy of fiscal and tax policies. Third, build a synergistic inter-departmental linkage mechanism to ensure win-win progress. Enhance the linkage between city and county to identify concrete measures for the work of tax and fee cuts; enhance the linkage between finance authorities and enterprises and encourage "thousands of cadres to reach out to thousands of enterprises"; enhance inter-departmental linkage, work with the city tax authorities in taking the initiative to report to the discipline inspection commission, the supervisory committee and the audit authorities on the implementation of tax and fee cut policies and report the implementation progress to the city people's congress. ■

64 Finance authorities of Henan Province adopted multiple measures to ensure the effectiveness of tax and fee cut policies

According to the news released by the Finance Department of Henan Province on August 6, since 2019, the finance authorities of Zhoukou City, Henan Province have actively played its role and adopted a number of effective measures to ensure that all policies and measures for tax and fee cuts are well-implemented. First, enhance political awareness and make early planning. The city finance, taxation, human resources and other departments have set up their respective leading taskforce for tax and fee cuts, formulated specific implementation plans, and established the mechanism for effective communication and coordination, in order to ensure that all the tax and fee cut policies are implemented without compromise. Second, strengthen publicity and correctly guide public opinion. Make comprehensive use of newspapers, magazines, internet, news media and WeChat public account to explain and publicize the tax and fee cut policy and raise public awareness of the policy. Third, make scientific planning and improve income calculation. Zhoukou finance and tax authorities work closely to analyze tax and fee cut policies such as tax cuts and exemption for small and micro enterprises, further VAT reform and cuts of social insurance rate, and to measure the impact on the city's enterprises and local fiscal revenue. Fourth, regulate fee collection and implement list-based management. Make public the city's administrative fees and the catalogue of governmental fund projects in 2019 through the portal websites of the city government and the finance bureau. Fifth, strengthen research and ensure the effectiveness of policy. Carry out field research of more than 10 enterprises in Shangshui, Huaiyang and other counties. Sixth, administer taxes in accordance with the law to ensure that all taxes are duly collected. Promote law-based tax administration and continuously improve the quality of revenue. ■

65 Finance Department of Yunnan Province actively implemented forest ecological benefit compensation in support of poverty alleviation

According to the news released by the Finance Department of Yunnan Province on August 13, in 2019, the Finance Department of Yunnan disbursed a total of 1.86 billion RMB of central and provincial forest ecological benefit compensation funds, in order to implement the "ecological civilization construction leader" strategy, support the fight against poverty and build the "Forest Yunnan". First, strengthen management and build mechanisms to maximize the benefits of compensation funds. Establish leading groups at the provincial, prefecture and county level, and create a platform for joint management from province to county, so as to carry out the work, release compensation tasks and funds and organize inspection and evaluation in a unified manner. Second, increase investment, offer compensation, and strive to protect the interests of farmers. Increase investment and achieve the same compensation standard at the provincial and national levels. The Yunnan Finance authorities have twice raised the compensation standard for provincial collective public welfare forests. Since 2012, the compensation has been 10 RMB per mu, and since 2014, the compensation has risen to 15 RMB per mu, achieving the parity with the national level in terms of the compensation for public welfare forests. Third, increase income and support the development of industries to boost poverty alleviation. The compensation for forest ecological benefits has directly increased the cash income of forest farmers. For example, there are 14 households in the Latudi Village of Shangpa Town, Fugong County, Nujiang Prefecture. By providing compensation funds for public welfare forests, farming household received a maximum of 8760 RMB and a minimum of 7,220 RMB, averaging 7,500 RMB per household. By combining management, protection and operation and promoting the local employment of forest farmers on the spot, more than 7 million farming households and 23.85 million people gained direct benefits, and 73,000 farmers directly participated in public welfare forest management and received labor income. Yunnan also actively guided forest farmers to rely on public welfare forest resources and vigorously developed industries such as undergrowth planting, livestock breeding, forest product processing and forest tourism. For example, the family of Nu Wenjun from Xiyuegu Group of Qida Village, Puladi Township, Gongshan County, Nujiang Prefecture used 2093.1 RMB of forest compensation funds to purchase seedlings of Amomum tsao-ko, and gained more than 30,000 RMB of annual income by growing 50 mu of Amomum tsao-ko. Diqing Prefecture has also developed forestry in the mountainous region and built a total of 800,000 mu of woody oil plant base centered on iron walnuts. ■

66 Finance Department of Guangdong Province developed innovative measures to improve the effectiveness of fiscal investment review

According to the news released by the Finance Department of Guangdong Province on August 14, since 2019, the Fiscal Investment Review Center of Zhongshan City, Guangdong Province, with the aim to improve the effectiveness of the use of fiscal funds, has strengthened fiscal review, actively explored innovative evaluation models, standardized and optimized the internal management system, and continuously improved the level of fiscal investment review. First, standardize internal review management and prevent and control corruption risks. In accordance with the actual work, the *Procedures for Internal Review of City-level Fiscal Investment Projects* were formulated and promulgated. The manager of Investment Review Center is responsible for organizing internal review and conducting internal collective review of the disputes in project evaluation. Second, perfect the review work paper and improve the quality of review. Issue the *Circular on Further Improving the Work Paper of Fiscal Investment Settlement Review,* further clarify the specific operational rules for number-checking, standardize the intermediary agencies' number-checking behavior, reduce review errors, improve the quality of fiscal investment review, and ensure the authoritativeness of the conclusions of fiscal investment review. Third, adjust the final confirmation model and optimize the workflow. Add the phase of comment-seeking for the conclusions of the preliminary review; remove the confirmation requirement for "estimate confirmation" and "final settlement confirmation", and add the requirement for signature confirmation. Fourth, strengthen the management of review experts and give play to their technical advantages. Strictly control the entry of experts to ensure their professional quality. Strictly vet the qualifications of experts, including professional competence, work experience, age and records of malpractices. ■

67 Finance authorities of Shaanxi Province took multiple measures to strengthen the city financial credit guarantee company

According to the news released by the Finance Department of Shaanxi Province on August 26, the Ankang Finance Bureau of Shaanxi Province has conscientiously implemented the series of policies of the central, provincial and city government on developing fiscal and financial services for real economy and has taken multiple measures to support the growth of the city's financial credit guarantee company, achieving remarkable results in serving local economic development. First, keep problem-oriented and make utmost efforts to solve the difficulties. The Ankang Finance Bureau attached great importance to the development of the financial credit guarantee company and actively fulfilled its duties as the regulator and capital contributor. Its principal leaders have conducted several field investigations of the financial credit guarantee company to help the company resolve practical problems and vigorously promote the company's capital increase, share increase, system development and new business operation. Second, strengthen financial support and enhance the company's strength. Innovate fiscal investment methods, make every effort to raise funds and support the financial credit guarantee company. With 9 rounds of capital increase over the past 14 years since 2005, the registered capital went up from 20 million RMB to 1.173 billion RMB, offering a cumulative of 87.88 million RMB of subsidies and reward funds. Third, strengthen policy support and improve the guarantee system. Tightly seize the policy opportunities for the construction of central and provincial government financing guarantee systems, coordinate the issuance of the

Implementation Plan for Ankang City Governmental Financing Guarantee System Construction in the name of the city government, and take the city financial credit guarantee company as the core to fully promote the construction of a governmental financing guarantee system with Ankang characteristics. Fourth, strengthen service awareness and boost economic development. Since the establishment of the company, it has provided 21.6 billion RMB of guaranteed loans for 2,175 enterprises and 3,966 projects, playing an indispensable role in supporting the development of Ankang's characteristic industries, industrial poverty alleviation and rural revitalization. ■

68 Finance authorities of Shandong Province reformed the fund management system to support the transition of growth drivers

According to the news released by the Finance Department of Shandong Province on August 27, in order to further promote investment by the Shandong Provincial Fund for the Transition of Growth Drivers and accurately support the implementation of major projects for the transition of growth drivers, the Shandong Finance Department proposed 20 policy measures to reform the management system and operational model, so as to improve the level of market-oriented operation of the Fund. First, reform the management system and improve the level of market-oriented operation. In terms of the mechanism for fund establishment, matters like the identification of cooperative institutions and the establishment of fund are to be independently decided by the Fund; on the mechanism for fund operation, "trusted management" is changed into "direct capital injection"; on the fund performance appraisal, a tiered fund evaluation system is established. Second, lower the threshold for establishment and enhance the attractiveness and competitiveness of the Fund. Lower the threshold for fund declaration, with the size of the fund to be determined by the fund company and the fund management institution through consultation; relax the fund return investment limit, and the proportion of fund invested in Shandong shall not be less than 1.5 times of the capital contribution of the guiding fund; increase the proportion of capital contribution of the guiding fund, and the proportion of guiding fund invested in industrial fund shall be no more than 25%. Third, adopt flexible operational models to achieve accurate support by the fund. Adjust the fund structure and change the three-level structure of "guiding fund, parent fund and sub-funds" into "guiding fund and sub-fund"; innovate the operational models, with the provincial guiding fund working together with the city and county guiding fund and private sector capital to develop customized project fund. Fourth, strengthen policy incentives and improve the efficiency of fund use. Encourage the guiding fund to make greater concession; encourage private investors to purchase the equity or share held by the guiding fund; provide fiscal incentives and offer up to 2 million RMB of rewards for the fund management institutions according to the progress of investment and the actual amount of investment within two years of fund establishment. Fifth, improve services and create a good environment for the development of fund. Improve the project screening and promotion mechanism, and enable the Fund company to take the lead in setting up the fund investment project pipeline; establish an accountability mechanism; improve the service mechanism and establish regular consultation and regular reporting systems. ■

69 Finance authorities of Shandong Province established a synergistic, well-coordinated and precise mechanism for budget performance management

According to the news released by the Finance Department of Shandong Province on September 2, the finance authorities of Jinan City of Shandong Province established a synergistic, well-coordinated and precise mechanism for budget performance management to promote the high-quality operation of the city's public finance. First, promote institutional innovation and explore a scientific and efficient budget performance management model. Formulate the *Measures for the Management of Budget Performance of City-level Departments in Jinan City and the Measures for the Management of Budget Performance of Sub-city Transfer Payment Funds in Jinan City,* which set out 17 reform measures from five aspects to basically establish a full-coverage, whole-process and all-round budget performance management system. Second, keep problem-oriented and create a precise mechanism for budget performance management. Set clear targets to improve the efficiency of budget implementation. In preparing the departmental budget for 2019, performance indicators covered more than 1,500 projects in 446 budget units of the city, involving about 60 billion RMB of special funds in departmental budget; "three links" between major policies and project budget preparation were achieved. In preparing the departmental budget for 2019, it took the lead in conducting pre-performance evaluation of 88 policies and projects in the fields of industrial policy and urban construction plan, involving 6.62 billion RMB of budgeted funds, deducted by 32.1% after being reviewed; track and monitor the effectiveness of funds and establish a "project performance tracking and evaluation + expenditure progress and idle fund warning and rectification + dynamic and accurate cleanup" mechanism; implement "three combinations" of performance evaluation, i.e., combination of performance self-evaluation and spot check and review, combination of performance evaluation and analysis feedback, and combination of performance accountability and rectification. Third, establish a synergistic, well-coordinated and precise mechanism for budget performance. Clarify the work responsibilities of all parties; establish a joint meeting system and urge all functional departments to support each other, closely cooperate to jointly push forward budget performance management; build an information sharing platform and gradually promote comprehensive, coordinated, open and shared big data application. ■

70 Finance authorities of Heilongjiang Province took multiple measures to strengthen the management of fiscal funds for poverty alleviation

According to the news released by the Finance Department of Heilongjiang Province on September 4, in recent years, the Finance Department of Heilongjiang Province has thoroughly implemented the decisions and plans of the Party Central Committee, the State Council, the Heilongjiang Provincial Party Committee and the Provincial Government on poverty alleviation, raised funds through multiple channels, and strengthened supervision in all aspects to provide sound and reliable financial support for the province to win the battle against poverty. First, strengthen organizational leadership and build up the work force. The Finance Department of Heilongjiang Province set up a leading group and office for poverty alleviation. The office consists of four teams: Policy Fund Team, Technical Support Team, Supervision and Verification Team, and Comprehensive Coordination Team. It also selected 17 key staff to work full-time on poverty alleviation. Second, build a monitoring platform and promote transformation and upgrading. The Finance Department of Heilongjiang Province clearly defined the work procedures, and formulated the *Procedures for the Dynamic Monitoring of Fiscal Funds for Poverty Alleviation of the Finance Department of Heilongjiang Province;* clarified the division of responsibilities, with the poverty alleviation office taking the lead in advancing the dynamic monitoring of fiscal funds for poverty alleviation; improved the platform functions and initiated the data connection between the platform and the fiscal production system. Third, strengthen the basic work and enhance process control. The Finance Department of Heilongjiang Province accelerated the implementation of budget and sped up the disbursement of all kinds of fiscal funds for poverty alleviation in the province through telephone reminders, letters and urges; conducted special inspection on the public disclosure of the management and use of the fiscal funds for poverty alleviation in 20 national-level poor counties; strengthened performance management and required the city and county finance authorities to simultaneously enter performance evaluation data into the dynamic monitoring platform of fiscal funds for poverty alleviation. Fourth, promote online and offline linkage to strengthen supervision. The online dynamic management platform is operating in real time. At present, the total amount of fiscal funds for poverty alleviation entering the monitoring scope of the platform reached 5.984 billion RMB in 2019 in the province; the offline supervision and verification was carried out in 20 national-level poor counties from June 17 to July 12. ■

71 Finance authorities of Sichuan Province conducted meticulous management of funds and comprehensively enforced the requirements of belt-tightening

According to the news released by the Finance Department of Sichuan Province on September 10, in order to conscientiously implement the requirements of central, provincial and city governments for tightening belt, exercising frugality and opposing waste, Dazhou City of Sichuan Province has refined budget preparation, strengthened budget constraints, optimized expenditure structure, enhanced resource mobilization, continued to reduce non-mandatory and non-priority project expenditures, promoted frugality and saving of Party and government organs and institutions at all levels, and strived to improve the life of people by tightening the belt of government. First, improve budget preparation and continue to reduce general expenditures. Consolidate and strengthen the management of the "three public expenses", further cut general expenditures, and resolutely reduce non-mandatory and non-priority special expenditures. Second, strengthen budget constraints and speed up budget implementation. Strictly control the adjustment and increase of budget, speed up budget implementation, and strictly conduct revenue and expenditure management. Third, strengthen comprehensive budgeting and enhance the coordination of fund use. Actively strengthen the mid-term evaluation of budget implementation, conduct item-by-item screening and case-by-case verification, and recover the long-term idle funds for coordinated use. Fourth, optimize the expenditure structure and enhance the funding support for improving people's livelihood. Strictly implement the requirements of "ensuring wage payment, basic operation and people's livelihood", constantly optimize the expenditure structure, and increase investment in people's livelihood. Fifth, conduct effective budget management and continuously improve the efficiency of fund use. Comprehensively strengthen performance target management, conduct in-depth performance evaluation, and strengthen the application of evaluation results. Sixth, enforce strict financial and economic discipline and make efforts to build a long-term mechanism. Strictly control the scope and standards of the "three public expenses", travel expenses, conference expenses and training expenses. ■

72 Finance authorities of Zhejiang Province effectively deepened budget management reform

According to the news released by the Finance Department of Zhejiang Province on September 11, the Finance Bureau of Jinhua City of Zhejiang Province has earnestly implemented the reform requirements of MOF and the Finance Department of Zhejiang Province, deepened budget management reform as an important component of fiscal work, and constantly improved the budget preparation system to effectively improve the budget management level. First, promote budget preparation with real effects. Deepen the zero-based budgeting, alter the concept of the base used in previous budget preparation, and strengthen the regulation of the use of fiscal funds through strict budget review from the original source. Improve the budget preparation system, compile comprehensive revenue budget, and compile substantive expenditure budget; promote the disclosure of budget information, and increase the disclosure of information on the process and results of the allocation of funds related to people's livelihood and the performance of fund use. Second, enforce strict budget implementation. Strengthen the budget constraints at the beginning of the year, and avoid the addition of budget expenditure except for the case of temporary and emergency expenditures; strictly tighten the belt, vigorously reduce and control general expenses such as conference expenses and training expenses; promote the coordinated use of the stock of fiscal funds and strengthen the dynamic monitoring of funds. Third, advance effective fund management. Pay attention to the management at the source, strengthen the principal responsibility of budget department, promote the transition from performance target management to budget performance review; carry out interim supervision, promote the reform of budget performance monitoring, improve the timeliness, balance and effectiveness of expenditure; increase the application of results, establish and improve the whole-process performance management mechanism for budget preparation, budget implementation, evaluation and supervision, and feedback the evaluation results in a timely manner to the budget preparation link, which may serve as an important basis for the next year's budget review. ■

73 Finance authorities of Liaoning Province took proactive and targeted measures to promote high-quality economic development of Liaoning

According to the news released by the Finance Department of Liaoning Province on September 16, since 2019, the Finance Department of Liaoning Province has focused on stabilizing the short-term growth, promoted the transition of growth drivers over the medium term, and made every effort to raise funds for the stable and sound development of Liaoning's economy. First, expand effective investment. Raise 6.06 billion RMB of capital construction funds to support the construction of a number of major infrastructure projects, and make good use of the newly added 20.1 billion RMB of bonds to support around 200 key projects, directly catalyzing over 100 billion RMB of private investment. Optimize industrial (entrepreneurial) investment to provide guidance for fund management, with a total investment of 3.612 billion RMB. Connect with the national fund, and set up 9 sub-funds and 165 direct investment projects, directly catalyzing over 29.3 billion RMB of private investment. Second, support innovation-driven development. Optimize the model of fiscal investment in science and technology, arrange 500 million RMB of funds to support the development, operation and maintenance of the Northeast Science and Technology Market, implement 30 major projects in the fields of electronic information and new materials as well as 116 key R&D programs in equipment manufacturing, energy and transportation, which is expected to catalyze 3.22 billion RMB of private R&D investment. Third, support industrial transformation and upgrading and the transition of growth drivers. Raise 150 million RMB of funds to support the development of new energy vehicles. Strengthen the development of the financing guarantee and re-guarantee system, allocate 270 million RMB of guarantee and re-guarantee risk compensation funds, and establish a provincial risk compensation mechanism for the re-guarantee system. Fourth, support coordinated regional development. Raise 780 million RMB of funds to support 48 projects related to high-tech industry, strategic emerging industry, modern service industry, and enterprise transformation and upgrading in the coastal economic zone. Offer 520 million RMB of rewards promised in the three-year action plan of the regional economic development strategy, raise 1 billion RMB respectively for the construction of Shenfu New District, for the development of northwest Liaoning, and for the promotion of the coordinated development of the regional economy. ■

74 Finance authorities of Anhui Province set up indicators to establish the standards for budget performance management

According to the news released by the Finance Department of Anhui Province on September 18, in order to lay a solid foundation for budget performance management and make performance management more standardized and regulated, the Finance Bureau of Hefei, Anhui adopted the approach of "framework building, index collection, refinement, and science evaluation", started with over 1,000 special funds and the good cases of performance targets and performance evaluation over the years, sorted through the applied performance indicators, and gradually established and improved the performance indicators and standard system by categories, sectors and fields. First, clear framework. Vertically, set up 80 sets of complete indicator systems according to the 80 purposes of the use of funds by taking into account the use of indicators in the various stages of preparation, implementation, supervision and evaluation; horizontally, make the indicators comparable and measurable, and set three levels of indicators that are both normative and practical. Second, scientific classification. The indicators are divided into two categories of general indicators and special indicators in light of the specific use of funds and the classification of government revenue and expenditure. General indicators are divided into 15 categories and 417 third-level indicators according to the general use of funds for economic operation. Special indicators are divided into 15 categories and 1304 third-level indicators based on the use of funds for special development and construction. Third, refined and quantitative setting of indicators. The setting of indicators considers common and special features; and the indicator value is determined by a combination of quantitative and qualitative methods. Fourth, dynamic adjustment. The indicator library is designed to provide reference for budget performance management. The indicators can be selected from the indicator library according to the actual work, and be expanded and improved as needed. ■

75 Finance authorities of Hunan Province made notable progress on the management of special funds

According to the news published by the Finance Department of Hunan Province on September 23, since 2019, the Finance Bureau of Chenzhou City of Hunan Province has vigorously promoted the reform of special fund management, and greatly improved the effectiveness of the use of special fiscal funds through measures such as zero-based budgeting, clean-up and consolidation, innovative investment and regulated use. First, persist in breaking new ground and renewing efforts to implement zero-based budgeting. The city finance authorities vigorously promoted the zero-based budgeting model. The "two types of special funds" were reduced by more than 30% from the previous year, and 270 million RMB of funds were freed up, effectively breaking the "base + growth" model of departmental projects. Second, keep problem-oriented and substantively promote the consolidation of special funds. At present, the city-level special funds have been greatly reduced, and the industry-guiding funds have been integrated into the four types of industry-supporting funds from the original seven categories; the departmental special funds arranged by city finance authorities have been consolidated from 82 to 38, a decrease of 44, or 53.7%. Third, promote innovative investment and link the funding arrangement to the contribution of fiscal and tax revenue. The city finance authorities revised and introduced new incentives to support industries and clarified the industry-supporting policies with the main elements of "contribution of fiscal and tax revenue, employment, scientific and technological innovation, and financing through public listing". Fourth, promote open and transparent operation and strictly regulate the management of special funds. Establish a fund management system featuring "special funds + task list" and implement the list-based management of special funds. ■

76 Finance authorities of Yunnan Province strengthened the management of poverty alleviation funds to support the fight against poverty

According to the news published by the Finance Department of Yunnan Province on September 24, the Finance Department of Yunnan Province, with the aim of comprehensively improving the effectiveness of the use of poverty alleviation funds, has implemented the performance management of poverty alleviation funds, deployed the dynamic monitoring platform for poverty alleviation funds, further clarified the responsibilities of major players, rationalized the division of responsibilities, strengthened dynamic supervision, and promoted the shift of the focus of performance management of poverty alleviation funds from full coverage to high quality. First, define the responsibilities of major players. Extend the dynamic monitoring system for poverty alleviation funds to departments (units) and townships, emphasize that the departments (units) that use funds are responsible for the performance management of poverty alleviation funds, and clarify that departments (units) and townships are responsible for reporting and reviewing performance data and the finance authorities of provinces, cities and counties are responsible for checking data. Second, implement the "four synchronized" management. The performance targets of projects supported by poverty alleviation funds and the project budget will be simultaneously submitted, reviewed, released and entered into the dynamic monitoring system for poverty alleviation funds. Third, implement "all-weather" supervision. Establish a rectification and feedback mechanism for problems, place focus on reviewing the 8 cities with heavy poverty-reduction tasks, submit a list of problems to the city every

5 working days, and urge the project implementing units to verify and rectify problems in a timely manner. Fourth, improve the quality of performance management of poverty alleviation funds. Adopt a new model of performance information management with the finance authorities initiating tasks, the departments (units) reporting performance information, and the finance authorities reviewing performance information. Fifth, strengthen field research. Strengthen business guidance and technical support for the finance authorities at the grass-root level, and establish a rapid feedback mechanism for reporting problems across the province. ■

77 Finance authorities of Guangdong Province established an equalization transfer payment system to add new impetus to coordinated regional development

According to the news released by the Finance Department of Guangdong Province on October 8, since 2019, the Finance Department of Guangdong Province has put in place an equalization transfer payment system and vigorously raised the standard to promote coordinated and balanced regional development. First, promote equalization and systematically construct a transfer payment system conducive to high-quality development. Establish an equalization transfer payment system with the goal of "promoting equalization", in order to "compensate the costs" for the northern ecological development zone, "strengthen industries" for the key areas of the eastern and western coastal economic belts, and "promote the revitalization" of the old revolutionary base areas and ethnic minority areas. Second, fundamentally shift the direction of transfer payment policy from providing incentives to offering basic safeguards. Delink the transfer payment distribution from GDP and fiscal revenue growth, and tilt the allocation of funds towards areas with large population, heavy expenditure burden and tight financial resources according to the principle of sustainability and safeguards through a new distribution mechanism. Third, promote full coverage and include the poor areas of the Pearl River Delta into policy support. The six Pearl River Delta counties and districts with financial resources lower than the provincial average, such as Taishan and Kaiping, were added to the policy support for the first time. After the full expansion, the equalization transfer payment was extended from the original 60 counties (cities) to 86 counties and districts, achieving the "full coverage and broad benefits" in all financially difficult counties and districts in the province. Fourth, address the problem of weak financial resources in underdeveloped areas. Include all the 22 city districts in the underdeveloped areas in the scope of equalization transfer payment policy; maintain the original transfer payment for five years for the 7 county-turned districts to alleviate the practical difficulties of insufficient financial resources during the transition period. Fifth, comprehensively support the implementation of the "three guarantees" policy in counties and districts to ensure smooth and stable operation. In 2019, the equalization transfer payment was 44.2 billion RMB, an increase of 15.7% over the previous year, and 5 percentage points higher than the growth of central-to-local equalization transfer payment. ■

78 Finance authorities of Shandong Province put in place six mechanisms to ensure the effective implementation of tax and fee cut policy

According to the news released by the Finance Department of Shandong Province on October 9, since 2019, Dongying City of Shandong Province has adopted a number of measures to cut taxes and fees, and cut 5.007 billion RMB of taxes and fees from January to July. First, improve political position and establish an efficient and effective leading mechanism. The Dongying Finance Bureau issued the *Work Plan for Implementing the Tax and Fee Cut Policy* to ensure the orderly progress of tax and fee reduction. Second, strengthen policy advocacy and establish a variety of publicity mechanisms. The city has carried out 29 editions of "physical + live broadcast" online classes, covering 130,000 taxpayers, and expanded the coverage of publicity and counseling. Third, stay problem-oriented and establish a monitoring mechanism for enterprise-related fees. Set up monitoring points for 49 selected enterprises, designate personnel to assist enterprises in keeping records, regularly report the relevant information on enterprise-related fees, and track the fee collection of related enterprises in real time. Fourth, standardize the collection procedures and establish a regulation mechanism for invoices. Adjust the invoicing authority of relevant invoice users in the invoice information management system in line with the suspension or cancellation of non-tax charges. Fifth, attach importance to the cultivation of financial resources and establish a mechanism for increasing revenues. Lead the development of 20 measures for cultivating financial resources, and encourage the relevant departments to refine 21 implementation plans according to their respective responsibilities. Sixth, carry out strict supervision and inspection and establish a standardized and orderly linkage mechanism. Set up a supervision team to carry out three rounds of inspection over the work of tax and fee cut in counties and districts. ■

79 Finance authorities of Yunnan Province unveiled measures to optimize the business environment to promote fair market competition in government procurement

According to the news released by the Finance Department of Yunnan Province on October 14, to further optimize the business environment in the government procurement sector and build a unified, open, competitive and orderly government procurement market system, 18 measures in 5 aspects have been proposed. First, remove all kinds of unreasonable barriers and restrictions and create a fair market competition environment for government procurement. In accordance with the principle of competitive neutrality, eliminate all kinds of unreasonable restrictions and barriers imposed on different market entities in the government procurement process, and ensure fair competition among government procurement suppliers in accordance with the law. Second, reduce the transaction costs of participating in government procurement activities and reduce the burden on enterprises. Comprehensively sort through local government procurement charges and exempt e-procurement documentation fees for government procurement projects that implement electronic procurement. Third, promote "internet + government procurement" to improve the efficiency of services. Fully implement online government procurement review, approval and filing, and actively promote the online processing of matters such as the registration of the information of suppliers and agencies at the Yunnan Provincial Online Government Service Center. Fourth, strengthen the policy function of government procurement and create conditions for the development of small and medium-sized enterprises. Encourage small and medium-sized enterprises to take out credit loans with government procurement contracts and electronic transaction records, in accordance with the principle of "government guidance, market operation, voluntary bank-enterprise cooperation, and mutual benefits". Fifth, strengthen interim and ex-post supervision of government procurement and implement measures to optimize business environment. Require all localities and departments in the province to establish a sound self-assessment mechanism for fair competition and establish and improve the internal control system for government procurement. ■

80 Finance authorities of the Inner Mongolia Autonomous Region focused on three aspects to promote high-quality development

According to the news released by the Finance Department of the Inner Mongolia Autonomous Region on October 15, the Finance Bureau of Baotou City has promoted high-quality development by supporting business development, eco-environmental protection and economic transformation and upgrading and made great efforts to strengthen the weak links and reinforce the advantages, in order to lay the foundation for the city's high-quality economic development. First, promote the transition of growth drivers by implementing demonstration projects. Implement the national comprehensive demonstration project for emission reduction, and invest 2.15 billion RMB of fiscal funds to leverage 10.8 times of private investment to participate in energy conservation and emission reduction. Implement 151 typical demonstration projects for energy conservation and emission reduction in three years and catalyze 20.8 billion RMB of investment. Implement national demonstration project for black and odorous water treatment and secure 400 million RMB of special subsidies from the central government from 2019 to 2020. Implement the national pilot project for rare earth transformation and upgrading, secure 700 million RMB of special subsidies from the central government, provide 198 million RMB of city-level matching funds, and leverage 8 times of private investment to support 96 projects of 80 rare earth enterprises in the city. Second, promote investment of industry funds and actively bring in capital and talents. Establish the Baotou City Key Industry Development Fund with an initial scale of 1.5 billion RMB and set up the Talent, Innovation and Entrepreneurship Investment Fund with an initial scale of 200 million RMB. Third, advance the "streamlining of administration, delegation of powers and improvement of services" to promote the improvement of business environment. Vigorously promote the "streamlining of administration, delegation of powers and improvement of services" in public finance, accelerate the development of smart public finance featuring internet + e-government procurement, internet + treasury centralized payment and internet + government investment project pipeline, and improve the management service level. ■

81 Finance authorities of Hebei Province introduced the working procedures for the dynamic monitoring of fiscal funds for poverty alleviation and deployed "two systems" to conduct thorough monitoring of poverty alleviation funds

According to the news released by the Finance Department of Hebei Province on October 21, in order to strengthen the supervision of fiscal funds for poverty alleviation, enhance risk prevention and control, and standardize the dynamic monitoring of fiscal funds for poverty alleviation, the Finance Department of Hebei Province formulated and issued the Working Procedures of the *Finance Department of Hebei Province for the Dynamic Monitoring of the Fiscal Funds for Poverty Alleviation* and deployed the MOF Monitoring Platform and the Hebei Monitoring System to carry out thorough monitoring of the allocation, disbursement and payment of fiscal funds for poverty alleviation as well as the implementation of the performance targets of project funds, with view to ensuring that the operation of funds is recorded, risks are early warned, responsibility is traced and performance is tracked. The *Working Procedures* clarify that the scope of funds for dynamic monitoring includes all kinds of fiscal funds for poverty alleviation at all levels in the province that are under the aggregate management of government poverty alleviation funds. The dynamic monitoring of poverty alleviation funds in Hebei Province is supported by the MOF monitoring platform and the Hebei monitoring system. In accordance with the requirements for the management of fiscal funds for poverty alleviation and the risk level of early warning, the dynamic monitoring of poverty alleviation funds implements three levels of early warning, namely yellow alarm warning, yellow light warning and red light warning. The Finance Department of Hebei Province is responsible for the organization of the dynamic monitoring of fiscal funds for poverty alleviation, establishing an integrated dynamic monitoring mechanism that operates efficiently, and giving full play to the role of dynamic monitoring in standardizing rectification, warning and deterrence. ■

82 Finance authorities of Shanxi Province improved mechanisms and strengthened review and assessment to continuously enhance the level of the development of beautiful villages

According to the news released by the Finance Department of Shanxi Province on October 22, in recent years, the Finance Bureau of Xinzhou City, Shanxi Province has actively explored and improved the mechanism to strengthen the review and assessment, in order to lay a solid foundation and accumulate practical experience for supporting the fight against poverty and promoting rural revitalization. First, continuously improve the new mechanism for project initiation. Establish a leading group to improve political position; pay attention to field visits and improve the quality of assessment, 8 counties have passed the preliminary assessment in 2018-2019; select assessment experts according to the content of project; and accept broad supervision and strive for fairness and justice. Second, continuously learn from and draw on the advanced and new ideas. In 2018, Xinzhou City organized 33 main leaders, heads of finance bureaus and township chiefs from 14 counties (cities and districts) in the city to study in Anji where they opened up their horizons and updated their minds. Third, continuously bring the assessment to a new level. The Finance Bureau of Xinzhou City entrusted the Budget Investment Evaluation Center of the Finance Bureau to conduct performance evaluation over the counties (cities and districts) involved, tracked the effectiveness, and produced a general report on the performance evaluation of the city and detailed reports for each county. Fourth, constantly explore a new model of beautiful villages in Xinzhou. The pilot counties (cities and districts) of the city organically combined the development of beautiful villages with the task of poverty alleviation and took the two-pronged approach to explore the Xinzhou model for the development of beautiful villages. ■

83 Finance authorities of Henan Province worked on four fronts to support the high-quality development of economy

According to the news released by the Finance Department of Henan Province on October 28, since 2019, the Finance Bureau of Xinxiang City, Henan Province has adopted a mix of measures on fiscal investment, reduction of taxes and fees, leverage of resources and "streamlining of administration, delegation of powers and improvement of services", thus helping promote the high-quality development of the city's economy with high-quality fiscal development. First, work on fiscal "addition" to support the city's economic and social development. Continue to focus on improving the quality and efficiency of economic development, support the expansion of the real economy, and improve the quality of the real economy. Second, work on fiscal "subtraction" to reduce the burden on the real economy. Conscientiously implement the central and provincial policies and measures for the reduction of taxes and fees to see to it that the burden of social security contributions for enterprises, especially small and micro enterprises, will be substantially reduced. Third, work on fiscal "multiplication" to crowd in private capital investment. Establish the Xinxiang City Industrial Transformation and Development Fund with a scale of 5 billion RMB to support the leading industries and key projects of Xinxiang and its counties (cities and districts). Fourth, work on fiscal "division" to improve the efficiency of government services. Deepen the reform of "streamlining of administration, delegation of powers and improvement of services", further rationalize the fiscal system at the city and county (city and district) level, and stimulate the enthusiasm for work at the grass-root level. ■

84 Finance authorities of Beijing Municipality promoted the high-quality development of public finance with the rule of law

According to the news released by the Finance Bureau of Beijing Municipality on October 29, in recent years, the Beijing Finance Bureau has tackled the mismatch of fiscal revenue and expenditure within the framework of the rule of law, moved forward the key tasks of reform, properly handled the interests of different entities, and focused on four aspects to promote the high-quality development of public finance with the rule of law. First, advance the legal outreach and education to lay the legal foundation for the high-quality development of public finance. Actively adopt various methods and means to promote the outreach and education of fiscal laws and combine such efforts with the key tasks of fiscal reform. Second, accelerate the legislative progress to consolidate the legal basis for the high-quality development of public finance. The Municipal Finance Bureau focused on the improvement of business environment to help accelerate the related legislative work by streamlining 50% of the administrative licenses and other services, streamlining the application materials submitted by the applicants, shortening the processing time limit, and increasing online processing. Third, conduct strict law enforcement to pave the legal way for the high-quality development of public finance. It has adopted disciplinary measures such as prohibiting participation in government procurement activities against nearly 200 entities for violation of laws. Fourth, carry out rigorous assessment to drive the high-quality development of public finance. It accorded no less than 4% of scores to the assessment of law-based fiscal management. The assessment of 2019 is mainly focused on the law-based implementation of key fiscal tasks and comprehensive regulation of the administrative behavior of finance authorities, with emphasis on 12 indicators such as regulating government financing and borrowing behavior. ■

85 Finance authorities of Hebei Province published the measures for the record filing of the city and county standards for basic public services to ensure the sustainability of basic public services

According to the news released by the Finance Department of Hebei Province on November 4, in order to regulate the formulation and implementation of the city and county standards for basic public services and accelerate the equalization of basic public services, the Finance Department of Hebei Province recently published the *Measures for the Record Filing of the City and County Standards for Basic Public Services in Hebei Province*. First, define the meaning of "standard". The basic public service standards of Hebei Province are divided into provincial standards as well as city and county standards. Among them, the provincial standards are further divided into provincial-level basic standards and provincial-level standards. The city and county standards are divided into city and county-level basic standards and city and county-level standards. The city and county standards shall not be lower than the basic standards of the upper level, nor shall they be divorced from reality, make excessive promise and offer excessive protection. Second, emphasize the "record-filing" requirements. In terms of standards record-filing, if the city-level standards are higher than the provincial-level basic standards, the city-level finance department and the relevant competent departments shall submit the standards to the Finance Department of Hebei Province and the relevant provincial-level competent departments for record filing; if the county-level standards are higher than the city-level basic standards, the county-level finance department and the relevant competent departments shall submit the standards to the city-level finance department and the relevant competent departments at the city level for record filing, and copy them to the Finance Department of Hebei Province if the counties' finance happen to be directly administered by the provincial finance department. Third, set out the elements for "record filing". The record filing of city and county-level standards is mainly done through a record-filing form, which includes the implementation of the basic standards of the previous year, the existing problems, the financial situation of the region, the government debt and its impact on the implementation of city-level standards. Fourth, clarify the main responsibilities. The city and county finance departments and relevant competent departments shall bear the main responsibility for the formulation of city and county-level standards, and shall strictly implement the requirements for the formulation of city and county standards and strengthen the review and control. ■

86 Finance authorities of Hubei Province adopted a mix of policies to reduce taxes and fees in support of the development of real economy

According to the news released by the Finance Department of Hubei Province on November 5, since 2019, Jingzhou City, Hubei Province has conscientiously implemented various tax and fee reduction policies, accurately implemented inclusive tax reduction and structural tax reduction, and effectively reduced the burden on enterprises; it has also fully played its fiscal functions, actively raised funds, supported the development of enterprises, unleashed the vitality of market players, stabilized market expectation, and offered enterprises a real sense of gain. First, raise funds to inject new impetus to development. Set up the real economy development fund to alleviate the working capital difficulty of key enterprises in urban areas. Change the approach for the use of major industrial fund to support the development of enterprises in the city or major investment projects. Second, expand the scope of subsidies to benefit small and micro enterprises. Implement central and provincial inclusive financial policies to serve small and micro enterprises. Continue to expand the scope of beneficiaries of the subsidy policy. In 2019, in the budget of the city-level unemployment insurance fund, the expenditure on subsidies for job stabilization was 21 million RMB, and 11.94 million RMB was allocated as of September. Third, enhance the cooperation between the government and banks to reduce the financing costs. In 2019, the city government arranged 100 million RMB of government risk compensation fund, and engaged with China Construction Bank, Industrial and Commercial Bank of China and rural commercial banks, carrying out the business of "helping to secure loans", "government-bank-insurance collective loans" and "new rural loans" to support the financing needs of small and medium-sized enterprises. Fourth, enforce strict supervision and administer taxes and fees in accordance with the law. Strengthen supervision and inspection, and resolutely put an end to the "excessive taxation" and other behaviors; strictly implement the "one list" system for enterprise-related charges and avoid "loss in dike and compensation outside dike" as well as the substantial increase in administrative charges. Fifth, reduce general expenditures and strengthen budgetary constraints. In the face of the impact of tax and fee reduction on fiscal revenue and expenditure, resolutely tighten the belt, cut general expenditures by 10% from the previous year and reduce the "three public" expenses further by 3% in 2019. ■

87 Finance Department of Guangxi Zhuang Autonomous Region took a mix of policies to accelerate budget implementation

According to the news released by the Finance Department of Guangxi Zhuang Autonomous Region on November 14, in the first half of 2019, the general public budget expenditure in Guangxi was 296.86 billion RMB, a year-on-year increase of 13.2%. The increase in expenditure was among the highest in the country, and the scale of expenditure reached a new high in the same period. First, strengthen awareness of the targets and make a good "first move". Accelerate the expenditure schedule as an important task to strengthen fiscal management, tap the potential of local expenditure, and enhance the expenditure responsibility of cities and counties. Second, strengthen the sense of overall planning and beef up the "safeguard network". Actively make up for the financial shortfall, accelerate the issuance of new bonds, and actively align with the central transfer payments. Third, strengthen awareness of priority tasks and make key steps. Optimize the expenditure structure, vigorously reduce non-mandatory and non-emergency expenditures, and cut or eliminate budget for inefficient and ineffective funds. Actively involve in the implementation of major projects in the autonomous region, timely report the government procurement process, and create favorable conditions for promoting the efficient use of funds. Accelerate the use of funds from the advance issuance of new general bonds in the first half of the year compared with the same period of the previous year. Fourth, strengthen awareness of efficiency and take the initiative to "win the battle". Accelerate the allocation of funds and create good conditions for accelerating the progress of expenditure. Accelerate the disbursement of funds, urge all departments and units of the autonomous region to prepare monthly fund-usage plans based on the annual budget and project implementation progress, timely submit payment applications, and timely review and disburse funds. Strengthen incentives and constraints, strictly implement the required documents, standardize budget implementation and management, and improve the efficiency of budget implementation. ■

88 Finance Department of Liaoning Province took multiple measures to support the fight against pollution

According to the news released by the Finance Department of Liaoning Province on November 11, as stated by the general requirements of "making breakthrough in tackling water pollution, consolidating the outcomes of tackling air pollution, and moving to treat soil pollution" proposed by the Liaoning Provincial People's Government, the Liaoning Finance Department and the relevant provincial departments have actively cooperated to raise funds, tackle the shortcomings and weaknesses, speed up the resolution of outstanding environmental issues, and focus on improving the quality of the ecological environment. First, raise funds to ensure adequate funding. In 2019, a total of 3.5 billion RMB of pollution prevention and control funds were raised, including 2.36 billion RMB for water pollution prevention and control, 310 million RMB for air pollution prevention and control, 380 million RMB for soil pollution prevention and control, and 450 million RMB for rural environmental management. Second, concentrate the funds on addressing the shortcomings and weaknesses. Highlight the key aspects, address the shortcomings, and spend the money on the priority areas, in accordance with the feedbacks from the central environmental protection inspection and the national ocean inspection. Third, consolidate the funds to enhance the synergy. In order to resolve the problem of scattered use of funds and fragmented management, the Liaoning Finance Department, in conjunction with other departments, consolidated the investment of funds on the basis of the special plans. Fourth, improve management and strengthen monitoring. While supporting the construction of pollution control facilities, the Liaoning Finance Department, in response to the unknown pollution sources in the province, arranged 60 million RMB of special funds in 2019 to support the construction of automatic water quality monitoring stations along the Liao River and the coastline of Bohai Sea as well as automatic air monitoring stations near key industrial parks. Fifth, step up supervision and assessment to promote rectification. Since 2019, the Liaoning Finance Department has actively cooperated with other relevant departments to carry out special inspections around the key issues identified by the central environmental protection inspection and the national ocean inspection as well as the key projects on pollution prevention and control that are of interest to people, and urged all localities to take effective measures to work expeditiously to accelerate the construction of various pollution prevention and control projects. ■

89 Finance authorities of Jiangxi Province took multiple measures to optimize the business environment

According to the news released by the Finance Department of Jiangxi Province on November 18, since 2019, Ganzhou City, Jiangxi Province has made efforts to create a business environment that is fair, equitable, high-quality, efficient, entrepreneurial, innovative, convenient and fast, in order to fully promote the high-quality development of Ganzhou's economy. First, create a fair and equitable market environment and give private investment greater market access. Vigorously dismantle the investment threshold and resolutely remove the hidden barriers. In response to the problem of the "exclusion of private capital access", it is ordered that no department in the city should separately impose additional conditions and discriminatory terms on private capital. Second, create a high-quality and efficient government service environment so that private enterprises can be "assured". Introduce policies to further improve development environment and strive to create an enabling business environment. Continue with self-reform and deepen the reform of "streamlining administration, delegating powers and improving services"; make full efforts to solve problems and boost the confidence of private enterprises; and continuously innovate the use of fiscal funds to reduce costs for private enterprises. Third, create a platform for entrepreneurship and innovation so as to invigorate the private economy. Continue to enable the government to set up platforms for engagement with enterprises, stimulate the vitality of private enterprises, and actively build platforms for incubation, cooperation and service. Fourth, create a convenient and fast tax environment to bring down the burden of enterprises. Actively promote tax and fee reduction and comprehensively publicize the policies of tax and fee reduction; continuously make it more convenient for taxpayers to pay tax and comprehensively implement tax refunds; strengthen supervision over implementation and track policy effectiveness; rely on big data platform for tax collection and management to simplify procedures and improve tax refund efficiency. ■

90 Finance authorities of Xinjiang Uygur Autonomous Region enhanced six aspects to deepen fiscal and tax reform and comprehensively carry out budget performance management

According to the news released by the Finance Department of Xinjiang Uygur Autonomous Region on November 19, since 2019, the Aksu region of Xinjiang has integrated performance concepts and methods into the whole process of budget preparation, implementation and supervision through "six enhancements", and initially established the ex-ante, interim and ex-post performance management system. First, enhance organizational leadership and improve the budget performance management system. The Aksu Party Committee strengthened the Party's leadership over the full implementation of budget performance management and clarified the timetable and roadmap for the full implementation of budget performance management in the region. Second, enhance the in-depth management and build a comprehensive budget performance management structure. Fully integrate the government revenue and expenditure budget into performance management; fully integrate the revenue and expenditure of department and unit budget into performance management; and fully integrate policies and projects into performance management. Third, enhance closed-loop management and establish a full-process budget performance management chain. Enable the closed-loop management of budget performance to run throughout the "all-round, full-process and full-coverage" budget performance management system. Establish a performance evaluation mechanism, strengthen performance target management, effectively monitor performance, and apply performance evaluation results. Fourth, enhance the coordination of the "four budgets" and improve the full-coverage budget performance management system. Strengthen the management of general public budget performance and establish other government budget performance management systems. Fifth, enhance information management and establish an IT-based platform for budget performance management. Purchase budget performance information system through open tendering, and realize IT-based management of whole-process budget performance in all counties (cities) as of May 30. Sixth, enhance basic management and establish a budget performance training mechanism. Invite professionals to carry out special training regarding budget performance management system, whole-process budget performance procedures and information platform operation. ■

91

Finance authorities of Tianjin Municipality actively explored a new 4G model of zero-based budget management

According to the news released by the Finance Bureau of Tianjin Municipality on November 25, starting from 2019, Tianjin Finance Bureau has worked to build a new 4G model of zero-based budget management with Tianjin characteristics featuring one Goal, two Guides, three Governs, and four Grips. First, break down the rigidity of departmental budgets around "one goal". For a long time, the Tianjin municipal expenditure budget has mainly adopted the "base + growth" model of preparation. Second, clarify the "two guides" to optimize the order of project funds. Establish the positive and negative lists of budgetary arrangements and implement the "cash flow" budget management. Third, implement the "three governs" and strengthen the control of the entire budget process. Since 2019, Tianjin has implemented "three governs" of enforcing total project budget control, hardening budget implementation constraints, and making overall planning and balance. Fourth, establish the "four grips" to advance the closed-loop management of budgetary funds. Propose "four grips" mechanisms that link budgetary arrangements with implementation progress, balance carry-over, audit issues, and idle assets in light of the specific state of budget implementation. ■

92

Finance authorities of Hunan Province focused on five aspects to promote the high-quality development of SMEs

According to the news released by the Finance Department of Hunan Province on November 26, since 2019, the finance authorities of Changsha City, Hunan Province have adopted a series of measures to effectively promote the high-quality development of SMEs in the city. First, implement inclusive policies to cultivate the "potential" of the economy. Comprehensively implement various tax and fee reduction policies, strictly investigate and deal with the arbitrary collection of taxes and fees, and strive to reduce the tax burden on all industries. Second, increase fiscal investment to enhance the "strength" of development. The city government arranged a budget of 735 million RMB for industrial development in 2019; a budget of 508 million RMB of special funds for scientific and technological development; and a budget of 225 million RMB of special funds for open economic development. Third, innovate financing models to assist the development of enterprises. Take the credit risk compensation fund for small and micro enterprises, the SME on-lending guidance fund and the angel investment guidance fund as the lever to vigorously encourage banking institutions to lower the credit threshold for enterprises. Fourth, focus on innovation and entrepreneurship to stimulate the "internal vitality" of enterprises. Timely implement the "22 New Policies for Talents" and other policies to promote the employment and entrepreneurship of various talents. Fifth, optimize the business environment and provide quality service. Further stimulate the vitality of enterprises and promote the development of a unified, open, competitive and orderly market system. ■

93 Finance authorities of Beijing Municipality took multiple measures to enhance the effectiveness of monitoring over the implementation of fiscal budget

According to the news released by the Finance Bureau of Beijing Municipality on December 2, since 2019, the Beijing Finance Bureau has further enhanced the effectiveness of monitoring by improving its dynamic monitoring mechanism. First, expand the scope of monitoring to achieve full coverage of fiscal funds. As of the end of September, the dynamic monitoring has horizontally covered 1387 grass-root budget units of 215 municipal budget departments, and vertically extended to 2348 budget units of 16 district-level finance departments and 550 budget units of 319 townships (streets). Second, clarify monitoring priorities and provide accurate and smart early warning. Formulate early warning rules to accurately monitor whether budget units are transferring fiscal funds against the rules and changing the purpose of the use of funds without authorization. Third, conduct fiscal supervision to spur the implementation of departmental budget management. The supervisory departments of finance authorities shall conduct on-site inspection of suspected violations identified by monitoring and early warning, and instruct the budget units to timely correct irregularities in financial management and gift collection. Fourth, raise awareness to regulate and correct problems. Carry out two-way monitoring of cash withdrawal and use, and add cash withdrawal early warning and official credit card settlement and payment reminder functions to the centralized payment system, in order to regulate the use and withdrawal of cash. ■

94 Finance authorities of Guangdong Province focused on the priority areas to put public finance at the service of public interests

According to the news released by the Finance Department of Guangdong Province on December 3, since 2019, the Finance Bureau of Zhuhai City, with a focus on the management of revenues and expenditures, has accelerated the reform of the fiscal management system and steadily advanced various fiscal tasks, so as to provide strong financial support for the city's high-quality development. First, raise revenues to build a solid foundation for economic and social development. Conduct research of the impact of tax and fee reduction on the city's revenues in a timely manner, and unite all departments at all levels to raise revenues. Second, stabilize expenditures and enhance the effectiveness of proactive fiscal policies. Vigorously reduce all unnecessary administrative expenses, and strengthen the monitoring over expenditures related to people's livelihood and major projects. Third, strengthen management to gradually improve the budget management system. Strictly review the increase of expenditure, and examine the items of increased expenditure one by one. Fourth, promote reforms to accelerate the establishment of a modern fiscal system. Accelerate the establishment of a fiscal system that matches the financial resources with the fiscal powers of cities and districts in accordance with the principles of concentrating financial resources for priority tasks, enhancing sustainable development and reducing dependence on land. ■

95 Finance authorities of Henan Province took four measures to push forward the comprehensive tax administration

According to the news released by the Finance Department of Henan Province on December 9, since 2019, Nanyang City has achieved remarkable results in advancing comprehensive tax administration. First, improve the system and enhance the basic administration capabilities. Formulate eight rules and regulations, and clarify the working process and division of responsibilities. Second, promote information sharing and improve the comprehensive tax administration system. Improve the tax-related information catalogue, strengthen the coordination of departments, disaggregate the reported tax-related information, clarify the information items, sharing cycle and sharing level, and refine the content of data items. Third, enhance coordination and carry out special programs. The Finance Bureau of Nanyang City actively communicated with relevant departments, and paid close attention to the developments of real estate and land transfer. Fourth, promote learning and work to solve the problem of comprehensive tax administration. Actively draw upon the advanced experience, continuously improve the level of law-based tax administration, and take the electronic invoices as a lever to close the loopholes and increase revenues and as a highlight of the work of tax and fee reduction. ■

96 Finance authorities of Guangxi Zhuang Autonomous Region concentrated efforts on implementing the "three checklists" of poverty alleviation through industrial development

According to the news released by the Finance Department of the Guangxi Zhuang Autonomous Region on December 11, since 2019, it has formulated the "three checklists" for poverty alleviation through industrial development, and promoted the transition of public finance in support of poverty reduction from being qualitative to quantitative and from being extensive to intensive. The first checklist is to promote the consolidation of agriculture-related funds and increase funding support. The consolidated funds are primarily spent on the industries that directly benefit the poor and to encourage the expansion of local specialty insurance products. The second checklist is to enlarge and strengthen the advantageous industries. Strengthen the support for county-level "5+2" and poverty-stricken village-level "3+1" industries, and comprehensively implement the policy of replacing subsidies with rewards to ensure that more than 90% of poor households are covered during the year. The third checklist is to vigorously develop new industries and new forms of business. Promote the development of poverty alleviation projects through tourism, nurture the advantageous industries of tourism, and create new products that integrate regional features such as rural cultural tourism, agricultural tourism, and forest tourism. ■

97 Finance authorities of Zhejiang Province mobilized tens of billions of funds to boost rural revitalization

According to the news released by the Finance Department of Zhejiang Province on December 16, Zhejiang Province has made "agriculture, rural areas and farmers" a top priority, and concentrated financial resources to promote the modernization of agriculture and rural areas and the high-quality development of the rural economy. First, focus efforts around a specific goal. Finance authorities of Zhejiang have set up special incentive funds for enhancing the performance of rural revitalization to spur cities and counties to work together and leverage private capital and financial capital to invest in rural revitalization. Second, adopt two methods of allocation to ensure that the incentive funds are properly used. The "factor method" allocates funds according to the results of the performance assessment of the rural revitalization strategy. The "competitive allocation method" allocates incentive funds to support cities and counties (cities and districts) to concentrate financial resources on addressing the key or difficult work in rural revitalization. Third, highlight the three key tasks and work to ensure greater quality and efficiency. Promote smart rural development, green agricultural development, and urban-rural integrated development, in order to boost the quality and efficiency of rural areas. ■

98

Finance authorities of Qingdao City worked on six fronts to expand financial resources in response to the pressure from tax and fee cut

According to the news released by the Finance Bureau of Qingdao City on December 18, since 2019, Qingdao has focused on six areas to expand the financial resources, effectively addressing the mismatch between fiscal revenues and expenditures and ensuring generally stable fiscal performance. First, issue bonds to make up for financial resources. Properly balance the relationship between borrowing and development as well as between current and long-term needs, and give full play to the role of bonds in stabilizing investment, expanding domestic demand and strengthening shortcomings. Second, make budgetary arrangements to concentrate financial resources. Make budget adjustment plans in a timely manner to increase the contribution of state-owned enterprises to public finance. Third, save financial resources by reducing expenditures. Cut general expenditures and the "three public" expenses to the extent possible and free up more funds to deliver more benefits to people and businesses. Fourth, revive the idle state-owned assets to put financial resources to good use. Carry out thorough investigation and put a total of 29.3 billion RMB of idle state-owned assets to good use. Fifth, strengthen the collection and administration of taxes. Improve the tax administration mechanism and enhance tax planning for investment projects. Sixth, adopt market-based means to leverage financial resources. Actively promote the use of PPP model to reduce the current financial pressure and fully leverage the government guiding fund. ■

99

Finance authorities of Tianjin Municipality accelerated budget implementation

According to the news released by the Finance Bureau of Tianjin Municipality on December 23, since 2019, it has implemented zero-based budgeting reforms, hardened budget implementation constraints, revitalized idle capital and assets, and effectively improved budget implementation efficiency, in order to ensure the high-quality and sustainable economic development of the municipality. First, build a "new engine" with zero-based budgeting. Fully implement the zero-based budgeting, readjust and optimize the expenditure structure, and further improve the efficiency of the allocation and use of fiscal funds. Second, strengthen management and control and keep the "steering wheel" stable. Firmly establish the consciousness of law-based budgeting, strengthen budget implementation management, harden budget implementation constraints, and effectively preserve the seriousness and binding force of government budget. Third, tap the potential and leverage the idle funds. Redouble efforts to sort through various types of surplus and carryover funds, revitalize and put to good use idle and low-efficient government assets, and strengthen the centralized management and unified use of fiscal and public funds. ■

100 Finance authorities of the Inner Mongolia Autonomous Region worked on three fronts to boost high-quality economic development

According to the news released by the Finance Department of the Inner Mongolia Autonomous Region on December 24, in recent years, the Finance Bureau of Baotou City, has worked on three fronts to shore up weak links and increase advantages, laying the foundation for the city's high-quality economic development. First, work on demonstration projects to promote the transition of new growth drivers. Implement the national comprehensive demonstration project for emission reduction, the demonstration project for treatment of dirty and odorous water, and the pilot demonstration project for rare earth transformation and upgrading, in order to facilitate the transition of growth drivers in advantageous industries and promote energy conservation, environmental protection and green development. Second, promote investment in industrial fund to bring in capital and talents. Actively explore ways to support the development of Baotou's real economy and resolve corporate financing difficulties, innovate fiscal investment methods, and guide the establishment of Baotou Key Industry Development Fund with an initial scale of 1.5 billion RMB and the Talent Innovation and Entrepreneurship Investment Fund with an initial scale of 200 million RMB. Third, advance the reform of "streamlining administration, delegating powers and improving services" and promote the improvement of business environment. Vigorously promote such reform in the public finance, accelerate the development of smart finance based on Internet + electronic government procurement, Internet + centralized treasury payment, and Internet + government investment project pipeline, so as to improve the level of management and services. ■

101 MOF published the 2018 local budget and final accounts openness ranking

According to the news released by the Supervision and Evaluation Bureau on December 31, MOF has published the 2018 local budget and final accounts openness ranking on the basis of the scores of various localities made through inspection. In 2019, MOF organized a special inspection over the disclosure of local budget and final accounts in 2018. The work of the disclosure of local budget and final accounts has achieved initial outcomes. In terms of the scope, the vast majority of local departments have made public their budget and final accounts. In 2018, local governments at all levels were basically able to disclose their budgets and accounts as required, and the inspection covered 267,800 departments and units at all levels, with the exception of only 8 departments and units. In terms of the effect, the relevant requirements of the system for disclosure of budget and final accounts were met, and the average completion rate of various indicators for the disclosure of local budget and final accounts increased year by year from 2015 to 2018. However, there are still some problems with the disclosure of local budget and final accounts. First, there are still problems in terms of completeness and standardization, and a few departments and units have failed to disclose their budget and final accounts. Second, the awareness of proactive disclosure is still not strong, and the relevant explanations and details are insufficient. Third, the quality of disclosure of budget and final accounts needs to be improved, the accuracy and readability are insufficient, and there are cases of false presentation of revenues and expenditures. In the next step, MOF will continue to promote the disclosure of budget and final accounts, and promote the transformation of disclosure from "form" to "substance". ■

102 Finance Authorities of Zhejiang Province explored the establishment of a fiscal policy system to concentrate financial resources on priority areas

According to the news released by Finance Department of Zhejiang Province on January 2, since 2019, Huzhou City, Zhejiang Province has made coordinated efforts to revitalize and consolidate financial resources in order to ensure that fiscal policies are tilted to the priority areas and fiscal funds are channeled toward important directions. First, carry out major tasks with strict use of financial resources. Strengthen organization and leadership, set up a city-level cross-departmental leading work group for the formulation of implementation program in order to improve the accuracy and reliability of formulation. Second, arrange projects in a tiered and classified manner. Clarify each direction of funding support, and concentrate funding support on project implementation and subsidy disbursement. Third, maintain a balance by preserving necessary expenditures and cutting unnecessary ones. With reference to the preparation method of the annual budget draft, adopt the "base period + growth rate" method and follow the principle of pro-activity and prudence to define the expected average level and bottom level for the fiscal revenues and corresponding financial resources during the planned period. ■

REMARKS & OPINIONS

01 Liu Kun: promote the establishment of a long-term and sustainable funding mechanism for medical care and health suited to China's national conditions

Source: MOF

On December 24, entrusted by the State Council, Finance Minister Liu Kun made a report to the Standing Committee of NPC on the allocation and use of the fiscal funds for medical care and health.

Minister Liu Kun said that the investment in basic medical care and health should be further increased at all levels of government, and the basic medical and health system should be provided to the general public as a public good. We must improve the way government invests to make it compatible with the development of public hospitals, fully implement the government's policy on investing in public hospitals that meet regional health plans, and guide local governments to steadily resolve long-term debts of eligible public hospitals after careful screening and sorting.

First, establish a well-structured and efficient medical service system, vigorously promote the pilot program of nationally centralized drug procurement and use, intensify reform efforts to control high-cost medical consumables, and further improve the efficiency of medical insurance funds, so as to give full play to market incentive mechanism, increase transparency of drug prices, and put in place a drug supply system with reasonable prices, adequate supply and regulated order.

Second, establish and improve the government-led and diversified funding mechanism for medical care and health to better meet the needs of the development of medical care and health. Further improve the management of non-profit and for-profit hospitals, refine the policies that support private sector's running of hospitals in terms of talent introduction, asset rights, tax incentives, and financing services, give full play to the role of market mechanisms, and incentivize private capital to invest in medical care and health.

Third, increase investment in poverty alleviation and take effective measures to improve the medical and health conditions of the poor people in rural areas and the medical and health service capacity of poor areas. Improve basic medical insurance, serious illness insurance and medical aid to reduce the burden of medical expenses for the rural poor and effectively prevent the lapse into poverty due to illness.

Fourth, strictly enforce the laws and regulations such as the budget law, strengthen the institutional building, and improve the scientific and regulated use and management of funds. Continue to optimize and consolidate health care projects to avoid duplication of investment and inefficient use of financial resources at the source. Comprehensively promote budget performance management, strengthen performance evaluation of major medical and health investment, improve performance management mechanisms that cover budget preparation and implementation, and link performance evaluation results to project fund allocation. ■

02 Liu Shangxi: the bedrock of market economy is property rights rather than ownership

Recently, Liu Shangxi, President of the China Academy of Fiscal Sciences, said that China's socialist economic development has entered a new era. Standing at a new historical starting point, China's economic development has achieved great success over the past 40 years. The most important element of the 40-year success is the integration of national development with market economy. In discussing China's economic development, we must return to a fundamental proposition: the socialist market economy.

First, to study the Chinese economy, we must proceed from the complete proposition of socialist market economy. Studying only the generality not the peculiarity of the market economy will result in market economics being divorced from the reality of China. Although there are many common features in market economy, yet it still varies across countries, not to mention countries with vastly different political structures.

Second, sets of the three logics and two major breakthroughs in China's economic development. (1) There are three logic in China's economic development: theoretical logic, historical logic and practical logic. China can draw upon and learn a lot of theoretical logics from the market economics of developed countries. But it is difficult to find clues of the practical logic and the historical logic from the history and practice of other countries. Because China's economic development is entirely based on its own logic, its practical logic and historical logic are completely different from those of other market economies. (2) Two breakthroughs in China's development theory. The combination of socialism and market economy has broken two dogmas: one is the dogma of planned economy and the other is the dogma of public ownership. With emancipation of mind and active exploration in practice, the above two dogmas were broken. However, from the theoretical and practical perspective, the above two problems have not been completely resolved.

Third, the bedrock of the market economy is property rights, not ownership. The market plays a decisive role in resource allocation, and its cornerstone lies in property rights. (1) Property rights relationship is the main form of property relationship in modern society, and ownership relationship is the main form of property relationship in traditional society. The two have historical links, but the property rights relationship has gradually become the foundation for the development of modern society. (2) As property rights move to the front and ownership retreats, the role of ownership rights and ownership in economic nature and distribution relationship needs to be re-recognized. ■

03 Liu Kun: intensify the proactive fiscal policies to boost high-quality economic growth

Recently, in the interview with the People's Daily, Xinhua News Agency, CCTV and Economic Daily, Finance Minister Liu Kun said that General Secretary Xi Jinping delivered an important speech at the Central Economic Work Conference held in December last year, which analyzed the current economic situation and planned the economic work of 2019. Premier Li Keqiang also made specific arrangements for economic work in 2019. In 2019, the proactive fiscal policy should be strengthened with its efficiency be improved.

Intensify reduction of taxes and fees and increase expenditures. First, intensify reduction of taxes and fees. On one hand, we must implement larger scale of tax cut, combine universal tax cut with structural tax cut, reduce the burden of manufacturing sector and small and micro enterprises, and support the development of the real economy. On the other hand, we must promote reduction of fees, clean up and regulate local collection of fees, and increase efforts to investigate and rectify arbitrary charges. Second, increase fiscal spending. In light of the economic situation and various spending needs, we must moderately expand the scale of fiscal spending. At the same time, we must increase the scale of local government special bonds to support the construction of major ongoing projects and shore up weak links.

Improve the efficiency and effectiveness of the allocation of fiscal funds. To improve the efficiency of fund allocation, we must focus on key areas and weak links and further adjust and optimize the expenditure structure. The funding of key areas must be well safeguarded, including poverty alleviation, agriculture, rural areas, farmers, structural adjustment, science and technology innovation, ecological protection and people's livelihood; the funding of non-essential areas must be reduced, and the government must tighten its belt, reduce general spending, strictly control the "three public expenditures", cut general spending by more than 5%, eliminate ineffective expenditures, and do not spend a single cent on unnecessary areas. To improve the effectiveness of the use of fiscal funds, we must carry out budget performance management throughout the budget preparation and implementation process and better promote the implementation of policies; continue to revitalize the stock of fiscal funds and recover the long-standing idle funds for the areas in urgent need of financial support.

As we intensify the proactive fiscal policies, instead of resorting to massive stimulus, we must implement countercyclical adjustment, actively pre-adjust and fine-tune policies, stabilize aggregate demand, and iron out cyclical fluctuations; we must resolutely prevent debt risks, strike a balance between stable growth and risk prevention, and appropriately expand the scale of fiscal spending on the basis of strengthening government debt management; instead of letting government take on everything, we must adopt more reform measures, use more market-oriented and law-based approaches to promote the sustained and healthy development of the Chinese economy. ■

04 Zhu Guangyao: the debt ratio of the Chinese government is at a low level among the major economies

Source: MOF

At the recent Asian Financial Forum, former Vice Finance Minister Zhu Guangyao said that the debt ratio of the Chinese government is slightly below 40%, which is at a low level among the major economies in the world. In the past year, China's supply-side reforms have made some progress in deleveraging. At the same time, it is faced with new challenges such as the external headwinds and increased downward pressure on the economy. The United States has 22 trillion USD of government debt, and the Japanese government has a debt ratio of more than 250%. In 2018, the combined central and local fiscal deficit of China added up to about 2.6%. China has always been very cautious in budgetary arrangements and requires the People's Congress to conduct review and deliberations. Therefore, China is confident of maintaining economic growth as the government has ample policy tools. At the same time, it must do so in accordance with market rules and laws. All arrangements are subject to the approval by the People's Congress. In order to maintain stable economic growth this year, China issued 1.9 trillion RMB of local special bonds in advance. It is evident that China has adopted prudent and stable measures in a targeted manner. In short, in accordance with the proactive fiscal policies deployed by the Party Central Committee and the State Council, we must play a more effective role and do a better job to maintain the stable and healthy development of the Chinese economy. ■

05 Zhu Guangyao: four uncertainties for China's economic development in 2019

On January 14, former Vice Finance Minister Zhu Guangyao said in a speech that the most important thing for China's economic development is to make progress while maintaining stability. How to follow the principle of making progress while maintaining stability would be essential for both China and the world. At the same time, it is necessary to objectively acknowledge that there are four uncertainties in the current global economy. First, can we maintain a stable and sustained development trend? Only the close integration of products, industry chains, value chains and supply chains can form a complete global supply chain, enabling the global economy to move forward steadily. But the unilateralism led by the United States is posing a real challenge. Second, the uncertainty of rules. Since WTO needs and is also determined to reform, artificial obstacles should not be created to the key appellate courts. In accordance with WTO regulations, there are only three incumbent members of the appellate court and only two will be left by the end of this year. This is indeed a matter of urgency. For the sake of keeping the general trend of global cooperation, WTO is expected to effectively push forward its reform in a way that respects its members and on a principled basis. Third, the British Parliament has to vote on the Brexit deal between UK and EU. UK is faced with a choice between hard Brexit and soft Brexit, either way it will have a great impact on the global economy in the short term. Fourth, the impact of the US monetary policy. Interest rate has been raised nine times since 2015, and from last October, the Fed began to trim its balance sheet. During the 2008 financial crisis, the Fed's balance sheet was only 1.5 trillion USD, but by the end of last year, it reached 4.5 trillion USD. Therefore, the Fed began to reduce its balance sheet in last October, which still stands at 4 trillion USD and is expected to fall to 2.2 trillion USD in 2022. ■

06 Gao Peiyong: the Central Economic Work Conference held from December 19 to 21, 2018 offered insights into the economic work under the new situation

Gao Peiyong, Vice President of the Chinese Academy of Social Sciences, said that the Central Economic Work Conference held from December 19 to 21, 2018 was guided by Xi Jinping's Thoughts on Socialism with Chinese Characteristics for a New Era and offered insights into the economic work under the new situation. First, the main contradiction in China's economy is still structural and on the supply side. Understanding the main contradictions in the high-quality development stage, coping with the problems and challenges of the supply system not being able to adapt to the changes in the demand structure and the difficulty of the economy in achieving a virtuous circle is essential for maintaining the sustained and healthy development of the Chinese economy and the overall social stability. Second, stick to the supply-side structural reforms as the key task. To fundamentally solve the problems and challenges facing the Chinese economy, it is imperative to continue on the path of supply-side structural reforms, consolidate the achievements of "cutting excess capacity, inventory and leverage, reducing costs and shoring up weak links", enhance the vitality of the market entities, upgrade the level of the industrial chain, remove the obstacles to the national economic cycle, and make it a central task to deepen the supply-side structural reforms and promote high-quality development of the economy in the current and future periods. Third, adopt more reforms and use more market-oriented and rule-of-law methods. Only under the centralized and unified leadership of the Party Central Committee and by deepening the reforms, invigorating the market entities, and driving growth with reforms can we win the tough battle of supply-side structural reforms. Fourth, maintain the focus of macroeconomic regulation and actively guide market expectations. Under the premise of maintaining the overall continuity and stability of macroeconomic policies, we must make preemptive adjustment, adhere to the objectives, follow our own pace of development, focus on getting things done, and turn pressure into the driving force for accelerating the development of high-quality economy. This is not only the important requirements put forward by the Central Economic Work Conference, but also the strategic choice that should be made to ensure the stability of economic operation. Of course, in the high-quality development stage, we must also maintain strategic focus and must have strategic confidence. ■

07 Shi Yaobin: deepen the fiscal and tax reform and comprehensively implement the Budget Law

Source: MOF

Shi Yaobin, Deputy Chairman of the Economic and Financial Committee of NPC (NPC) and Chairman of the Budgetary Affairs Commission of NPC, said that it is necessary to further comprehensively implement the Budget Law, strengthen the review and supervision of budget by NPC, promote the government's standard management of budget, and deepen budget reform, in order to enable public finance to play its role as the foundation and important pillar for state governance. First, further enhance the understanding of the importance of implementing the Budget Law. Leading cadres of the Party and governments at all levels should further enhance their sense of responsibility and mission, take the lead in studying the Budget Law, actively publicize and strictly implement the Budget Law, earnestly harden budget constraints, and embed the concept of law-based governance of state and law-based management of public finance into all aspects of policy formulation and work planning. Second, accelerate the improvement of the supporting laws and regulations of the Budget Law. Enact and implement the *Regulations on the Implementation of the Budget Law* as soon as possible. Amend the relevant laws in accordance with the requirements of the Party Central Committee on addressing the problem of linking key expenditures with the increase of fiscal revenues or the total value of production. Speed up the improvement of specific measures or regulations that should be formulated under the authorization of the Budget Law. Provincial people's congress should speed up the formulation or revision of local regulations such as those for budget review and supervision. Third, further strengthen government budget management. (1) Make budget preparation more complete and scientific. (2) Make budget implementation more rule-based. (3) Fully implement performance management, deeply embed the performance concepts and methods into the whole process of budget preparation, implementation and supervision, and improve the performance of fund use and the effects of policy implementation. (4) Speed up the promotion of taxation by law. (5) Comprehensively promote the disclosure of budget and final accounts. (6) Strengthen local government debt management. Fourth, further deepen fiscal and tax reform. (1) Accelerate the reform of intergovernmental fiscal relations, scientifically define the central and local fiscal mandates and expenditure responsibilities, form a rational structure of financial resource allocation between the central and local governments, and accelerate the equalization of basic public services. (2) Improve the transfer payment system. (3) Gradually establish a stable and sustainable local tax system. Fifth, further strengthen the review and supervision of budget by NPC. (1) Strengthen the comprehensive review and supervision of budget. Promote the complete and detailed budget preparation, promote the standardization of budget implementation, and enhance the seriousness and authority of budget. (2) Closely focus on the overall interests of the Party and the state, focus on the major policies, plans and decisions of the Party Central Committee, focus on the hotspots and difficult issues that concern the NPC deputies and the people, grasp the key points and sticking issues, and intensify review and supervision. (3) Actively implement the important reform measures of the Party Central Committee and promote the implementation of the Budget Law. (4) Implement the Budget Law amid the active promotion of budget network supervision. (5) Improve the budget review and supervision work mechanism. ■

08 Liu Shangxi: full implementation of budget performance management should avoid widening the income distribution gap

On February 23, Liu Shangxi, President of the Chinese Academy of Fiscal Sciences, said at the Forum on State Governance and Fiscal Performance that the full implementation of budget performance management should give priority to the following issues. First, the dependence of expenditure arrangements on base numbers. Only by breaking this dependence and optimizing the expenditure structure can the 22 trillion RMB of fiscal funds be effectively used and truly meet the expectation of people. Second, the use of funds should be integrated to avoid fragmentation of the use of special funds. The fragmentation of the use of funds is an important cause of the disconnect between money and mandate. The fragmentation of the use of funds is one of the risk factors we are facing now. This determines the effectiveness of state governance, and the effectiveness of state governance can be judged by the degree of fragmentation and the degree of integration of the use of funds. Third, conduct fair competition review over funds that support industrial transformation and upgrading. If government departments only support certain enterprises or a single industry, it will lead to unfair competition in the market, impede the market from playing a decisive role in resource allocation, and greatly lower the overall economic efficiency. Fourth, social expenditures on the protection and improvement of people's livelihood should be analyzed from the scope of beneficiary groups to avoid widening the income distribution gap and social injustice. In reality, the social inequality brought about by social expenditures is caused by the uncertain perception and the unscientific methods of government departments. ■

09 Liu Kun: government will tighten its belt and cut the general fiscal expenditures at the central level by 5%

At the Press Conference held at the Press Center of the Second Session of the 13th National People's Congress, Finance Minister Liu Kun said that the financial authorities should work on "addition, subtraction, multiplication and division" in order to implement a proactive fiscal policy with greater intensity and better performance as emphasized by Premier Li Keqiang in the *Report on the Work of Government.* First, work on "multiplication" to "lighten the burden of market entities and cultivate revenues", deploy tax and fee cut to energize market players, and strengthen the spending power of residents. Tax and fee cut is the top priority of the proactive fiscal policy in this year. Larger-scale tax cut and more significant fee reduction will be implemented to better guide corporate expectations, enhance market confidence and stabilize economic growth. Second, work on "addition" and step up fiscal expenditures. The fiscal expenditures exceeded 22 trillion RMB last year. In this year, we will continue to moderately expand the scale of fiscal expenditures, and set the central general public budget expenditures at 11.13 trillion RMB, an increase of 8.7% year on year, with a focus on increasing support for poverty alleviation, "agriculture, rural areas and farmers", structural adjustment, technological innovation, eco-environmental protection and people's livelihood. Third, work on "subtraction" and spend the saved money on people. The government will tighten its belt, vigorously reduce general expenditures, strictly curb the budget of the "three public expenses", and eliminate inefficient and ineffective expenses. The central government will take the lead in strictly managing departmental expenditures. The general expenditures will be reduced by more than 5%, the "three public expenses" will be cut by about 3%, and the long-idling funds will be put to good use. Fourth, work on "division", remove the institutional hindrances, and comprehensively deepen the reform of the fiscal and taxation institution. In particular, it is necessary to fully implement budget performance management throughout the budget preparation and execution process, accelerate the pace of budget execution, enhance the monitoring of budget performance, and give full play to the role of fiscal funds. Fifth, to pursue a proactive fiscal policy with greater intensity and better performance, it is important to implement counter-cyclical adjustment, better apply market-oriented and rule-of-law methods, adopt reform measures, work hard to "consolidate, strengthen, enhance and smooth out" economic operation, and concentrate efforts on promoting China's high-quality economic development. ■

10 Cai Fang: an unemployment rate of over 5% calls for more proactive macroeconomic policy response

Cai Fang, the Deputy of NPC and the Vice President of the Chinese Academy of Social Sciences, said at the final "Deputy Channel" of the 2nd Session of the 13th National People's Congress that placing employment-first policy at the macro policy level is an upgraded version of the employment-first policy, or the 3.0 edition of the proactive employment policy. At the same time, the macro policy system has also been upgraded and improved. The main basis for the formulation of macroeconomic policies in the past was the rate of economic growth and employment. The coefficient relationship between economic growth and employment expansion can be called employment elasticity. As China enters a new stage of economic development, the elasticity coefficient will also change. Instead of indirectly seeking employment targets, it is better to directly use employment as the basis for adjusting and implementing macroeconomic policies, thus developing an inherent connection between employment targets and macroeconomic policy objectives and means. The 5% surveyed urban unemployment rate mentioned by Premier Li Keqiang is a rate suggesting relatively full employment, i.e. such unemployment rate does not contain cyclical factors and primarily indicates structural and frictional unemployment. Structural unemployment means that personal skills and the labor demand are not completely matched, so it takes a certain amount of time to train and upgrade skills of jobseekers; frictional unemployment means that demand for labor and the labor have not yet met, which is due to the function of the labor market and the mechanism of information transmission. Therefore, a proactive employment policy should be implemented to address structural and frictional unemployment, and improve market functions in terms of training, education, and provision of better public employment services, so that job seekers and employers can be better connected. At present, China faces a complicated external environment. Once the demand side is impacted and the economic growth rate is affected, economic growth may be lower than the potential growth and unemployment may rise. An unemployment rate of over 5% is a cyclical unemployment phenomenon. Therefore, more proactive macroeconomic, monetary and fiscal policies should be implemented. This is also the reason why the government work report set the employment target below the surveyed unemployment rate of 5.5%. ■

11 Liu Kun: new measures of proactive fiscal policy

At the 2019 Annual Meeting of the China Development Forum on March 24, Finance Minister Liu Kun said that the current Chinese economy has transitioned from a stage of high-speed growth to a stage of high-quality development, and is in a critical process of transforming the development model, optimizing the economic structure and shifting the growth drivers. In accordance with the requirements of the Central Economic Work Conference and the plan of the *Government Work Report,* this year's proactive fiscal policy will be strengthened to further enhance its important role in supporting the real economy, unlocking domestic demand potential, optimizing the economic structure, and improving people's well-being. First, implement a larger scale of tax and fee cut to support the development of real economy. In order to support the development of real economy, we must undergo the "subtraction" of government revenues in exchange for the "addition" of corporate benefits and the "multiplication" of market vitality. Last year, China's scale of tax cut and its share of the total economy were among the highest in the world. This year, a larger-scale tax cut and more significant reduction of fees will be implemented. The burden of corporate tax and social insurance contributions will be reduced by nearly 2 trillion RMB, which is significantly more than last year. Second, support the deepening of supply-side structural reforms and promote high-quality economic development. Deepening the supply-side structural reforms is the fundamental way to adjust the economic structure and transform the economic development model, the only way to improve the quality of the supply system and achieve high-quality development. While deploying the proactive fiscal policy to properly expand the domestic demand, we will continue to push forward supply-side structural reforms, adopt more reform measures, use more market-oriented and rule-of-law methods to ensure solid, enhanced and smooth economic performance, and work hard to improve the quality of China's economic growth. We will consolidate the outcomes of "cutting overcapacity, deleveraging, reducing inventory, lowering costs and strengthening weak links", continue to dispose of zombie enterprises, and speed up the exit of enterprises in overcapacity industries. Third, appropriately expand the scale of fiscal expenditures and promote the formation of a strong domestic market.

Due to factors such as the downward pressure on the economy and the implementation of tax and fee cut, the growth rate of fiscal revenues will slow down this year, whereas the fiscal expenditures keep growing and the pressure on balanced budget will increase. Faced with the pressure of balanced budget, we will firmly stay mindful of the bottom line, further optimize the expenditure structure, use the limited funds on the key areas, and accurately focus on enhancing the support for the overall economic and social development of the country; carry out budget performance management to ensure that "every penny" is spent well and used safely, and give full play to the role of fiscal funds to support the enforcement of policies. Fourth, strengthen policy support and financial support to resolutely win the three critical battles. We will fight the three critical battles of preventing and defusing major risks, precision poverty alleviation, and pollution prevention and control, which are all related to the overall development of the country, and are not only the realistic needs for solving development problems and promoting high-quality economic development, but also the necessary requirements for achieving the goal of building a moderately prosperous society in all respects. On the basis of consolidating the existing achievements, we will focus on outstanding problems, tackle the challenges head on, and concentrate efforts on fighting the key battles. Fifth, make every effort to ensure and improve people's wellbeing. Public finances are taken from the people and must be used for the people. The finance authorities should adhere to the people-centered thinking, highlight the public nature and fairness of public finance, and enable more people to share the benefits of reform and development in a fair way. This year, despite of the pressure of balanced fiscal budget, we will ensure that spending on people's basic livelihood will only increase, and improve the design of expenditure policies and mechanisms in relevant fields in order to improve people's wellbeing. ■

12 Zou Jiayi: Belt and Road Initiative offers a Chinese solution to address the challenges of globalization

Source: MOF

On March 27, Vice Finance Minister Zou Jiayi made a keynote speech at the Belt and Road Sub-forum of the 2019 Annual Meeting of the Boao Forum for Asia where she made three points on the Belt and Road. First, BRI reflects China's thinking on the basic laws of economic globalization and offers a Chinese solution to address the challenges of globalization. In recent years, there have been many new challenges in the process of globalization, such as unequal income distribution and backlash against globalization in some countries. The international community needs to establish a broader and deeper cooperation platform for promoting globalization in a more inclusive direction and enabling more people to participate in and share the benefits of globalization. The BRI proposed by President Xi Jinping is based on the idea of building a community of shared future for mankind. It essentially champions the global governance featuring consultation and cooperation for shared benefits and is an open and inclusive platform for cooperation. Any country that recognizes the principle of mutual benefit and win-win cooperation in advancing globalization would be aligned with the spirit of BRI. We welcome countries at different stages of development to participate in the development of the "five connectivity" under the Belt and Road. Second, the Belt and Road has absorbed the development experiences of China and other countries and is a platform for international development cooperation. The experience and achievements of China's 40 years of reform and opening-up show that infrastructure is the material basis for the development of market economy, and the leading role of infrastructure construction should be given full play. The business model of inclusive development works precisely because of the underpinning of strong infrastructure and the support of a well-developed logistics system. At present, one of the bottlenecks facing the development of the world economy is the serious shortage of infrastructure. China's development experience and BRI would help tackle the infrastructure bottlenecks facing the world today. In promoting the development of the Belt and Road, MOF has mainly worked on three aspects: (1) It forged the broad consensus of the international community and built a policy framework for the high-quality development of Belt and Road infrastructure financing. MOF of China and the finance authorities of 27 countries jointly endorsed the *Guiding Principles on Financing the Development of Belt and Road,* and also signed the *Memorandum of Cooperation on Collaboration on Matters of Common Interest under BRI* with six major multilateral development banks. (2) It committed to the openness of the Belt and Road cooperation and supported funds from multiple channels to participate in the long-term financing of infrastructure. Through multilateral and bilateral cooperation platforms, it encouraged multilateral development institutions to conduct co-financing with the Belt and Road countries, encouraged third-party cooperation and multi-party cooperation, and mobilized long-term capital and private sector capital to achieve diversified financing. (3) It improved project risk management and promoted the steady development of the Belt and Road. On the one hand, China is establishing and improving the debt sustainability analysis framework and the credit risk management framework to improve the risk management level of Chinese financing institutions; on the other hand, debtor countries should also enhance their debt management capabilities. China will work with all countries to promote the high-quality development of the Belt and Road. ■

13 Gao Peiyong: this year's proactive fiscal policy can be interpreted from two angles

Gao Peiyong, Vice President of the Chinese Academy of Social Sciences, recently said that a series of fiscal policy arrangements, including the deficit ratio is only 0.2 percentage point higher than last year, suggest that this year's tax and fee cut in the context of supply-side structural reform is not underpinned by substantially increasing deficit and expanding issuance of government bonds but by reducing government's expenditures and saving money for the people. First, the nearly 2 trillion RMB of tax and fee cut is the manifestation of the strengthened proactive fiscal policy with better effects, and is also this year's goal of combining inclusive tax cut with structural tax cut. The configuration of this year's fiscal policy is different from the past in that the policy background focuses on high-quality development and supply-side structural reform. Second, the expansion of fiscal deficit not only depends on the total size, but also on the increment. We may interpret this year's proactive fiscal policy from two aspects: we must recognize that in order to cope with the downward pressure on economy, it is necessary to expand the deficit scale and moderately increase the deficit ratio; at the same time, we should also be conscious that the increase of deficit scale and deficit ratio is limited and has not yet reached the 3% warning line. Third, the above-mentioned deployment reflects the policy logic of strengthening counter-cyclical adjustment in the context of supply-side structural reforms. In the current sequencing of macroeconomic regulation policies, when two requirements are put forward at the same time, fiscal policy should not only consider the urgency of supply-side structural reform but also the necessity of risk prevention. Fourth, under different target orientations, the operating mechanism and action route of tax and fee cut are also completely different. In the stage of transition toward high-quality development, tax and fee cut is setting its sight on reducing costs, with a focus on not just reducing the costs of enterprises, but also the production and operation costs of enterprises. The 2 trillion RMB of tax and fee cut is mainly about value-added tax and social security contributions rather than corporate income tax. On the one hand, as corporate income tax is closest to the needs of enterprises, it would help reduce costs for enterprises rather than expanding demand of enterprises; on the other hand, China's tax reform requires further reduction of the proportion of turnover tax or indirect tax to the overall tax and increase of the proportion of direct tax to the overall tax. Fifth, the current tax and fee cut adopted the approach of cutting government expenditure in exchange for lighter burden and greater benefits of enterprises and people. This is a very important perspective for understanding the current configuration of macroeconomic policies. ■

14 Liu Kun: China will continue to substantially ease market access

From April 12 to 13, Finance Minister Liu Kun addressed the 99th Development Committee meeting in Washington, DC. Liu Kun pointed out that the current world economic growth is slowing down, the downside risks are more prominent, and global development cooperation is facing severe challenges. As the most important multilateral development institution in the world, the World Bank should uphold the principle of multilateralism, encourage all members to support the rule-based multilateral trading system, adhere to the purpose of serving all members, and adopt a differentiated aid strategy that targets each country's domestic conditions. It should deepen its understanding of the trend of global development in the 21st century and provide solutions to the major development problems of the 21st century. It should increase investment in global and regional cooperation, advance South-South and North-South cooperation, and promote constructive development cooperation among countries at different stages of development to achieve common development. Facing with the rapid development of the scientific and technological revolution, the World Bank should promote the innovation-driven development, and help member countries to adopt cutting-edge technology to promote the transfer of innovative technologies to developing members. At the same time, it should support member countries to improve the business and investment environment, help developing members to improve total factor productivity, and achieve sustainable and leapfrog development.

The current Chinese economy is accelerating the transition from high-speed growth to high-quality development. The economic structure continues to be optimized and upgraded, the new growth drivers continue to expand significantly, and the consumption, as engine of growth, continues to strengthen. This year, China's proactive fiscal policy has been intensified and substantial tax and fee cut has been implemented. The economic growth in the first quarter achieved a good start. China will continue to greatly ease market access, strengthen the protection of intellectual property rights, strictly enforce the newly introduced *Foreign Investment Law,* implement larger-scale tax and fee cut, and create a more attractive investment and business environment. These measures are both independent choice for meeting China's own development needs and positive effort to promote global economic growth. China and the World Bank are important development partners. As a developing country, China still faces the problem of inadequate and imbalanced development as well as many difficulties and challenges in the field of economic and social development. China hopes to continue to use the World Bank's loan program and knowledge cooperation as a vehicle to bring in international experience in key areas of reform and opening up, in order to promote innovation-driven and high-quality development. China is willing to make positive contributions to the realization of the World Bank's twin goals and the UN's 2030 Sustainable Development Agenda through platforms such as the Belt and Road Initiative, regional cooperation and South-South cooperation.

During the meeting, Liu Kun also met with David Malpass, the new President of the World Bank, and exchanged views on issues such as China's cooperation with the World Bank. Liu Kun said that as the largest developing country and the World Bank's important development partner, China's potential for future cooperation with the World Bank is immense. China is willing to continue deepening its loan and knowledge cooperation with the World Bank. It is willing to cooperate with the World Bank to summarize China's successful experience in poverty alleviation and share it with other developing countries. China hopes that the World Bank will continue to carry out loan cooperation with China in accordance with the consensus and agreed principles reached under the capital increase package, and improve the innovativeness, demonstration effects and value-added of projects. The Chinese side also looks forward to cooperating with the World Bank in the area of business environment and high-standard development of the Multilateral Cooperation Center for Development Finance. ■

15 Zou Jiayi: global infrastructure financing is facing a huge gap and is especially short of long-term capital

On April 22, Vice Finance Minister Zou Jiayi said at the Seminar on Opportunities for Collaboration on High-quality and Sustainable Infrastructure Connectivity that high-quality and high-standard infrastructure must take into account the development stage and actual situation of project countries, suit their development strategy, and meet their development needs. At the same time, we must pay attention to cost-effectiveness and strike a balance between the financial, economic and social benefits of project. At present, the infrastructure level in developing countries is generally low, and there still exists a large gap in global infrastructure financing. There is a long way to go for building high-quality and sustainable infrastructure. The main problem is the lack of long-term capital for investment infrastructure. There is no shortage of capital and infrastructure projects, but most of the capital is pursuing short-term high returns and is thus unwilling to invest in infrastructure. As an important force for promoting international development cooperation, the multilateral development banks such as the AIIB should fully leverage the advantages of development finance as a long-term and stable source of investment and conduct more infrastructure projects that the private sector is unwilling and afraid to but are urgently needed by developing countries and can drive industrial development. ■

16 Liu Kun: building a policy framework for high-quality financing to promote high-standard Belt and Road projects

On April 25, Finance Minister Liu Kun delivered a keynote speech at the Thematic Forum on Financial Connectivity of the Second Belt and Road Forum for International Cooperation. First, implement the Guiding Principles on Financing the Development of BRI jointly endorsed by the finance authorities of 28 countries, work with the World Bank to study the environmental and social standards of BRI, give play to the role of the Multilateral Cooperation Center for Development Finance jointly established by China and 8 multilateral development institutions such as AIIB to support high-quality project preparation and capacity building, and encourage all parties to follow the international rules, adapt to the needs of developing countries, observe market principles and practice high-quality, high-standard, affordable and sustainable financing of Belt and Road development. Second, establish a debt sustainability framework to prevent and resolve debt risks. To achieve the development goals of BRI, we must strike a balance between the effective implementation of development measures and the maintenance of debt sustainability. On the basis of IMF and the World Bank's debt sustainability analysis framework of low-income countries, China published the Debt Sustainability Framework for Participating Countries of the Belt and Road Initiative, which encourages Chinese financial institutions, the participating countries of BRI, and international organizations to voluntarily use this tool to make their investment and financing decision more scientific and improve the debt management level in order to achieve sustainable and inclusive growth. Third, support funds from multiple channels to participate in long-term infrastructure financing, promote the openness of Belt and Road cooperation, encourage multilateral development institutions to carry out co-financing with the participating countries of BRI through multilateral and bilateral cooperation platforms, encourage third-party cooperation and multi-party cooperation, promote equity financing and PPP project financing, leverage public funds and mobilize long-term capital and private capital to participate in the financing of BRI, and further improve the diversified, inclusive and sustainable Belt and Road financing system. ■

17 Liu Kun: fiscal policy in 2019 will have greater intensity and effectiveness

On May 16, Finance Minister Liu Kun published an article to explain the fiscal policy with greater intensity and effectiveness. It is mentioned in the article that the fiscal policy in 2019 is still proactive, but the intensity and focus are different as the policy is of greater intensity and effectiveness compared with previous years. "Greater intensity" is mainly about stepping up tax and fee cut as well as expenditures, implementing larger-scale tax reduction, and promoting more notable reduction of fees to guide corporate expectations, enhance market confidence and better serve the real economy. "Greater effectiveness" is mainly about improving the efficiency and effectiveness of fund allocation, reviving the stock of funds, making good use of new funds, further optimizing the structure of fiscal expenditures, supporting the fight of the three critical battles, technological innovation, supply-side structural reform, and work related to agriculture, rural areas and farmers, improving people's livelihood, and improvingthe performance of fiscal expenditures. The article is comprised of six parts. First, why is it necessary to work harder to implement a proactive fiscal policy with greater intensity and effectiveness. Second, what benefits are delivered by tax and fee cut. Third, the role of public finance in supporting the fight of the three critical battles. Fourth, strong financial backing for supply-side structural reforms. Fifth, the fiscal measures in promoting the formation of a strong domestic market. Sixth, the focus of fiscal policy on safeguarding and improving people's livelihood. ■

18 Liu Shangxi: cut taxes and fees to achieve the policy goal of stabilizing expectations

Liu Shangxi, President of the China Academy of Fiscal Sciences, recently said that tax and fee cut is an important part of the proactive fiscal policy. The focus of this round of tax and fee cut has shifted from tax base to tax rate and is organically meshed with tax reforms, which will help stabilize the expectations of micro entities. From a global perspective, especially in light of China's situation, the current risks are mainly brought about by structural shift and the dynamics of this structural shift largely spring from the vitality of micro entities. However, in the process of this structural shift, the micro entities are faced with various uncertainties, which may lead to the unstable expectation of micro entities about the future. Therefore, keeping expectations stable is the key. How tax and fee cut, as a major move of the proactive fiscal policy, works to promote the stable expectation of micro entities is both a theoretical question and a policy question. At present, micro entities are faced with various risks and these risks cannot be pre-dissolved, which is leading to the unstable expectation. In this case, it is necessary to enforce the tax and fee cut that can stabilize expectations in order to change the state and hedge against uncertainties. The tax and fee cut that can stabilize expectations will expand domestic demand and reduce costs. Therefore, for the sake of stabilizing expectations, the shift of tax cut from tax base to tax rate is the right choice. Tax and fee cut should take into account policies, tax system, collection and administration system, social security system and payment system to form an integrated and comprehensive solution. Only in this way can we help shape the correct expectation of tax and fee cut, and avoid the misconception and misunderstanding of the market. ■

19 Jia Kang: China's tax and fee cut should be advanced with the support of tax reforms

Jia Kang, Chief Economist of China Academy of New Supply-side Economics, recently said that China's tax and fee cut, combined with the supporting tax reforms, is not only a matter of reducing the burden of taxpayers, but also need to consider tax structure optimization and formation of a reasonable reform plan in increasing the proportion of direct tax. After years of efforts to reduce taxes, China should further the space for possible tax cut, move forward the supporting tax reforms, and continue to optimize the tax reduction effects and arrangements. In terms of turnover tax, in addition to reducing the VAT burden and refining the implementation rules after the VAT reform, the reform of consumption tax, which is a local source of tax, has become an important task that must be considered in actively constructing a local tax system. In terms of personal income tax, we should consider expanding the coverage to some non-labor income in the next round of tax reform, and actively consider lowering the highest marginal tax rate. In terms of the reform of resource tax, we must actively summarize the management experience of environmental tax, further refine the operational mechanism of environmental tax, and take other relevant measures into account, in order to give better play to the role of environmental tax in promoting the rational development and intensive use of natural resources. In the design of the specific reform plan of property tax, we must have enough patience and ensure full public participation, so that the tax can better adapt to China's national circumstances and specific conditions at this stage. After the framework is established, it can be gradually refined and improved in the future. ■

20 Yu Yongding: six possibilities of trade war escalation by the US

Yu Yongding, Member of the Chinese Academy of Social Sciences, recently said that the United States has breached the bottom line of China in terms of "quantitative target, sovereignty and dignity", which China cannot accept. At present, Sino-US trade negotiations have stalled, and there are six possibilities of trade war escalation by the US. First, the tariff escalation. The tax hike would make the United States suffer certain losses in the early period, but China would suffer even greater losses in the later period. Second, the investment war. Foreign-funded enterprises would speed up their withdrawal from China, and some Chinese companies may also leave. For the US capital, we should make our best efforts to meet their reasonable requirements and retain them, rather than jumping from one extreme to the other. Third, the United States may cut off the global value chain to stifle China's high-tech industries. China should allow high-tech enterprises to make their own choices, while the government should listen to the opinions of various enterprises, coordinate the positions of different parties, and strive for as much time as possible for the adjustment of enterprises. Fourth, the foreign exchange rate war. China may be vilified by the United States as the "manipulator of foreign exchange rate". Fifth, the financial sanctions. Once China is included in the US Specially Designated Nationals and Blocked Persons List, it will be kicked out of the settlement system by the United States. Not only would it be unable to use the US dollar, but its US dollar assets may even be seized. We must consider the countermeasures. Europe used the "blocking statute" to deal with US financial sanctions. Although the effect is not necessarily obvious, they had, at least, laws to follow. China should push forward the relevant legislation to protect the interests of its domestic enterprises. Sixth, freeze China's overseas assets, including foreign exchange reserves. Therefore, in the short run, China should actively negotiate, but should not accept ultimatums or sacrifice its sovereignty and dignity. Instead, China should pursue proactive fiscal policies and accommodative monetary policies to offset the adverse effects of trade war on the Chinese economy; promote the reform of the exchange rate system and improve the management of cross-border capital flows; and further improve the competitive environment of foreign capital and try to retain foreign capital in China. In the long run, we should adjust our long-term strategy, develop more domestic markets, and reduce external dependence. At the same time, the government should offer companies the necessary support to ease the difficulties companies face in adjusting their position in the global industrial chain. ■

21 Liu Kun: high-quality infrastructure investment should be development-oriented

From June 8 to 9, the G20 Finance Ministers and Central Bank Governors' Meeting was held in Fukuoka, Japan. Finance Minister Liu Kun attended the meeting and delivered a speech. Liu Kun pointed out that the uncertainties in the world economy have increased, and protectionism is still a major challenge facing the world. All parties should pay close attention to potential downside risks, jointly safeguard the rule-based multilateral system, and deal with trade disputes in an equal and rational way. At present, global imbalances are mainly concentrated in advanced economies, and these countries should play a greater role in addressing imbalances. Adopting trade protectionist measures on bilateral occasions would not help address the imbalance under the multilateral system, but would harm the world economic growth. This year, China's economy has maintained a steady momentum of growth. The Chinese government will take a series of major measures related to reform and opening up to promote higher-level opening up and advance the high-quality development of China's economy and the prosperity of the global economy. Liu Kun stressed that development financing is the main bottleneck faced by low-income countries. G20 should fully respect the national conditions and financing needs of LICs and improve their debt sustainability in a constructive manner. High-quality infrastructure investment should be development-oriented, fully respect the national conditions of each country, pay equal attention to quantity and quality, and fully integrate the concept of sustainable development into high-quality infrastructure investment. China is willing to work with all parties to support the development of high-quality, sustainable, resilient, reasonably priced, inclusive and accessible infrastructure to enable countries to better integrate into global supply chain, industrial chain and value chain to achieve inter-connected economic development. ■

22 Xie Fuzhan: economic and trade frictions provoked by US are groundless

On June 20, Xie Fuzhan, President of the Chinese Academy of Social Sciences, said in his published article that since March last year, some people in the United States have deliberately provoked China-US economic and trade frictions and assertively claimed that the US is "being taken advantage of", accusing China of "unfair trade", "forced technology transfer", "stealing US technology", and "not fulfilling WTO commitments". These accusations are groundless and simply untenable. First, the bilateral trade surplus is on China's side but the benefits are shared by both sides. The US trade deficit with China is a reflection of the division of labor in the global value chain and the resulting layout of supply chain and industrial chain, which are formed in the process of economic globalization. Discussing the bilateral trade imbalances in this context requires understanding the multilateral factors behind it, and it is obviously one-sided to talk about trade imbalances from a bilateral perspective. China-US economic and trade cooperation is essentially mutually beneficial and win-win. The so-called "US is being taken advantage of" is not in line with reality. For the US, China-US economic and trade cooperation will not only help it achieve static gains such as trade and investment growth, but also bring about dynamic gains in economic growth and industrial upgrading. Second, the US accusation against China's technological progress is contrary to the facts. China's scientific and technological progress is mainly due to independent innovation, and foreign companies fully recognize the protection of intellectual property rights in China. The suppression of Chinese high-tech enterprises by some people in the US will seriously undermine the innovation ecology of global open cooperation. Third, China is a top student among the members of WTO. The current US government's evaluation of China's accession to the WTO is politically motivated and not objective. Some people in the US accuse China's economic model of harming the interests of other WTO members. The fact is that since China's accession to the WTO, its average contribution to world economic growth has approached 30%, making it an important engine for driving world economic growth. At a time when the WTO and other members of the WTO recognize China's performance after its accession to the WTO, the US, in order to come to the conclusion about China's non-compliance with WTO rules, can only move to judge China's performance on the basis of its own standards set higher than WTO rules and whether the US benefits the most from it. This is obviously unreasonable. Fourth, the economic and trade frictions provoked by US go against the trend of the times. Peace, development, cooperation, and win-win are the trend of the times. The economic and trade frictions provoked by US are contrary to the trend of the times and have been resolutely opposed by the people of China and US as well as the people of the world. Unilateralism and protectionism harm both oneself and others, and would only lead to a dead end. Some people in the US should abandon their wrong practices and meet China halfway to jointly promote the China-US relations based on coordination, cooperation and stability, and enhance the well-being of the people of the two countries and the world. ■

23 Liu Kun: report on the central government final accounts for the year of 2018

Source: MOF

On June 26, the 11th meeting of the Standing Committee of the 13th National People's Congress held its second plenary meeting. Entrusted by the State Council, Finance Minister Liu Kun made a report on the 2018 central final accounts. The full text is as follows.

Standing Committee of the National People's Congress,

Entrusted by the State Council, I hereby submit the 2018 central final accounts report and the draft central final accounts to the Standing Committee of NPC for review.

I. Final accounts of the central government's fiscal revenues and expenditures in 2018

In 2018, in the face of the complicated international environment and the arduous domestic tasks of reform, development and stability, and under the strong leadership of the Party Central Committee with Comrade Xi Jinping as the core, all localities and departments, guided by the Xi Jinping Thought on Socialism with Chinese Characteristics for a New Era, fully implemented the requirements of the 19th CPC National Congress and the Second and Third Plenary Sessions of the 19th Central Committee, adhered to the general principle of striving for progress while maintaining stability, followed through the new development concepts, enforced high-quality development requirements, pursued the supply-side structural reform as the main task, and conscientiously implemented the resolutions of the First Session of the 13th National People's Congress in accordance with the decisions of the Party Central Committee and the State Council. As a result, we have maintained the sustained and healthy economic development and the overall stability of the society, and made new progress toward building a moderately prosperous society in all respects. On this basis, new stride has been made in the work of fiscal reform and development, and the central final accounts are generally in good shape. According to the relevant provisions of the Budget Law, the following highlights are mainly reported.

(1) The final accounts of the revenues and expenditures of the central general public budget

In 2018, the central general public budget revenue was 8.545646 trillion RMB, or 100.1% of the budgeted amount. With the addition of 245.3 billion RMB of funds transferred from the central budget stabilization fund, the central government fund budget, and the central state-owned capital operating budget, the total revenue reached 8.790946 trillion RMB. The central general public budget expenditure was 10.238847 trillion RMB, completing 99.1% of the budget. With the addition of 102.099 billion RMB of funds transferred to the central budget stabilization fund, the total expenditure reached 10.340946 trillion RMB. The central government's fiscal deficit was 1.55 trillion RMB when the total revenues were offset against the total expenditures, which was in line with the budgeted amount.

Compared with the figure reported to the 2nd Session of the 13th National People's Congress, the central general public budget revenue saw an increase of 912 million RMB. This is mainly due to the increase in non-tax revenue during the settlement period. The central general public budget expenditure increased by 667 million RMB, mainly due to the central government's tax return to local governments. The above balance of revenue and expenditure was 245 million RMB, which was already included in the above-mentioned 102.099 billion RMB of the central budget stabilization fund.

In terms of the final accounts of revenues, due to the implementation of the tax and fee cut policy and the new downward pressure on the economy, the central general public budget revenue increased by 5.3%, an increase of 1.8 percentage points over the previous year. Among them, the tax revenue was 8.044807 trillion RMB, which was 100.3% of the budgeted amount, representing an increase of 6.3% and 4.3 percentage points lower than that of the previous year; the non-tax revenue was 500.839 billion RMB, which was 97.2% of the budgeted amount, down by 8.7%. Among the tax revenues, the domestic value-added tax was 3.075332 trillion RMB, or 104% of the budgeted amount; the domestic consumption tax was 1.063175 trillion RMB, or 100.6% of the budgeted amount; the value-added tax, consumption tax and customs duties of imported goods totaled 1.972675 trillion RMB, accounting for 97.7% of the budgeted amount; corporate income tax was 2.224211 trillion RMB, accounting for 101.6% of the budgeted amount; personal income tax was 832.442 billion RMB, accounting for 107.4% of the budgeted amount, mainly because the personal income tax went up rapidly with the increase of the residents' wage income before the rise of basic deduction standard on October 1, 2018; the vehicle purchase tax was 345.253 billion RMB, which was 96.4% of the budgeted amount; the value-added tax and the consumption tax return of export goods was 1.591393 trillion RMB, which was 107.7% of the budgeted amount, mainly because that the export tax rebate rate for some products was raised twice in the middle of the year.

In terms of the final accounts of expenditures, the central government's expenditure was 3.270781 trillion RMB, completing 100.7% of the budget; the central government's tax return and transfer payment to local governments was 6.968066 trillion RMB, completing 99.1% of the budget. Among the central expenditures, education expenditure was 173.123 billion RMB, completing 101.2% of the budget; science and technology expenditure was 312.027 billion RMB, completing 100.2% of the budget; diplomatic expenditure was 58.337 billion RMB, completing 9.1% of the budget; defense expenditure was 1.10697 trillion RMB, completing 100% of the budget; public safety expenditure was 204.151 billion RMB, completing 102.5% of the budget; general public service expenditure was 150.368 billion RMB, completing 103.4% of the budget; grain and oil reserve expenditure was 137.564 billion RMB, completing 100.3% of the budget; debt service expenditure was 416.165 billion RMB, completing 97.1% of the budget. Among the central government's tax return and transfer payment to local governments, the tax return was 803.151 billion RMB, completing 98.7% of the budget; the general transfer payment was 3.872206 trillion RMB, completing 99.3% of the budget;

the special transfer payment was 2.292709 trillion RMB, completing 98.8% of the budget. The central government transferred 5.258335 trillion RMB to the central and western regions, accounting for 85.3% of the total transfer payments.

The central reserve budget was 50 billion RMB, and the actual expenditure was 1.748 billion RMB. It was mainly used to support local efforts to strengthen the prevention and control of African swine fever, and the remaining 48.252 billion RMB has been transferred to the central budget stabilization fund. The balance of central general public budget expenditure was 92.153 billion RMB (including the 48.252 billion RMB of central reserve fund balance), which totaled 102.099 billion RMB with the addition of 9.946 billion RMB of surplus and was all used to supplement the central budget stabilization fund. At the beginning of 2018, the balance of the central budget stabilization fund was 270.846 billion RMB. With the addition of the above-mentioned 102.099 billion RMB and the 3.369 billion RMB of carryover funds from the central government-managed fund, the balance of the central budget stabilization fund at the end of 2018 was 376.644 billion RMB. After the transfer of 280 billion RMB to the budget in 2019, the balance was 96.644 billion RMB.

In 2018, the central general public budget used 115.364 billion RMB of expenditures from the previous years' carry-over funds. Among them, 18.709 billion RMB was used by the central government, and 96.655 billion RMB was used as the central government transfer payment to local government. The scale of the central budget working capital has not changed, the balance of which at the end of 2018 was 35.403 billion RMB and was mainly used to adjust the seasonal payments within the budget year.

In 2018, the central government's "three public" expenses were 3.992 billion RMB (including basic expenditures and project expenditures), which was 1.714 billion RMB less than the budgeted amount. This was mainly because the central government implemented the spirit of the Eight-point Regulations, strictly controlled and reduced the "three public" expenditures, as well as partly due to the fact that some official overseas trips and hospitality expenses did not materialize and official car spending decreased. Among them, official overseas travel expenditure was 1.484 billion RMB, a drop of 279 million RMB; official vehicle purchase and operation expenditure was 2.233 billion RMB, a fall of 1.082 billion RMB; official hospitality expenditure was 275 million RMB, a decrease of 353 million RMB.

In 2018, the central infrastructure investment expenditure was 537.6 billion RMB. Among them, the central level expenditure was 126.733 billion RMB, and the local transfer payment was 410.867 billion RMB, which was mainly used for the development of "agriculture, rural areas and farmers", major infrastructure projects, innovation, and structural adjustment, subsidized housing projects, social undertakings and social governance, energy conservation and environmental protection, and ecological development. The expenditure helped further enhance investment efficiency, playing a positive role in optimizing the supply structure, strengthening the infrastructure sector, and stabilizing effective investment. In the actual implementation, the central infrastructure investment projects greatly deviate from the budgeted amount, which is mainly because of the increased support to key projects such as Beijing Daxing International Airport and the power supply project for Sichuan-Tibet Railway Lhasa-Ningchi section in accordance with the arrangement of the Party Central Committee and the State Council.

In 2018, the central government issued 3.709231 trillion RMB of government bonds, including 3.677558 trillion RMB of domestic debts and 31.673 billion RMB of foreign debts. The funds raised were used by the central government after the repayment of the principal of maturing debts. The treasury bonds were used to repay 2.226472 trillion RMB of principal, of which the 2.201439 trillion RMB was for domestic debts and 25.33 billion RMB was for foreign debts. The balance of the government debts at the end of the year was 14.960741 trillion RMB, including the balance of domestic debts of 14.820862 trillion RMB and the balance of foreign debts of 139.879 billion RMB, and was kept within the limit of 15.690835 trillion RMB approved by NPC.

(2) The final accounts of the revenues and expenditures of the central government-managed fund budget

In 2018, the revenue of central government-managed fund was 403.481 billion RMB, accounting for 104.4% of the budgeted amount. Added with the carry-over revenue of 38.559 billion RMB in 2017, the total revenue was 442.04 billion RMB. The central government-managed fund expenditure was 402.155 billion RMB, completing 94.7% of the budget, which was mainly due to the fact that some projects failed to meet the implementation criteria in the Civil Aviation Development Fund and the Lottery Public Welfare Fund. Among them, the central government's expenditure at the central level was 308.929 billion RMB, and the local transfer payment was 93.226 billion RMB. A total of 146 million RMB was transferred to the general public budget. The final accounts of central government-managed fund revenue increased by 216 million RMB compared with the figure of implementation, and the final accounts figure for expenditure was equal to the implementation figure.

The central government-managed fund revenue was 39.739 billion RMB more than expenditure, of which, 36.04 billion RMB was carried over to be used in the next year; the carryovers of government-managed fund that exceed 30% of the revenue of the current year totaled 3.699 billion RMB and were used to supplement the central budget stabilization fund according to regulations.

(3) The final accounts of the revenues and expenditures of central state-owned capital operating budget

In 2018, the central state-owned capital operating revenue was 132.638 billion RMB, which was 96.3% of the budgeted amount. Added with 11.359 billion RMB of carry-over revenue of 2017, the total revenue was 143.997 billion RMB. The central state-owned capital operating expenditure was 111.173 billion RMB, completing 95.1% of the budget, which was mainly due to the corresponding reduction in expenditures in the unfinished budget. Among them, the central government's expenditure was 102.485 billion RMB, and the local transfer payment was 8.688 billion RMB. A total of 32.154 billion RMB was transferred to the general public budget. The carryover for the expenditure of next year was 670 million RMB. The final accounts figure of central state-owned capital operating revenue increased by 107 million RMB compared with the implementation figure, and the final accounts figure of expenditure was equal to the implementation figure.

(4) The final accounts of revenues and expenditures of the central social insurance fund budget

In 2018, the central social insurance fund revenue was 58.967 billion RMB, accounting for 87.2% of the budgeted amount, of which, insurance premium revenue was 30.833 billion RMB and fiscal subsidy revenue was 27.487 billion RMB. Added with 241.33 billion RMB of the central adjustment fund revenue paid by the local government, the total revenue was 300.297 billion RMB. The central social insurance fund expenditure was 53.249 billion RMB, completing 81.3% of the budget. Added with 240.68 billion RMB of the central adjustment fund expenditure arranged for the local government, the total expenditure was 293.929 billion RMB. The balance of revenue and expenditure for the current year was 6.368 billion RMB, and the accumulated balance at the end of the year was 33.044 billion RMB. The final accounts figure of the central social insurance fund increased by 756 million RMB compared with the implementation figure, and the final accounts figure of expenditure increased by 36 million RMB over the implementation figure.

In accordance with the Budget Law and the relevant provisions of the State Council, the accrual accounting was implemented for some of the revenues and expenditures of the central government in 2018, including the salary and social insurance funds that have been allocated but not yet spent in the current year, the treasury centralized payment at the end of the year, and other special matters approved by the State Council. The specific information has been reported to the Standing Committee of NPC. For the above-mentioned funds, MOF will strengthen the management of budget implementation, make timely disbursement, and maximize the benefits of funds.

The budgeted amount, the final accounts and their comparative analysis regarding the central general public budget, the government-managed fund budget, the state-owned capital operating budget, the social insurance fund budget in 2018 are detailed in the draft central final accounts. Before the draft was submitted to the Party Central Committee and the State Council for approval and to the Standing Committee of NPC for review, it had been audited by the National Audit Office and revised accordingly.

II. Earnestly implement various fiscal and tax policies to promote high-quality development

In 2018, we conscientiously implemented the decisions of the Party Central Committee and the State Council, and in accordance with the relevant resolutions of NPC and approved budgets, we worked to implement a proactive fiscal policy, vigorously implemented the tax and fee cut policy, increased support to the three critical battles and supply-side structural reforms, stepped up support to innovation, "agriculture, rural areas and farmers" and people's livelihood, deepened the reform of the fiscal and tax system, strengthened budget execution management, and promoted the sustained and healthy economic development and overall social stability.

(1) Vigorously implemented tax and fee cut

On top of the 1.1 trillion RMB tax and fee cut determined at the beginning of 2018, we made adjustments in light of the macroeconomic situation in the middle of the year, and implemented a number of preferential tax and fee policies. The annual tax and fee reduction was about 1.3 trillion RMB. First, improve the VAT system. The VAT rate was lowered starting from May 1, 2018 and adjusted to 16%, 10% and 6%. The annual sales standard for small-scale taxpayers of industrial enterprises and commercial enterprises was raised from 500,000 RMB and 800,000 RMB to 5 million RMB. For the eligible enterprises in advanced manufacturing, R&D and other modern service industries as well as power grid firms, whose input tax have not been fully deducted within a certain period of time, they should get refunded at one time. Second, implement personal income tax reform. The first step of reform was implemented starting from October 1, 2018, as the basic deduction standard was raised from 3,500 RMB/month to 5,000 RMB/month, and the new tax rate table was applied. As a result, the taxpayers with monthly wage income of less than 20,000 RMB saw their tax burden fall by more than 50%. The second step of reform was implemented starting from January 1, 2019, and six special additional deductions were introduced for children's education, continuing education, major medical care, mortgage loan interest, housing rent, and care for the elderly. Third, increase the tax support for small and micro enterprises. The maximum annual taxable income of small and micro-profit enterprises that enjoy the preferential policy of halving the corporate income tax was raised from 500,000 RMB to 1 million RMB. Fourth, encourage enterprises to increase investment in research and development. The unit value ceiling for the purchase of research and development equipments by companies that enjoy one-time pre-tax deduction was raised from 1 million RMB to 5 million RMB. The policy of increasing the extra deduction of R&D expenses to 75% was expanded from the technology-based SMEs to all enterprises. The loss carryover period of high-tech enterprises and high-tech SMEs was extended from 5 years to 10 years. Restrictions on the extra deduction of entrusted overseas R&D expenses were removed. Fifth, adjust and improve the import and export tax policy. The export tax rebate rate was increased for more than 4,000 products, and the seven brackets of tax rebate rate were reduced to five. We improved the preferential corporate income tax policies for foreign investors that make direct investment with their profits. We increased the upper limit of the goods that enjoy preferential import tax policies for cross-border e-commerce retailing and expand the scope of goods. The cross-border e-commerce retail export tax policy was extended to all cross-border e-commerce comprehensive pilot zones. The implementation of the departure tax rebate policy was extended to 26 provinces. At the same time, we cleaned up and regulated administrative fees, reduced the collection standards of some government funds, and accelerated the cleaning-up of port charges.

(2) Support the three critical battles

We adhere to the basic principles, concentrate on key tasks, maintain steady focus, and resolutely support the three critical battles. First, focus on preventing and mitigating the hidden debt risks of local governments. We opened the "front door" and strictly blocked the "back door" to firmly forestall systemic risks. We strictly implemented local government debt limit management and budget management, basically completed the target of government debt swaps, strengthened special bond management, promoted local government debt information disclosure, and effectively kept government debt risks within statutory limits. In 2018, local government bond issuance reached 4.165168 trillion RMB, repaying 838.937 billion RMB of bonds due in the year. The balance of local government debts at the end of the year was 18.461867 trillion RMB, which was kept within the limit of 20.99743 trillion RMB approved by NPC. We continued to maintain the regulatory high pressure, and resolutely curb the increase in hidden debt. We strengthened the guidance for local government, stably and orderly resolved hidden debt stocks, and urged high-risk areas to reduce debt risk through multiple channels. The illegal borrowing behaviors and those responsible in some cities, counties and financial institutions were seriously dealt with and publicly censured in 9 batches of public notices. We actively cooperated in the efforts to establish the lifelong accountability and investigation mechanisms of local governments. Second, vigorously support poverty alleviation. The central government allocated 106.059 billion RMB of special subsidies for local poverty alleviation, an increase of 23.2%. The increased funds were mainly used for deeply poor areas such as "three regions and three prefectures". The transfer payments for education and the transfer payments for key ecological functional areas have increased in the deeply poor areas. We comprehensively promoted the pilot projects for the consolidation of agriculture-related funds in poverty-stricken counties, with the annual consolidated funds exceeding 300 billion RMB. We strengthened the supervision of poverty alleviation funds at all levels, conducted special inspections of poverty alleviation funds in "three regions and three prefectures", and significantly reduced the cases of violations of laws and regulations. Performance management basically covered all the funds for poverty alleviation projects.

In the year, 2.8 million documented poor people were relocated, and 13.86 million rural poor people were lifted out of poverty. Third, actively support pollution prevention and control. We increased investment, changed approaches and created new mechanisms to support the prevention and control of pollution. The central government allocated 255.5 billion RMB for pollution prevention and control, an increase of 13.9%. The investment in prevention and control of atmospheric, water and soil pollution was the largest in recent years. The number of pilot cities supported by central government funding in promoting clean winter heating in the northern region increased from 12 to 35. The air quality of Beijing, Tianjin, Hebei and surrounding areas further improved. The demonstration program of black and odorous water treatment was carried out in 20 cities. We supported the improvement of urban sewage treatment in the central and western regions, and strengthened the comprehensive management of the Bohai Sea. We strengthened soil pollution control and promoted the rehabilitation and treatment of farmland contaminated by heavy metal. We expanded pilot projects such as comprehensive utilization of crop straws and utilization of livestock and poultry manure, and strengthened agricultural non-point source pollution control. 14 projects, including Ningxia Helan Mountain Range, Guizhou Wumeng Mountain Area and Inner Mongolia Wuliangsuhai Basin, were included in the third batch of landscape ecological protection and restoration pilot projects, with the pilot scope basically covering China's important ecological function areas.

(3) Support the deepening of the supply-side structural reform

We intensify efforts to overhaul the economic structure, promote the innovation-driven development of the real economy, strengthen support for manufacturing sector, private enterprises, and SMEs, unleash the vitality of market players, and foster new growth drivers. First, support the high-quality development of manufacturing sector. Conduct the pilot program of insurance compensation for the first (set) major technical equipment and new materials. Second, enhance scientific and technological innovation. Safeguard the funding for public science and technology activities and continue to increase support for basic research. Further expand the autonomy of research institutions and central colleges in the use of funds, and streamline the reporting and inspection process. Third, promote the growth of new drivers. Support 100 national and provincial-level real economic development zones to create special platforms for innovation of SMEs. Improve the tax policy for technology enterprise incubator, university science park and public creation space, and promote nationwide the personal tax incentives for venture capital enterprises and angel investment. Give full play to the role of the National Emerging Industry Venture Capital Guidance Fund to support the development of innovative enterprises in their early and middle stages. Fourth, strengthen support for private enterprises and small and micro enterprises. Make comprehensive use of financing, credit enhancement, rewards and tax incentives to encourage financial institutions to increase financing for enterprises. Establish a national financing guarantee fund to leverage more than 270 billion RMB in credit. Make good use of the special funds of financial inclusion to reward the increase of about 100 billion RMB of agriculture-related loans. Implement the policy of offering rewards and subsidies for the reduction of financing guarantee fees to small and micro enterprises, in order to cut the financing costs of small and micro enterprises. Fifth, consolidate the achievements of "cutting overcapacity, deleveraging, destocking, reducing costs and shoring up weak links". Continue to support the steel and coal industry to cut excess capacity, complete the overcapacity-cutting targets of the "13th Five-Year Plan" two years ahead of schedule, and allocate subsidies to support the resettlement of about 1.2 million people. Seek solutions to resolve the legacy problems of state-owned enterprises, and support the central enterprises in the disposal of "zombie enterprises" and the management of extremely difficult enterprises. Increase efforts to shore up weak links in the key areas, promote the orderly PPP cooperation, and steadily increase the participation of private enterprises.

(4) Support the continuous improvement of the people's livelihood

Coordinate economic development with the improvement of people's livelihood, and improve the management of spending policies related to people's livelihood, while increasing spending on people's livelihood. First, improve and implement the measures to stabilize employment. Introduce a number of policies to support enterprises to keep employment stable, and expand the scope of apprenticeship subsidies. Support the grass-root employment of college graduates, the resettlement of workers in industries that cut excess production capacity, and the training of new professional farmers. Spend about 45 billion RMB of unemployment insurance fund to ensure the basic living of 4.523 million unemployed people, and create 13.61 million new jobs in urban areas. Second, support the development of fair and quality education. Allocate about 84% of the central government's education transfer payments to the central and western regions in 2018. Increase the supply of the resources of inclusive pre-school education, and increase the pre-school education gross enrollment rate to 81.7%. Consolidate the funding mechanism for integrated compulsory education in urban and rural areas with a focus on rural areas. Raise the nine-year compulsory education rate to 94.2%, and reduce the proportion of large classes and super-large classes. Support the accelerated development of modern vocational education and promote the development of "double first-class". Third, advance the reform of the pension insurance system. Establish and implement the centrally managed system for the basic pension insurance of enterprise employees starting from July 1, 2018, and mobilize a total of 242.23 billion RMB of funds, benefiting 22 provinces. Steadily promote the pilot program of transferring some state-owned capital to replenish the social security fund at the proportion of 10% of the state-owned shares of the enterprise. Establish the mechanism for setting and adjusting the basic pension insurance benefits for urban and rural residents. Raise the minimum basic pensions to 88 RMB, and raise the basic pension standard for retirees by about 5%. Fourth, promote the development of healthy China. Raise the fiscal subsidy for medical insurance of urban and rural residents to 490 RMB per person per year, and spend half of the increase of 40 RMB to strengthen the capacity for insuring against major illness. Keep the actual compensation rate for major illness insurance at no less than 50%. Support the reduction of taxes and prices for anti-cancer drugs, and include 17 kinds of anti-cancer drugs in the medical insurance catalogue, with an average price reduction of 56.7%. Support centralized drug procurement pilots, and cut the average price of 25 selected drugs by 52%. Raise the per capita fiscal subsidy standard for basic public health service projects to 55 RMB, and further increase the number of service projects. Consolidate the results and continue to deepen the comprehensive reform of public hospitals. Fifth, strengthen the policy to improve people's livelihood. Increase the subsidy funds for the needy people, and support the local governments to provide assistance for the low-income people with special difficulties, beggars and orphans. Continue to raise the standard of pension and living allowances for recipients of special care, benefiting more than 8.6 million people in the country. Strengthen the basic housing security, start the renovation of 6.26 million units of houses in the shantytown and 1.9 million units of rural dilapidated houses. Sixth, promote the development of cultural undertakings. Promote the free admission of more than 50,000 museums, memorials, art galleries, cultural centers, and other public cultural facilities. Support the implementation of more than 2,000 protection programs by national key cultural relic protection units and world cultural heritage sites. Strengthen support for the development of media integration and enhance the influence of mainstream media.

(5) Promote coordinated development of urban and rural areas

Focus on the implementation of the rural revitalization strategy and the major regional strategy, strengthen fiscal and tax policy support, narrow the urban-rural development gap, and optimize urban and rural resource allocation. First, support the implementation of the rural revitalization strategy. Establish cross-provincial farmland and construction land coordinating mechanism, and raise funds to support rural revitalization and poverty alleviation. Strengthen the protection of cultivated farmland, promote the advanced agricultural technology, increase the area of high-efficiency water-saving irrigation by 21.38 million mu, and raise the comprehensive mechanization rate of agriculture to over 67%. Deepen the supply-side structural reform of agriculture, support the trial of 29 million mu of land rotation, comprehensively promote the high-quality grain project, and improve the price formation mechanism for rice and other grains. Extend the national agricultural credit guarantee system to cover nearly 50% of the counties and cities nationwide, and provide over 64 billion RMB of secured loans for 190,000 agricultural projects. Use policy-based agricultural insurance to provide 3.46 trillion RMB of risk protection for 195 million households throughout the year. Promote the improvement of rural living environment with emphasis on wastewater treatment, toilet revolution, and village appearance. Expand the scope of pilot projects to support village-level collective economic development. Second, support the implementation of major regional strategies. Use fiscal and tax policy tools to support the implementation of major regional strategies. Develop a supportive fiscal policy system for the initial stage of the planning and construction of Xiong'an New District. Introduce fiscal policies to support the comprehensive reform and opening up of Hainan. Implement incentive policies for promoting ecological protection and restoration of the Yangtze River Economic Belt, and start the compensation for the fishing ban of the key waters of the Yangtze River Basin. Formulate the fiscal and taxation policies for the construction of The Guangdong-Hong Kong-Macao Greater Bay Area. Third, support the improvement of the level of equalization of basic public services. Significantly increase the size of the general transfer payment to the central and western regions. Raise the equalization transfer payment by 9.2%, and increase the rewards and subsidies for county-level basic funding by 10% and the transfer payment to old-revolutionary bases, ethnic minority regions, border areas and poor areas by 15.7%. Arrange 40 billion RMB of phased fiscal subsidies to support the livelihood of people in the resource-depleted areas and the Northeast region.

(6) Deepen the fiscal and tax reforms

Keep goal-oriented and problem-oriented, further refine policy measures, pay more attention to the implementation and effectiveness of the fiscal and tax system while introducing new reform measures. First, accelerate the reform of fiscal system. Introduce the reform plan for the division of joint fiscal mandates and expenditure responsibilities between the central and local governments in the basic public service field, and the reform plan for the division of fiscal mandates and expenditure responsibilities in the medical and health fields, and actively promote reforms in the fields of education, science and technology, and transportation. Second, deepen the reform of the budget management system. Deeply implement the Opinions of the Central Committee of the Communist Party of China and the State Council on the Comprehensive Implementation of Budget Performance Management, and basically establish a central-level budget performance management system focused on project expenditure. Make the disclosure of the central budget and final accounts more detailed, and further advance the disclosure of the budgets and final accounts of the provincial, city, and county governments and departments. Third, improve the tax system. While promoting tax and fee reduction, basically establish an individual income tax system that is both comprehensive and classified, reform and improve the VAT system. Accelerate the tax legislation process, successfully implement the Environmental Protection Tax Law, the Ship Tonnage Tax Law, and the Tobacco Leaf Tax law, complete the review and passage of the farmland occupation tax law and the vehicle purchase tax Law by the Standing Committee of NPC, and submit the Resource Tax Law to the Standing Committee of NPC for initial review.

In addition, actively deploy fiscal and tax policies to support reforms in key areas. First, spare no effort to ensure the smooth progress of the reform of Party and state institutions. In line with the reform plan of Party and state institutions, release the 2018 departmental budget to the departments involved in reform, handle budget transfer in accordance with the law, and timely disburse funds to the newly formed departments to ensure the normal operation and performance of duties and smooth implementation of the reform. Second, implement reform measures related to opening up. Implement zero tariffs on most imported drugs, including anti-cancer drugs, in service of opening up and the needs of domestic production and living. Reduce import tariffs on automobile vehicles and parts, 1,449 daily consumer goods, and 1,585 industrial products, cutting the overall tariff level of China from 9.8% in the previous year to 7.5%. Third, deepen the reform of state-owned assets and state-owned enterprises. Introduce the implementation opinions on the pilot of state-owned capital investment and operating company reform. Improve state-owned financial capital management. Present, for the first time, to the Standing Committee of National People's Congress a comprehensive report on the management of state-owned assets and a special report on state-owned assets of financial enterprises.

III. Highlight problems and further strengthen fiscal budget management

The 2018 final accounts are generally in good shape, yet there are also some problems that need to be resolved. Relevant parties from NPC and the National Audit Office also made suggestions.

We attached great importance to these issues, thoroughly implemented the spirit of the important speech of the General Secretary Xi Jinping at the Central Audit Committee, followed the arrangement of the State Council on the audit and rectification work, seriously rectified the outstanding problems identified by the audit, took effective measures to solve the problems, strengthened management, improved the system, and strived to prevent problems before they happen. At the same time, we conscientiously implemented the opinions and suggestions of NPC on the budgetary work, and continuously improved the scientific budget management.

(1) Optimize the preparation of final accounts

Implement the suggestions of NPC on shifting the focus of budget review and supervision toward expenditure budgets and policies, fully take up the opinions and suggestions of NPC deputies and CPPCC members, continuously improve the preparation of the final accounts, and raise the quality and readability of the report. Enable the 2019 Budget Report to strictly follow the arrangement of the Central Economic Work Conference, make the expenditure policies and expenditure budgets more specific and detailed, and add annexes to enrich the form of report. Make the draft preparation more detailed, and add more notes. For the first time, include the central government-managed fund budget and the transfer payment from the state-owned capital operating budget, and include the income and expenditure of central adjustment fund into the social insurance fund budget, further increase the materials related to the performance targets of central to local transfer payment budget and government-managed fund budget, and continue to increase the number of central department projects submitted to NPC for review compared with the previous year.

(2) Strengthen budget performance management

Steadily promote a result-oriented and full-process budget performance management model. Expand the performance target management scope from general public budget projects to some central government-managed fund budgets and central state-owned capital operating budget projects. Allow the performance targets of central department-level projects and special transfer payments to be simultaneously reported, reviewed and released as the budgets, carry out "double monitoring" over the budget execution and performance achievement of all departmental expenditures, timely correct the deviations in implementation, conduct self-assessment of performance after implementation, and check and review the results of self-assessment. Intensify the key performance evaluations. Carry out performance evaluation for 38 key expenditures related to people's livelihood in 2018, involving more than 550 billion RMB of funds. Continue to arrange funds or increase fiscal spending for some policies and projects with good performance evaluations, and cut budget and urge relevant departments to improve policies and improve management in case of poor performance evaluation. Submit over 260 project performance self-assessment results and 20 key performance evaluation reports to the Standing Committee of NPC for review or reference, and promote the disclosure to the public.

(3) Reform and improve the transfer payment system

Amend more than 50 central-to-local transfer payment funds management methods, optimize distribution factors and weights, and adjust and refine subsidy standards. In accordance with the reform requirements of the central and local fiscal mandates and expenditure responsibilities and in light of the problems identified by the audit, merge the projects that belong to the basic public service field with joint central and local fiscal mandates in the current general transfer payments and special transfer payments, set up joint-fiscal-mandate transfer payments starting from 2019, and enhance the local capabilities in providing basic public services. Accelerate the release of transfer payment budget, and strengthen transfer payment management. When it comes to general transfer payment, study and simplify distribution factors, and encourage local governments to retain more financial resources. In terms of joint-fiscal-mandate transfer payment, promote the establishment of a separate management system, and gradually promote the list-based management and establishment of control mechanisms. In terms of special transfer payments, further standardize the allocation management, improve the regular assessment and exit mechanism, and cancel or adjust the special payment based on the evaluation results.

(4) Improve departmental budget management

Supervise and guide the central government departments to optimize the expenditure structure, strictly control the general expenditure, and use more funds for important undertakings. Further expand the evaluation scope of central department projects, continue to organize and carry out dynamic evaluation of major projects, and strive to change the pattern where project expenditures keep increasing. Strengthen budget monitoring, and accelerate the pace of budget execution. Further link budgetary arrangement with budget implementation, and reduce the budgetary arrangements for the next year for departments with slow implementation progress in the previous year. Enable central departments to publicize the budget and final accounts on a unified platform and actively respond to public concerns.

(5) Strengthen the coordination of budget management

Strengthen the coordination of government-managed fund budgets, state-owned capital operating budgets and general public budgets when arranging related expenditures. Remove the requirements regarding the use of funds for intended purpose in the general public budget. Raise the proportion of central state-owned capital operating budget funds transferred to the general public budget to 25%, an increase of 3 percentage points over 2017. Raise the central infrastructure investment budget disbursement rate to 94.8% at the beginning of 2018. Release the local transfer payment budget in advance for the first time, and compile the budget performance targets for the first time. Strengthen inter-departmental communication and coordination, implement project double-checking mechanism, further optimize investment direction and structure, and give better play to the guiding role of government investment.

Since the beginning of this year, in accordance with the decisions of the Party Central Committee and the State Council, major fiscal and tax policies have been implemented in a faster manner, and policies, such as deepening the reform of value-added tax, inclusive tax reduction for small and micro enterprises, and lowering the rate of social security contribution, have been implemented. The local governments have made cumulative issuance of 1.4596 trillion RMB of new bonds in the first five months, which effectively promoted the smooth performance of China's economy and significantly improved market confidence. From January to May, the national general public budget revenue was 8.9919 trillion RMB, a year-on-year increase of 3.8%. Among them, tax revenue increased by 2.2%, down by 13.6 percentage points. The increase of value-added tax revenue in tax revenue fell by 12.2 percentage points, and personal income tax revenue fell by 30.7%, the increase in the value-added tax and consumption tax revenue of imported goods fell by 16.4 percentage points, and the increase in tariff revenue fell by 11.4 percentage points; the special revenue among the non-tax revenues related to education fees decreased by 2.9%, and the revenue from administrative fees fell by a further 1.3% on top of the 20.7% decrease in the same period of last year. The national general public budget expenditure was 9.3023 trillion RMB, an increase of 12.5%. Expenditures on poverty alleviation, eco-environmental protection, education, and health care went up rapidly. The central general public budget revenue was 4.3397 trillion RMB, an increase of 3.6%; the central general public budget expenditure was 1.3439 trillion RMB, an increase of 12.5%.

In the next step, we will closely implement the spirit of the Central Economic Work Conference, strictly follow the requirements of the Government Work Report, strictly implement the budget approved by NPC, strive for progress while maintaining stability, highlight the central task, adhere to the overall principle of keeping macro policies stable, micro policies flexible and social policies sound, work harder to implement effective proactive fiscal policies, stimulate market vitality and promote high quality development. At the same time, we will firmly establish the awareness and enforce diligence and frugality in all aspects of fiscal work. We will tighten the belt, adopt a simple work style, and vigorously reduce administrative expenses. Focus will be put on the following work. First, ensure that the large-scale tax and fee cut is put in place. Strictly implement the VAT cut policies such as reducing the VAT rate, expanding the scope of input tax deduction, refunding the tax credit, as well as the inclusive tax reduction measures for small and micro enterprises. Strengthen non-tax revenue management, and further clean up and standardize administrative fees and government-managed fund. Supervise and guide local government to mobilize financial resources and cut expenditures, strengthen budget management of fiscal revenue and expenditure, revitalize existing assets, strive to further reduce general expenditures by more than 10%, and support the implementation of tax and fee cut policies. Closely follow the reaction of market participants in the implementation of policy, improve policies and services in a timely manner, and strengthen supervision and inspection, so that enterprises and the masses can truly gain the benefits. Second, strengthen spending in key areas. Continue to support the fight against the three critical battles, and focus efforts on tackling the outstanding issues. Promote the employment of key groups of people, implement the subsidy policies for elderly care, medical care and social protection, and continuously address the shortcomings of people's livelihood. Improve the management mechanism for expenditures on areas related to people's livelihood and timely correct the expenditure policies or projects that are unrealistic and unaffordable. Improve the basic funding mechanism at the county level and enhance the financial ability of regions suffering from financial difficulties. Supervise and guide the local authorities to ensure the "three guarantees", and prohibit the local governments from engaging in illegal borrowing no matter the financial difficulty. Third, improve the ability and level of budget implementation. Accelerate the budget release, especially the budget not allocated to departments and localities at the beginning of the year. Accelerate the local government's new bond issuance, and strive to complete the basic issuance before the end of September. Strengthen the analysis and assessment of budget implementation, and urge local governments and departments to implement the principal responsibility for budget implementation. Promptly establish a comprehensive, full-process and full-coverage budget performance management system, reduce inefficient and ineffective expenditures, and improve the efficiency of fund allocation and effectiveness of fund use. Fourth, promote the implementation of key reform tasks. Promptly formulate reform plans for the division of fiscal mandates and expenditures responsibilities in areas such as emergency rescue and natural resources. Steadily promote the reform of the revenue sharing between central and local governments. Further expand the scope of the implementation of the central state-owned capital operating budget. Increase efforts to promote tax legislation. Improve the submitting of comprehensive report on the management of state-owned assets and the special oral report on the management of state-owned assets in administrative institutions to the Standing Committee of NPC. Fifth, continue to intensively rectify the problems identified in audit. Clarify the responsibility for rectification, increase the efforts of rectification, adhere to the principle of "treating the disease and preventing the potential disease", and at the same time, deepen the reform and improve the system, further strengthen management and supervision of budget implementation and fiscal expenditure, and establish and improve the long-term mechanism.

We will be more closely united around the Party Central Committee with Comrade Xi Jinping as the core, be guided by Xi Jinping Thought on Socialism with Chinese Characteristics for a New Era, firmly adhere to the "four consciousnesses", strengthen the "four self-confidence", and resolutely ensure the "two safeguards", consciously accept the supervision of the Standing Committee of NPC, conscientiously enforce the suggestions and comments of this meeting, do a good job in fiscal budget management, promote sustained and healthy economic development and overall social stability, in order to lay a decisive foundation for the building of a moderately prosperous society in all respects and celebrate the 70th anniversary of the founding of the People's Republic of China with excellent achievements. ■

24 Liu Shangxi: fiscal reform during the 14th Five-Year Plan Period should tilt more toward the division of expenditure responsibilities

On June 26, Liu Shangxi, President of the China Academy of Fiscal Sciences, said at the Workshop on China's Fiscal Reform during the 14th Five-Year Plan Period that China's fiscal reform should be compatible with the current stage of development and be adapted to the overall goal of reform. First, the targets of fiscal reform should be diverse. Fiscal reform must focus not only on economic targets, but also on social targets; it should consider not only economic issues, but also social, ecological and global governance issues. It is necessary not only to unleash the vitality of the local economy, but also to promote social development, support poor areas and improve the ecological environment. Second, in a dynamic society, fiscal reform should tilt towards the division of expenditure responsibilities. In view of the increasingly integrated development of the dynamic society, the central and provincial governments need to take on more fiscal mandates and gradually increase the proportion of central government expenditures to the total expenditure. Third, we must consider fiscal sustainability from the perspective of public risks. To achieve fiscal sustainability, we must not only control the risks of the financial sector itself, but also balance the relationship between public risks and fiscal risks. Fourth, the core of the 14th Five-Year Plan is people-centered. It is necessary to shift investment from material capital to human capital and provide better public services, with a view to addressing inequality and promoting fair opportunities. The future development of China should be centered on people, which is also at the core of the 14th Five-Year Plan. ■

25 Jin Liqun: Asian countries need to invest in high-quality infrastructure

On July 12, at the 4th Annual Meeting of the AIIB, AIIB President Jin Liqun said that global growth is stabilizing, but protectionism and disruption of trade and cross-border investments constitute a major risk to many countries. Many low-income countries are particularly vulnerable to market turbulence as their exports are likely to suffer setbacks and their debt sustainability adversely affected. A well-coordinated investment program in infrastructure and other productive sectors should be established in low-income countries to boost growth, create jobs, reduce poverty, empower women, and then drive a higher level of economic and social achievement. AIIB and other MDBs have a crucial role to play in this regard. Asian investment markets are still at an early stage of development in terms of depth, breadth and impact. Lack of infrastructure investment is still one of the constraints affecting growth in developing Asia. Asian countries need to invest in high-quality infrastructure, choose projects with high economic returns, design them well and finance them sustainably. At the same time, it should be ensured that projects benefit the local population, do no harm to people or the environment and leave no chance for corruption. This is what it means to be lean, clean and green. ■

26 Jia Kang: leave space for the innovation of the manufacturing sector

On July 17, Jia Kang, President of the China Academy of New Supply-side Economics, said that since the beginning of this year, China's fixed asset investment has maintained an overall growth trend, but the momentum is weak. At present, against the backdrop of complicated external changes and accumulated internal problems, China's manufacturing enterprises have shown strong conservative wait-and-see sentiment, and are more likely to endure the difficult stage than make any investment. Therefore, enterprises should be incentivized to invest in manufacturing. First, encourage enterprises to get bold and seize opportunities for development. Second, stimulate effective investment through large-scale projects, so that enterprises can feel the realistic relevance of their production capacity. The production capacity of large and medium-sized equipment manufacturing enterprises must be connected with investment projects of a certain scale. In the face of the current external uncertainties, we must enhance our own certainty, and as we expand domestic demand and increase effective investment, we should properly increase infrastructure construction, such as roads and railways, in support of China's economic development. Third, create a high-standard and law-based business environment, so that enterprises have more confidence in property rights protection and fair competition. Fourth, achieve an upgraded version of high-quality development in the unavoidable competition by turning "pressure into power". We need to guide and motivate small and medium-sized enterprises to complement each other in competition and cooperation and to support large-scale social production. As a result, the unleashed potential will become active investment and expanded the scale of production and operation, i.e., boost dynamism through institutional supply and promote technological innovation through institutional innovation. ■

27 Bai Jingming: tax cut and increased expenditure are lightening the burden of businesses and strengthening the basis for sustained growth

On July 23, Bai Jingming, Vice President of the China Academy of Fiscal Sciences, said that aggressive tax cut and further increase in expenditure is a prominent feature of the proactive fiscal policy which aims to stabilize growth, i.e., adopting accommodative measures to lighten the burden of businesses and strengthen the basis for sustained growth. Specifically, this move intends to transfer more resources to market entities and individuals through tax cut; and expand current effective consumption demand and effective investment through increased spending. The tax cut would lead to an increase in potential demand, and the increase in expenditure would result in an increase in the actual purchasing power. The interaction between the two ultimately would push up total supply growth and structural adjustment, and the synergy would strongly boost economic growth. The macroeconomic data for the first half of 2019 suggest that the policy objectives of aggressive tax cut and increased expenditure have been achieved, which are manifested in three aspects: First, the VAT reform is focused on promoting the healthy development of the real economy, especially the manufacturing industry. VAT cut directly increased the cash flow of manufacturing companies, thus supporting manufacturing development to a certain extent. Second, structural adjustment is the focus of tax cut and increased expenditure. In 2019, China once again increased the pre-tax deduction ratio of R&D expenses for enterprises, which greatly lowered the growth of corporate income tax. Third, aggressive tax cut and increased expenditure have expanded employment and stimulated consumption. The macroeconomic data of 2019 showed that the selection of the focus of aggressive tax cut and increased expenditure has paid off. In the first half of the year, the growth rate of resident income exceeded the GDP growth rate by 2.5 percentage points. The number of newly-employed people in urban areas was 7.37 million, accounting for 67% of the annual target. The growth rate of total retail sales of consumer goods exceeded the GDP growth rate by 2.1 percentage points. As a result, the macroeconomy has maintained a virtuous interaction between employment, consumption and GDP. ■

28 Liu Shangxi: establish new fiscal policy thinking from the perspective of risk-based decision-making

On July 26, at the Publication of *Blue Book of Public Finance: China's Fiscal Policy Report (2019)* & Seminar on the Macroeconomic Situation and Fiscal Policy in the First Half of the Year, Liu Shangxi, President of the China Academy of Fiscal Sciences, said that the traditional method of economic situation analysis is to look at the performance of the "troika" of investment, consumption and export, but this analytical framework based on deterministic thinking can no longer meet the needs of realistic macroeconomic policies. He thus proposed new fiscal policy thinking from the perspective of risk-based decision-making: First, establish a fiscal policy concept underpinned by un-deterministic thinking. It is necessary to think out of the traditional deterministic policy analysis framework, formulate, adjust and improve fiscal policies in the trade-off between public risks and fiscal risks, and incorporate uncertainty into the policy analysis framework. Second, inject macro certainty into fiscal policies to stabilize market expectations. Stable expectations will stabilize the overall situation, thereby minimizing the public risks we face and bring uncertainty into market control. Third, innovate fiscal policy on the basis of public risk management. Fiscal policies from the perspective of public risk management include economic and social policies, and fiscal policies aim to address public risks in the economic and social fields. The measure of the effects of fiscal policies is to help micro-entities to avoid market risks and bring down public risks. (1) Achieve a virtuous cycle of aggregate social supply and demand by stabilizing expectation of micro-entities; (2) Achieve a virtuous cycle of public service supply and demand by promoting employment and human capital accumulation; (3) Achieve a virtuous cycle of financial supply and demand by maintaining liquidity and long-term financing. In addition, he also proposed the concept of institutional change based on public risks. If institutional change is lagging behind and policies are not perfect, then the risks in the market cannot be cleared out and may transform into public risks, resulting in a general increase of the costs of micro entities. Preventing and mitigating major risks is aimed at public risks. We should have a thorough understanding of risks, and promote reforms to better optimize institutional arrangement and resolve public risks. ■

29 Liu Kun:work hard to firmly move forward the tasks of fiscal reform and development in the spirit of diligence and frugality

Recently, Finance Minister Liu Kun published a signed article entitled *Work Hard to Firmly Move Forward the Tasks of Fiscal Reform and Development in the Spirit of Diligence and Frugality* in the 15th issue of *China Finance* in 2019. The full text is as follows:

Source: MOF

Hard work, diligence and frugality are the traditional virtues of the Chinese nation, the political nature and fine traditions of the Communists, and the source of strength of the Party and our country's great undertakings. As General Secretary Xi Jinping pointed out, "the great rejuvenation of the Chinese nation can never be achieved easily, and the whole Party must be prepared to make more arduous and harder efforts to that end." Our Party must rally and lead the people to effectively cope with major challenges, tackle major risks, overcome major obstacles, resolve major contradictions, and address major problems. We must always uphold and carry forward the spirit of hard work, diligence and frugality to prevent any hedonistic and negative thoughts and behaviors. The finance authorities shoulder important responsibilities in implementing the important instructions of General Secretary Xi Jinping and the decisions of the Party Central Committee. It is necessary to firmly work hard in a spirit of diligence and frugality and do a good job in all aspects of fiscal reform and development.

I. Firmly working hard in a spirit of diligence and frugality is of great significance for remaining true to our original aspiration, fulfilling our mission, and advancing the great cause of socialism with Chinese characteristics

The report of the 19th CPC National Congress emphasized the original aspiration and mission of the Communists, which is "to seek happiness for the Chinese people and seek rejuvenation for the Chinese nation". This original aspiration and mission are the fundamental driving force for the Chinese Communists to keep moving forward. Hard work, diligence and frugality are of crucial importance for our Party to stay closely in touch with the masses, pursue our original aspiration and mission, and advance the great cause of socialism with Chinese characteristics. Since the 18th CPC National Congress, General Secretary Xi Jinping has repeatedly made important instructions on diligence and frugality. During the Two Sessions of this year, he once again stressed the need to guide work with the spirit of hard work, diligence and frugality. We must profoundly understand the importance of working hard in the spirit of diligence and frugality in the new era, and lay a solid mental foundation for practicing diligence and frugality.

First, we must profoundly realize that working hard in the spirit of diligence and frugality is an inevitable requirement for inheriting and carrying forward the Party's fine traditions and working style. The Party Central Committee has always emphasized that Party and government agencies at all levels should work hard, strive to save money, and oppose extravagance and waste. Whether it is in the revolutionary war era, or the period of socialist construction and reform and opening-up, the reason why our Party can win the true support of the people and make remarkable achievement is largely because our Party follows the fine tradition of diligence and frugality, and share weal and woe with the people. It is fair to say that the history of the Chinese Communist Party is the history of hard work of the Party.

In 1936 and 1939, American journalist Snow twice went to Yan'an and other northern Shaanxi revolutionary bases for interview. He saw Mao Zedong living in a simple cave dwelling, Zhou Enlai sleeping in an earthen bed, and Peng Dehuai wearing a vest made from a captured parachute. On these small things, he felt that the Chinese Communists had an invincible "Oriental Magic", and asserted that this is the symbol of the rejuvenation of the country and the foundation of victory. On the eve of the national victory of the Liberation War, Comrade Mao Zedong, at the Second Plenary

Session of the 7th CPC National Congress, required the entire Party to remain clear-headed in the face of victory, and "the comrades must be taught to remain modest and prudent and refrain from arrogance and rashness in their style of work; the comrades must be taught to preserve the style of plain living and hard struggle." In 1957, when Comrade Mao Zedong expounded on the major issues of socialist construction, he further emphasized that "it will take decades of hard work to make our country prosperous and strong, including implementing a policy of exercising frugality and opposing waste " , and "we must strive to save and do more with less money".

In January 1954, Comrade Deng Xiaoping, then Deputy Premier and Finance Minister of the Government Council, pointed out at the National Meeting of the Director-Generals of Finance Department that "in order to put the state finance on a solid foundation and safeguard the construction of socialist industry, all expenditures that can be cut must be cut and any waste must be avoided". Later, when he talked about achieving the goals of "four modernization", he stressed that "if you do not advocate hard work, diligence and frugality, this goal cannot be achieved. We must adhere to our tradition of hard work. Otherwise, there is no hope for our cause".

Comrade Jiang Zemin said that "our fiscal work must be done in a way that is within our means, and we must exercise frugality, increase revenue, reduce expenditure, and do the right thing". He pointed out that "it is necessary to vigorously advocate the noble socialist ideology and morality and the fine traditions of the Chinese nation across the whole Party and the whole society, take proud in hard work, diligence and frugality, and be ashamed of extravagance and waste", and went on to emphasize that this is a test of the political stance, political views, and political discernment of Party member cadres.

Comrade Hu Jintao pointed out that "hard work and diligence, as our Party's fine tradition and work style as well as the political essence of our Marxist political Party, is a powerful spiritual force that unites the Party and the people and encourages the whole Party and all the people to achieve common prosperity and national rejuvenation. It is an important magical weapon for our Party to maintain close ties with the people. The more we reform and open up and develop the socialist market economy, the more we must carry forward the spirit of hard work and diligence".

General Secretary Xi Jinping, whether working in Liangjiahe of North Shaanxi, Zhengding of Hebei, Fujian, Zhejiang, Shanghai or working in the central government, has always adhered to and practiced the fine traditions and style of hard work, diligence and frugality. He warned us that "the whole Party must preserve the style of hard work and diligence, refrain from arrogance and rashness, and strive to take the long march of the new era with a sense of urgency".

It can be seen from these important expositions of the Party's main leaders that our Party's thoughts on hard work, diligence and frugality have been consistent. The spirit of Jinggangshan, the spirit of the Long March, the spirit of Yan'an, the spirit of Yimeng, the spirit of Xibaipo, the spirit of Daqing, the spirit of "two bombs and one satellite", the spirit of fighting floods and the spirit of manned space mission are all vivid manifestation of this precious spiritual asset. In the new era, as we remain true to our original aspiration and keep our mission firmly in mind, we must always preserve the political qualities of the Communists, and inherit and carry forward this fine tradition and style.

Second, we must profoundly realize that working hard in the spirit of diligence and frugality is required by the studying and implementation of Xi Jinping Thought on Socialism with Chinese

Characteristics for a New Era.

Since the 18th CPC National Congress, General Secretary Xi Jinping has repeatedly stressed the need to work hard in the spirit of diligence and frugality, and put forward clear requirements for the Party and the government to tighten the belt. On November 15, 2012, General Secretary Xi Jinping emphasized at the First Plenary Session of the 18th CPC National Congress that "we must always be in close touch with the people, share weal and woe with the people, work diligently, and strive to offer people a satisfactory answer sheet". On December 4, 2012, General Secretary Xi Jinping presided over the meeting of the Political Bureau of the Central Committee, and deliberated and adopted the *Eight-Point Regulations on Austerity* to improve work style and link closely to the masses. On January 17, 2013, General Secretary Xi Jinping made important instructions on practicing frugality and opposing extravagance and waste. He called for targeted, operable and guiding measures to strengthen supervision and inspection, encourage savings, and rectify wasteful practices. On January 22, General Secretary Xi Jinping pointed out at the Second Plenary Session of the 18th Central Commission for Discipline Inspection that "it is important to improve work style, but the most fundamental thing is to uphold and carry forward the spirit of hard work and diligence". On October 29, 2013, General Secretary Xi Jinping presided over the meeting of the Political Bureau of the Central Committee , which deliberated and passed the *Regulations of the Party and Government on Promoting Saving and Opposing Waste,* and stressed that it is necessary to promptly formulate implementation rules and supporting measures to put in place a comprehensive system to promote saving and oppose waste. Since then, General Secretary Xi Jinping has repeatedly made important instructions on hard work, diligence and frugality and put forward clear requirements for the implementation of relevant work, effectively promoting the change of the Party's work style and the transformation of social ethos.

General Secretary Xi Jinping's series of important expositions on hard work, diligence and frugality are insightful and significant. They are important components of Xi Jinping Thought on Socialism with Chinese Characteristics for a New Era, pointing the direction and providing the guidance for the carrying forward the spirit of hard work, diligence and frugality for a new era. If we are to study and implement Xi Jinping Thought on Socialism with Chinese Characteristics for a New Era and realize the "two centenary goals" and the great rejuvenation of the Chinese nation, we must thoroughly understand and accurately grasp the important guiding instructions of General Secretary Xi Jinping on hard work, diligence and frugality, further deepen the ideological understanding, improve the political awareness, integrate the thoughts into the whole process of theoretical thinking and practical exploration, and consciously reflect and implement them in practical work.

How to deepen understanding and improve the awareness? I have four points of feelings and views. First, working hard in the spirit of diligence and frugality concerns the success of the Party and the people's undertakings. On March 5 this year, General Secretary Xi Jinping pointed out during the meeting with the Inner Mongolia Delegation that "hard work, diligence and frugality are not only an important guarantee for us to grow from strength to strength over the years, but also an important guarantee for us to carry forward and create greater glories". "The ability to work hard in the spirit of diligence and frugality is of crucial importance for the success of the Party and the people". We must understand the paramount importance of working hard in the spirit of diligence and frugality from the height of the ruling basis and ruling status of the Party and from the height of the rise and fall of the Party and the people's undertakings. Second, working hard in the spirit of diligence and frugality reflects the purpose and nature of our Party. General Secretary Xi Jinping said that "people's longing for a better life is our goal". He emphasized that "the Party and the government taking the lead in tightening the belt is aimed to enable people to lead a good life. This is determined by the purpose and nature of our Party". The CPC is a Marxist political party, the vanguard of the Chinese working class, the vanguard of the Chinese people and the Chinese nation, and the leading core of the socialist cause with Chinese characteristics; therefore, serving the people whole-heartedly is the Party's fundamental purpose. The fundamental purpose of working hard in the spirit of diligence and frugality is to make unremitting efforts for the fundamental interests of the overwhelming majority of the people, to solve the most direct and most realistic issues that the masses care most about, and to better meet the people's growing needs for a better life. Only by firmly governing the Party for the public and for the people, working hard in the spirit of diligence and frugality, and always linking closely to the people can we maintain the close ties between our Party and the people and better realize the aim of serving people whole-heartedly. Third, working hard in the spirit of diligence and frugality is the heirloom of our Party and must be adhered to for a long time. General Secretary Xi Jinping said that "in the past, our party relied on hard work, diligence and frugality to accomplish great achievements; now we still need to guide our work with this kind of thinking." "No matter what level of development our country may attain, no matter how much the people's life may improve, the spirit of hard work, diligence and frugality can never be abandoned". We must be soberly aware that China's basic national condition of being still in and long remaining in the primary stage of socialism has not changed, many important issues concerning the well-being of people's livelihood need further investment, and many things still need to be done for national construction, we must, therefore, avoid the thought of "taking a breath and resting for a while". We must always work hard in the spirit of diligence and frugality, use the "family heirloom" well, manage the "money bag" well, and keep persevering for a long time. Fourth, working hard in the spirit of diligence and frugality is striving to be careful and frugal in all undertakings. General Secretary Xi Jinping demanded that the Party and the government at all levels should firmly establish the idea of belt-tightening and emphasized that "our financial resources are constantly increasing, but we must not squander and waste them. We must practice frugality in all the work, and resolutely resist hedonism and extravagance". Under the new historical conditions, although the material conditions and living standards have improved, the contradiction between income and expenditure and between demand and supply remains eternal. Therefore, we must continue to work hard in the spirit of diligence and frugality, enhance the sense of urgency, plan ahead, and strengthen coordination, "be mindful of the worst, make the best preparation, work hard in the good direction, and strive for the best results", resolutely oppose extravagance and waste, resolutely resist squandering and hedonism, adhere to the glorious tradition of saving, and practice diligence and frugality in all work.

Third, we must profoundly realize that working hard in the spirit of diligence and frugality is an objective need for doing a good job in all aspects of fiscal reform and development. The spirit of hard work, diligence and frugality are to be upheld by the Party for the management of public finance and the basic principles must be followed for budgetary revenue and expenditure arrangements. All along, the fiscal work has always adhered to the correct political direction, resolutely implemented the decisions of the Party Central Committee, focused on the center and served the overall situation, and strived to maximize the effects of precious fiscal resources to provide a strong backing for the cause of revolution and construction. At present, socialism with Chinese characteristics has entered a new era, and economic development has shifted from a period high-spced growth to a stage of high-quality development. The main contradiction in our society has evolved into a contradiction between the growing needs of people for a better life and the inadequate and unbalanced development. Compared with the past, the connotation and focus, the concepts and methods, the environment and conditions, and the level and the requirements of development are all very different from the past, and the people's yearning for a better life has become more intense. The environment facing economic and social development is more complex, with growing uncertainty and more risks. Effectively responding to these risk and challenges and addressing the problem of inadequate and unbalanced development has put forward new and higher requirements for optimizing the allocation of fiscal resources and exercising fiscal regulation.

Public finance is taken from the people and used by the people. The fiscal system arrangement reflects the relationship between government and market, local and overall, current and long-term, and priority and non-priority, and is closely related to the needs of people in all aspects of their good life. In order to better play the role of public finance in the new era, we must firmly establish the awareness of working hard in the spirit of diligence and frugality, properly balance and handle various relationships, cut back on unnecessary expenditures, constantly optimize the structure of fiscal expenditures, focus on supporting the deepening of supply-side structural reforms, and put more energy and resources into promoting reform and development, safeguarding key areas and strengthening weak links. We must keep people-oriented, highlight the public nature and fairness of public finance, fully consider the level of economic development and financial resources, arrange the expenditures related to people's livelihood according to the principle of sustainability and basic protection, and make more effective institutional arrangements to bring more benefits of reform and development to all people.

II. Implement the spirit of hard work, diligence and frugality from the political position and height of providing important guarantee for the success of undertakings

Public finance is the foundation and an important pillar of state governance. MOF is in charge of the "money bag" and the specific service work for the Party Central Committee. We must profoundly understand the rich meaning of General Secretary Xi Jinping's exposition on hard work, diligence and frugality, and implement them in line with the reality of fiscal work.

(1) Enhance political position and raise the ideological consciousness for implementing the instructions of General Secretary Xi Jinping on working hard in the spirit of diligence and frugality. The important instructions of General Secretary Xi Jinping are the political requirements of the Party. Resolutely implementing the important instructions of General Secretary Xi Jinping is the basic political rule of the Party and an important political responsibility. The national fiscal system should thoroughly study and profoundly comprehend the general principles and practical requirements of General Secretary Xi Jinping's expositions on hard work, diligence and frugality, strive to achieve the unity between knowledge and practice, and continuously improve the consciousness and firmness in implementation. It is necessary to further improve political position, work hard in the spirit of diligence and frugality from the height of "four awareness", "four self-confidence" and "two safeguards", make belt-tightening of the Party and government a long-term policy of fiscal work, effectively implement and reflect it in the whole process and all aspects of fiscal reform and development, open up new sources of revenue, practice frugality, and oppose extravagance.

(2) Adhere to the development ideology centered on people, and do everything possible within our means to ensure and improve people's livelihood. General Secretary Xi Jinping pointed out that "to protect and improve people's livelihood, we must focus on the most direct and most realistic issues that people care most about, and do everything possible within our means." In recent years, we have continuously increased investment in people's livelihood, focused on improving and implementing

the policy of keeping employment stable, and introduced a number of policies to support the stable employment of enterprises and increase employment apprentice subsidies. We will vigorously support the development of fair and quality education, and maintain sustained and steady growth of fiscal investment in education. We will promote the improvement of the pension insurance system, and have introduced a central adjustment system for basic pension insurance funds of enterprise employees to ensure that pensions are paid in full and on time. We will support the Healthy China initiative, and raise the fiscal subsidy standards for urban and rural residents' medical insurance and basic public health service projects. We will consolidate the results of drug price reform and continue to deepen the comprehensive reform of public hospitals. At the same time, we must strengthen the management of policies related to people's livelihood, establish and improve the fiscal constraint mechanism, strengthen the performance evaluation of expenditures related to people's livelihood, timely adjust the budget and improve policies in light of the evaluation results, and strive to do things better and more effectively. However, there are still some problems in the field of safeguarding and improving people's livelihood. For example, there are policies introduced in violation of laws and regulations, blind expansion of the scope of government protection, over-increase of the fiscal subsidy standards, and construction of projects that go ahead of the stage of development.

We must do everything possible within our means and properly deal with the relationship between developing the economy and safeguarding people's livelihood. We must constantly increase the protection of people's livelihood on the basis of sustaining economic development, while avoiding making unrealistic commitments that exceed financial capacity, and make sure the policy is based on a more stable and sustainable foundation. First, we must further increase fiscal investment in people's livelihood. We will benchmark the binding tasks of building a moderately prosperous society in all respects, make fiscal arrangements and long-term development plans for the next two years, and provide sufficient financial support to make up for the shortcomings in areas related to people's livelihood. In response to the public concern, we will work to resolve outstanding problems in the fields of employment, education, elderly care and medical services. Second, we must ensure that policies are sustainable. We will make comprehensive consideration of factors such as the stage of economic development, financial affordability and the practical needs of people, in order to effectively prevent the unsustainable system due to unscientific design of policies related to people's livelihood. It is necessary to reasonably guide the expectations and take care to prevent the loss of public trust because of the failure to fulfill policy objectives on time and excessive commitment and excessive publicity. Third, we must strengthen the inter-regional coordination of policies related to people's livelihood. We will not only encourage the fast-growing regions to take the lead and play a leading role, but also strengthen macro-control and avoid problems caused by excessive disparities in basic public service level between regions.

(3) We will deepen the reform of budget management system and harden the budget constraints. In the report of the 19th CPC National Congress, General Secretary Xi Jinping proposed to establish a comprehensive, rule-based and transparent budget system that uses scientific standards and imposes effective constraints. In accordance with the requirements of the *General Plan for Deepening the Reform of the Fiscal and Tax System* reviewed and approved by the Third Plenary Session of the 18th CPC Central Committee and the meeting of the Political Bureau of Central Committee, we have implemented a series of regulations in terms of budget openness, budget control methods and local government debt management, basically putting in place a scientific and complete budget management system. The central government will release local transfer payments in advance to promote the integrity of local fiscal budgeting. We will strictly control the expenditure policy and

rigorously control the adjustment in budget execution. We will resolutely curb the increase in local government debt, and actively and properly bring down the debt stock, playing an important role in promoting the belt-tightening and strengthening budget constraints.

In the next step, in view of the low accuracy of local and unit budget preparation, the lack of solid budget execution, and the slow progress of expenditure, we must further improve the awareness of budgetary rules and laws and consolidate the reform results, so as to lay a solid foundation for working hard in a spirit of diligence and frugality. First, constantly improve the budget law and legal system. We will actively cooperate with relevant departments to complete the revision of the implementation rules of Budget Law as soon as possible. We will improve the basic expenditure standards system, and classify and study the fiscal security policy. We will study and put forward the framework and overall plan of the project expenditure standards system, formulate the annual development plan, and effectively implement it. Second, further strengthen budget preparation and execution management. We will promote all-round government budget management, speed up the unified budget allocation, and strictly control the scope and scale of budget at the beginning of the year. We will adhere to the principle of "budget first, expenditure later", prohibit unbudgeted expenditure, and strictly control budget adjustment. Third, continue to move forward the disclosure of final accounts. We will constantly expand and standardize the content, scope and methods of disclosure, further improve the transparency of budget and final accounts, take the initiative to accept the supervision of the NPC and the CPPCC, accept the audit supervision and public supervision, and force the government at all levels to change their idea of spending money through open and transparent supervision. Fourth, accelerate the IT-based processing of fiscal information. We will benchmark advanced experience, find existing gaps, keep both goal-oriented and problem-oriented, and construct a unified system for core fiscal work in accordance with the work plan that has been issued, so as to provide strong technical support for strengthening budget management.

(4) We will strengthen the development of the system for promoting saving and opposing waste, and put an end to extravagance and waste at the source. General Secretary Xi Jinping pointed out that "we must vigorously carry forward the fine tradition of diligence and frugality of the Chinese nation, vigorously advocate for the virtue of saving and shame of waste, and strive to foster the atmosphere of saving in the society". Since the 18th CPC National Congress, MOF has resolutely implemented the instructions of General Secretary Xi Jinping on promoting saving and opposing waste, actively played its role in coordinating the formulation and revision of the *Regulations of the Party and Government Agencies on Promoting Saving and Opposing Waste* as well as more than 20 supporting policies related to the management of conference expenses, travel expenses and training expenses, established and improved a scientific and reasonable public service expenditure standards system, and provided an operable system for implementing the spirit of the Eight-Point Regulations and putting an end to extravagance and waste at the source.

Through years of cutting back on spending, the central government's "three public" expenditures have decreased year by year, and decreased by 46.2% in 2018 compared with 2012, effectively reducing administrative operating costs. This year, we also formulated and issued the *Circular on Implementing the Requirements of "Belt-Tightening" to Further Strengthen and Regulate the Budget Management of the Central Departments and the Administrative Measures for the Management of State-owned Assets of Central Administrative Institutions* and other documents. We also introduced further regulations on departmental budget compilation, departmental asset management and the disclosure of information on budget and final accounts.

Conduct building has no end. The removal of the root cause of "formalism, bureaucratism, hedonism and extravagance" will be a long-term process, and the problem of hedonism and extravagance must continue to be tackled. In the next step, we must continue to take effective measures in accordance with the important instructions of General Secretary Xi Jinping and the decisions of the Party Central Committee and make unremitting efforts to promote saving and oppose waste. First, we must improve the institutional arrangement. In view of the actual situation and changes in market prices, we will continue to improve the management system and standards system of public expenditure. We will strengthen guidance for local system construction, strengthen supervision, and promote the formation of a long-term mechanism where people are unable and unwilling to practice waste and extravagance. Second, we must work to ensure effective implementation of measures. We will strengthen planning and approval management, strictly control the total amount of official activities and scope and standards of expenditure, and enforce requirements on daily management and supervision. Third, we must make efforts to cut expenditures. We will further reduce general expenditures and continue to strictly control the "three public" expenditures.

(5) We will fully implement budget performance management and effectively manage the use of fiscal funds. General Secretary Xi Jinping pointed out that "the government's money can't be squandered, so it is necessary to control the expenditure", and repeatedly stressed that "the money should be spent on priority matters". Implementing budget performance management is an important step to optimize the allocation of fiscal resources and improve the effectiveness of the use of fiscal funds. It is also an important starting point for the Party and the government to take the lead in tightening the belt. In recent years, the finance authorities have actively explored budget performance management, and have done a lot of work in performance target setting and performance evaluation mechanism construction. The basic framework of budget performance management system has been initially established.

In the next step, we must follow the requirements of the *Opinions of the Party Central Committee and the State Council on the Comprehensive Implementation of Budget Performance Management* to promote the establishment of a comprehensive, full-process and full-coverage budget performance management system to achieve regular, institutionalized and standardized budget performance management. First, expand the scope of implementation. We will gradually extend performance management to cover all fiscal funds as well as all grassroots units and end-users of funds, and strengthen the performance accountability of fund users. Second, optimize business processes. We will deepen the integration of budget and performance management, and deeply embed performance management in budget management to achieve an organic integration. We will accelerate the development of core performance indicators and standards by different industries, fields and levels. Third, improve the quality of evaluation. We will take strong measures rectify the problems of unscientific performance target setting, low-quality self-assessment and insufficient role of third-party evaluation, strictly review performance targets, and urge the relevant departments to conduct performance self-evaluation in a way that objectively reflects performance. Fourth, strengthen the application of results. We must do a good job in rectifying performance problems, and on the basis of the results of performance evaluation, vigorously reduce inefficient and ineffective expenditures and establish a clear incentive and disincentive mechanism.

(6) We will strengthen financial discipline to ensure the safe and efficient use of funds. General Secretary Xi Jinping once pointed out that "whether it is the life discipline, organizational discipline, or financial and economic discipline, political discipline, the problem is that the disciplines are not

implemented well. Some people think that discipline is a scarecrow and don't care about it. Now it is time to enforce strict discipline", and went on to emphasize that "we must strengthen financial and economic discipline, enhance fund management, step up discipline inspection and audit supervision, and strictly investigate malpractices and corrupt behaviors. Since the 18th CPC National Congress, we have vigorously enhanced the financial and economic discipline, formulated and issued the *Circular of the Ministry of Finance on Comprehensively and Strictly Enforcing Financial and Economic Discipline and Strictly Managing Central Departmental Budget,* organized the campaign on the implementation of the *Eight-Point Regulations on Austerity,* the strict enforcement of financial and economic discipline, the special supervision and management of public finance and the special inspection of fiscal funds for poverty reduction, made great efforts to address the outstanding problems in the implementation of financial and economic discipline, sent out a strong and deterring warning signal, and vigorously tackled corruption at the source and promoted the construction of a long-term mechanism.

Although we have achieved positive results in the strict enforcement of financial and economic discipline, cases of the violation of financial and economic discipline still occur from time to time, and some have resulted in financial losses and waste. In the next step, we must follow the important instructions of General Secretary Xi Jinping, ensure the strict use of power, and effectively curb various cases of the violation of laws and regulations with binding institutional constraints and strict disciplinary mechanism. First, make efforts to strengthen institutional constraints. We will work to establish an institutional management system that meets the new requirements by starting with the improvement of the system of official reception, financial budget, assessment and accountability, and supervision. With a focus on key links such as budget allocation, implementation and policy formulation, we will promptly revise the internal control measures for budget preparation and budget execution, and urge the relevant departments to strengthen internal control, in order to effectively prevent operational and integrity risks. Second, strengthen the supervision of funds in key areas and the constraints on the exercise of core power. MOF is the department that manages money, and is prone to power rent-seeking. We must pay close attention to the management and use of funds in key areas such as poverty alleviation, improve the dynamic monitoring mechanism of fiscal funds, and adopt various forms such as daily supervision and special inspection to track policy implementation and problem rectification. When it comes to major project layout, financial allocation and work arrangement, we must earnestly comply with the laws and serve the public interest, and must not use the public resources under management to seek unfair benefits for any individuals and agencies. We must strictly require family members, children, relatives and friends not to interfere in political affairs and use their own official powers to influence matters. Third, seriously rectify the problems identified by the audit. We will keep records of and rectify the problems identified by the audit, and earnestly assume the responsibility for reviewing and supervising the budget management of the relevant departments. On the one hand, it is necessary to supervise and guide the departments to rectify specific problems. On the other hand, it is also necessary to profoundly analyze the causes of problems and to propose rectification measures to tackle both the symptoms and the root causes. Fourth, seriously investigate and deal with violations of law and discipline. We will continue to maintain high-pressure of the anti-corruption struggle, and enforce full coverage and zero tolerance, so that the economic and financial discipline would be a red line that shall not be crossed.

III. Adhere to the two-pronged approach and strive to do a good job in all aspects of fiscal reform and development

Since the beginning of this year, the macroe-conomic situation has been complicated, the global economic growth expectation has weakened, the external uncertainty has increased, and the risk and challenges facing the global economy have increased. The domestic economic operation is generally stable, and the main indicators are still in a reasonable range. However, the foundation for economic stability still needs to be consolidated. In accordance with the decisions of the Party Central Committee and the State Council, we must continue to adhere to the general principle of making progress while maintaining stability, promote high-quality development, pursue the supply-side structural reform as the main task, implement the "consolidation, enhancement, upgrading and unblocking" policy, make overall plans to promote steady growth, reform, structural adjustment, improvement of people's livelihood, prevention of risks and maintenance of stability, implement various measures of proactive fiscal policy, further stabilize employment, finance, foreign trade, foreign investment, investment and expectations, and better promote the sustained and healthy development of the economy and society. At the same time, we will continue to carry out the thematic education of "remaining true to the original aspiration and keeping the mission firmly in mind", bear in mind the fundamental purpose of serving the people whole-heartedly, earnestly implement the general requirements of "keeping the original aspiration, shouldering the mission, finding the gap and working on the implementation", combine the thematic education with the "two learning and one action" as well as the central fiscal work to ensure progress on both fronts.

(1) Intensify efforts to implement proactive fiscal policies to ensure the implementation of various policies for tax and fee cut. Implementing a larger-scale tax and fee cut is a major strategic move made by the Party Central Committee. It is an important measure to deepen supply-side structural reforms and a key step to deal with the current economic downturn and external pressure. Since the beginning of this year, the MOF leadership has attached great importance to tax and fee cut, and carried out coordinated planning and meticulous organization to implement tax and fee cut as an important political task as well as the primary measure to strengthen the effectiveness of the implementation of proactive fiscal policy in 2019. From January to June this year, China has registered a total of 1.17 trillion RMB of tax and fee cut, including a tax cut of 1.04 trillion RMB. Enterprises and the general public believe that this year's tax and fee cut is very aggressive, and their sense of gain and satisfaction is high.

In the next step, we must strictly follow the important instructions of General Secretary Xi Jinping, and continue to implement the measures for tax and fee cut in greater details with relevant departments. First, strengthen communication, coordination and inspection. Promote the sharing of data on tax and fee cut, track and improve performance monitoring and analysis, and increase the guidance for and supervision of the work of local finance departments. Second, strengthen the budget management of fiscal revenues and expenditures. Supervise and guide local governments to increase revenues and reduce expenditures, raise revenues through multiple channels, further reduce general expenditures, and support the implementation of tax and fee cut policies. Strengthen guidance for regions that find it difficult to complete the annual revenue and expenditure budget, and adjust the budget according to the law when budget adjustment conditions are triggered. Third, strengthen publicity and training. Innovate publicity methods, provide targeted training for corporate finance personnel, and help companies to make good use of policies. Fourth, conduct timely research of policy response plan. On the basis of extensive research, promptly respond to the new situation and new problems that arise during the implementation of policy and ensure the decrease of tax burden of all industries.

(2) Pay close attention to reforms and implementation, and make policy preparation for further the deepening of reforms. General Secretary Xi Jinping required that "we must continue to hold high banner of reform, stand at a higher starting point to plan and promote reforms, strengthen the resolve and courage of reform, summarize and apply the new experience accumulated since the 18th CPC National Congress, and make persistent efforts to unswervingly carry out the reforms". We must further strengthen our responsibility, follow the important instructions of General Secretary Xi Jinping and the decisions of the Party Central Committee, and continue to move forward the various reform tasks involving MOF. First, accelerate the reform of the division of fiscal powers and expenditure responsibilities between central and local government. At present, the reform plan for the division of fiscal powers and expenditure responsibilities in the fields of science and technology, education and transportation has been promulgated, and reform plans in the fields of ecological environment, emergency rescue and natural resources are being researched and formulated. It is necessary to pay close attention to the revision and improvement work and introduce the reform plan as soon as possible. At the same time, it is important to do a good job in reforming the central-local revenue division and improving the transfer payment system. Second, conscientiously implement the principle of law-based taxation. Among the 18 types of taxes currently in force, there are 8 types of taxes for which laws have been enacted. We must actively cooperate with the NPC to speed up the work related to the legislation of resource tax, deed tax, urban maintenance and construction tax, stamp duty, VAT, land appreciation tax, customs duty and consumption tax. Third, speed up the pilot project of state-owned capital investment and operation companies directly authorized by the State Council, as well as the pilot project of centralized and unified supervision of the operational state-owned assets of the central Party and government organs and institutions. Do a good job in reporting to the Standing Committee of the NPC on the management of state-owned assets. Fourth, on the basis of systematically reviewing the progress of reform tasks, work to study the issues related to the further deepening of reform, with a focus on advancing the modernization of the state governance system and governance capacity and establishing a modern fiscal system.

(3) Block the "back door" and effectively prevent and defuse local government debt risks. Since the 18th CPC National Congress, in accordance with the decisions of the Party Central Committee and the State Council, we have adhered to the principle of "opening the front door and strictly blocking the back door", strengthened and standardized local government debt management while meeting the needs of debt financing for local economic and social development in accordance with the law. At present, China has basically established a local government debt management system and the risks are generally controllable. In the next step, we must implement the important instructions of General Secretary Xi Jinping and the decisions of the Party Central Committee, further improve the system, pay close attention to implementation, work more on "opening the front door", risk monitoring, due debt response, supervision and accountability, and make efforts to prevent systemic risks.

(4) Continue to consolidate and improve the outcomes of the central special inspection of poverty alleviation and support the fight against poverty. Last year, the Tenth Central Inspection Team conducted a special inspection of MOF on poverty alleviation. The MOF Party Group attached great importance to it, earnestly worked on the rectification of problems in accordance with inspection feedbacks, and achieved phased progress in rectification. In the next step, we must conscientiously study and implement the important exposition of General Secretary Xi Jinping on poverty alleviation, further enhance the sense of responsibility and urgency of poverty alleviation, strive to give full play to the role of the public finance, and resolutely support the fight against poverty. First, concentrate resources to speed up efforts of strengthening the weak links in the field of poverty alleviation. We

will fully support the resolution of outstanding problems in compulsory education, basic medical care, housing security and drinking water safety, with a focus on the areas of extreme poverty. Second, optimize the fiscal policy system for poverty alleviation. Improve the support for poor areas and poor people, and enhance the precision of fiscal policies for poverty alleviation. Further promote the pilot projects on the consolidation of agriculture-related funds in poverty-stricken counties and improve the effectiveness of consolidation policies. Third, comprehensively implement performance management to further improve the management level of poverty alleviation funds. Conduct real-time and dynamic monitoring of all types of poverty alleviation funds at all levels as soon as possible, and carry out ex-ante, interim and ex-post performance management of poverty alleviation project funds. Fourth, conscientiously summarize and refine advanced practices and successful models, and propose policy recommendations on public finance supporting poverty alleviation and the implementation of rural revitalization strategy. At the same time, conscientiously implement the relevant MOF arrangements of poverty alleviation work and continue to provide assistance to the poor areas supported by MOF.

(5) Enhance the sense of political responsibility and mission, and carry out the thematic education of "remaining true to the original aspiration and keeping the mission firmly in mind" in a solid and orderly manner. In the early stage, under the strong supervision and guidance of the 23rd Central Guiding Group, the MOF Party Group earnestly fulfilled its principal responsibilities, played a leading and demonstrative role, kept firmly in mind the objectives and tasks of the thematic education, and moved forward various work in a solid and orderly manner. In the next step, we must strictly follow the important instructions of General Secretary Xi Jinping, strictly implement the requirements of the Party Central Committee and the Central Guiding Group, and ensure the effectiveness of thematic education activities.

First, make further efforts to raise awareness. Seriously study and implement General Secretary Xi Jinping's important exposition on "remaining true to the original aspiration and keeping the mission firmly in mind", study General Secretary Xi Jinping's speeches at the Thematic Education Work Conference, the 15th Collective Study of the Central Political Bureau, and the Party Building Work Conference of Central and State Organs as well as his important speech delivered during the inspection in Inner Mongolia, thoroughly read the Party Constitution and *the Compendium of Xi Jinping Thought on Socialism with Chinese Characteristics for a New Era,* deepen the understanding of our Party's original aspiration and mission, enhance the awareness of the risks and test faced by the Party, develop a firm belief and a strong sense of responsibility, and practice the acquired knowledge in day-to-day work to promote fiscal reform and development.

Second, make greater efforts to find the gap. The MOF Party Group and the leadership of all units must listen to opinions and suggestions in various ways on the basis of previous investigation and research, solicitation of opinions and identification of problems, work to identify problems in the political construction, ideological construction, organizational construction, work style construction and discipline construction of Party, and figure out specific measures to rectify the problems. Comprehensively and systematically sort through the performance in implementing the important instructions of General Secretary Xi Jinping, and keep detailed records. Carefully analyze the root causes of existing problems, hold high-quality thematic democratic life meetings, and effectively enhance the ability of self-purification, self-perfection, self-innovation, and self-improvement.

Third, make greater efforts on rectification. The MOF Party Group and the leadership of all units must strengthen the consciousness of facing the problems head on and the courage of rectifying the problems, adhere to the problem-oriented approach, and solve the problem with real efforts. Make systemic efforts to rectify the outstanding problems identified in this thematic education, and to carry out special rectification work in accordance with the actual situation of MOF. The comrades of the MOF Party Group must earnestly implement the "two responsibilities" and give full play to the "leading role". The responsible persons of all units should, while doing a good job of rectifying their own problems, take the initiative to shoulder the responsibility for the problems existing in their units. The identified problems must be rectified and remedied. The system and mechanism that ought to be perfected should be perfected, the loopholes that ought to be closed should be closed, those that ought to be criticized should be seriously criticized, and those that ought to be held accountable should be dealt with seriously.

Fourth, make greater efforts to strengthen supervision and guidance. The comrades of the MOF Party Group should fulfill the "one post and two responsibilities" and strengthen supervision and guidance of thematic education in the units under their charge. The guiding groups within MOF should strengthen their responsibility and strictly handle the key tasks such as study session, investigation and research, review and rectification and special democratic life meetings, in order to enhance the effectiveness of work. The Office of the MOF Leading Group for Thematic Education should improve the working mechanism, keep abreast of the progress of work, and strengthen coordination and supervision.

Struggle in the past created history and current hard work will shape the future. In the new journey of comprehensively building socialist modernization, the finance authorities should be more closely united around the Party Central Committee with Comrade Xi Jinping as the core, and follow the guidance of Xi Jinping Thought on Socialism with Chinese Characteristics for a New Era, strengthen the "four consciousnesses" and the "four self-confidence", ensure the "two safeguards", make in-depth study and implementation of General Secretary Xi Jinping's important guiding instructions on hard work, diligence and frugality, remain true to the original aspiration and keep the mission firmly in mind, give full play to the role of the public finance, and effectively promote the sustained and healthy development of economy and society and the stability of the overall society, in order to lay a decisive foundation for the completion of the task of building a moderately prosperous society in all respects and celebrate the 70th anniversary of the founding of the People's Republic of China with outstanding achievements! ■

30 Liu Kun: finance authorities of China and Russia should actively promote cooperation in the economic and financial field

On August 22, Finance Minister Liu Kun and Russian First Deputy Prime Minister and Finance Minister Anton Siluanov co-chaired the 8th China-Russia Financial Dialogue in Moscow, Russia. Minister Liu Kun said that this year marks the 70th anniversary of the establishment of diplomatic relations between China and Russia. This dialogue is conducive to the implementation of the important consensus reached by President Xi Jinping and President Putin in the economic and financial field in June this year, and provides impetus to the development of China-Russia relations in the new era. In order to implement the consensus of the heads of state of China and Russia, the finance authorities of the two countries should actively promote cooperation in the economic and financial field. First, strengthen communication and coordination of macroeconomic policies. Adopt effective macroeconomic policies, accelerate structural reforms, enhance macroeconomic policy communication and coordination, jointly safeguard multilateralism and the free trade system, and promote the stable and healthy economic development of the two countries and the world. Second, support each other on major international economic and financial issues. China actively supports Russia in hosting the 2020 BRICS Leaders Summit and is willing to strengthen cooperation with Russia under the G20 framework and on MDBs such as NDB and AIIB, work together to call on IMF and the World Bank to accelerate the reform process, jointly safeguard the interests of developing countries, and promote the improvement of global economic governance. Third, explore new areas of innovation and cooperation. China is willing to further strengthen exchanges and cooperation on fiscal and tax policies with Russia, share experiences on issues such as budget management, tax policies and treasury management, promote accounting standards equivalence and audit regulatory cooperation, and provide policy support for local fiscal and tax cooperation. ■

31 Liu Shangxi: it is important to enhance knowledge dissemination and expand the influence of fiscal communication

On August 7 and 8, 2019, Liu Shangxi, President of the Chinese Academy of Fiscal Sciences, said at the 2019 National Workshop on Fiscal Research and Publicity that it is important to enhance knowledge dissemination and expand the influence of fiscal communication. First, fiscal communication has continued to innovate, and the influence of communication has been continuously expanded with remarkable achievements. The innovation of journals has led to a benign interaction between readers, authors and editors; the innovation of methods has created new communication models such as online live broadcast salon, university cooperation forum, internet debut launch and WeChat public account; and organizational innovation has established a correspondent system and strengthened interaction and exchange. Second, fiscal communication is faced with new circumstances and needs to keep pace with the times. Public finance is now newly defined as the foundation and important pillar of state governance. We must think outside the box, re-understand public finance by moving beyond the departmental mentality, and re-recognize fiscal communication. The uncertainties facing fiscal operation have increased, and stabilizing expectation has become a top priority. Effective fiscal communication is essential for stabilizing expectation. The dissemination of fiscal knowledge is first and foremost the dissemination of fiscal theories, and only in doing so can new fiscal theories adapt to the new economic reality. Fiscal theoretical innovation is of utmost importance and urgency at this moment. Third, improve knowledge dissemination and contribute to the fiscal communication of the new era. (1) Improve fiscal communication between the government and the people. Knowledge dissemination requires innovative approaches to enhance its readability and attractiveness, and needs to provide more services from the perspective of readers and demanders. (2) Build a community of fiscal communication and work together to enhance the public recognition of public finance. (3) Adopt a holistic approach to coordinate different models of communication and deploy digital technologies such as big data, cloud computing and artificial intelligence to develop three-dimensional, all-round, timely and effective means of communication, and further expand the influence of fiscal communication. ■

32 Zhu Guangyao: in the face of global economic challenges, the G20 must play a coordinating role

From September 6 to 7, Zhu Guangyao, the former Vice Finance Minister, said at the 2019 Special Session of the China Development Forum that the downward pressure on the global economy is increasing, global trade growth is lower than global economic growth, and global trade disputes have become a major drag on the global economy. In the face of severe global challenges, the G20 must play a key coordinating role in the following three areas. First, the coordination of exchange rate policies. At the G20 Finance Ministers and Central Bank Governors' Meeting held in Shanghai in March 2016, China and the United States jointly promoted the formation of a mechanism to prevent competitive devaluation, and designated the IMF as the central institution for global exchange rate coordination. However, in August 2019, the United States took the lead in breaking the G20 consensus between China and the United States, and labeled China a "currency manipulator", which not only disrupted the international financial order, but also undermined the three criteria for affecting exchange rate set by the United States itself. Second, there is an urgent need to coordinate the international tax policy of the digital economy. On the issue of taxing the digital economy, the OECD has been authorized by the G20 to formulate policies on issues such as BEPS. China and the United States may coordinate the international tax policy of the digital economy with the help of the G20 framework. Third, the firewall of the IMF for preventing risks. Previously, under the G20 framework, the IMF put in place a firewall of over 1 trillion USD to cope with the global financial crisis, but it is now faced with major challenges in sustaining this mechanism. All in all, China and the United States should restart cooperation under the G20 framework, as this is being responsible for China and the United States and for the cause of global peace and development. ■

33 Zhang Qi: China's poverty alleviation has made decisive progress

On September 10, Zhang Qi, Member of the Expert Advisory Committee of the Leading Group for Poverty Alleviation and Development of the State Council, said that China's poverty alleviation has made decisive progress. The outcomes of poverty alleviation are mainly reflected as follows. The number of rural poor population in China fell from 98.99 million at the end of 2012 to 16.6 million, a cumulative decrease of 82.39 million; the rural poverty incidence rate dropped from 10.2% in 2012 to 1.7%, a cumulative decrease of 8.5 percentage points; of the 832 poor counties in China, 436 were lifted out of poverty, accounting for 52.4% of all poor counties; and the number of documented poor villages fell to around 26,000 at the end of 2018. China's poverty alleviation experience mainly includes: first, give play to China's institutional advantages, concentrate efforts on doing big things, and fully mobilize all social resources to tackle poverty. Second, promote targeted poverty alleviation, strengthen the assistance for the documented poor people in villages, implement tailored poverty alleviation policies on a case-by-case basis, identify the real causes of poverty, enforce a combination of sound policies, multiply the effects of assistance, and at the same time, step up inspection and assessment to ensure the quality of poverty alleviation. Third, increase inputs. From 2013 to 2018, the central government invested more than 280 billion RMB of special poverty alleviation funds. Fourth, mobilize social participation. China has tackled poverty through special programs, industrial development, and social participation. Fifth, promote the participation of masses and enable the masses to play a principal role. In general, China has established the responsibility system, policy system, input system, mobilization system, and supervision and evaluation system centered on targeted poverty alleviation, which have ensured the steady progress of the work of poverty alleviation. ■

34 Gao Peiyong: the evolution, historical logics and trend of the fiscal and tax reform of the People's Republic of China

On September 24, Gao Peiyong, Deputy President of the Chinese Academy of Social Sciences, said that public finance in the new era should have a broader and higher perspective, and the deepening of the reform of fiscal and tax system should focus on the systematic reconstruction of the long-term mechanism. China's modern fiscal system is linked to the socialist market economy, and it is connected with modern state governance. It is actually a product of the combination of the socialist market economy and the modern state governance. To deepen the reform of the fiscal and tax system, first, it must be recognized that only the "publicity" of public finance can match the "marketization" of economy. The modern fiscal system that matches the socialist market economic system must adhere to the essential attribute of public finance—"public". Second, it must be recognized that only the modernization of public finance can match the modernization of state governance. The modern fiscal system that matches modern state governance must follow the essential definition of public finance—the foundation and important pillar of state governance. In short, establishing a modern fiscal system based on the public finance system, adding fiscal modernization to fiscal publicity, allowing the public finance to play a fundamental and supporting role in state governance at a higher level and in a wider scope, and supporting and promoting the modernization of state governance system and governance capacity with the modernization of the fiscal governance system and governance capacity are not only the defining theme of China's public finance in the new era, but also the mission of China's public finance in the new era and the manifestation of the socialist system with Chinese characteristics. ■

35 Bai Jingming: accelerate the implementation of budget performance management for basic expenditures

On September 19-20, Bai Jingming, Vice President of the Chinese Academy of Fiscal Sciences, said at the 2019 International Seminar on Budget Performance Management that it is important to accelerate the implementation of budget performance management for basic expenditures. The budget performance reform for basic expenditures is not only about the need to implement comprehensive budget performance management, but also the requirement to improve the budget management level in the context of tax reduction. Implementing budget performance management for basic expenditures is an important part of the comprehensive implementation of budget performance management, and needs to be coordinated and harmonized with the deepening of institutional reform. The key to accelerating the implementation of budget performance management for basic expenditures is: First, continue to deepen institutional reform. Deepening institutional reform is an important means of optimizing cost control. Cost expenditures are directly proportional to the number of institutions, and the greater the number of institutions, the higher the cost of expenditure. Deepening institutional reform is a fundamental question facing basic expenditure performance management. Second, explore reforms in the way of spending. In order to further strengthen budget performance management, it is necessary to consider whether some services can adopt the way of government procurement of services and how the public institutions can optimize costs through "allocation-to-purchase reform". As the number of institutions remains unchanged, the change in the way of spending may also play a role in optimizing the reform of budget performance for basic expenditures. Third, the reform of basic expenditures should be combined with the staffing reform. It is necessary to strengthen the staffing reform, strictly control the number of formal staff for administrative agencies, and pay special attention to the basic expenditures of informal and retired staff. ■

36 Gao Peiyong: establishing a modern fiscal system based on the public finance system

On October 2, Gao Peiyong, Deputy President of the Chinese Academy of Social Sciences, said that the importance and particularity of the public finance of the People's Republic of China are reflected in the fact that it is the economic foundation of all the activities undertaken by the government and its natural connection with state governance as it is the foundation and important pillar of state governance. As socialism with Chinese characteristics is entering a new era and China's economy is entering a stage of high-quality development, in the face of the new situation and new tasks, public finance in the new era should have a broader and higher perspective. Establishing a modern fiscal system based on the public finance system, adding fiscal modernization to fiscal publicization, allowing the public finance to play a fundamental and supporting role in state governance at a higher level and in a wider scope, and supporting and promoting the modernization of state governance system and governance capacity with the modernization of the fiscal governance system and governance capacity are not only the defining theme of China's public finance in the new era, but also the mission of China's public finance in the new era and the manifestation of the socialist system with Chinese characteristics and its enforcement capability. ■

37 Zhu Guangyao: the world economy is currently faced with four major challenges of the trade war, negative interest rate, geopolitical risks and Brexit

On October 12, Zhu Guangyao, the former Vice Finance Minister, said at the 4th China-Australia Belt and Road Roundtable Dialogue on Investment and Financial Cooperation that the world economy is currently faced with four major challenges of the trade war, negative interest rate, geopolitical risks and Brexit. First, trade war. The trade war also exists between U.S. and Europe. How Europe should deal with the U.S. tariffs on goods imported from Europe merit particular attention. Second, negative interest rate. We must pay close attention to the spread of negative interest rate in the world and the impact on the global market. Third, geopolitical risks. Geopolitical risks in the Middle East and other regions would have a very negative impact on the global financial market, which in turn would impact the global economy. Responding to geopolitical risks requires the major countries in the world to further strengthen policy coordination. Fourth, Brexit. There is great uncertainty to Brexit, and the direction of future relationship between UK and EU is worthy of attention. It is hoped that UK and EU can properly resolve the Brexit before the deadline through in-depth policy communication. In general, the global economy faces four major risks which pose challenges to maintaining global economic growth, safeguarding world peace, and delivering benefits to people and nations around the world. It is especially important to have in-depth and effective policy communication if we are to deal with these challenges. ■

38

Zou Jiayi: promote the high-quality reform and development of PPP

Source: MOF

On October 29, the 5th China PPP Development (Financing) Forum was held in Zhengzhou, Henan Province. Vice Finance Minister Zou Jiayi attended the forum and delivered a keynote speech.

Vice Finance Minister Zou Jiayi said that PPP is a concrete step to implement the decision of the Third Plenary Session of the 18th CPC Central Committee on comprehensively deepening reform and promoting the modernization of state governance. By liberalizing market access, encouraging competition, enforcing life-cycle management, risk sharing and paying by performance, PPP offers an innovative model for public service supply, stimulates market vitality and social creativity, spurs the changes of growth quality, efficiency and growth drivers, delivers diversified and high-quality public service supply, and meets people's needs for a better life.

Vice Finance Minister Zou Jiayi pointed out that over the past five years, MOF, together with relevant competent authorities, in accordance with the decisions and arrangements of the Party Central Committee and the State Council, and on the basis of China's basic national conditions and development stage, have drawn upon international experiences and engaged in institutional design, comprehensive capacity building, promotion of demonstration projects and pragmatic international cooperation. As a result, MOF has achieved the objectives of the reform in a phased way, and basically put in place a unified, standardized, transparent and efficient PPP market. At the same time, PPP has also played a role in advancing reform, providing new opportunities for the development of private enterprises, and creating new drivers for economic development. China's PPP reform has been widely recognized and highly praised by the international community.

Vice Finance Minister Zou Jiayi said that some trends in the PPP reform process should merit our attention. For example, increasing local government debts under disguise and packaging unqualified projects into PPP. In order to prevent and resolve major risks, and promote the sustainable development of PPP, we must: first, adhere to the original purpose of reform and stay mindful of the risks; second, strengthen supervisory measures to prevent financial risks; third, ensure the quality of projects and improve the efficiency of PPP development; fourth, clarify the responsibilities of all parties and promote win-win cooperation.

Vice Finance Minister Zou Jiayi emphasized that in the new stage of PPP development, we should take the Xi Jinping Thought on Socialism with Chinese Characteristics for a New Era as the guide, follow the principle of "making best effort according to our capability", and remain mindful of fiscal performance, in order to increase the supply of high-quality public services. First, promote high-quality development of PPP by improving the institutional arrangement, standards and policy system; second, strengthen the life-cycle project management to improve the capacity for PPP risk prevention and control; third, optimize the business environment to create conditions for the high-quality development of PPP; fourth, innovate the financing model and make good use of the two resources of government and market; fifth, deepen pragmatic international cooperation in support of the Belt and Road Initiative. ■

39

Gao Yan: China's pace of opening-up will not be affected by China-U.S. economic and trade frictions

On November 8, Gao Yan, Chair of the China Council for the Promotion of International Trade, said at "the 10th Caixin Summit: Opening up China and the World" held in Beijing that China's opening up will not be affected by China-U.S. economic and trade frictions, China's determination to open up to a higher level will not change, and the pace of opening up will not slow down. China's door of opening-up will only grow wider. At present, the global economic and trade landscape is undergoing profound adjustment as economic globalization and the growth of world economy and trade are slowing down and international trade frictions and tussles over international trade rules are increasing. The world economy may enter into the era of frictions. The international trade friction will be long-term, normalized and complicated, entailing wider fields, new means and deeper impact. However, as long as all the parties seek common ground while shelving differences, expand consensus and strengthen cooperation, they will be able to minimize the impact of economic and trade friction on the world economy and globalization, and jointly build an open, cooperative, innovative and inclusive world economy. While promoting a higher level of opening up to the outside world, China will advance the high-quality development and diversification of trade, so that imports and exports, trade in goods and trade in services will develop in a coordinated manner. China will also continue to properly handle international trade frictions through dialogue, consultation and mutually beneficial cooperation. China will actively negotiate high-standard free trade agreements with more countries on top of 17 free trade agreements that have been signed. The Chinese business community is pleased to see that 15 countries taking part in RCEP concluded text-based negotiations, and expects the agreement to be signed and enter into force at an early date, so that the free trade zone with the most population, the most diversified energy structure and the greatest development potential in the world will inject new impetus into the economic development of the region and the world. ■

40

Zou Jiayi: China's successful issuance of euro-denominated sovereign bonds created a new platform for China-EU financial cooperation

On November 6, Vice Finance Minister Zou Jiayi attended and addressed the celebration ceremony of the successful issuance of the euro-denominated sovereign bonds of the People's Republic of China in Paris, France.

Zou Jiayi pointed out that this year we just celebrated the 70th anniversary of the founding of the People's Republic of China. Over the past 70 years, China's development has been a result of independent and open development. As part of the opening-up process, China will increasingly integrate into the international financial market. After a lapse of 15 years, China restarted euro financing and made it in Paris, which reflected our emphasis on and support for euro and Paris as the international financial center, and will help deepen the financial cooperation between China and France, as well as China and Europe. First of all, the successful issuance of euro-denominated sovereign bonds is a concrete action for us to build an economy of higher-level openness. The Chinese government has continuously introduced new opening-up measures. While welcoming foreign investment into the domestic market, China is also actively moving into the international market. China's resumption of the issuance of euro-bonds not only added high-quality sovereign issuers to the euro international market, but also established a benchmark for euro financing by Chinese issuers, which is of far-reaching significance for furthering China's participation in the development of international financial market. Second, the successful issuance of euro sovereign bonds demonstrates that the Chinese economy is entering a new phase of high-quality growth. The industrial structure of the Chinese economy has been continuously optimized and adjusted, the new drivers of economic growth have been continuously cultivated, and China's international ranking of the business environment has been continuously improved, laying a good foundation for the long-term healthy development of the economy. In this issuance of euro-bonds, 4 billion euros of sovereign bonds were actively subscribed by international investors, with a total subscription of 20 billion euros, which is five times the amount of issuance. Among the subscription, 57% comes from Europe and 43% comes from outside Europe, with a wide range of investors, broad geographical distribution, and better-than-expected results, reflecting not only the international investors' high recognition of the Chinese government's efforts to further reform and open up its economy and integrate into the international economic system, but also the international investors' strong confidence in China's sovereign creditworthiness. Third, the successful issuance of euro sovereign bonds has created a new platform for China-France and China-Europe financial cooperation. At present, high-level interactions between the two countries are frequent, political mutual trust is being continuously consolidated, and economic and trade cooperation is getting more pragmatic. In order to consolidate the comprehensive strategic partnership between China and France, we will implement the important consensus of our state leaders with more pragmatic and effective actions to support the development of the Paris international financial center.

Zou Jiayi emphasized that in recent years, China-EU cooperation has progressed in an orderly manner and the cooperation mechanism has been continuously improved. The momentum of China-EU relations is encouraging. China's restart of the euro financing not only reflects our confidence in the euro, but also provides high-quality investment products for euro investors. We look forward to attracting more Chinese issuers to finance and invest in Europe in the future and continue to deepen bilateral economic and trade cooperation, and hope China-EU cooperation could become an important driver and underpinning for world economic growth. ■

41 Shi Yaobin: make active exploration to take PPP development to a new level

On November 12, Shi Yaobin, Commissioner of the Budgetary Affairs Commission of the Standing Committee of the NPC, attended and addressed the second annual meeting of the 2019 Global PPP50 Forum of Peking University. Shi Yaobin said that the Budgetary Affairs Commission of the Standing

Source: MOF

Committee of the NPC will support and promote the development of PPP in the following aspects:

First, make in-depth understanding of the significance of PPP. We need to further understand the significance of PPP development for promoting high-quality economic development, serving the people, and innovating social governance model from the perspective of transforming the advantages of the socialist system into the efficiency of national governance. We must give full play to the positive role of PPP in promoting supply-side structural reforms and achieving high-quality economic development, in order to break monopoly, increase supply, improve efficiency, allow the market to play a decisive role in resource allocation, and better play the role of government. We must always adhere to PPP's essential characteristics of being people-oriented and serving the people, innovate the way public services are provided, encourage and support private forces to run social undertakings, so as to meet the diverse needs of people and move toward the goal of building a society where everyone is responsible and stands to benefit from social progress.

Second, strengthen the rule of law. PPP is a long-term project involving the relationship between government and market players. Sound rule-of-law environment is the fundamental guarantee for the sustainable and healthy development of PPP. In accordance with the principle of "legal guarantee, sound system and policy guidance", we will revise and improve laws and regulations related to budget management and government procurement, and study and formulate PPP laws and regulations. Through the formulation and revision of relevant laws and regulations, we will effectively deal with and take into account the interests of all parties involved, regulate the behaviors of government and market entities, strengthen communication and collaboration between departments, and create a sound rule-of-law environment for win-win cooperation.

Third, promote regulated development of PPP. We will carry out the overall requirements of "not only regulating but also developing PPP", further align understanding, build consensus, and promote the return of PPP to its original purpose and its regulated development. The standard PPP projects should be unswervingly promoted. The non-standard PPP projects should be rectified within a time limit. The PPP projects that constitute illegal borrowing must resolutely be held accountable and the hidden debt risks of local government must be prevented. We must strengthen the life cycle management of PPP projects, use modern IT and big data to strengthen supervision, and improve project management and performance of fund usage. It is necessary to strengthen the disclosure of PPP information, make further detailed disclosure, allow private enterprises greater market access, promote the transparent operation of projects, and actively accept the supervision of people's congress and general public at all levels. By transmitting clear signals, we will stabilize market expectations, boost market confidence, and promote steady progress of PPP.

Fourth, promote the real effects of PPP. We will implement the requirements of the Party Central Committee on expanding the focus of NPC's budget review and supervision to expenditure budget and policies, strengthen the review and supervision of key expenditures and major investment projects, and promote the implementation of the major decisions of the Party Central Committee. In the field of PPP, we need to set great store by the development of project pipeline, pay attention to the implementation of key projects in such key areas as poverty alleviation, ecological and environmental protection, and people's livelihood, and pay attention to project risk management and sustainable development, in order to enable PPP to better play its role in stabilizing growth, advancing reform, improving weak links and benefiting people's livelihood. ■

42 Liu Kun: benchmarking against the best international standards to optimize China's business environment

On November 22, at the opening ceremony of the High-level International Seminar on Optimizing the Business Environment, Finance Minister Liu Kun said that in recent years, MOF, in accordance with the decisions of the Party Central Committee and the State Council, has taken the lead in coordinating with the relevant departments and the Beijing and Shanghai municipal governments to improve the business environment. By leveraging the opportunity of the World Bank's business environment assessment and benchmarking against the best international standards, MOF has promoted a series of drastic reforms. As a result, China's global ranking of business environment moved up 15 places to the 31st this year on top of the substantial rise of 32 places last year, making China one of the 10 economies with the largest improvement in the business environment for two consecutive years.

In accordance with the unified arrangement of the Party Central Committee and the State Council, MOF will require relevant parties to be guided by the best practice in the world, promote reform with opening-up, and create a business environment in line with international norms; enforce policies to meet corporate demands, highlight practical effectiveness, and further enhance the corporate sense of gains and satisfaction; tackle the weak links reflected in the *Doing Business Report* to accurately implement policies and continue to optimize the business environment in China with greater efforts and more pragmatic measures. ■

43 Zhu Guangyao: it is important to tackle challenges in four areas in the year 2020

On December 1, Zhu Guangyao, Counselor of the State Council and former Vice Finance Minister, stated at the 4th (2019) China New Finance Summit Forum that the key to promoting global economic growth and coping with the uncertainty and complexity of the international environment in 2020 is tackling challenges in four areas. First, we must safeguard the multilateral trading system as much as we can. The 164 members of WTO should proceed from the easier issues to advance WTO reforms on the basis of consultation and communication. Second, we must accelerate the formulation of international rules related to the digital economy, including digital taxation, digital currency and digital cash. Third, international policy coordination is required in such important fields as artificial intelligence, but the most critical aspect of macroeconomic policy coordination is the coordination of monetary and fiscal policies. Fourth, we must respond to the impact of geopolitical emergencies. In the face of international political and economic challenges, the most important thing for China is to manage its own affairs well, adhere to the general policy of making progress while maintaining stability, continuously deepen reform and expand opening up, and drive the sustained and healthy development of China's economy through reform, opening up and innovation. ■

44 Wang Yiming: better promote the high-quality development of economy

On December 9, Wang Yiming, Deputy Director of the Development Research Center of the State Council, wrote in the *Economic Daily* that in order to promote high-quality economic development, we must make supply-side structural reform our central task and work faster to build and improve the institutional environment that is compatible with high-quality development. First, strengthen the foundational role of competition policy, coordinate related policies on the basis of the competition policy, and accelerate the establishment of a fair competition review system. Second, further improve the property rights system and build an institutional environment that promotes the equal use of production factors, the open and fair participation in market competition, and the equal protection of law for entities of all ownership. Third, deepen the reform of the land system, speed up the reform of collectively-owned land for construction use, and promote the two-way flow of urban and rural production factors. Fourth, explore the market-oriented incentive mechanism for scientific and technological findings, explore the granting of ownership over scientific and technological findings to scientific research personnel, and promote the reform of the allocation of the initial rights and interests of scientific and technological findings. Fifth, accelerate the reform of state-owned assets and state-owned enterprises, advance the optimization and structural adjustment of the state-owned economy, and invest more in the important industries and key areas related to national security and national economy. Sixth, deepen the reform of the fiscal, tax and financial system, regulate local governments' debt financing mechanism, increase the proportion of direct financing, especially equity financing, improve the transaction system, and strengthen the vitality of the capital market. ■

45 Liu Kun: take General Secretary Xi Jinping's important exposition as guide to lend full support to "agriculture, rural areas and farmers" in the new era

On December 16, Finance Minister Liu Kun wrote in *China Finance* that the finance authorities should thoroughly study and implement General Secretary Xi Jinping's important exposition on the work of "agriculture, rural areas and farmers", give full play to the role of public finance, and support the work of "agriculture, rural areas and farmers" in the new era with greater determination, clearer objectives and stronger measures.

The article pointed out that public finance is the foundation and an important pillar of state governance, and the finance authorities shoulder important responsibilities in implementing General Secretary Jinping's important instructions and the decisions of the Party Central Committee to promote agricultural and rural development. We must adhere to the guidance of General Secretary Xi Jinping's important exposition on the work of "agriculture, rural areas and farmers", conscientiously implement the spirit of the Fourth Plenary Session of the 19th Party Central Committee, implement the relevant requirements of the *Regulations on Rural Work of the Communist Party of China*, strive to build and improve the policy system and institutional mechanism of public finance supporting the enforcement of rural rejuvenation strategy, enhance the effectiveness of work, and take the work of "agriculture, rural areas and farmers" to a new level.

(1) Prioritize the development of agriculture and rural areas, and continue to increase fiscal input.

We must always adhere to the general policy of prioritizing agricultural and rural development, make best efforts within our capacity, further improve the input system, innovate investment and financing mechanisms, broaden financing channels, and promote the formation of a diversified financing pattern featuring fiscal and financial support as well as private participation. First, continue to increase investment in "agriculture, rural areas and farmers". We will provide strong fiscal support for poverty alleviation, take rural rejuvenation as an important factor in fiscal budget arrangement, implement agriculture-related tax cut policies, and continue to tilt government investment towards agriculture and rural areas. We will advance the reform of the division of fiscal powers and expenditure responsibilities in the agriculture-related fields, clarify and strengthen the responsibilities of governments at all levels regarding investment in "agriculture, rural areas and farmers", and promote the implementation of accountabilities. Second, broaden the input channels for "agriculture, rural areas and farmers". We will adjust the scope of the use of land transfer income, and increase the proportion of investment in agriculture and rural areas. We will use the newly-added farmland quotas for high-standard farmland development, implement the policy for the inter-provincial allocation of urban-rural construction land quotas, and use the income from such allocation for consolidating the results of poverty alleviation and supporting rural revitalization. We will actively leverage the national financing guarantee fund, improve the agricultural credit guarantee system, and work to resolve the problem of difficult and expensive financing for new agri-businesses. We will explore the possible models and mechanisms for the application of PPP for public welfare projects with stable returns in the agricultural and rural areas by deploying subsidies, rewards and subsidized loans. Third, accelerate the establishment of a long-term mechanism for the consolidation of agriculture-related funds. We will improve the management mechanism featuring "special project + task list", release task lists in tandem with funds, reasonably define the binding tasks and the guiding tasks, and promote the establishment of an implementation mechanism for sub-provincial level task lists.

(2) Adhere to the policy of focusing on domestic needs and ensuring self-sufficiency, and support high-quality agricultural development. We must actively give play to fiscal functions, continue to make national food security a top priority, strengthen support for the production of key agricultural products and livestock products, enhance China's comprehensive agricultural efficiency and competitiveness, and promote the transformation from a major agricultural country to a strong agricultural country. First, consolidate and improve comprehensive agricultural production capacity. We will accelerate the development of high-standard farmland, strengthen the protection of cultivated land, enhance land fertility, vigorously promote the innovative development of seed industry, and support the improvement of science and technology in service of agriculture. We will speed up efforts to strengthen the weak links of water conservancy, and support the management of small and medium rivers, the reinforcement of small and dangerous reservoirs, the construction of flood prevention and early warning systems for rural grass-root units, and the prevention and control of flash floods. Second, support the deepening of agricultural supply-side structural reforms. We will give overall consideration to the regional distribution of productivity and market-oriented direction, and promote the construction of a modern agricultural structure that integrates grain, cash crops and feed, planting, raising and processing as well as farming, herding and fishing. We will steadily push forward the establishment of the national modern agricultural industrial park, and the leading demonstration platform for quality agriculture. We will support the campaign of boosting the prosperity of villages and counties through industrial development, promote the integrated development of rural primary, secondary and tertiary industries, accelerate the reform of grain and cotton collection and storage system, and deepen the implementation of high-quality grain projects.

Third, improve the agricultural support and protection system. We will implement and improve the agricultural subsidy system, and consolidate the results of the "three agricultural subsidies" reform. We will strongly support the development of social services throughout the agricultural production process, and promote the organic connection between small-scale farmers and modern agricultural development. We will improve the benefit compensation mechanism in major grain producing areas, continue to implement subsidy policies for corn and soybean producers, and improve the cotton target price subsidy policies. We will innovate and improve the subsidy policies for agricultural insurance premiums, and strengthen the agricultural risk prevention and protection systems.

(3) Adhere to the direction of prioritizing ecological and green development, and support the promotion of rural ecological revitalization. We must consciously practice the concept of green development, strengthen agricultural and rural pollution control and ecological environment protection, and make good ecological environment an underpinning of rural revitalization. First, support green agricultural development movement. We will promote the establishment of a green ecology-oriented agricultural subsidy system, vigorously promote the development of green, circular, quality and efficient agriculture, expand the trials of cropland rotation and fallow system in an orderly manner, establish a compensation mechanism for banning fishing in key waters of the Yangtze River Basin, and step up efforts to support the use of livestock and poultry waste and the trial for the comprehensive use of crop stalks. Second, promote water saving in agriculture. We will accelerate the development of water-saving agricultural projects such as efficient and water-saving irrigation, step up the comprehensive reform of agricultural water prices, and establish a precision subsidy mechanism for agricultural use of water. We will support the implementation of the river chief system, the lake chief system and the most stringent water resource management system, support the expansion of the scope for the comprehensive management of groundwater over-exploited areas, accelerate the comprehensive management of soil erosion, carry out the trials for providing rewards instead of subsidies for soil and water conservation, and work to promote the connectivity of rivers, lakes and reservoirs. Third, support the strengthening of forestry and grassland ecological development. We will arrange funds to support the launch of large-scale land greening operations, vigorously support the major forestry ecological protection and restoration projects such as natural forest protection and a new round of farmland conversion to forest and grassland, strengthen wetland protection and restoration, and continue to provide a new round of subsidies and rewards for grassland ecological protection. Fourth, promote the improvement of rural living environment. We will support the implementation of the three-year action for the improvement of the rural living environment, provide solid fiscal subsidies and rewards for carrying out the rural "toilet revolution", further upgrade the ecologically livable and beautiful rural areas, actively and steadily carry out the pilot demonstration programs of the construction of a pastoral complex, and accelerate the construction of an ecological and circular pastoral production system. Fifth, strengthen the construction of key ecological function zones. We will implement the transfer payment policy for key ecological function zones, guide local governments to strengthen ecological environment protection, promote the development of ecological civilization, and improve the basic public service delivery capabilities of local governments in the key ecological function zones.

(4) Continue to safeguard and improve rural people's livelihood, and vigorously support the equalization of basic public services in urban and rural areas. We will continue to support the equalization of basic public services in urban and rural areas, make it an important focus of fiscal policies, continue to increase fiscal input, and provide solid guarantee for the urban and rural integration. First, strengthen rural infrastructure construction. We will strengthen funding for

infrastructure construction including rural roads, water supply, gas supply, environmental protection, power grids, logistics, information, radio and television, and postal services, and promote urban and rural infrastructure interconnectivity. Second, give priority to the development of rural education. We will consolidate and improve the funding mechanism for compulsory education in urban and rural areas, vigorously support the reform and development of vocational education, promote pre-school education in rural areas with a combination of public and private participation, continue to support the development of special education, and implement a plan for advancing universal education in senior high school. Third, support the construction of a rural social security system. We will further improve the mechanism for determining the basic pension insurance benefits of urban and rural residents. We will integrate the basic medical insurance system for urban and rural residents, rationally determine the government subsidy standards, and implement urban and rural medical assistance policies. We will improve social assistance and welfare policies such as the rural minimum living allowance, the renovation of dilapidated houses, and the protection of the disabled. Fourth, support later-period resettlement of large and medium-sized reservoirs. We will implement resettlement subsidy policies to support infrastructure construction and economic and social development in the reservoir area and resettlement area.

(5) Adhere to the path of good governance in rural areas and promote the establishment and improvement of a modern rural social governance system. We must vigorously support all aspects of rural social governance, promote innovation in rural governance, and make rural areas vibrant and harmonious. First, further promote comprehensive rural reform. In line with the implementation of the rural revitalization strategy, we will explore and push forward the pilot demonstration of comprehensive rural reform. We will develop the rural collective economy, and improve the fiscal reward and subsidy policies for rural public welfare undertakings. Second, promote the reform of agricultural reclamation, the reform of collective forest tenure system and the reform of state-owned forest farms and forest areas, and cooperate with the rural land system reform, rural collective property rights system reform, and the reform of economically developed towns. Third, support the promotion of rural talents. We will support new business entities such as major grain growers, family farms, farmers' cooperatives, and agricultural enterprises according to local conditions, implement programs for cultivating new type of professional farmers, support the cultivation of rural scientific and technological personnels, and nurture various specialized market-oriented service providers. Fourth, improve the stable funding guarantee system for village-level organizations centered on fiscal input, and ensure that village-level organizations have human and financial resources to get things done.

(6) Adhere to the basic strategy of targeted poverty alleviation, and give full support to winning the battle against poverty. We must fully implement the Guiding Opinions of the CPC Central Committee and the State Council on the Three-year Action to Win the Battle against Poverty, ensure that the battle against poverty is won by 2020 as scheduled, and strengthen the connection with the rural revitalization strategy after the task of poverty alleviation is completed. First, improve the input mechanism that suits the task of poverty alleviation. We will increase special poverty alleviation funds and related transfer payment to poor areas, tilt resources towards the extremely poor areas of the "three regions and three prefectures", regulate the financing in the field of poverty alleviation, and support poor areas to shore up the weak links in poverty alleviation as soon as possible. Second, standardize and deepen the pilot projects for consolidating agriculture-related funds in poor counties. We will effectively decentralize the review and approval authority for fund projects to poor counties,

supervise and guide poor counties to carry out consolidation within the prescribed scope, adjust the scope of use according to the requirements of the Party Central Committee, arrange expenditures, and make good use of the consolidated funds. Third, refine and implement the fund management policies. We will strictly abide by the targets and standards for poverty alleviation, and will neither raise the targets blindly nor lower the standards at will. We will strengthen the supervision and management over the allocation and use of funds, urge and guide poor areas to strengthen budget constraints and guidance, and constantly improve the accuracy of the use of poverty alleviation funds to ensure that money is spent on the key areas. Fourth, make scientific planning to consolidate and expand the outcomes of poverty alleviation and to enhance synergy with the rural revitalization strategy. We will accelerate policy research, summarize the advanced practices and successful models, put forward and enforce policy measures regarding fiscal support to consolidate and expand the outcomes of poverty alleviation and to better implement rural rejuvenation strategy, and establish a long-term mechanism to tackle relative poverty.

46 Liu Kun: continue to implement various tax and fee cut policies to unleash its effects

Source: MOF

On December 25, at the 15th meeting of the Standing Committee of the 13th NPC, Finance Minister Liu Kun made a report to the Standing Committee of NPC on the work of tax and fee cut. The full text is as follows.

The Standing Committee of NPC,

Entrusted by the State Council, I now report to the Standing Committee of NPC on the work of tax and fee cut in 2019.

I. Implementation of various tax and fee cut policies and measures in 2019

Implementing larger-scale tax and fee cut is a major decision made by the Party Central Committee and the State Council. General Secretary Xi Jinping emphasized that macro policies should strengthen counter-cyclical adjustments, proactive fiscal policies should be strengthened to improve effectiveness, and tax and fee cut policies and measures should take root to lighten the burden of enterprises. Premier Li Keqiang pointed out that tax and fee cut directly addresses the difficulties of current market players, and is thus a fair and efficient policy. In accordance with the decisions of the Party Central Committee and the State Council, the largest tax and fee cut policy unprecedented in history has been rolled out in this year.

(1) Make meticulous research and planning to ensure the timely introduction of tax and fee cut policy

This year's *Government Work Report* explicitly required that the burden of corporate taxes and social security contributions be reduced by nearly 2 trillion RMB throughout the year. The policy of inclusive tax cut for small and micro enterprises and special additional deductions for personal income tax was implemented starting from January 1; measures to deepen VAT reform were implemented starting from April 1; reduction of social insurance premium rates was implemented starting from May 1; and measures to regulate administrative fees and governmental fund were implemented starting from July 1.

First, deepen the reform of VAT. According to the decisions of the executive meeting of the State Council, the 16% VAT rate of the manufacturing and other industries was reduced to 13%, the 10% VAT rate of the transportation and construction industries was reduced to 9%, and the export tax rebate for some goods and services and the deduction rate applicable to the purchase of agricultural products were adjusted accordingly; the scope of input tax deductions was further expanded to include passenger transport services, and the input tax paid by taxpayers to obtain real property was changed from two-year deduction to one-time full deduction; for taxpayers whose principal business is postal, telecommunication, modern services and consumer services, extra 10% of the input tax amount was deducted from the taxable amount (the rate for the consumer services industry was further raised to 15% starting from October 1).

Second, implement inclusive tax cut for small and micro enterprises. In accordance with the decisions of the executive meeting of the State Council, a number of new inclusive tax cut measures for small and micro enterprises were introduced. For small-scale taxpayers, the threshold for VAT was raised from monthly sales of 30,000 RMB to 100,000 RMB; the criteria for small and micro enterprises to enjoy corporate income tax benefits was greatly relaxed and the corporate income tax benefits were raised; the people's government of provinces, autonomous regions and municipalities may reduce up to 50% of "six taxes and two fees" (i.e., resource tax, urban maintenance and construction tax, real estate tax, urban land use tax, stamp tax, farmland occupation tax and education surcharge, and local education surcharge) for small-scale VAT taxpayers according to the local situation; the scope for start-up science and technology enterprises to enjoy preferential policies for investment was expanded.

Third, implement special additional deductions for personal income tax. On August 31, 2018, the 5th session of the 13th session of the Standing Committee of NPC passed the newly revised *Personal Income Tax Law of the People's Republic of China*. The Article 6 of the new personal income tax law set out 6 special additional deduction policies for children's education, continuing education, medical treatment of major illness, mortgage loan interest, housing rent, and caring for elderly dependents. On this basis, the State Council issued the *Interim Measures for Special Additional Deductions of Personal Income Tax*, and officially implemented 6 special additional deduction policies from January 1 this year.

Fourth, reduce social insurance premium rates. After review and approval by the State Council executive meeting, the General Office of the State Council issued the *Comprehensive Plan for Reducing Social Insurance Premium Rates*, which clearly reduced the proportion of basic pension insurance paid by urban employers for their employees. If the employers' share of contribution in provinces, autonomous regions and Xinjiang Production and Construction Corps (hereinafter collectively referred to as provinces) is higher than 16%, the share may be reduced to 16%; continue to gradually reduce the unemployment insurance and work-related injury insurance premium rates; adjust the social insurance payment base policy, and all provinces may determine the upper and lower limits of the individual payment of social insurance on the basis of the average salary of urban employees, and industrial and commercial proprietorships and the flexibly employed may voluntarily choose the payment base set at between 60% and 300% of the average salary of urban employees in their provinces.

Fifth, clean up and regulate administrative fees and governmental fund. In accordance with the arrangement of the State Council executive meeting, policies and measures were introduced to further clean up and regulate administrative fees and governmental fund, explicitly reduce and exempt real estate registration fees and cultural undertaking construction fees, and expand the scope of reduction for patent application fees and annual fees; reduce the charge for private passports, registration of some trademarks, and occupation of radio frequency; reduce the charge for major water conservancy construction fund and airline civil aviation development fund by half; deduct 30% of investment against payable education surcharge and local education surcharge if the investment is made by enterprises under the pilot production-education integration program into vocational education.

In addition, NDRC, MCA, MIIT, GAMS, CBIRC and other departments have also formulated measures to reduce the costs of energy, logistics and telecommunication for enterprises, further reduce the electricity prices and telecommunication fees for general industrial and commercial enterprises, promote the reduction of tolls for roads, railways and ports, and clean up and regulate the charges for banking and intermediary services, in order to effectively reduce the burden on enterprises and society.

(2) Make meticulous organization and implementation to ensure that the tax and fee cut policies take root

First, strengthen organizational leadership and improve working mechanisms. MOF, SAT, MOHRSS, and other departments have established special taskforce for tax and fee cut to coordinate the various tasks of tax and fee cut, focused efforts on program formulation, publicity, supervision and inspection, budget support, and overall coordination, refined and broke down work tasks, clarified timetables and roadmaps, and rigorously benchmarked and compared notes, so as to ensure that all work progress in a steady way; guided and urged all provinces, autonomous regions, and municipalities to strengthen the leadership and efforts of tax and fee cut in line with local conditions, established and improved working mechanisms, clarified their work responsibilities, and built joint synergy.

Second, conduct in-depth research and strengthen policy evaluation. Relevant departments in various regions actively carried out research on tax and fee cut, collected information on the implementation of policies, listened to the opinions of enterprises and the public on the implementation of tax and fee cut policy, followed up and evaluated in a timely manner, strengthened the analysis of policy effects, and studied and addressed the new situations and problems arising in the course of policy implementation; carried out in-depth accounting and calculation for tax and fee cut to ensure meticulous book-keeping.

Third, strengthen the interpretation of policies to ensure the effectiveness of publicity. Relevant departments in various regions explained tax and fee cut through multiple channels and platforms of press conference, government websites, WeChat, Weibo, mobile portal, and tax service hotlines; proactively explained policies, interpreted data, responded to and addressed social concerns in a timely manner, and actively created a favorable public opinion environment; organized multiple rounds of special counselling and training on tax and fee cut policies to help taxpayers and fee-payers to make full use of the tax and fee cut policies and enhanced the sense of gain for taxpayers and fee-payers.

Fourth, optimize tax payment services and simplify tax procedures. In accordance with the requirements of "streamlining administration, delegating powers and improving services", the tax authorities promptly introduced new measures to facilitate tax payment, and rolled out specific tax services that target the inclusive tax cut for small and micro enterprises, VAT reform and reduction of social insurance rates. 60 tax-related certificates were canceled and functions of electronic tax bureau were improved, to allow taxpayers and fee-payers to go online to access tax services.

Fifth, strengthen supervision and inspection to ensure effective implementation. Relevant departments in various regions focused on the effects of the tax and fee cut policies, continued to strengthen supervision and inspection, seriously investigated and dealt with inaction and misconduct, and resolutely punished the cases that compromised the effects of tax and fee cut, in order to make sure that enterprises truly enjoy the policy benefits of tax and fee cut.

(3) Strengthen budget management of fiscal revenues and expenditures to support the implementation of tax and fee cut policies

First, increase local transfer payments. In order to support the stable operation of local finances, the central government provided 7.54 trillion RMB of local transfer payment in this year, up by 9% over the previous year, representing the largest increase in recent years. At the same time, the allocation of equalization transfer payments and the subsidies for county-level finances was tilted toward areas with financial difficulties at the grass-root level and areas affected by tax and fee cut, in order to strengthen their financial capabilities. At the same time, the provincial governments' principal responsibilities should be enforced to enhance the "three guarantees" at the grass-root level (wage payment, basic operation and people's livelihood).

Second, guide local governments to raise funds through multiple channels to make up for reduced income. As the central government increases transfer payment to local government, it also guided local finance departments to take into account local realities, studied the use of budget stabilization funds, the increased transfer of state capital operating budget into general public budget, and the revival of the stock of funds and state-owned resources and assets to raise funds to mitigate the impact of tax and fee cut on the fall of fiscal revenues, in order to strive to achieve a balanced budget.

Third, urge local governments to reduce general expenditures. All regions are required to firmly tighten their belt, and strive to cut over 10% of expenditures on top of the 5% reduction of general expenditures specified in the *Government Work Report*. The saved funds would be used to finance the expenditures related to the "three guarantees", and support the fight against the three critical battles. At the same time, the budget implementation constraints will be hardened and budget adjustments be strictly controlled.

Fourth, study and implement the plan for reforming and advancing the central-local revenue division. The State Council issued the *Plan for the Reform of the Central-Local Revenue Division after the Implementation of Larger-scale Tax and Fee Cut,* which kept the "50-50" ratio for sharing the revenue of VAT and further stabilized local expectations; adjusted and improved the mechanism for sharing VAT rebates to make the sharing mechanism more fair and reasonable; moved backward the stage for the collection of consumption tax and steadily delegated it to the localities so as to strengthen local financial capabilities.

Fifth, increase central adjustments and subsidies for basic pension insurance funds of enterprise employees. In order to balance the burden of basic pension insurance funds for enterprise employees between regions, the central government further increased the transfer rate in 2019 to 3.5%. The scale of annual fund transfer reached more than 630 billion RMB, and 22 central and western regions and the old industrial base provinces received over 150 billion RMB of benefits. At the same time, the basic pension insurance fund subsidies for enterprise employees were increased. In this year, the central government budget allocated 528.5 billion RMB of such subsidies, a year-on-year increase of 9.4%.

II. Principal effects of tax and fee cut

In accordance with the decisions of the Party Central Committee and the State Council, and with the concerted efforts of all relevant parties, the various tax and fee cut measures are well implemented and the effects are gradually showing.

(1) Effectively reduce the costs and burdens of enterprises. From January to October, tax and fee cut reached 1.968894 trillion RMB nationwide, of which tax cut was 1.647326 trillion RMB and the cut of social insurance premiums was 321.568 billion RMB. The annual tax and fee cut will exceed 2 trillion RMB, accounting for more than 2% of GDP, which is significantly higher than that of other countries in the world. After the VAT reform, the higher bracket rate of VAT dropped from 16% to 13%, which is at the lower-middle level among G20 countries and is lower than some developed countries and emerging market countries.

(2) Basically meet the "three guarantees" requirement. Since the implementation of the policy of deepening VAT reform on April 1, we have firmly grasped the requirements of the "three guarantees". First, ensure that the tax burden of major industries such as manufacturing is significantly reduced. From April to October, the VAT cut for manufacturing and wholesale industries was 459.883 billion RMB, a reduction of 25.7%. Second, ensure that the tax burden on industries such as construction and transportation is reduced. From April to October, the construction industry reduced taxes by 18.819 billion RMB, a fall of 6.2%; the transportation industry reduced taxes by 3.563 billion RMB, a fall of 7.5%. Third, ensure that the tax burden of other industries is reduced or not increased. From April to October, the tax cut of modern services industry and consumer services industry was 32.196 billion RMB and 13.49 billion RMB respectively, a fall of 12.3% and 6.6% respectively. With the implementation of policies such as the increase of deduction from 10% to 15%, the consumer services industry will continue to see larger scale of tax cut.

(3) Focus on supporting private and small and micro enterprises. Place equal emphasis on inclusive tax cut and structural tax cut, with a focus on reducing the tax burden on small and micro enterprises. Since the implementation of the inclusive tax cut policy for small and micro enterprises on January 1, as of the end of October, the tax cut for small and micro enterprises reached 186.089 billion RMB. After the standard was relaxed, the number of taxpayers who actually enjoy corporate income tax cut reached 4.6892 million, and the small-scale taxpayers who enjoy VAT exemption increased by 4.0264 million. Private enterprises are the principal beneficiaries of the tax cut policy. From January to October, the total tax cut from various policies for private enterprises reached 1.051184 trillion RMB, accounting for 63.8% of the total tax reduction.

(4) Effectively promote enterprises to increase investment in research and development. Accelerate

the implementation of the policy of deducting 75% of R&D expenses before taxes to reduce taxes by 87.796 billion RMB. With the implementation of other policies to reduce taxes and fees, enterprises were spurred to use the saved costs for reinvestment in R&D and technological upgrading. From January to October, despite the overall decline of investment, investment in high-tech industries increased by 14.2% year on year, an increase of 1.2 percentage points from the previous three quarters, and 9 percentage points higher than the total investment.

(5) Notably increase residents' income and consumption capacity. From January to October, the special additional tax deduction policy has cut personal income tax by 52.194 billion RMB. With the increase in basic deduction standards for personal income tax and the optimization of the tax rate structure on October 1 of last year, the total tax cut was 448.084 billion RMB; the per capita tax reduction for personal income taxpayer was 1,786 RMB, which directly increased residents' income and boosted consumption capacity.

Judging from the response of various sectors, the tax and fee cut policy has been well implemented, and enterprises and the general public are satisfied as the tax and fee cut policy implemented this year has exceeded expectations and delivered most direct, effective and fair benefits to enterprises. According to the estimate of the fiscal and tax departments, tax and fee cut boosted GDP growth by 0.8 percentage point in the current year, fixed asset investment growth by 0.5 percentage point, and total retail sales of consumer goods by 1.1 percentage point. Currently, economic operation is in a reasonable range and maintains the overall trend of stable and steady development, which is largely owed to the important role of the tax and fee cut policy.

While acknowledging the effectiveness of tax and fee cut, we must also recognize that there are still some difficulties and problems in the implementation of the policy. First, increased pressure on fiscal revenues. From January to October, due to higher-than-expected tax and fee cut, the national general public budget revenues increased by 3.8%, of which tax revenues only increased by 0.4%. Central and local fiscal revenues are under great pressure, making it difficult to complete the annual revenue budget. In addition, the pressure on the balance of revenue and expenditure of social insurance funds in some provinces is also rising, leading to a deficit between current revenues and expenditures. Second, the burden reduction of a few enterprises is not obvious. Judging from the implementation of VAT reform, the tax burden of all industries has declined, but the benefit transmission mechanism of tax and fee cut is not smooth and some enterprises in the "mezzanine layer" of the industrial chain could only access relatively limited policy dividends. A small number of enterprises have experienced a small increase in taxes due to inconsistent tax rate reductions at sales and purchase and imperfect self-management. Third, the problems of arbitrary charges, fines and apportionment involving enterprises cannot be ignored. Some enterprises reported that the problem of random charging by industry associations and intermediaries still exists. In the context of large fall in fiscal revenues, non-tax revenues, especially fines and confiscated incomes, have increased significantly in some localities, and it is necessary to prevent arbitrary fines and apportionment.

III. Thoughts on the work of tax and fee cut in the next step

In view of the difficulties and problems in tax and fee cut, the finance and tax authorities will take Xi Jinping Thought on Socialism with Chinese Characteristics for a New Era as the guide, conscientiously implement the requirements of the 19th National Congress of the CPC, the 2nd, 3rd and 4th Plenary Sessions of the 19th CPC Central Committee, and the Central Economic Work

Conference, adhere to the problem-oriented approach, continue to implement the various tax and fee cut policies on the basis of ensuring sustainable financial operation, and promote the continued effects of tax and fee cut policies.

(1) Resolutely implement the tax and fee cut policy. We will earnestly implement the tax and fee cut measures arranged by the Party Central Committee and the State Council to ensure that enterprises and general public reap real gains. We will firmly grasp the requirements of the "three guarantees", strengthen departmental coordination and cooperation, step up local guidance and supervision, continue to pay close attention to changes in the tax burden of various industries, follow up on effect monitoring and analysis, and organize the summary and assessment of the effects of policy implementation. We will further increase publicity and policy interpretation, increase the policy awareness of taxpayers and fee-payers, and help enterprises to make the most of the policies. We will urge local government to resolutely clean up and regulate fees related to enterprises, seriously investigate and deal with problems such as the failure to implement policies, the increased burden on enterprises, and the damage to the interests of the people, and ensure that all measures are put in place.

(2) Effectively strengthen fiscal budget management. We will continue to pay close attention to the implementation of budgets at all levels, and guide and urge local governments to increase revenues and reduce expenditures to support tax and fee cut. We will strengthen budget management of fiscal revenues, carefully study and assess the fiscal revenues, analyze in depth the impact of tax and fee cut policies, and where appropriate, require state-owned financial institutions and state-owned enterprises to turn in profits in accordance with laws and regulations in an orderly manner, and step up efforts to revive state-owned resources and assets. As things stand now, it is expected that local fiscal revenues may see a large shortfall in this year; the central fiscal revenues may basically complete the budgeted target, and if there are changes in expenditures caused by a small shortfall in revenues, a balanced will still be achieved by saving non-emergency expenditures.

(3) Adjust and optimize the structure of fiscal expenditures. We will firmly tighten the belt and strictly reduce general expenditures. We will enhance provincial government's principal responsibilities, delegate more financial resources, work on supporting grass-root "three guarantees", and focus on helping areas with difficulties of ensuring "three guarantees" and where the impact of tax and fee cut is big. We will implement the plan for reforming the division of revenues between the central and local government after a larger-scale tax and fee cut, and ensure that the mechanism for sharing VAT rebate burden is well calibrated, so as to effectively reduce the financial pressure on some areas, especially the ones at the grass-root level.

Chairman, Deputy Chairman, Secretary General, and Members of the NPC Standing Committee, implementing tax and fee cut is an important step to deepen supply-side structural reforms, and plays a critical role in reducing the burden on enterprises, stimulating the vitality of market players, and boosting economic growth. We must unite more closely around the Party Central Committee with Comrade Xi Jinping as the core, strengthen the "Four Consciousnesses", reinforce the "four self-confidence", ensure the "two safeguards", conscientiously implement the decisions of the Party Central Committee and the State Council, follow up on the opinions of the NPC Standing Committee, do a good job in reducing taxes and fees, in order to adhere to and improve the socialist system with Chinese characteristics, promote the modernization of the state governance system and governance capabilities, strive to achieve the "two centenary" goals, and realize the Chinese dream of the great rejuvenation of Chinese nation. ■

47 Liu Kun: proactive fiscal policies in 2020 must vigorously enhance quality and effectiveness and do a good job in 5 key areas and 8 aspects

At the National Fiscal Work Conference held on December 26, Finance Minister Liu Kun put forward the guiding principles and preliminary arrangements for fiscal work in 2020, and elaborated the principal tasks of fiscal work. He pointed out that, in accordance with the decisions of the Party Central Committee and the State Council, proactive fiscal policies in 2020 must vigorously enhance quality and effectiveness, pay more attention to structural adjustment, and work on both "quality" and "quantity". At the same time, we will endeavor to save fiscal resources and increase funding support for local government, especially those in difficult areas. We must keep macro policies stable, micro policies flexible, and social policies sound, adhere to the problem-oriented, goal-oriented, and result-oriented approach, and solidly move forward tasks in 5 key tasks and 8 aspects.

Solidly move forward 5 key areas

First, resolutely implement the decisions of the Central Economic Work Conference. It is necessary to further clarify the priority direction of fiscal expenditures and step up structural adjustment. General expenditure must be vigorously reduced, unnecessary project expenditures must be resolutely phased out, new project expenditures must be strictly controlled, and in principle, no new expenditures should be made. We will effectively fund the key expenditures, ensure that general transfer payments are significantly higher than the growth rate of central government expenditures, and see to it that equalization transfer payments, subsidy and reward funds for basic financial capacity at the county level, and transfer payments to old revolutionary base, ethnic minority, border and poor areas register relatively strong increase. Each locality must, in light of the actual situation in the region, clarify the priorities of fiscal spending, pinpoint shortcomings and weak links, and concentrate policies and funds to ensure targeted support. We will do a good job of budget performance management, embed the concept of performance into the entire process of budget management, improve the fiscal management level, and ensure that the fiscal policies are of greater quality and efficiency and are more sustainable.

Second, consolidate and expand the effects of tax and fee cut. The tax and fee cut is institutionalized and sustained. After years of implementation, the cumulative effects are immense, and the reduction of burden for enterprises will become increasingly notable. At the same time, relevant tax policies will be studied and improved around promoting high-quality development, encouraging technological innovation, attracting high-end talents, and promoting export growth. During the process of implementation, it is important to strengthen the sharing of information on tax and fee cut, closely watch the changes in the tax burden of various industries, firmly follow the "three guarantees" requirement, timely study and resolve outstanding problems flagged by enterprises, and continue to maximize the effects of tax and fee cut policies. Tax and fee cut is the most important manifestation of proactive fiscal policies. The transfer of more resources to market entities is also a way to increase expenditures. We will resolutely cut taxes and fees that ought to be reduced.

Third, do a good job of saving expenses. We must determine expenditures according to revenues and improve fiscal balance by reducing expenditures. The general fiscal expenditures of local governments should be further reduced on the basis of the reductions already made in 2019, and various stock funds and assets will continue to be revived. In the implementation of budget, we must save expenses as much as we can. We must strictly control the disbursement of fiscal funds. Basic expenditures already included in the budget must be funded in accordance with state regulations, project expenditures must save expenses, and disbursement must be made in strict accordance with project progress, contractual agreement and prescribed procedures. Over-scheduled advances beyond contract are strictly prohibited. It is also strictly forbidden to push up budget implementation progress by means of false presentation of expenditures. For projects that do not meet the conditions for implementation, with slow pace of progress, and may fail to make expenditures, no funds shall be disbursed.

Fourth, give full play to the role of fiscal capital in making up for the shortcomings and protecting people's livelihood. We must do a good job of protecting people's livelihood. When allocating funds for people's livelihood, we must give priority to support the basic livelihood of people living with difficulties and make targeted efforts at the right time to address the living difficulties of people. We will focus on the unemployed, urban and rural households with minimum living allowances, recipients of social assistance, disaster-affected people, and people with special hardships, pay close attention to the changes in the number, scope and degree of difficulties of the disadvantaged people, and take timely measures to effectively protect their livelihood to the extent possible. It is necessary to make good use of the special bonds of local government, adhere to the principle of "funds following projects", optimize the bond investment structure, implement policies to expand the use of special bonds, speed up the establishment of mechanisms for project preparation, evaluation and selection, develop, build and implement a batch of non-profit construction projects, and actively leverage the advantages of special bonds regarding low financing cost and direct and rapid policy effectiveness to expand effective investment as soon as possible to boost the economy.

Fifth, strengthen fiscal support for localities, especially those in difficult areas. In order to support the normal operation of localities, especially those in difficult areas, the central government has continued to increase general transfer payments to local government, with a focus on the old revolutionary base areas, ethnic minority areas, border areas and poor areas. Provincial finance departments should further increase sub-provincial transfer payments, strengthen the financial capabilities of relevant areas, and support grass-root and difficult areas to do a good job of "three guarantees" and implement the central government decisions.

Plan and carry out eight tasks

First, vigorously support the fight against the three critical battles and promote the construction of a moderately prosperous society in all respects as scheduled. On the basis of consolidating the existing outcomes, we will continue to focus on priority areas, make up for shortcomings, strengthen weak links, complete relevant qualitative and quantitative indicators, and continue to work on outstanding issues. We will continue to increase fiscal investment in poverty alleviation to ensure that the goals and tasks of poverty alleviation are achieved. We will focus on supporting the efforts to preserve the blue sky, clear water and clean land, and promote the realization of the phased targets for the prevention and control of pollution. We will strengthen supervision and accountability, strictly rectify disorderly debt borrowing, effectively curb the increase of hidden debts, and prevent and resolve the hidden debt risks of local government.

Second, spur innovation and industrial upgrading, and vigorously promote the healthy development of the real economy. We will adhere to the principles of "consolidating, enhancing, upgrading and unblocking" the economy, give full play to the role of fiscal and tax policies in structural adjustment, and advance supply-side structural reforms to comprehensively improve the overall economic competitiveness. We will promote industrial transformation and upgrading, support the development of new energy vehicles, and research and establish government procurement transaction system as well as cost management and risk sharing mechanisms that are suited for supporting innovation. We will support scientific and technological innovation, and improve the institutions and mechanisms that encourage and support basic research and original innovation. We will support the development of small and medium-sized enterprises, and work to clear the arrears owed to private enterprises and small and medium-sized enterprises.

Third, implement the strategy of rural revitalization and accelerate the modernization of agriculture and rural areas. We will establish and improve the policy system and institutional mechanisms for public finance to support the implementation of the strategy of rural rejuvenation, concentrate resources, strengthen support, and implement precise policies to take the work of "agriculture, rural areas and farmers" to a new level. We will vigorously support the development of modern agriculture, continue to promote the in-depth integration and development of rural primary, secondary and tertiary industries, further advance agricultural supply-side structural reforms, support the advancement of rural reform and development, and take the work of "agriculture, rural areas and farmers" to a new level.

Fourth, promote the equalization of financial resources across regions and promote the formation of a new pattern of coordinated regional development. We will accelerate the implementation of regional development strategies, improve relevant fiscal and tax policies, give full play to the comparative advantages of various areas, and promote the formation of a pattern of regional economic development with complementary advantages and high-quality development. We will improve the cost-sharing mechanism for the urban residency of farming population, strengthen the synergy between the policies related to the urban residency of farming population and the new type of urbanization, support the implementation of major regional strategies of the state, and promote the implementation of fiscal and tax policies to support high-standard construction and development of Xiong'an New District, development of The Guangdong-Hong Kong-Macao Greater Bay Area, revitalization of Northeast China, and the development of the western region.

Fifth, make effort to protect and improve people's livelihood, and effectively enhance the well-being of people. We will adhere to the people-centered development philosophy, give play to the role of government in protecting people's basic livelihood, pay attention to inclusiveness and basic needs, and make targeted efforts at the right time to address the living difficulties of people. We will take employment stabilization as the top priority, and support the employment of key groups of people such as college graduates and veterans. We will further optimize the structure of education spending and support the development of fair and quality education. We will actively promote the strategy of healthy China, steadily increase the level of old-age security, improve the basic housing security system, promote cultural prosperity, and provide solid funding support for the hosting of Beijing Winter Olympics and the preparation of the national team.

Sixth, promote the reform of fiscal and tax system and accelerate the establishment and improvement of the modern fiscal system. With a focus on advancing the modernization of state governance system and capability, we will continue to resolutely and steadily deepen the reform of fiscal and tax system. We will accelerate the reform of fiscal system, basically complete the division of fiscal mandates and expenditure responsibilities between the central and local governments in major areas, and actively promote the sub-provincial reform of fiscal system. We will improve the budget management system, accelerate the establishment of a comprehensive, full-process and full-coverage budget performance management system, deepen the reform of treasury management system, and further advance the market-oriented reform of the management of treasury bonds. We will deepen the reform of tax system, steadily advance the reform of the local tax system, adjust and optimize the tariff policy system, and vigorously advance tax legislation. At the same time, the reform of state-owned assets and state-owned enterprises will be accelerated to form a state-owned asset supervision system focusing on managing capital.

Seventh, strengthen fiscal management and supervision and earnestly improve the effectiveness of the use of fiscal funds. We will pay close attention to system construction and implementation, plug loopholes, enhance supervision, and continuously improve the efficiency of fiscal management and fund performance. We will improve the supervision ability with IT-based fiscal management, and improve the supervision mechanism with traceability of responsibilities in the allocation and use of fiscal funds. We will strengthen the management and supervision of budget execution, and continuously improve the efficiency of fiscal management and fund performance.

Eighth, deepen international economic and financial cooperation and promote higher level of opening up. We will take into account and make comprehensive use of international and domestic markets, resources and rules, actively engage in multilateral and bilateral exchanges and cooperation, and actively participate in the transformation of global economic governance. We will support the expansion of opening up, optimize the import tax policy system, and continue to improve the business environment in China. We will actively carry out multilateral and bilateral exchanges and cooperation to promote the in-depth development of multilateral and bilateral financial cooperation. ■

IEFI 国际财经中心
International Economics and Finance Institute

Mailing Address: *IEFI, Ministry of Finance, China, 100820*
Telephone: *86-10-68141100*
Fax: *86-10-68527620*
E-mail: *iefi@iefi.org.cn*
Website: *http://iefi.mof.gov.cn/*

Brief Introduction to IEFI

The International Economics and Finance Institute (**IEFI**) is the think tank affiliated to the Ministry of Finance of China.

Founded in 2007, **IEFI** carries out economic research on a wide range of issues and topics both domestic and international, including the world economy analysis, country studies, globalization, and international development cooperation. **IEFI** provides strategic and overarching policy recommendations to the top decision-makers of the Ministry of Finance and other governmental bodies of China.

IEFI maintains a strong partnership with other major think tanks and the academia both at home and abroad. Extensive and in-depth exchanges and co-operations are conducted.

IEFI works closely with global and regional multilateral financial institutions, including the WBG, the IMF, the OECD, the ADB, the AIIB, the NDB and etc.

IEFI also reaches out to the governmental agencies of other countries, and establishes close exchange and cooperation in one way or another.

Besides its research papers, **IEFI** has several annual publications.

Backed by its strong team and connections, **IEFI** has now become a renowned think tank both in China and the rest of the world.